CLOCK
IDENTIFICATION AND PRICE GUIDE, BOOK 3

INTRODUCTION

This book consists of new and different material not included in **Clock Identification and Price Guide, Book 1**, published in 1977, or **Book 2**, published in 1979. It contains carefully selected actual pages from original factory sales catalogs, factory advertisements, supply house catalogs, and sales brochures; and covers American and some imported clocks from 1881 to the 1950's. The following information is given for each clock:

— THE YEAR IT WAS OFFERED FOR SALE —

— THE FACTORY DESCRIPTION —

— THE PRICE IT SOLD FOR ORIGINALLY —

— THE PRESENT RETAIL VALUE —

— 1,966 CLOCKS PICTURED OR DESCRIBED —

— BOTH AMERICAN AND FRENCH —

Over 95% of all clocks manufactured or sold in the United States since 1850 can be identified and a reasonably close retail value determined by comparing your clock with a picture of it or a similar one in this book, or Book 1 or Book 2.

You are holding a very unique book. The original antique and historic material has not been altered. Long after the current retail prices no longer apply to the clocks shown herein, it will still be very valuable to anyone interested in clocks for research and identification.

ROY EHRHARDT — Author

MALVERN "RED" RABENECK — Technical Editor & Historian

SHIRLEY K. SHELLEY — Copy Editor

SHERRY L. EHRHARDT — Graphic Artist

Send orders to:
HEART OF AMERICA PRESS
10101 Blue Ridge Blvd.
Kansas City, MO 64134
(816) 761-0080
We sell reliable information

Second Printing February 1987

ISBN 0-913902-50-0

DESCRIPTION OF CLOCKS & PRICES (Clocks shown left to right)

PHOTO No. 1

French — Crystal Regulator	$1,550.00
French — L. Bouchet Set.	2,500.00
Bailey Banks & Biddle — Meissen China	1,750.00

PHOTO No. 2

Gustav Becker — Chime	$375.00
Ansonia — Royal Bonn	625.00
New Haven — Banjo	275.00
Boston — China	625.00
Kroeber — "Kansas"	395.00

PHOTO No. 3
(Top Row)

Ballerina — United	50.00
Jennings Bros. — Silver	125.00
Sessions — Onyx	75.00
Japan — Min. Grandather	35.00

PHOTO No. 3 (Cont.)
(Middle row)

Waltham — 8-Day	$ 65.00
Ansonia — Tambour	75.00
Gravity Clock	250.00
Lux — Harvestime	150.00

(Bottom Row)

Waltham — Electric	35.00
Parker — Alarm	40.00
United — Horse	25.00
Hamilton — Civil Time	125.00
French — Art Deco	40.00
Boston — Brass	125.00
Big Ben — Alarm	25.00
Gilbert — Min. Alarm	40.00
United — Fisherman	80.00
Sessions — Glossnia	50.00

ACKNOWLEDGEMENTS

The values shown in this book have been supplied by collectors and dealers from all over the United States. I'd like to take this opportunity to say thanks for the help they have given me.

Special recognition is given to "Red" Rabeneck, Clock Historian, a long-time collector and researcher of American Clocks. "Red" has worked closely with me on each of my clock books, spending many hours in consultations and pricing sessions. He is the contributor of the historical text in this book.

John Adams, Jr.
Springfield, IL

Gene Anderson
St. Louis, MO

Bill Andrus
Bossier City, LA

Fred Andrus
Auburn, ME

Don Bass
Sandusky, OH

Dr. Douglas Beck
Baton Rouge, LA

Steve Berger
Buffalo Grove, IL

Marion Blevins
Bettendorf, IA

Jane A. Brinkmeyer
Manchester, MO

Clyde & Betty Brown
Akron, OH

Dr. Warner Bundens
Woodbury, NJ

Jo Burt
Bloomfield Hills, MI

George Collard
Portland, ME

Patrick Cullen
Natick, MA

Rene Desjardins
Hollywood, CA

Roger & Alice Dankert
Aurora, CO

Jerry Faier
Overland Park, KS

Eldon Falke
Kansas City, MO

Michael "Mike" Ehrhardt
Kansas City, MO

Sherry L. Ehrhardt
Grandview, MO

James Eller
Greensboro, NC

Ed Getman
Newton, MA

Jonathan Giunchedi
Lake Forest, IL

Roy Good
Memphis, TN

Fred Hansen
Montgomery, NY

Robert Hansen
New Hampton, NY

Russell Henschel
Fairview Heights, IL

Howard Klein
St. Louis, MO

Jerome Levin
Creve Coeur, MO

Fred Linker
Fort Wayne, IN

Tran Du Ly
Arlington, VA

Mrs. L. McCormack
Portland, OR

Wiley McNeil
Greensboro, NC

Tom Maker
North Andover, MA

Bill Mather
Randolph Center, VT

William "Bill" Meggers
Ridgecrest, CA

Paul J. Morrissey
Waterbury, CT

Harry Neames
Baton Rouge, LA

Daryl Penniston
Lake Charles, LA

T.R. Pritts
Decatur, IL

Sal Provenzano
Bronx, NY

Gregg Reddick
Dubuque, IA

Roger Rees
Rockford, IL

Shirley Shelley
Belton, MO

Royce Shepard
Battle Creek, MI

Dr. Sam Simmons
Atlanta, GA

H.A. Soper (Deceased)
Harrison, AR

Ron Starnes
Tulsa, OK

Douglas Thomas
Tullhoma, TN

Larry Thompson
Green Lawn, NY

Col. George Townsend (Deceased)
Alma, MI

David M. Warner
Manchester, MO

Bobby Webber
Hampton, NH

James B. West
Houston, TX

Ralph Whitmer
Springfield, VA

Col. Henry Williamson
Topeka, KS

Stacy B.C. Wood, Curator
NAWCC, Inc. Museum
Columbia, PA

Richard "Dick" Ziebell
Ipswich, MA

INDEX
CLOCK IDENTIFICATION & PRICE GUIDE, BOOK 3

Acrobat Novelty 49
Advertising. 197-203

Admiral Electric 153

Airplane 122,123
Alarm
   Electric 56,57,133,146,154,156
   195-197
   Imported. 141
   Miniature. 42
   Musical 42,86
   Spring. . .28,29,40,45,47-57,81,85-87
   136,171,176,181,182,195-197
Anniversary 400D 48,94,137,194
Antimated 42,49,50,61,81,175,177
   181,182,195-196

Ansonia
   Alarm 40,45,50
   Alarm, Square. 53
   Art Noveau 41
   Bobbing Doll 36
   Cabinet 41,112
   Jumper 36
   Kitchen 39,40,44,72
   Mantel, Black 41,46
   Mantel, Wood 41
   Novelty 41
   Onyx 41
   Plush. 40
   Porcelain 45,46
   Regulators
      Octagon Top 43,111,112
      Parlor 44,112
      Round Top 111
   Wall, Square. 112

Art Deco 113-117,126-128
  131-156,167
Art Glo 143
Art Noveau 41,95-98
Atlas. 143

Attleboro Clock Co. 48

Autocrat Alarm. 50
Automobile 102,110,122,123,154
Automobile Novelty 58
Baby Ben. 53,54
Banjo 58,59,103-107,120-124
   170,195,197
Barometer Novelty 49
Barrel Novelty 58,61
Battery 86,131
Ben Hur Chariot 143
Bent Glass 151
Bicycle 154
Big Ben 53,54
Big Ben Electric 54
Bobbing Doll 36

Boston Clock Co. 102

Boudoir. 126

Box Chronometer 121
Bracket, English 108
Brass. 68,77,101
Briar 140
Bronze 62,63,116
Cabinet 41,67,68,76,77,86,94,112
   125,166,168
Calendar, Double Dial 27,44
Calendar, Simple 64,65,77,182
Capitol Dome Novelty 58
Carriage, Domestic. 29,81
Carriage, French 86,87,109

Carson, Pirie, Scott Co. 134

Chelsea 101,102

Chrome 128
Chronart 136
Chronometer 121
Clear Plastic 194
Cloisonne. 140

Colonial Hall Clock 183-190

Connecticut Shelf 13-16
Cromwellian. 108
Crystal Regulator 94
Cuckoo 37,38,48,52,93,179
Delf Plate. 136
Desk 126,131,146,149,152,156,193
Dice Clock 58
Direct Reading 150,156,194
Duplex 194
Electric 131-168, 175
Eli Terry (Type) 194

Eltime
   Electric Alarm 56
   Jump Hour. 57

Empire 94
Enamel Inlay 113
English 108-110
Flying Pendulum. 67
Fountain Novelty 49
Four Hundred Day 48,94,137,194

French Clocks
   Alarms 85-87
   Alarms, Musical 86
   Cabinet 86,94
   Cabinet, Musical 86
   Carriage. 87
   Carriage Alarms. 86
   Crystal Regulator 94
   Cuckoo 93
   Empire 94
   400 Day 94
   Gallery 88
   Louis XVI 95-99
   Marine. 93
   Novelty 89
   Open Swinger 86,90
   Picture Frame. 88
   Porcelain 89
   Regency 95-99

French Clocks (Cont.)
   Regulators
      Box 92
      Special 90
      Standing 91
      Sweep Second. 90
      Vienna 90,91
      Westminster 91,92
   Renninance 95-99
   Statue, Large 97-100
   Swing Arm. 89
   Wall Decorated 88
   Watch Holders 89

French Clock Signatures
   Bruchon 97
   Carra. 97
   Lavergne 100
   Levy 100
   Moreau, A. 97
   Moreau, F. 97
   Moreau, H. 100
   Moreau, L. 100
   Paladine. 97
   Picault, C. 100
   Rancoulet 97
   Ruchon 100
   Scotte 100
   Vienis, H. 100

French (type) Regulators 82,83,91
French Stag Case. 39
Fussee. 108

Fyart 151

Gallery 77
Giant Alarm 52

Gilbert Clock Co.
   Alarm 28,45,55-57
   Alarm, Thin 52
   Connecticut Shelf, Column & O.G.
      Column Spring 15
      Column Weight 15
      O.G. Weight 14
   Connecticut Shelf, Cottage
      Cottage No.2 15
      Coupon 15
      Favorite. 15
      Haidee. 15
      Rose 15
      Rose & Gilt 15
   Connecticut Shelf, Octagon Top
      Clyde 16
      Comet. 16
      Pilot Extra 16
   Connecticut Shelf, Round Top
      Keystone 16
      Round Top 14
      Round Top Extra 16
      Star Extra 16
   Connecticut Shelf, Split Top
      Advocate 17
      Coupon Extra. 17
      Gem Extra 17
      Hero 17

Gilbert Clock Co. (Cont.)
  Connecticut Shelf, Split Top (Cont.)
    Obelisk 17
    Rocket 17
  Connecticut Shelf, Steeple (Gothic)
    Sharp Gothic 14
    Winsted Gothic 14
  Kitchen . See Walnut Mantel .17-33,44
  Mantel, Black 35
  Mantel, Oak 34
  Maranville Calendar 27
  Novelty 57
  Regulators
    Octagon Top 27,35,43
    Parlor 24,27,28,44
    Round Top 27,43
    Sweep Seconds 23
  Scribe Ink 57
  Tambour 55
  Walnut Mantel & Kitchen . . .17-33,44

Glass 127,128,151
Glossnia 139
Grandfather 109,183-192
Grandfather Miniature 58
Grandmother 130,185
Hall 109,183-190
Hammond Electric .134,138,144,147,149
Hanging Kitchen 26,44
Heart Beat 172,175,176

Herchede
  Grandfather 195
  Hall 191,192

Imperial Clock Co.
  Battery 131
  Electric 142

Ingraham
  Alarm 51,55
  Alarm, Electric 56,57
  Box Clock 46
  Kitchen 39
  Wall 52
  Western Union 46

Ivory, French 47,50
Jumper 36

Junghans
  Cabinet 168
  Tambour 168
  Westminster 168

Keebler (See Lux) 169-182

Kenmore Electric
  Art Deco 167
  Mantel 167
  Table 167
  Tambour 167
  Wall 167

Kienzle
  Hall 185
  Mantel 161
  Tambour 161
  Westminster 161

Kitchen 17-33,39,40,44,46,66,67
  . . . . 69,72,74.75
Knight Novelty 59

Kroeber, Florence T. 73-81
  Alarm 81
  Antimated 81
  Brass 77
  Cabinet 76,77
  Calendar, Simple 77
  Carriage Alarm 81
  Cuckoo Mantel 80
  Gallery 77
  Kitchen 74,75
  Mirror Side 76
  Noiseless Rotary 80
  Novelty 80
  Plush 80
  Porcelene, Iron 80
  Regulators
    Octagon Top 78
    Parlor 78,79
    Round Top 78
    Seconds Bit 79
    Sweep Second 78
    Vienna 79

Ku-Ku Novelty 59
Lantern 108
Library 116,117

Lincoln Electric 131

Louis XVI 95-99

Lux 169-182
  Alarms 171,176,181,182
  Antimated 174,175,177,181,182
  Art 171,172,173,176
  Art Deco 152
  Banjo 170
  Calendar 182
  Cuckoo 179
  Electric 175
  Heart Beat 171,175,176
  Lamp 170
  Mickey Mouse 177
  Minute Minders 180,182
  Mirror 152
  Novelty 152,172,176,178
  Pendulettes 170-182
  Popeye 177
  Rotary 174
  Three Little Pigs 177
  Timers 182
  Wall 175,176

Madison 194

Mantel . . .34,40,41,62,63,125, 129,140
 146,157,158,167,195-201

Maranville Calendar 27

Marble 62,63,96-99,140,144,157
  Imitation 62,63
Marine 90,101

Marston Electric 131

Mauthe
  Mantel 160
  Tambour 160
  Westminster 160

Miller, Herman
  Mantel 157,158
  Tambour 159
  Westminster 157,158

Miller Plate 52,133,136

Minute Minders 180,182
Mirror 128,146-155
Mirror Side 76
Mission 46
Musical 57,42

New Haven
  Abbey Desk 131
  Alarm 50,56
    Electric 57,154,156
    Ideal 154,156
  Art Deco 146,148,152
  Automobile 154
  Bicycle 154
  Brass 68
  Cabinet 67,68
  Desk 152
  Direct Reading 150
  Gothic Desk 131
  Ignatz 68
  Keyless Pullwind 154,156
  Kitchen 67,69
  Mirror 146,148,150
  Novelty 68
  Radio 152
  Rear View Mirror 154
  Regulators
    Octagon Top 43
    Parlor 44,67

Nicholas Muller's Sons 62-65
  Bronze, Real 62,63
  Calendar, Simple 64,65
  Mantel, Black 62,63
  Marble, Imitation 62,63
  Marble, Red 62,63
  Nickel & Bronze 64
  Novelty 64
  Plaque 62
  Plush 62,65

Nite Glo 143
Noisless Rotary 80
Novelty 41,57,58,61,64,68,80,88
 152,169-182,193,198-201
Numeral Rolling 150,156,194
Onyx 41,126,132,144,157,158
Open Swinger 86,90
Ormolu & Marble 109
Parlor Standing 70
Pendulette 57,170-182

Penwood 150,156

Phinney-Walker
   Ship Wheel. 156

Picture 114,115
Picture Frame. 88
Plaque. 62
Plate Wall. 52,136

Plato. 47

Plush. 40,62,65,80
Political. 59,61
Porcelain 44-46, 89
Porcelene, Iron 80
Pullwind 154,156
Radio 129,152
Radio Imitation 57
Rear View Mirror 154
Regency 95-99
Regulators
   Box 46
   Drop Octagon. . 27,35,43,78,111,112
   French 82,83,91
   Parlor . .24,27,44,67,78,79,90,91,112
   Round Top 27,43,78,111
   Seconds Bit 79
   Sweep Second. 23,78,90
   Vienna 79,90-92
   Westminster 92
Renaissance 95-99

Revere Telechron
   Cabinet 166
   Hall 186
   Tambour 166
   Westminster 166

Roosevelt Political. 59,61
Rotary 174
Royal Bonn 46

Sangamo Electric
   Mantel. 163
   Tambour 162,163
   Wall Round 163
   Wall Square 163
   Westminster 162

Sessions
   Alarm 56,136
      Electric 56,146
   Art Deco 139,150
   "Cap-Maid" . . . . !39
   Desk 146,156,193
   Glossnia. 139
   Mantel. 146
   Mirror 150
   Mission 46
   Novelty 193
   Tambour 55
   Wall, Octagon 136
      Round Electric 193
      Square Electric 193

Seth Thomas
   Alarm 28,29
   Art Deco 152

Seth Thomas (Cont.)
   Calendar Double Dial 44
   Carriage Alarm 29
   Desk 152
   Kitchen 44,46
   Mantel, Black 40
   Radio 152
   Regulator No. 2 43
   Regulator, Octagon Top 43
   Tambour 55

Sets 94-99,137
Ships Bells 102
Silver 115

Silvercraft 132,135

Simplex Alarm 50,53

Standard Time Stamp. 36

Statue, Large 97-100
Swing Arm 49,89
Table 195-197
Tambour 55,117,125,129,159-168
Tape 174

Terry Clock Co. 71

Timers. 182
Time Stamp 36
Travel Alarms 109,126,128,195-197
Travel Imported 141
Trumpeter Cuckoo 80
Twin Face 127,193

United. 195-196
   Antimated 195-196
   Mantel. 195-196
   Novelty 195-196
   Wall 195-196

Usalite. 143

Vienna Regulators. . . . 79,82,83,90,91

Wakemaster Alarm. 133

Waldorf Wall 143

Wall 52,88,93,175,176
   Octagon. 136
   Round. . . 119,124,129,163,165,193
   Square. . . 119,124,129,163,165,193

Waltham
   Airplane 122,123
   Art Deco 113-117,126-128
   Automobile 122,123
   Banjo 120,121
   Boudoir 126
   Bronze 116
   Chromium 128
   Chronometer 121
   Colonial. 116,119
   Desk 126
   Enamel Inlay 113
   Glass Keywind 127,128,151
   Grandmother 130

Waltham (Cont.)
   Library 116,117
   Mirror 128
   Onyx 126
   Oriental 118
   Picture 114,115
   Silver 115
   Tambour 117
   Travel 126,128
   Twin Face 127
   Wall Round 119
   Wall Square 119

Waltham Electric
   Automobile 123
   Art Deco 148-152
   Banjo 124
   Cabinet 125
   Desk 149,150,152
   Electric Kit 124
   Glass. 151
   Mantel. 125,129
   Novelty 152
   Radio 152
   Tambour 125,129
   Tambour Round 124,129
   Wall Square 124,129
   Westminster 149

Warren Telechron 164,165
   Mantel. 164,165
   Tambour 164
   Wall Round 165
   Wall Square 165

Watch Holders 89

Waterbury
   Alarm 48,57
      Electric 133
   Calendar Double Dial 44
   Kitchen 70
      Wall 44
   Parlor, Standing 70
   Porcelain 45
   Regulators
      Octagon Top 43
      Parlor 44
      Round Top 43

Welch, EN.
   Kitchen 66
   Patti 66

Westclox Alarms 53,54

Western Union 46
Westminster 149,157-162,166,168
White House Alarm 56

Windsor
   Coach & Horses. 60
   Pagoda & Rickshaw 60
   Paperclip 61
   Sailing Ship 60
   Storm, The. 60,61
   Ukulele 60

Windsor Electric 153

THE REASON FOR
CLOCK IDENTIFICATION & PRICE GUIDE, BOOK 3

It is with pleasure that we present Clock Identification & Price Guide, Book 3, with the realization that many clock collectors have appreciated the immeasurable value of having a reliable guide to the originality of their clocks. For the past year we have had an increasing number of collectors ask that we expand the number of original pictures available to them by putting out this book. The average collector is no longer content to find a clock "similar" to one for which he desires a value guide. He wants to find the exact clock, to have an idea of the years of production, and to compare the catalog picture with the clock to check originality. Collectors will no longer accept books which have "non-original" clocks pictured that simply confuse the issue.

Clock Identification & Price Guide, Book 2 was published in 1979, and since that time the country has fallen into a recession, from which it is just now emerging, and this has had its effects on the market for clocks. While we have seen a 10% to 20% drop in the prices of some clocks (especially when hard times or bad luck has forced a collector to sell), the main effect of the recession has been a decrease in the number of sales observed. Trading seems to have increased but cash buying has definitely decreased. This has made it more difficult to establish some prices, but as times have seemed to get better in early 1983, activity has increased and the upward trend in prices seems to be re-establishing itself.

Probably due in part to the difficult economic factors, and probably due also to other factors, the young collectors and the beginning collectors have been conspicuous by their absence. This must be corrected if the hobby is to survive, and to do our part we will try to include many of the lower priced (but collectible) clocks in this and future price books. Even the affluent collector does not always feel like parting with a large sum at every NAWCC Regional he attends, but would like to join in the fun by buying some lower priced clocks that are still interesting, rare, and collectible. Therefore, we feel that all categories of collecting will be helped by the inclusion of lower priced collectibles without, of course, neglecting the higher priced treasures we all desire.

RELATIONSHIP OF CLOCK BOOK 3 TO
CLOCK BOOKS 1 AND 2

At the risk of becoming repetitious, certain facts must be emphasized. Book 3 is *NOT* a repeat of either Book 1 or Book 2. Every effort has been made not to repeat any of the clocks shown in Books 1 and 2, even to the point of cutting previously shown clocks out of the catalog pages. Any repetition found is usually due to necessity because of the layout of the old catalogs. And, look carefully before you assume that a certain clock is shown. It may be a different but similar model. Again, it may be a model previously shown but of a different year's production with subtle changes.

Again, Book 3 is an entirely *NEW* book, showing different clocks, taken (in many cases) from different catalogs than those used for Books 1 and 2, with current prices shown. The information to be given in the text of this book is new information, some of it dug out of many old books in bits and pieces and assembled here to provide a convenient reference in one place. So, if you do not have Books 1 and 2, do not expect to find that information here. Rather, use all the books together to have a complete information file.

IMPORTANT — IMPORTANT: EXPLANATION OF PRICING
PLEASE REVIEW THIS SECTION

ALL THE VALUES GIVEN IN THIS BOOK ARE FOR MINT, ORIGINAL CLOCKS, AND ARE RETAIL.

Understand this statement before you proceed. It is the basis for all prices given. Go back to Book 2 and read again the definitions of "Mint", "Original", and "Restored to Original." Granted, few clocks are mint, original clocks, and so will not command the price shown. If a clock is restored, use the appropriate pictures in Books 1, 2, or 3 to judge how well it has been returned to original. You must be your own judge as to how much to adjust the price you will pay according to the condition of the clock. It is human nature that most sellers will price their clock as mint, original, even though they know it is not. In their heart they know how much they will reduce the price because of the lack of perfection, so use your own judgment and make them an offer. You may be in agreement.

RETAIL VALUE: The "top price" that a serious collector, investor, or housewife who wants the clock and has the money will pay another who knows the value.

This definition is repeated in this book so that it will be remembered by the users of this book. An arm's length transaction between a knowledgeable buyer and a knowledgeable seller who has no pressures to buy or not buy, to sell or not sell, will establish a true value at that moment. Like all definitions, this one may not fit all cases. If the seller has pressure to sell, even if forced to sell, you may still see a true value established by two or more knowledgeable buyers bidding for the clock, as long as the competition does not create a compulsive pressure to buy. This definition of "Retail Value" is used at all times to screen the prices given in these books.

PRICE TRENDS SINCE BOOK 2

The price trends of recent months may be summed up in one sentence: "Now is the time to buy." If you are reading this later than 1983 you may already have missed your best opportunities, and, of course, it naturally follows that if you feel you must sell some clocks now (in the summer of 1983) you may not readily get the top price.

To summarize the price trends since 1979, when Book 2 was published, prices rose steadily until 1981 when sales slowed. The slowing of sales continued in 1982, with prices weakening and showing some decrease in parts of the country. Antique shops particularly reported very slow sales, due largely to poor specimens at high prices. The Marts at the NAWCC Regionals, from the fall of 1982 through the spring of 1983, showed falling prices. I believe the collectors in general were showing more selectivity in their purchases, since during this period certain clocks seemed to sell very readily but more common clocks were carted back home by the owners.

AUCTIONS: Normally, auctions are a rather poor indicator of values when considering prices for a clock price book, and have been almost disregarded in the past because the transactions will not fit our definition of retail value: the price that will be paid in an arm's length transaction when a knowledgeable collector, investor, dealer, or housewife who wants the clock and has the money, buys from a seller who knows the value. Auctions can generally be put into two classifications: honest and otherwise.

Honest, true auctions are those in which the auction bill gives an accurate description of the clock and its condition; the bidders are given ample time to check and examine the clock; there is *NO reserve, minimum bid, or bidders for the auctioneer or owner; and the auctioneer does not try to run the bidder up by faking an opposing bidder.* With a little thought, you can easily see why (usually) most auctions of the honest sort are estate auctions when the heirs are disinterested and the auctioneer is scrupulously honest.

In late 1982, at a time of dwindling sales and lowering prices due to the economic conditions, a noteworthy auction was held in Harrison, Arkansas, when, due to failing health, long-time collector H.A. "Dutch" Soper sold all the clocks from his clock shop and a portion of his collection, resulting in a two-day sale of 450 clocks that ran the gamut from poor condition to excellent; from old wood-works to modern; from American to English, French & German; from common to rare. Although "Dutch" was alive at that time, his condition was such that he was unable to lift a clock, required oxygen to be available at all times, and traveled in a wheelchair. Therefore, his desire was to sell the clocks with no sale restrictions whatsoever.

The auctioneer was the well-known "Col." Glen LaRue of Sweet Springs, Missouri, who has a spotless reputation and refuses to take an auction that is not completely honest, and consequently has such a following that he has been known to have 400-500 registered buyers at what would otherwise have been a routine farm sale. His larger antique auctions normally and routinely draw dealers from as many as 15 to 20 states.

This, then, was the background of "Dutch" Soper's auction, which drew an assortment of registered buyers from 27 states. These bidders and buyers represented every category of persons interested in clocks: from housewives to large and small dealers; from specialized collectors to general collectors; from newcomers to old timers; from those looking for a bargain to those determined to get one certain clock; and included both NAWCC members and non-members. So, this became a good indicator of present prices, since the buyers had more time to examine the clocks than they would normally have in a Mart. The buyers were generally of the type who would not overbid from emotion; the good clocks were in a price range that would preclude careless, reckless, or emotional bidding; and there were no dishonest factors involved to run up the bidding.

In a very few cases where specialized collectors were after one particular clock, I was able to sound out the collectors involved to find out how high they were willing to go for the clocks.

For all these reasons, this auction was a unique and accurate indicator of the prices at a time when sales at the Marts had decreased to the point that prices on many clocks were difficult to determine. Auctions of this type are beneficial to the hobby, and "Dutch" Soper is to be commended for having the courage to have an honest auction. The "win some, lose some" action resulted in satisfaction to both buyer and seller.

The prices paid indicated that collectors were still ready and able to pay the high retail value for the very rare and more desirable clocks. The auction was well-planned and efficiently managed, with few complaints, and a good time was had by all.

Final word on "Dutch": he passed away on April 28, 1983, and the final auction of his personal clocks that he called "My Museum" will be held in June 1983.

By the spring of 1983, prices on many common clocks had sagged to the point that the prices in Books 1 and 2 were again accurate. But the signs are clear that the increasing competition for a decreasing supply will soon begin to drive the prices up again. The spring Marts were indeed slow, with excellent buys abounding. But on the way home from one spring meeting, I stopped at a clock auction with many varied clocks. It included a number that had been "built" from bits and pieces by a well-known "artisan" (now deceased). This collector had been well known, and both his collection and his proclivity to play around "building" clocks were famous. His estate had sold all the remains of his many years of indulgence in the hobby, and many of the corpses and Trojan Horses ended up in this auction. While there was not an extremely large crowd of bidders, it included both collectors and dealers. Most of the collectors checked the clocks and knew which were original and which were not. Most even knew the history of the clocks. But some, probably dealers, did not, and a "built-up" mirrorside went for top market price for an original, and some "built-up" swinging arms also brought high prices for "non-original" merchandise. Moral: let the buyer beware. Always check the clock before you buy. Do not hesitate to ask the seller any questions that you may have, and never hesitate to ask other collectors for their opinion of the clock. Many old-timers will not offer their knowledge unless asked, but are usually glad to help. Many beginners are afraid to ask about a clock, feeling that the dealers or old-timers may buy it quickly, but the dealer or old-timer probably already has several. Most dealers and old-timers, as a matter of principle, will not try to snatch it away from someone else. Also, most reputable dealers and old-timers will not take fakes to a Mart. (The public "stop and swap" places and flea markets are used to unload the fakes.) For the beginner, the safest place to buy a clock is usually the NAWCC Marts. If the beginner will ask other collectors about the reputation of various dealers and buy only from the ones of good reputation, he will probably never be stuck with a fake.

FEATURES THAT MAKE A CLOCK VALUABLE

For most collectibles, rarity is everything: the main determining factor in the price at which the collectible is sold. But this is not true with clocks. Most clocks when purchased, are taken into the home and become part of the furnishings. With the homemaker (of whatever sex) looking at the clock day in and day out, if it does not have enduring beauty it is soon gone. This is particularly true with the beginning collectors and with the "interior decorators" who enter the market solely to equip a room. Therefore, from long observation, I am forced to say that beauty is the greatest, strongest feature affecting the value of a clock.

The second strongest determining factor is the interest that the clock arouses in the observer. Features of interest are, (1) motion of some king; (2) unusual shape; (3) unusual or special case material; (4) special or unusual strike; (5) special or unusual name (of clock or maker). To explain:

(1) Motion — A pendulum clock is usually more sought after than a balance wheel clock. An antimated clock is the most sought after of all. If the motion is interesting enough, the clock is sought after even if it is faulty as a timekeeper. Witness the popularity of the "Ignatz", the "Dickory-Dickory Dock", the "Foliots", and the bouncing and swinging dolls.

(2) Unusual Shape — An unusual shape that is still appealing is much sought after. Witness the "acorn" clocks, the "banjos", the "figure eights", and others.

(3) Unusual or special case materials — In this category we must include the marbles, onyx, marquety, exotic veneers, the metal cases (iron, brass, bronze, zinc, pewter, etc.), and others such as the so-called "plush cases".

(4) Special or unusual strike — This category includes the quarter-hour strikes, the various chimes, the musical clocks, the coo-coos, and many others you will think of immediately.

(5) Special or unusual name — This category is more elusive, as it can be attributed to both snob appeal and historical interest. Some names, such as Howard, fall into both categories, and in addition are high grade clocks. The names of makers were more important in the clocks of the individual makers, before 1850, but most collectors today develop preferences among the seven giants of the industry, and the names of some of the smaller clockmakers (such as George B. Owen, Florence T. Kroeber, the Mullers, Jennings Brothers, Bailey, Banks & Biddle) tend to raise the price of a clock, even though they were all primarily case modifiers, importers, and sales agents, not movement manufacturers, and so are not always considered true clockmakers. Waltham, Boston, Chelsea and Howard were all true manufacturers of complete, high grade clocks, and all have very loyal followers among the collectors.

When restoring clock cases it often becomes necessary to discuss the restoration on the phone, and, to facilitate complete understanding, the terminology becomes important. Therefore, the following definitions are presented as examples of the most common points of discussion.

Apron: The decorative piece below the base of a case; can be between the legs of a shelf or floor clock, or on the bottom of the case of a shelf clock.

Banding: Strip of veneer around a panel or door, strictly for decoration.

Boss: A projection.

Capital: The trim terminating the top of a column.

Cornice: Topmost moulding of a case.

Dowel: A wooden peg used to hold two pieces together, or to reinforce a joint.

Escutcheon: The trim around a keghole.

Types of Feet: (a) **Ball foot** — ball, may have small flat on top or bottom, or both; (b) **Block foot** — a block or cube; (c) **Bracket foot** — a small addition or bracket on the side of the main support; (d) **Bun foot** — ball flattened to an oval shape; (e) **Chinese foot** — rounded flat foot, a flat turning; (f) **Claw foot** — foot carved from a wood block or cast from metal to resemble an animals foot with claws, usually extended claws.

Finial: The turnings projecting above a clock case for decoration. Types: acorn, pineapple, ball, flambeau (a flaming torch), urn, Terry-type (the distinctive brass finials as used on the pillar and scroll.)

Mask: A face used as a decoration.

Medallion: On American clocks, usually refers to a small, flat turning, glued to the surface of the case for decoration.

Patina: The smooth sheen and aged coloration of antique wood. Technically, any surface of antique appearance.

Pediment: Used to indicate the decorative top of a case; that structure above the cornice.

These few definitions of case parts will suffice for our purposes. The natural finishes used in the 19th Century also need definition:

Japanning: Refers to finishing a decorative wood object with colored or black lacquer. Often used as a finish for clocks.

Lacquer: The sap of a tree cultivated in China and Japan. This resin has been in use in China since legendary times and in Japan since the 6th Century.

Shellac: A resinous secretion (or excretion) of the lac insect. When dissolved in acetone or alcohol, sometimes called shellac varnish. The natural orange shellac is bleached to form white shellac.

Varnish: Technically, any finish that produces a hard, transparent, shiny coating on the painted object, which explains the use of the terms "shellac varnish" and "lacquer varnish". Varnish dates from prehistoric times, with the Egyptians using a hot varnish on the mummy cases. About the middle of the 18th Century, linseed oil varnish began to be used and was used throughout the 19th Century. This will be the finish referred to in our text as "varnish". It usually consisted of linseed oil thinned with turpentine, with litharge as a drier. Any varnish is usually composed of: (a) a resin or gum (gives hardness and luster); (b) a drier, usually a drying oil (to give flexibility and toughness), with other driers to control the drying rate and luster; and (c) volatile solvents (to thin to the proper consistency for the particular method of application). The solvent must be volatile so as to leave only the oil and resin on the surface after application.

DETAILED INFORMATION ON CASE MATERIAL

ONYX AND MARBLE CASES

Before starting to repair an onyx or marble case, be sure that you understand the composition of these cases, particularly if you need to replace a portion of the case.

MARBLE: Technically speaking, the term SHOULD only be applied to metamorphosed, recrystallized limestones and dolomites. Practically speaking, the term is used to designate any limestone that is hard enough to take a polish. As a trade term, it is generally used for ANY crystalline calcium carbonate rock of pleasing pattern and color when cut and polished. All marble is composed of crystals of the minerals calcite ($CaCO_3$) and/or dolomite ($CaMg(CO_3)_2$) usually mixed with other minerals that give it the great variety of colors.

ONYX: Technically speaking, the term should only be applied to a striped agate in which white layers alternate with either black or darker layers of other colors. Practically speaking, (and for our purposes as clock collectors) it is generally applied to a quartz agate that is dyed black. As a trade term, it is loosely applied to both banded agate and banded marble.

ONXY MARBLE: For our purposes, any marble that is called "Onyx", e.g. "Mexican Onyx." Usually marble that is striped in more or less parallel layers that somewhat resemble true onyx.

Both marble and agate have been known and used since ancient times, and the terms "onyx" and "onyx marble" were also used in ancient times. The Germans developed a method of dying agate black, and now most commercial agate is artificially dyed in many different colors. The method used for coloring onyx black consisted of soaking the onyx in either oil (olive) or a sugar solution for a long period, then "carburizing" the onyx with sulphuric acid. The acid left the carbon from the oil or sugar in the onyx and thus colored it black. If some of the layers were particularly hard and impermeable, they would not absorb as much sugar or oil, and thus the color would not be as deep, so that the bands could still be distinguished after the coloring.

Black marble is found near Shoreham, Vermont and Glen Falls, New York. Marble can also be artificially colored black, but whether this was done by the nineteenth century clock factories, I do not know.

The "imitation black marble" clocks were generally iron cases finished with a very hard Japanned black finish and can, of course, be detected with a magnet. We have also found some black mantels in what appears to be slate, but so far I have been unable to find references to this in the old catalogs.

ONYX & MARBLE CASES (Cont.)

Now for the $64,000 question: How do you distinguish black onyx from black marble? In appearance, black onyx is usually more translucent than marble, but this cannot be used as a positive test to determine of which material a specimen is composed, since the characteristics of different specimens vary so greatly. Qualitative chemical analysis cannot be used due to the heterogeneous composition of the minerals. Quantitative tests of a large portion would be indicative. Acid will attack and destroy marble, although the harder dolomites will resist diluted sulphuric acid, while agate or onyx will resist acid. So, sulphuric acid, or preferably, hydrochloric acid, may be used to determine if a rock or clock case is marble or true onyx.

The easiest practical test is a hardness test. In a scale of hardness from 1 to 10, with talc as 1 and diamond as 10, marble has a hardness of 3 to 4, while true onyx has a hardness of 6 to 7. Since iron or mild steel has a hardness of 4 to 5, you can use a scratch test with a nail, and it should scratch marble but will not touch onyx.

This is about the extent of the tests available to check the composition of a case. Any test will be somewhat damaging to a clock case.

Once, while on vacation, I had a lot of fun asking antique dealers if they could tell me the difference between black marble and black onyx. The most common answer was that you just know from experience. One practical dealer said, "I just ask the customer what he thinks it is, and that's what it is." Another practical dealer said, "I just look it up in the book, and if it says "onyx", that's what it is." I have not yet determined if the old catalogs are always accurate when they show black onyx clock cases, but from the original prices as compared to the original prices of the black marble, I suspect that they are usually referring to true onyx. In the case of the green onyx cases, they are not accurate as these are marble, or, if you prefer, marble onyx.

VENEERED WOODEN CASES

Probably a majority of wooden clock cases are veneered, since this allowed the maker to get any grain desired at a much lower price. Even in the Victorian Period, solid walnut was not cheap. A 1902 book reports that a very large walnut tree would bring as much as $5,000. Convert that to today's prices and you will see that the trees will not bring that much today. Veneer was used by the Greeks and Romans, and the use of veneer has seemed to vary with the degree of civilization. The greater the degree of civilization, the greater the use of veneer. There was little veneer used during the dark ages. In the early 1800's, veneer was still made by hand methods. During the mid-1800's, more and more sophisticated saws were developed for sawing thin sheets from logs to make veneer, and eventually very thin saws were capable of cutting sheets that were less than 1/16" thickness, so that some sanding to finish the surface was all that was left to do after the sawing.

In the last 25 years of the 19th Century, the techniques of slicing, rolling, and "reverse rolling" came to be common techniques for making veneer, although sawing was still used for ebony, rose, olive, and quarter-sawed oak and sycamore. Surprisingly, at the turn of the century New York was the greatest veneer producing center, ahead of Boston, Grand Rapids, Cincinnati, and Chicago, in that order.

Razor-sharp knives were used for slicing a log into thin sheets. It is easy to see that both sawing and slicing could be used in a variety of ways to produce the desired grain effects. Logs could be sawed, or sliced lengthwise or crosswise, or the log could be cut into quarters, halves, or sections, and the veneer taken from these to get the desired figure.

To make veneer by rolling, the log was first boiled in large vats which were covered and heated by steam pipes. When thoroughly cooked the log was hoisted out (with a big cloud of steam) and put into a lathe large enough to take up to a 16 foot log. Then a razor-sharp knife as long as the log was fed into the log. As soon as the log was perfectly round the knife was adjusted to slice off exactly the thickness of veneer needed, which could be as thin as 1/32" and as thick as 1/4" or more. It is easy to see that this does not produce much figure or pattern in the grain, so this method is usually used to make plywood layers.

"Reverse Rolling" to make veneer is a variation of rolling in which the log is sawed lengthwise in halves and the centers of the lathe are set near the bark side so that as the log is rolled, the knife is shaving the veneer off across the grain, which gives a much more figured veneer than plain rolling.

This discussion of how veneer is made is designed to make the collector aware of the different types of grain and figure that he might see on a clock. And, if you are attempting to replace a missing piece of veneer, it is easy to see you must obtain a replacement piece made by the same method as the original if you desire a close match.

TO REPAIR VENEER: When possible, always glue the old veneer back in place, preferably without cracking it. The joints and cracks will leave lines in the surface that will show through the finish. Use slick shellac to fill the cracks and joints as described in Clock Book 2. If it is necessary to replace some of the veneer, you must use material of the same color, grain and thickness. An old piece of veneer from an old piece of furniture will usually be easiest to match.

When cutting a piece of veneer for a patch, trim the edges with a bevel slanting somewhat inward on the bottom so that the top edges are tight when it is pushed into place and clamped. Veneer always darkens with age, which is why new material must be stained to match old. Stain a patch before trimming, as the stain may expand the veneer. After trimming, sand the edges of the patch lightly until smooth, then stain the edges. Use a sharp, thin-pointed blade of a knife or a suitable carving chisel to remove all dirt and old glue from the area under the patch, as new glue will not stick properly to old. Neither will the patch lay properly in place if the surface is not clean and smooth.

Cover the hole and the bottom of the patch with a thin layer of glue, then lay the patch in place. Cover the area with waxed paper or a piece of plastic film from the kitchen to keep the glue from sticking to your blocks, weights, or clamps. If you used slightly too much glue so that it will be oozing up around the patch, a little wax on the wood around the patch will keep it from sticking so tight and reduce the sanding you must do later. A small patch on a flat area will require only a block and a weight or clamp to hold it in place until dry. A larger patch may require a sandbag or several clamps, or a press to hold it, and a curved surface may require that you make a mold beforehand so that it will properly hold the patch in place.

Let the glue dry for at least 24 hours, then remove the weights, clamps, waxed paper or plastic, and any excess glue not stuck to the clock, then finish sanding with 8/0 or 6/0 sandpaper until smooth.

If you have a loose edge, and when you lift it slightly adequate glue remains under the veneer, spray a little water on the glue (an atomizer works very well), then use an almost hot thin metal spatula to slide under the veneer and heat the water and glue until they mix and soften the glue. Then lay a sheet of foil over the veneer and weight it down with a very warm, old-fashioned flat iron for 24 hours. If you are careful enough and lucky enough not to break or crack the veneer, you will have a perfect repair. Do not use this method if there is dirt or inadequate glue under the veneer. In this case, carefully scrape the dirt and glue from under the veneer, put new glue on a spatula blade, and carefully spread the new glue under the veneer with the spatula blade. Then press the veneer down, roll it with a roller (roll toward the edge) if necessary to squeeze out all excess glue, wipe off the excess with a damp cloth, cover the area with a piece of plastic film, then a block and a weight for 24 hours.

If you have a blister or wave in the veneer (a place where

the veneer has raised from the surface), read the following methods of repair and choose the one that fits the conditions:

(a) If the veneer is not cracked or broken, cover the blister with a piece of smooth foil and very gently place a moderately hot old-fashioned flat iron on the blister. Be gentle — do not crack the veneer. The iron should not be hot enough to ruin the finish. Leave the iron in place for 24 hours. If the condition of the old glue is satisfactory and there is enough moisture in the wood below the veneer, the heat should draw out sufficient moisture from the wood to soften the old glue and make it stick.

(b) If the veneer is broken or cracked at the blister, lay a damp blotter over the blister and put the moderately hot flat iron over the blotter and blister. Leave for 24 hours, then if you had a broken piece that had fallen out or had been removed, glue it in place as in patching, put the weight on it and let set 24 hours.

Another method for a blister with cracked or broken veneer: Put vinegar in the blister and allow to stand for 8-12 hours to soften the glue, then pour out any remaining vinegar from the blister and place a dry blotter and the hot flat iron over the blister. The blotter will absorb the moisture and the heat should shrink the veneer back to the flat position. If any edges remain ungued, carefully raise the loose veneer and reglue as described for repairing loose edges.

(c) If the veneer over the blister is cracked and there is dirt under the veneer, take a razor blade knife and cut down the crack to open it to the edges of the blister, then make a similar cut at right angles to the crack so that you now have an X crossing the blister. Carefully lift the points of the flaps at the center of the X, clean out all dirt from underneath, then glue down by one of the above methods or by inserting new glue. If there is too much dirt or old glue, to easily remove as above cut a "barn door" flat instead of the X. This is done by making two cuts with the grain and one across the grain to make a square or rectangular flap which you can lift higher for heavy duty cleaning.

(d) If all the above methods are inadequate, cut out the blister and patch with an inlay. Always cut two sides of the veneer along the grain. Use a straight edge to cut out the veneer so that the edges of the patch are easier to fit. After cutting out the veneer, lay a piece of paper over the recess and rub your finger or a pencil lead around the edge of the recess so that it makes a line on the paper. Carefully lay the paper on a piece of veneer so that the grain runs correctly for the patch and cut out the patch with a large pair of scissors. Glue in place as described at the first of this section. Please review the information on glue in Book 2.

NOTE: An eye dropper and a large hypodermic needle (veterinarian style) are almost indispensible tools for applying glue when repairing veneer or loose glued joints. They save enough time to be worth the cleaning it takes later.

To get a stock of old veneer for use in repairing clock cases, go around the junk stores and secondhand furniture stores and buy some pieces of veneered furniture. Get the flat surfaces for easier working. Remove the finish from the old veneer and sand with 3/0 or finer sandpaper to open the grain. Soak the surface with a wet cloth for 12 hours, moistening the cloth frequently. Start at an edge, lift the veneer with a knife and remove. If it does not come off easily, continue soaking until it does. After removing the veneer, place it on a flat surface (while still wet) with the underside up. Use a scraper to remove all the remaining old glue. When dry, sand carefully with 3/0 or finer sandpaper until thoroughly clean and ready to use. Store in a dry place pressed between two flat surfaces with sufficient weight to keep the veneer from wrinkling and curling. Note that you will rarely need a piece of old veneer larger than this page. The above techniques are passed on to you in memory of my dad, A. F. Rabeneck, a true artist who spent 40 years restoring antique furniture, and could make patches and repairs in veneer that were practically invisible.

HINTS FOR THE NEW COLLECTOR

New and young collectors are necessary for the survival of our hobby, so we would like to offer a few hints to them to help make the hobby profitable as well as interesting and enjoyable. As one old collector remarked, "more profit means more enjoyment". Young collectors appear to become discouraged at the marts at the high prices for clocks, especially when they hear the old-timers tell of how cheap the prices were only a few (ten or twenty) years ago. If you fall in this category, take heart and read on. You have the greatest opportunity of all if you are young, for you have time in your favor. The law of supply and demand cannot be repealed, as much as some politicians would like to try. In our case, the supply is decreasing due to attrition (attrition in this case means destruction, both by forces beyond our control, such as fire, and also by the hand of man as when an unskilled person attempts a repair, or by poor storage, etc.). The demand is constantly increasing with the increase in our population, due both to new collectors and to the desire of housewives to have an antique clock in the furnishings of the house. Therefore, the value of a collector's clocks MUST increase with time — and will. So, all the new collector has to do is buy wisely and wait. Roy Ehrhardt, in his lectures, says that you make money when you buy, not when you sell. This is true. If you do not buy wisely the profit is gone, and the hobby has no room for a con man who will try to recoup profits by getting others to repeat his mistakes.

The young collector should remember that as anything becomes rare it becomes collectible. As it gets older it becomes more collectible. After an item reaches the age of 100 it is considered a "real antique". At present (in 1983) an item made in the 1930's is not considered a "real" antique, but in the 21st Century it will be considered so. Therefore, if you don't have much money to spend and you are looking for help for your retirement in the 21st Century, buy what will at that time be collector's items from the 1920's and 30's. In 20 years you can be telling new collectors how much cheaper they were a few years ago.

History tells you which clocks will be the collector's clocks of the future. Novelty items will probably increase in value first, then stabilize for the long haul. Clocks that are true art with great beauty will always be in demand and will probably be fairly stable in price at first, then show a steady increase for the long haul, with the greatest increase in value at the age of 100 or more. Any clock that shows movement has always been liked by collectors, therefore, good antimated clocks will definitely be collector's items in the future. Visible pendulums, visible escapements, and visible balance wheels in the movements are always preferred over clocks with invisible works hidden in the case. Even a seconds hand helps. High quality does not change with time. If a clock is of high quality today it will be high quality in the future, and it will command a higher price, both today and in the future.

Rarity will always win in the end. The extreme high prices that have been paid for some antiques and works of art are always for the rare ones. So the greatest increase in value will be for the rare clock that has other desired features, such as high quality, a desired maker, beauty, motion or animation, and novelty.

So, as a young collector if you do not have much money to spend, analyze the low priced clock that you find in the flea markets from the 20's, 30's and 40's. If it has several desired features, buy it, take it home, and wait; and while you wait, document the clock. Write down when and where it was purchased, from whom, and all of the history of the clock that you can get. Add to this information the history of the company that made the clock and any production estimates you can obtain. (In less than 50 years, this information will be impossible to get.) Put this documentation with the clock and in 50 years it will increase the value of the clock considerably at no cost to you.

If you are a new collector who is older, or a young collector who has more money to spend, apply the preceding principles to clocks that are already collector's items. Learn their present value and look for clocks that are underpriced. Follow the example of the dealers who cruise through the Marts looking for clocks that are underpriced or whose owners are willing to take considerably less before the final hours of the Mart, and buy them. Remember that the owner facing the work of packing and hauling a number of heavy clocks becomes much more anxious to sell.

The real collector's items that you buy at less than the market price can be sold at a profit tomorrow, next week, next month, or next year, when and if you find a buyer. In this category you must do your homework. Study the price books and other clock books so that you know the current market price and "why" the clock is desired by collectors.

CLOCKS THAT MAY BE DESIRABLE IN 20 YEARS

We will now take a brief look at clocks that are not at present greatly sought out by collectors, but seem to have great short-term potential for the next 20 years. These are general classes of clocks that seem to be overlooked by collectors at present, but have features for collectors that make them seem underpriced today. Admittedly, this is guessing, and investing in these types of clocks for short-term profit is risky; but these are probably the most interesting risk investments you will ever make as these are interesting clocks.

The first class of clocks that must be mentioned here are the old handmade American clocks produced before 1850. The transition wood-works and the triple deckers of the 1830-50 era have been fairly stable in price for the last five or ten years, going (in many cases) for $300 to $500 in the Marts. Many have carved columns and splats and are grossly underpriced in today's market. The wood-works, O.G.'s, and 8-Day O.G's are in the same category, with prices from $135 to $250 in the Marts. All of these clocks are historically important, with many interesting labels but with styles that are not favored today for home furnishings. Housewives do not want them in the house. This, along with the present intense interest in Victorian clocks, has caused their prices to be depressed. Many of these should now be museum pieces. The low prices give you the opportunity to build your own museum.

The next large class of clocks that show the promise of great opportunity for collectors are the electric clocks. Interest in electrics has been slowly building for years. At present, the greatest interest is in the spring-operated, electrically wound clocks — the so-called "self-winding clocks". There are a number of makers of these clocks. Most collectors are only familiar with the "Self-winding Clock Co." Many collectors do not realize that the early Sangamo electric clocks were high grade, jeweled, spring movements, wound by electric motors. Other companies, such as Herchede, also produced this type of clock. Low prices give great opportunities in this area.

Do not overlook the synchronous electric clocks, ignored and sneered at by many collectors. Many of these have all the qualities that will make them great collector items in the future. From the early hand-started models (historically important) to the late quartz movements, low prices and opportunities are numerous. Already, some of the quartz chronometers are being seen in the Marts. Clocks of beauty are plentiful in electrics, since the small works allowed flexibility in design. Novelty and animation (or motion) are also available. United electric clocks have animated designs such as the "Ballerina", the "Fisherman", and other clocks that have a clock section combined with a lighted animated section. These can be bought for a range of $15 to $150 today and will definitely be the collector's items of tomorrow. Many are shown in this book.

The last class to be mentioned here is the small clocks: the bedroom or boudoir clocks, the travel clocks, the car clocks,

and the alarms. Many of these are high quality clocks, but a look at the prices in this book will show low prices. Waltham made many high quality clocks called "travel", "bedroom", and "car" clocks, but while collectors have snatched up the small banjos and pillar and scroll models (and driven the prices up accordingly), they have largely ignored the other small clocks made by Waltham. This will not be true in the future. Waltham, Boston, Chelsea, the Rimwind companies, and most of the seven giants of the clock industry all made high quality car clocks. Westclox and others made low quality car clocks. Keywinds, stemwinds, backwinds, rimwinds, and pullwind models all seem to abound at low prices. But, at the auto swap meets the supplies have dried up and prices are rising. The same will be true in the Marts.

CURRENTLY PRODUCED CLOCKS THAT SHOULD BE COLLECTOR'S ITEMS IN THE FUTURE

Most collectors tend to ignore currently produced clocks as not being worthy of attention. However, past experience teaches us that if the clock is rare enough, or interesting enough, or beautiful enough, it will be a collector's item before waiting a century — some in only five or ten years. Certainly, no collector would turn down the chance to own one of the reproductions (replicas in some cases) put out by Howard, Chelsea, and the Boston Division of Chelsea. If the price is right, they change hands readily and quickly. However, there are other clocks that may be in great demand a few years in the future, such as Edward Cielascyk's decimal clock put out in 1979 by Westclox, and Hamilton Clock Co.'s cube clock put out in 1980, called the "Forecast Q" (which was a cube that swiveled on a base and had time, temp, humidity, and barometric pressure on the four sides of the cube), should also make collector status some day. A man named Chipley of Prescott, Arizona, supposedly during the last three years has been making wooden geared clocks in different case styles with a production goal of 50 clocks. These should be rare enough to attain collector status. And last but not least, the Atmos clock, produced currently and in production since 1925, has already attained collector status due to the interesting perpetual motion drive used by the clock.

OF INTEREST TO COLLECTORS

SHIP'S CHRONOMETER — WATCH OR CLOCK?

These timepieces are collected by both watch and clock collectors, since they have some of the characteristics of both. Watch collectors in general call the movement a watch movement but the faces (dials) are as large as a small clock. The ship's chronometers are too large to be carried on your person as a watch, and when mounted on the gimbals in a box becomes an armful for carrying, but they do present a nice appearance on a shelf. With their extreme accuracy, undisturbed by being moved around (because of the gimbal mounting), the ship's chronometer is very suitable for a clock collector to carry around as a time standard for setting his clocks accurately.

In this country, Waltham, Elgin, and Hamilton made many chronometers, with Waltham using their 8-Day lever movement; Elgin and Hamilton using a detent escapement. Elgin made about 200 of these but according to reports these were never used by the Navy.

Ship's chronometers can serve to educate clock collectors to the fact that serial numbers allow production dates and production totals to be closely estimated, thus age and rarity can be determined. With clocks in general, age and rarity are usually determined by guesswork tempered by wishful thinking.

No clock collector should be without a ship's chronometer, as its nice appearance on the shelf in the wooden box and its portability, combined with accuracy, makes it both decorative and useful as well as interesting.

FRENCH CLOCKS

A section of French clocks produced after the turn of the century is included in this book. French clocks have a long history that differs from that in other countries. In this country, the great need was for timepieces at an affordable price, and the clocks developed accordingly. In England and Germany, the emphasis was mostly on high quality movements, and the cases were primarily that—cases for the movements. In France, clocks were considered another art form and the movements were something that had to be integrated into the art form. Guilds (analogous to our unions) were developed, and maintained high standards and strict rules for the artisans of the clock craft. The clockmakers had their guild first and eventually this became the guild of the movement makers. France was almost the only country that gave casemakers a status equal to that of the clockmakers. The casemakers guild, by about 1750, required the casemaker to sign the wooden cases. The trend toward metal cases and fancy castings was evident by 1760 and this led to much friction between the casemakers guild and the casters guild. This type of friction became more common as the case finishers and other specialized crafts had their own guilds. The guilds could have stifled the development of clocks except for one unusual situation: a master clockmaker could progress to "Horologers du Roi", or, "Clockmakers to the King". The guild rules did not apply to the Clockmakers to the King. The status seemed to give almost unlimited latitude, which perhaps explains why they produced such extraordinary clocks.

In France, the King and his Court seemed to have more influence on the styles and arts of the country than was perhaps the case in other countries, and with a lavish, extravagant royalty the styles in art were rather extravagant, which resulted in the artistic clocks that are so prized today.

TIME PULSES, TIME BALLS
AND WESTERN UNION CLOCKS

At the turn of the century Standard Time for the United States was supplied by the Naval Observatory in Washington. The exact time at 12:00 Noon was determined every day, supposedly by astronomical observation, and the precise time was transmitted by wire to the clocks of government departments and to the telegraph company. Three minutes before noon each day the telegraph company cleared its lines of all business throughout the United States so that the time pulse would have complete priority. It was estimated that due to transmission time San Francisco would register the time within one-fifth of a second after it was taken at Washington, D.C.

For a charge of $15 per clock per year (ca 1900) a private or business clock could be connected to the telegraph system to receive the automatic time pulse. It was estimated that more than 10,000 clocks were regulated in this manner in New York City alone. And the telegraph company increased its income by 1—1/2 million dollars a year with this service, which was a lot of money in 1900.

Time balls were also set up at major ports so that any ship in the harbor could set their ship's chronometer by the time ball. This was particularly important for a ship waiting to depart. Originally, canon shots were used but the slow speed at which sound travels caused errors in setting the time and resulted in errors at sea in determining their position, so the time ball system was adopted. Time balls were installed as follows:

Washington, D.C., 1844 or 45: At the old Naval Observatory. Hand-operated until 1886, then rebuilt and electrically operated.

Boston, 1878-81: Time and control from Harvard Observatory.

San Francisco, 1885: On Telegraph Hill on Castellated Building. In 1898: Moved to top of Ferry Building. In 1909: Moved to top of Fairmount Hotel. In 1937: Discontinued

entirely.

New York City, 1870: Ball dropped on Western Union Building, corner of Broadway & Dey St. Last one in NYC put in operation 12-1-1913 at Seaman's Church Institute.

Cincinnati, St. Louis, Denver: All had time balls sometime after 1881.

Philadelphia: Put in operation in 1900, discontinued 1934.

Mystic Seaport, Connecticut: Put in operation in 1955.

In 1908, the ball that is used on New Year's Eve was installed on the old Times Tower Building in New York City. This time ball was different in that it ended its fall precisely at the desired time. The other time balls started their fall precisely at 12:00 Noon.

This bit of history brings us to that extra wire in Western Union clocks that has bugged collectors for so long. Most Western Union clocks were of the self-winding variety, and while extremely accurate they did not have compensated pendulums, nor did Western Union at that time have precise temperature control in their offices. Therefore, the rate of the clocks would vary slightly. This was taken care of by that extra wire through which the time pulse came at noon every day, precisely resetting the clock to the correct time, and while doing so lighting the small red bulb peeking out of the hole in the dial. This allowed the office personnel to observe that the time pulse was received by the clock.

Now, to take another look at the big picture, imagine if you will the scene at noon every day. At three minutes before twelve noon all communication via telegraph ceased, while it seemed the entire country waited with bated breath and ships' captains in the major ports shaded their eyes watching the time balls. At exactly noon the Naval Observatory sent the pulse, clocks in government buildings corrected, time balls fell while ships' captains set the chronometers, lights flashed on the faces of Western Union clocks while they corrected, whistles blew at the factories, and then the entire country started breathing again as the routine day continued.

THUMBNAIL SKETCHES OF SOME
INTERESTING COMPANIES

The **Daniel Pratt Clock Companies:** Daniel Pratt was born in 1797 in Redding, Massachusetts and eventually was putting out wooden works clocks. The label usually reads, "Extra Clocks manufactured and sold by Daniel Pratt, Jr." Most of these clocks have manufacturing dates on them. He used brass movements after 1838, and from 1846 to 1871 had a store at 49 Union St., Boston. He died in 1871. Many of his clocks are still around and can occasionally be seen in the Marts.

His business was continued after his death as "Daniel Pratts Sons", and you will find a few clocks with this label from the period 1871-1880. These labels are rare.

It has been reported that the business was continued under other names from 1880-1895, but after 1895 became known as "Daniel Pratt, Son, 339 Washington St., Boston", operated by Frank W. B. Pratt. The business was discontinued in 1915 with the death of Frank Pratt. After being in operation for well over three-quarters of a century, the clocks the business produced should have been better known by collectors.

Bristol Company, Waterbury, Conn.: Organized about 1892 and operated by the Bristol family, exists today as the Bristol-Babcock Company. Made recording temperature and pressure gauges and some electrical recording instruments. Bought Seth Thomas movements until the flood of 1955 put Seth Thomas out of business, then used German movements and some Lux movements. Also used some electric drives.

NOTE: This company is included because it is often confused with the Bristol Brass and Clock Company, Bristol, Connecticut, and has been thought (by some collectors) to be a branch of one of the seven giant companies.

Boston Clock Company. Formed in 1880 by Joseph H. Eastman, who had learned the clock trade from E. Howard. Best known for making mantel clocks with Eastman's single-wind mechanism. In 1897 the company became the Chelsea Clock Company. Today, Boston Clock Company is shown as a division of Chelsea.

Chelsea Clock Co., 284 Everett Ave., Chelsea, Mass. 1897 to present. Famous for high grade marine and ship's bell clocks. It was once said that Chelsea was recognized internationally and in military and scientific circles, but not as well recognized by collectors. This has changed, as evidenced by the prices of Chelsea clocks shown in this book.

Derry Clock Co., incorporated in Maine in 1908. Closed in 1910. Charter suspended in 1911 for non-payment of fees. Dissolved in 1912. All machinery and equipment sold to Herchede Hall Clock Company.

Howard. (NOTE: The history of Edward Howard has been given in various books. This short article is for quick reference only.) Edward Howard, born 1813, learned clockmaking as an apprentice to Aaron Willard, Jr. In 1842, formed the company of Stephenson, Howard & Davis. They made scales, balances, and clocks. Some references say they made church clocks. In 1847 or 1848, the company became Howard & Davis, still making scales, balances, and high grade clocks. About 1856 to 1858 (according to which reference you use), the company became E. Howard & Co. Some writers claim that wall clocks were made under this name from 1842 to 1858. In 1860, "E. Howard & Co." became their official trademark. In 1903, the company was reorganized under the name of E. Howard Clock Co. They were then making tower clocks, electric time systems, parts, and continuing to make high grade clocks. In the late 20's, the company began to look into synchronous clocks, moved into the Howard Watch Building in the 30's, and reorganized in 1934 as Howard Clock Products, Inc. The company then made precision parts, electrical instruments, aircraft instruments, and other instruments; and also produced a few high grade synchronous electric clocks and slave systems. In 1958, clock production ceased, except that the tower clocks were made until 1964. In the 50's and 60's, 80% of the company's output was for government contracts. In 1975, the company started making a few models of classic clocks and at present are making seven models. All models are given serial numbers. Howard clocks have always been among the most respected by collectors and this respect is shown by the high prices in these price books. NOTE: References to Howard watches have been purposely omitted.

Herchede. Herchede was first organized in 1885 and made cases, while importing movements and hall clocks. Their first catalog was issued about 1886 to 1890. Their first tubular chime clocks were made in the 1890's, with either the movements or complete clocks obtained through Durfee, made by J. J. Elliot, London. In 1902, a court decision ended Durfee's monopoly in this country on tubular chimes, and the Herchede Hall Clock Co. was incorporated. In 1903, Frank Herchede sold all his clock material to the corporation. In 1904, Herchede won a silver medal at the St. Louis World's Fair for their tubular chime clocks. In 1909, the company obtained a building for a movement factory, and in 1910 made the first 100 movements and issued a catalog showing "Crown Hall Clocks" with their own movements. In 1911, 180 to 200 hall clocks were sold, and in 1912 they bought the machinery and stock of the Derry Clock Co. The Canterbury Chimes were introduced in 1913, and in 1914 the company started recording each sale. They entered all known information on previous sales in a ledger. NOTE: No. 6 and No. 7 were sold to Daniel Pratt.

In 1915, awards were won by their clocks at the Panama-Pacific International Exposition. The company became so prosperous after this that in 1919 they paid a 20% dividend to the common stockholders. In the 20's, as electric clocks became ever more popular, the Herchede Co. decided to go into the electric clock business. In 1926, they organized the Revere Clock Co. to make electric clocks, but did not publicize the connection for fear of hurting their reputation for high grade clocks. In 1927, they contracted with G.E. to make a line of electric clocks for G.E. These had a red alert dot in the face to show power interruption. In 1929, Herchede announced electrically wound movements with a chime mechanism operated by an electric motor.

As electric clocks became accepted, Revere was absorbed by the company and all production was in one building. In 1960, the company moved to Starkville, Mississippi, and today they are still making high grade clocks at this location.

Revere Clock Co.: Organized by Herchede as a marketing company for electric clocks. They made electric clocks with an auxiliary 36-Hour spring mechanism that would keep the clock running when the electric power went off and start the synchronous motor when power returned.

Warren Telechron Co., Ashland, Mass.: Organized about 1916 when Warren devised the synchronous electric clock motor. Warren was the first to adapt the synchronous motor to clocks but it was not self-starting. In 1927, Telechron introduced the self-starting synchronous motor. In 1946, Telechron was purchased by G.E.

CONCLUSION OF CLOCK BOOK 3

Clock Book 3 represents a rather new approach, with an even wider spread of types of clocks than has been offered before. Yet, this book continues to develop the idea of Clock Book 1, published in 1977, which for the first time gave collectors authentic, original pictures of Victorian clocks, widening the horizon of knowledge visible to collectors. In Clock Book 2, published in 1979, we remarked that many books would not be able to show all models of the millions of clocks produced in the Victorian Period. As we began to include the clocks of the Modern and Contemporary Periods, it became an almost impossible task to show all the clocks about which collectors would like information. Most of the many letters we receive include the statement, "I can't find my clock in your books." This indicates a hunger for more information and more pictures.

This book attempts to give the new collector a little more to think about when considering which clocks to collect. It gives him an option of lower priced clocks to choose from, and, hopefully, will encourage many new collectors to stay with us in our hobby. In an old 60's NAWCC Bulletin in an account of a meeting of New York Chapter 2, it was reported that Brooks Palmer "now refers to them as 'sleepers', and promised never again to use the word 'junk' in such cases." There are indeed "sleepers" for the new collector and there is also junk in abundance in the flea markets and "stop and swaps." We hope that this book will help the new collector to recognize the sleepers, and still provide an abundance of the information desired by the experienced collectors.

In our enthusiasm in assembling the information for this book we discovered that we had accumulated more than can be used, so until the economic climate becomes more beneficial and until the enthusiasm of collectors dictates otherwise, the excess information and catalog pages will be used in Book 4, planned for release in 1984.

By: RED RABENECK

Wm. L. Gilbert

1881

8D. . . $175.00
1DS. . . 140.00

$160.00

8D. . . $180.00
1DS. . . 145.00

SHARP GOTHIC EXTRA
8D or 1D Strike
Height, 19½ inches

SHARP GOTHIC
8D or 1D Strike
Height, 19½ inches

SMALL SHARP GOTHIC
1D Strike, 1D Time
Height, 14¾ inches

8D. . $190.00
1DS. . 160.00

WINSTED GOTHIC EXTRA
8D or 1D Strike
Height, 17¼ inches

$150.00

8D. . . $160.00
1DS. . . 135.00

8D. . $160.00
1DS. . 130.00

O. G. WEIGHT
1D Strike
Height, 25-7/8 inches

O.O.G. SPRING
8D or 1D Strike
Height, 18-3/8 inches

ROUND TOP
8D or 1D Strike
Height, 13-3/8 inches

Wm. L. Gilbert

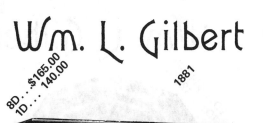

1881

ROSE COTTAGE (Rose Sash)
ROSE AND GILT (Gilt Sash) $95.00
1D Time, 1D Time, Alarm
Height, 9¾ inches

8D . . . $165.00
1D . . . 140.00

8D . . . $145.00
1D . . . 130.00

HAIDEE
8D or 1D Strike
Height, 13½ inches

COLUMN SPRING
8D or 1D Strike
Height, 15 inches

COTTAGE NO. 2 $95.00
1D Strike, 1D Time
Height, 12 inches

8D . . . $135.00
1D . . . 120.00

FAVORITE
8D or 1D Strike
Height, 13½ inches

8D . . . $150.00
1D . . . 130.00

$140.00

8D . . . $130.00
1D . . . 120.00

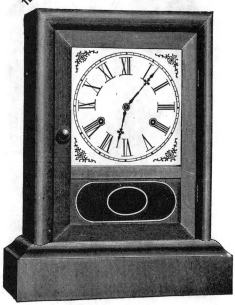

PARAGON
8D or 1D Strike
Height, 15 inches

COLUMN WEIGHT
1D Strike
Rose, Shell or Gilt Columns
Height, 25 inches

COUPON
8D or 1D Strike
Height, 13¼ inches

Wm. L. Gilbert

PILOT EXTRA

8D Strike	Height, 20½ inches
1D Strike	Height, 16 inches

8D . . . $145.00
1D . . . 120.00

COMET
8D or 1D Strike
Height, 14¾ inches

8D . . . $170.00
1D . . . 135.00

CLYDE
8D Strike
Height, 19 inches
1D Strike
Height, 15 inches

8D . . . $175.00
1D . . . 140.00

8D . . . $165.00
1D . . . 145.00

STAR ROUND TOP EXTRA
8D or 1D Strike
Height, 16¾ inches

$125.00

1881

COMET
1D Time, 1D Time, Alarm
Height, 11 inches

8D . . $145.00
1D . . 130.00

ROUND TOP EXTRA
8D Time, 1D Time,
or Time, Alarm
Height, 11 inches

8D . . $225.00
1D . . 210.00

KEYSTONE
8D or 1D Strike
Height, 17¾ inches

1881

CHROMO
1D Time, 1D Time, Alarm
Height, 14 inches

$155.00

8D . . $145.00
1D . . 135.00

OBELISK
8D or 1D Strike
Height, 16½ inches

8D . $150.00
1D . . 140.00

ADVOCATE
8D or 1D Strike
Height, 17 inches

GILBERT GEM EXTRA
8D or 1D Strike
Height, 17½ inches

8D . . $135.00
1D . . 125.00

ROCKET
8D or 1D Strike
Height, 15½ inches

8D . . $140.00
1D . . 130.00

8D . . $180.00
1D . . 160.00

HERO
8D or 1D Strike
Height, 17 inches

$250.00

PARACHUTE
8D Pendulum, Time
Height, 15¼ inches

8D . . $140.00
1D . . 130.00

COUPON EXTRA
8D or 1D Strike
Height, 15½ inches

Wm. L. Gilbert Clock Co.

1881

$185.00

THEBES
8D or 1D Strike
Height, 19 inches - 6 inch Dial

$345.00

CHAMPION
8D Strike
Height, 25 inches - 6 inch Dial

$190.00

TERN
8D or 1D Strike
Height, 19 inches - 6 inch Dial

$295.00

SHELL
8D Strike
Height, 21¾ inches - 6 inch Dial

$300.00

BARONET
8D Strike
Height, 21¼ inches - 5 inch Dial

$205.00

SCORER
8D Strike
Height, 21 inches - 6 inch Dial

$395.00

OCCIDENTAL
8D Strike
Height, 24 inches - 6 inch Dial

$180.00

LEDA
1D Strike
Height, 17 inches - 5 inch Dial

$290.00

METEOR
8D Strike
Height, 20½ inches - 5 inch Dial

$345.00

1881

CAPITAL
8D Strike
Height, 23 inches - 6 inch Dial - Glass sides

$310.00

ENTERPRISE
8D Strike
Height, 22 inches - 6 inch Dial

$180.00

CLINTON
8D or 1D Strike
Height, 20 inches - 6 inch Dial

$170.00

PLUTO
1D Strike
Height, 17½ inches - 5 inch Dial

$210.00

ENID
1D Strike
Height, 21½ inches - 6 inch Dial

$355.00

PSYCHE
8D Strike
Height, 24½ inches - 6 inch Dial

$210.00

NIOBE
8D Strike
Height, 20¼ inches - 5 inch Dial

Wm. L. Gilbert

1881

$215.00

CIPANGO
1D Strike
Height, 19¾ inches - 6 inch dial

$220.00

STORK
8D Strike
Height, 20 inches - 5 inch Dial

$220.00

SIGNAL
8D Strike
Height, 21¼ inches - 6 inch Dial

$200.00

ARGUS
8D Strike
Height, 20¼ inches - 6 inch Dial

$185.00

EDINA
1D Strike
Height, 18¾ inches - 5 inch Dial

$205.00

JANUS
8D Strike
Height, 22½ inches - 6 inch Dial

1881

$185.00

LESBIA
1D Strike
Height, 16½ inches - 5 inch Dial

$270.00

AVALON
8D Strike
Height, 21 inches - 6 inch Dial

$185.00

AMPHRITRITE
1D Time, 1D Time Alarm
Height, 17½ inches - 5 inch Dial

$195.00

NECHO
8D Strike
Height, 21 inches - 6 inch Dial

$195.00

PAROLE
8D Strike
Height, 20 inches - 6 inch Dial

$290.00

NYSA
8D Strike
Height, 21 inches - 5 inch Dial

$290.00

CASELLA
8D Strike
Height, 22 inches - 6 inch Dial

$280.00

MANITOBA
8D Strike
Height, 22½ inches - 6 inch Dial

Wm. L. Gilbert

$300.00

$325.00

$290.00

THEKLA
8D Strike
Height, 21½ inches - 6 inch Dial

CALIOPE
8D Strike
Height, 25 inches - 6 inch Dial - Glass sides

NUCLEUS
8D Strike
Height, 21 inches - 6 inch Dial

1881

$310.00

$310.00

$275.00

GALLIA
8D Strike
Height, 22 inches - 6 inch Dial

TURRET
8D Strike
Height, 22 inches - 6 inch Dial

NEREID
8D Strike
Height, 22¾ inches - 6 inch Dial

1881

$240.00

$125.00

$280.00

JET
(Ebony)
8D or 1D Strike
Height, 19 inches - 6 inch Dial

MEDAL
1D Pendulum, Time
Height, 9 inches

LAPWING
8D Strike
Height, 22½ inches - 6 inch Dial

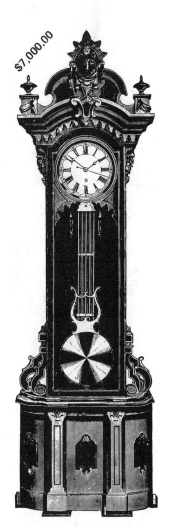

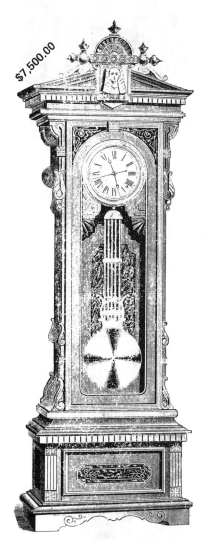

$7,000.00

$7,500.00

$6,500.00

REGULATOR NO. 7
8D Time. Weight. Glass Sides.
Swiss Movement.
Height, 8½ feet - 12 inch Dial

REGULATOR NO. 8
8D Time. Weight. Glass Sides.
Swiss Movement.
Height, 8 ft. 10 in. - 12 inch Dial

REGULATOR NO. 8 (Hanging)
8D Time. Weight. Glass Sides.
Swiss Movement.
Height, 8 ft. 7 in. - 12 inch Dial.

Wm. L. Gilbert

1881

$650.00

EUNOMIA
8D Time, 8D Strike, Spring
Height, 40 inches - 8 inch Dial

$650.00

COLUMBIA
8D Time. 8D Strike, Spring.
Height, 37½ inches - 8 inch Dial

$550.00

AMERICA
8D Time, 80D Strike, Spring
Height, 32 inches - 6 inch Dial

ROUND CORNER LEVER
4, 6, 8, 10 and 12 inch Dial

WOOD LEVER

4'' - 1D . . .	$135.00
6'' - 1D . . .	145.00
6'' - 1DA . .	155.00
6'' - 1DS . .	165.00
8'' - 1D . . .	165.00
8'' - 1DA . .	175.00
8'' - 1DS . .	185.00
10'' - 1D . . .	185.00
10'' - 1DS . .	195.00
6'' - 8D . . .	175.00
8'' - 8D . . .	185.00
8'' - 8DS . .	195.00
10'' - 8D . . .	185.00
10'' - 8DS . .	195.00
12'' - 8D . . .	195.00
12'' - 8DS . .	205.00

$450.00

SHIELD
8D Spring, Strike
Height, 29 inches - 6 inch Dial

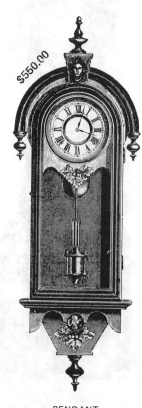

$550.00

PENDANT
8D Time. 8D Strike, Spring.
Height, 34¾ inches - 6 inch Dial

1881

$1,100.00

REGULATOR NO. 3
8D Time. Weight.
Dead-Beat Escapement.
Height, 51 inches - 8 inch Dial

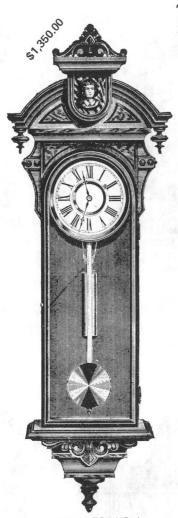

$1,350.00

REGULATOR NO. 4
8D Time. Weight. Glass Sides.
Dead-Beat Escapement.
8 inch Dial

$700.00

ITASCA
8D Time. 8D Strike, Spring.
Height, 46 inches - 8 inch Dial

$1,450.00

REGULATOR NO. 6
8D Time. Weight. Glass Sides.
Dead-Beat Escapement.
Height, 52 inches - 8 inch Dial.

8D..$185.00
1D.. 160.00

CHROMO
8D or 1D Strike
Height, 20¾ inches

8D..$150.00
1D.. 135.00

DRUID
8D Time, 1D Time,
or Time, Alarm
Height, 14 inches

8D..$190.00
1D.. 165.00

MERIDIAN
8D Time, 1D Time,
or Time, Alarm
Height, 18 inches

8D..$185.00
1D.. 160.00

TALLADEGA
(Walnut or Ebony)
8D or 1D Strike
Height, 17½ inches

Wm. L. Gilbert

1881

$180.00

ELIA
8D Strike
Height, 20 inches - 5 inch Dial

$175.00

IRIS
8D Strike
Height, 19½ inches - 5 inch Dial

$185.00

VARUNA
8D Strike
Height, 22 inches - 6 inch Dial

$990.00

REGULATOR NO. 5
8D Time. Weight. Glass Sides.
Dead-Beat Escapement.
Height, 46 inches - 8 inch Dial

$275.00

30 Hour OG Mvt.
& Modified Case
VERY RARE!

WALNUT MANTEL WEIGHT
Height, 35 inches - 8 inch Dial

$350.00

UNA DROP
8D Spring, Strike
Height, 28¾ inches - 6 inch Dial

1881

$800.00

8DT $460.00
8DS. 485.00

8DT. $275.00
8DS. 300.00

OFFICE DROP CALENDAR
8D Time. 8D Strike, Spring.
Height, 34 inches - 12 inch Dial

OCTAGON DROP
8D Time. 8D Strike, Spring.
Height, 25½ inches - 12 inch Dial

CIRCLE DROP
8D Time. 8D Strike, Spring.
Height, 32 inches - 12 inch Dial

8DT. $390.00
8DS. 415.00

8DT. $365.00
8DS. 390.00

$950.00

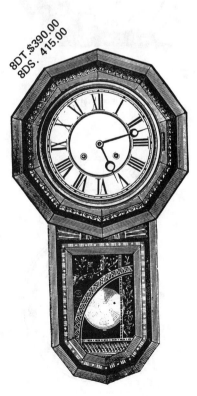

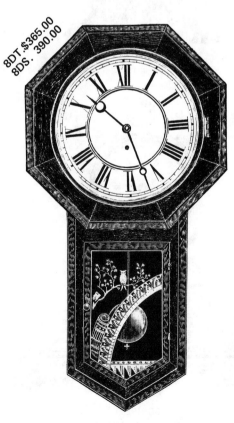

STAR DROP (Walnut)
8D Time. 8D Strike, Spring.
Height, 32½ inches - 12 inch Dial

RESOLUTE
8D Time. 8D Strike, Spring.
Height, 31½ inches - 12 inch Dial

REGULATOR NO. 2
8D Time. Weight.
Dead-Beat Escapement
Height, 33½ inches - 12 inch Dial

Wm. L. Gilbert

$40.00

WAKE-UP ALARM
1D Nickel
3½ inch Dial

1D.... $60.00
1DA ... 75.00

WATCH LEVER
1D Time or Time Alarm
3½ inch Dial

1881

$75.00

CHUB LEVER
1D Time or Time Alarm
Height, 7¼ inches - 3 inch Dial

$90.00

ANCHOR LEVER
1D Time
Height, 14 inches - 3½ inch Dial

$45.00

WAKE-UP ALARM
(With Call Bell)
1D Nickel
3½ inch Dial

Seth Thomas
$45.00

ECHO
1D Nickel, Time, or Time Alarm
4½ inch Dial

$60.00

NO. 8044
1D Nickel, Lever, Time
3½ inch Dial

1D.... $60.00
1DA .. 70.00

SPRITE
1D Nickel, Time, Calendar
1D Nickel, Alarm, Calendar
3½ inch Dial

1D.... $80.00
1DA .. 90.00
1DS... 100.00

MASONIC LEVER
1D Time, Time Alarm or Strike
Height, 14 inches - 4 inch Dial

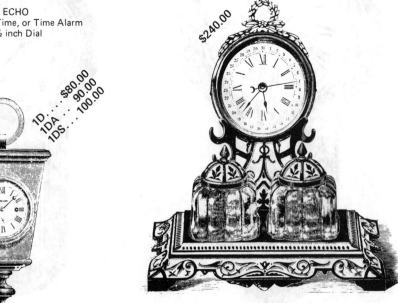

$240.00

SCRIBE
1D Nickel, Time, Calendar
nkstand finished in Black or Bronze
Entire Height, 8½ inches
3½ inch Dial

$40.00

NO. 8065
1D Nickel, Time, Alarm
3½ inch Dial

1891

$140.00

HELLO.—Leatherette.
NICKEL CASE.
ONE DAY TIME, ALARM.
Height, 9 inches ; 2½-inch Dial.

$160.00

ALL RIGHT.
ONE DAY TIME, ALARM, TWO BELLS.
Height, 10 inches ; 2½-inch Dial.
Made in Oxidised Copper, Oxidised Silver or Brass.
Will not tarnish.   Opens front and back.

$150.00

HELLO.
ONE DAY TIME, ALARM.
Height, 9 inches ; 2½-inch Dial.

$130.00

GRADUATE.
ONE DAY TIME, ALARM.
NICKEL PLATED FRAME AND SIDES.
Height, 9 inches; 3-inch Dial; Gold Gilt Front.
Movement can be taken out, and front sash and glass removed
to get at the hands, without disturbing case.

$40.00

WAKE-UP—With Call Bell.
ONE DAY NICKEL ALARM.
4-inch Dial.

$150.00

TURNOUT.
ONE DAY TIME, ALARM.
TWO BELLS   NICKEL PLATED FRAME AND SIDES.
Height, 9 inches ; 3-inch Dial ; Gold Gilt Front.
Movement can be taken out, and front sash and glass removed
to get at the hands, without disturbing case.

$165.00

'76 ALARM.—Rolling Bell.
ONE DAY TIME, ALARM.
Height, 10½ inches ; 2½-inch Dial.

1DC...$60.00
1DAC.. 75.00

OSSA.
ONE DAY NICKEL TIME, CALENDAR.
ONE DAY NICKEL ALARM, CALENDAR.
4½-inch Dial.

$35.00

WAKE-UP.
ONE DAY NICKEL ALARM.
4-inch Dial.

$175.00

BELFRY ALARM.—Rolling Bell.
ONE DAY TIME, ALARM.
Height, 11 inches ; 2½-inch Dial.
Made in Brass or Bronze Finish.

Wm. L. Gilbert

1891

$175.00

SPOKANE.—Walnut or Oak.
EIGHT DAY STRIKE.
Height, 20½ inches; 6-inch Dial.

$165.00

ALTAI.—Walnut, Ash with Walnut Trimmings, or Oak.
EIGHT DAY STRIKE. GONG ONLY.
Height, 20 inches; 6-inch Dial.

$295.00

GENERAL.—Oak or Walnut.
EIGHT DAY STRIKE.
Height, 29 inches.   Width, 15 inches.   8-inch Dial.

$175.00

PUCK.—Walnut or Oak.
ONE DAY STRIKE.
Height, 19 inches; 6-inch Dial.

$160.00

MERL.—Ebonized.
EIGHT DAY OR ONE DAY STRIKE.
Height, 20 inches; 6-inch Dial.

$170.00

DACCA.—Walnut, Ash with Walnut Trimmings, or Oak.
EIGHT DAY STRIKE. GONG ONLY.
Height, 21 inches; 6-inch Dial.

Spring $325.00
Weight 650.00

LATONA.—Walnut.
EIGHT DAY SPRING STRIKE. GONG ONLY.
Height, 30½ inches; 8-inch Dial.

$175.00

MITRA.—Ash, Walnut, Cherry or Oak.
EIGHT DAY STRIKE.
Height, 22½ inches; 7-inch Dial; Wooden Rod; Brass Ball.

ONE SET OF FISH.
All Eight Day Movements.   6-inch Dials.   Average Height, 22 inches.

ONE SET OF ANIMALS.
All Eight Day Movements.   6-inch Dials   Average Height, 21 inches.

1891

$175.00

$175.00

$175.00 $175.00

TROUT.

PIKE.

HYENA.

LEOPARD.

Two Clocks in each Set are fitted with Strike Wire Bell, two Strike Cathedral Gong, and two Strike Wire Bell Alarm.

$175.00

 $175.00

$175.00

$175.00

BASS.

SALMON

BUFFALO.

LION.

NOTE.—Each Set is made up of Six New Designs, of which three are finished in Walnut and three in Oak.

$175.00

 $175.00

$175.00

$175.00

CARP.

SHARK.

TIGER.

PANTHER.

Wm. L. Gilbert Clock Co.

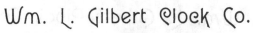

$175.00

$450.00
Glass Pen.—$500.00

1891

$175.00

DELOS.—Walnut.
EIGHT DAY STRIKE
Height, 22½ inches; 6-inch Dial.

AMPHION.—Walnut or Oak.
Cut Beveled Glass Mirror Panels in Sides and Base.
EIGHT DAY STRIKE, GONG ONLY.
Height, 25 inches; 7-inch Dial.

BRONTE.—Walnut.
EIGHT DAY STRIKE
Height, 22 inches; 6-inch Dial.

$165.00

$175.00

$170.00

$175.00

ELIA.—Walnut, Ash or Oak.
EIGHT DAY STRIKE.
Height, 20 inches; 6-inch Dial.

MEDEA.—Walnut or Oak.
EIGHT DAY STRIKE.
Height, 20 inches; 6-inch Dial.

ACHERON.—Walnut or Oak.
ONE DAY STRIKE.
Height, 19½ inches; 6-inch Dial.

MANOLA.—Walnut or Oak.
EIGHT DAY STRIKE.
Height, 20½ inches; 6-inch Dial.

$185.00

Ash
$180.00

$170.00

$185.00

FOREST.—Walnut or Oak.
EIGHT DAY STRIKE.
Height, 24½ inches; 7-inch Dial.

ABANA.—Ash with Walnut Trimmings.
EIGHT DAY STRIKE, GONG ONLY.
Height, 22 inches; 6-inch Dial.

ABANA.—Walnut or Oak.
EIGHT DAY STRIKE, GONG ONLY.
Height, 22 inches; 6-inch Dial.

VINTAGE.—Walnut or Oak.
EIGHT DAY STRIKE.
Height, 24½ inches; 7-inch Dial.

ONE SET OF BIRDS

1891

All Eight Day Movements.   6-inch Dials.   Average Height, 22 inches.

NOTE.—Each Set contains three Walnut and three Oak Clocks.

One Set of **Birds** are fitted with three Wire Bell and three Wire Bell Alarm in each box.
One Set of **Gong Birds** are fitted with four Cathedral Gong and two Cathedral Gong Alarm in each box.
One Set of **Alarm Birds** are fitted all with Wire Bell Alarm in each box.

$175.00

EAGLE.

$175.00

HAWK.

$175.00

$175.00

MECCA.—Walnut.
EIGHT DAY STRIKE.
Height, 20¼ inches; 6-inch Dial.

JUDGE.—Walnut or Oak.
ONE DAY STRIKE.
Height, 20½ inches; 6-inch Dial.

$175.00

QUAIL.

$175.00

SWAN.

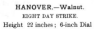

$175.00

$175.00

HANOVER.—Walnut.
EIGHT DAY STRIKE.
Height 22 inches; 6-inch Dial

RACELAND.—Walnut or Oak.
EIGHT DAY STRIKE.
Height, 21½ inches; 6-inch Dial.

$175.00

OWL.

$175.00

DOVE.

$175.00

$175.00

IRIS.—Walnut.
EIGHT DAY STRIKE.
Height, 22 inches; 6-inch Dial.

METIS.—Walnut or Oak.
EIGHT DAY STRIKE.
Height, 22 inches; 6-inch Dial.

Wm. L. Gilbert

1891

$135.00

EXILE.—Walnut or Oak
EIGHT DAY STRIKE.
Height, 21 inches ; 6-inch Dial.

$180.00

HERA.—Oak only.
EIGHT DAY. ONE-HALF HOUR STRIKE. GONG. DEAD-BEAT ESCAPEMENT. LONG-ROD MOVEMENT.
Height, 10½ inches ; Length, 17½ inches ; 5-inch Dial.
Regulates on Dial. Fitted with French Sash and French Sash Visible Escapement.

1D . . $150.00
8D . . 160.00

JET.—Ebonized.
EIGHT DAY OR ONE DAY STRIKE.
Height, 19 inches ; 6 inch Dial.

$160.00

THALBA.—Walnut or Oak.
ONE DAY STRIKE.
Height, 16 inches ; 5-inch Dial.

Add $50.00 for Visible Escapement.

$135.00

VEDA.—Oak only.
EIGHT DAY. ONE-HALF HOUR STRIKE. GONG. DEAD-BEAT ESCAPEMENT. LONG-ROD MOVEMENT.
Height, 10 inches ; Length, 15½ inches ; 5-inch Dial.
Regulates on Dial. Fitted with French Sash and French Sash Visible Escapement.

$170.00

MAHUTA.—Walnut.
ONE DAY STRIKE.
Height, 18½ inches ; 6-inch Dial.

$185.00

NOTE: Case is ash.

NEBO.—Ash only.
EIGHT DAY STRIKE, GONG ONLY.
Height, 22 inches. 6-inch Dial.

Movement has Dead Beat Escapement.

$135.00

RHEA.—Oak only.
EIGHT DAY. ONE-HALF HOUR STRIKE. GONG. DEAD-BEAT ESCAPEMENT. LONG-ROD MOVEMENT.
Height, 10 inches ; Length, 16 inches ; 5-inch Dial.
Regulates on Dial. Fitted with French Sash and French Sash Visible Escapement.

$170.00

CALLA.—Walnut or Oak.
EIGHT DAY STRIKE.
Height, 21 inches ; 6-inch Dial.

1891

$300.00

$375.00

$275.00

JUPITER.—Walnut with Oak Trimmings.
EIGHT DAY STRIKE.
Height, 24 inches ; 6-inch Dial.

OCCIDENTAL.—Walnut or Oak.
EIGHT DAY STRIKE.
Height, 24 inches ; 6-inch Dial.

PARISIAN.—Walnut or Oak.
EIGHT DAY STRIKE.
Height, 24 inches ; 6-inch Dial.

$80.00

$75.00

$135.00

$135.00

BURL.—Stained.
ONE DAY TIME. ONE DAY TIME. ALARM
Height, 11 inches ; 4-inch Dial.

DESDEMONA
Plastic Marble, Onyx or Marble Trimmings.
Length, 10½ inches ; Height, 10 inches.

DESDEMONA.
Plastic Marble, Onyx or Marble Trimmings.
Length, 10½ inches ; Height, 10 inches.

IAGO.
Plastic Marble, Half Columns.
Length, 10½ inches ; Height, 10 inches.

THE ABOVE CLOCKS ARE ALL EIGHT DAY. ONE-HALF HOUR STRIKE. CATHEDRAL GONG ON SOUNDING BOARD.

12″
T.....$225.00
TS.... 250.00
TC.... 275.00
TSC... 300.00

10″
T.....$200.00
TS.... 225.00
TC.... 250.00
TSC... 275.00

8″
T.....$175.00
TS.... 200.00
TC.... 225.00
TSC... 250.00

$135.00

ALAMO.—Veneered.
ONE DAY STRIKE.
Height, 18 inches ; 6-inch Dial.

OCTAGON DROP—Veneered ; Gilt.
EIGHT DAY TIME. EIGHT DAY STRIKE.
EIGHT DAY TIME. CALENDAR.
EIGHT DAY STRIKE. CALENDAR.
Height, 25½ inches ; 12-inch Dial.

OCTAGON DROP.—Veneered.
EIGHT DAY TIME. EIGHT DAY STRIKE.
Height, 23½ inches ; 10-inch Dial.

OCTAGON DROP.—Veneered.
EIGHT DAY TIME. EIGHT DAY STRIKE.
Height, 20½ inches ; 8-inch Dial.

$375.00

CUCKOO AND WACHTEL.—No. 6.
QUARTER HOUR STRIKE   ONE DAY, HANGING, WEIGHT.
Height, 24 inches.
Also fitted with Cornetist Movement. See list under **Cornetist No. 1.**

$425.00

MANTEL CUCKOO.—No. 4876.
ONE-HALF HOUR STRIKE. SPRING.
Height, 24 inches ; Width, 17 inches.

$175.00

CUCKOO.—No. 4.
ONE DAY, HANGING, WEIGHT.   ONE-HALF HOUR STRIKE.
Height, 20 inches.

1891

$325.00

CUCKOO AND WACHTEL.—No. 7.
QUARTER HOUR STRIKE.   ONE DAY, HANGING, WEIGHT.
Height, 19 inches.

$400.00

CORNETIST.—No. 2.
HANGING. ONE-HALF HOUR STRIKE, WEIGHT.
Height, 25 inches.

$225.00

CUCKOO.—No. 3.
ONE DAY, HANGING, WEIGHT.   ONE-HALF HOUR STRIKE.
Height, 18 inches.

$185.00

CUCKOO, NO. 4
1D Hanging, Weight.
Height, 20 inches. — German

These are 1881 clocks, and similar clocks of a later date would not be as high.

1881

$135.00

CUCKOO, NO. 2
1D Hanging, Weight.
Height, 20 inches — German

$250.00

CUCKOO, NO. 3
1D Hanging, Weight.
Height, 18 inches — German

$450.00

MANTEL CUCKOO, NO. 101
8D Spring. ½ Hour Strike.
Height, 22 inches — German

$175.00

CUCKOO, NO. 5
1D Hanging, Weight.
Height, 16½ inches. — German

$100.00

CUCKOO, NO. 1
1D Hanging, Weight.
Height, 15½ inches — German

$400.00

CUCKOO & WACHTEL, NO. 6
¼ Hour Strike. 1D Hanging, Weight.
Height, 24 inches — German

$350.00

CUCKOO & WACHTEL, NO. 7
¼ Hour Strike. 1D Hanging, Weight.
Height, 19 inches — German

OUR "1893 LEADER" CLOCK ASSORTMENT.

The greatest bargains in standard clocks ever offered in America. The prices below show that the "assortment plan" is **the** way to sell clocks cheap. Assortment comprises five Ansonia clocks, all safely packed in case.

$130.00 Cottage Extra. $180.00 Canada. $160.00 Gothic. $265.00 Africa. $215.00 Aden.

	Each.
Cottage Extra—1-day, time, veneered case, 13 inches high	$0 75
Canada—One-day strike, walnut case, height 21 inches, 6-inch dial	1 40
Gothic—1-day, alarm, neat gothic pattern, 15 inches high, veneered case	1 50
Africa—8-day, strike, oak case, 21 inches high, 6-inch dial	2 25
Aden—8-day, strike, walnut case, 20 inches high, 6-inch dial	2 35

(Total of 5 clocks, sold only by assortment.) **Total for Assortment, $8.25**

OUR NEW "BANKERS" CLOCK ASSORTMENT.

Comprising 6 Ansonia clocks, one each Belmont, Berkeley, Bedford, Buffalo, Beaver and Burton. They are all 8-day strike clocks, 4 time and 2 alarm. Uniform height 22½ inches, 6-inch dials. 3 with oak cases and 3 with walnut as specified under cuts herewith. The 6 clocks safely packed in case. No charge for case. We positively cannot break the assortment to supply single clocks.

Total for Assortment, $12.50.

Belmont, Oak Case, Time, $2.00 Each. Berkely, Walnut Case, Time, $2.00 Each. Bedford, Oak Case, Time, $2.05 Each. Buffalo, Walnut Case, Time, $2.05 Each. Beaver, Walnut Case, Alarm, $2.20 Each. Burton, Oak Case, Alarm, $2.20 Each.

1893 Butler Bros. New York

WOOD MANTEL CLOCKS

J5550, $1.65 Each. J2360, $2.10 Each.

J2354, $2.50 Each.

J5550—Fine oak finished embossed case, scroll design, ornaments each side, embossed lion in center, gold decorated hinged glass door. Well known Ingraham movement, 8 day, ½ hour strike, 6 in. dial. Ht. 22 in., 14½ wide. Each in case. **$1.65**

J2360—Solid oak. 24 in., 6 in. dial, 8 day, ½ hour strike. With calendar, barometer, thermometer. In case. Each, **$2.10**

J2354, "King"—Ansonia. Oak case, 24 in., 6 in. dial, 8 day, ½ hour strike, cathedral gong. Wt. 15 lbs. Each, **$2.50**

FRENCH STAG CASE CLOCK.

J8655: Scalloped octagon pattern, stag case, fine 30 hour movement, guaranteed, 2 in. celluloid dial, ornamented center, stag horn standard with gold plated scroll ornamentation, length 7⅝ in. width 5 in. Each in box. Each, **$2.00**

"MANTEL" WOOD CLOCK ASSORTMENTS.

Each $175.00

J6977 and J6978

J6977—Beauty asst. Extra value. Consisting of 6 highly finished oak clocks. Embossed top, side and base ornaments gold decorations on glass, hinged doors, 6 in. dial, Ingraham movement, 8 day, ½ hour strike, each guaranteed. 6 in case, no less sold. Total case, **$8.20**

J6978—Beauty *alarm* asst. As J6977, with alarm. 6 in case, no less sold. 75 lbs. Total case, **$9.40**

Each $180.00

J6798, $9.96 Case.

J6798—Embossed, 6 designs in oak finish, one of the best makes, guaranteed first grade, Ht. 22 in., 6 in. dial, 8 day, ½ hour strike alarm. Gold decorated glass hinged doors. Sold only in case of 6 clocks. Total, **$9.96** (6 at $1.66)

1893 Butler Bros. New York

1905 Butler Bros. New York

SETH THOMAS CLOCKS.

$55.00

$65.00

$1.95 Each.   Pansy, $2.12 Each.

$135.00

No. 781, $4.75 Each.

$145.00

No. 750, $5.20 Each.

$150.00

No. 744, $5.90 Each.

$145.00

No. 745, $5.50 Each.

Admittedly the best timekeepers made. All except the first one below are in the famous "Adamantine" finish, in exact copy of the French patterns in marble and onyx which are sold at very high prices. This Adamantine finish is extremely hard and everlasting, finely polished and finished in perfect imitation of marble.

Each.

"Lodge Lever" Seth Thomas Clock—Gold gilt front, nickel plated frame, glass sides, height 7 inches, 3-inch dia., 1-day time, alarm.............. $1 95

"Pansy" Seth Thomas Clock—Adamantine finish with gold columns, height 4 inches, width at base, 6 inches, 2-inch dial, 1-day time................... 2 12

No. 781, Seth Thomas Clock—Adamantine case in deep black with Adamantine marble trimmings, 11 inches high, 13 inches wide at base, heads and feet, 8-day, half-hour strike, cathedral bell. Each in case 4 75

No. 750, Seth Thomas Clock—Same as above only larger case, 11 inches high, width at base 17 inches. 5 20

No. 745, Seth Thomas Clock—Adamantine case in imitation tortoise shell, rich gilt trimmings, heads and feet, 11 inches high, width at base 17 inches, 8-day, half-hour strike, cathedral bell,... .... 5 50

No. 744, Seth Thomas Clock—Adamantine case in imitation marble, gilt trimmings, 13 inches high, 17 wide at base, 8-day, half-hour strike, cathedral gong... 5 90

CLOCKS IN PLUSH CASES.

All of the standard "Ansonia" make.

$70.00 $80.00 $100.00 $90.00

No. 3015, $1.00 Each.   No. 3000, $1.39 Each.   No. 4760, $1.75 Each.   No. 608, $1.40 Each.

Each.

No. 3015, Plush Case Clock—Nickel time clock in plush case 7½ inches square with four silver ornaments... $1 00

No. 3000, Columbus Bell Clock—*A ringing bargain.* Clever design plush case, with silver ornament, fitted with Ansonia nickel alarm clock................ 1 39

No. 608, Plush Case Clock—Princess nickel time clock in fancy wood case 11 inches high and covered with *fine quality* silk plush, silver trimmed. Colors red, violet, blue and mahogany Each in box... 1 40

No. 4760, Finest Plush Case Clock—10 inches high, very fine plush, two ⅞-inch silvered bands, 30-hour nickel clock. Colors red, violet, blue and mahogany. Very rich.... .... 1 75

"ANSONIA" NICKEL ALARM CLOCKS.

$40.00 $135.00 $85.00 $95.00

67c Each. $1.18 Each. $1.20 Each. $1.50 Each.

Each.

Ansonia "Pirate" Alarm—Nickel plated seamless case, 4-inch dial. Every one is examined by an expert before leaving our house to see that it is in perfect running order. We do not guarantee, however, to keep clocks in repair for customers...................... $0 67

The "Flirt" Alarm—The standard nickel alarm clock with enameled dial, on which, in colors, is the face of a pretty girl moving a fan back and forth before her face............ 1 18

No. 60, "Razzle Dazzle" Alarm—2-inch dial, French bevel plate glass. Double roller escapement. Clock nickel plated. *Very* loud 3¾-inch alarm bell. Each in box........... 1 20

"Climax" Square Nickel Frame Carriage Clock—Glass sides and front with drop handle. 5½ inches high. One-day time, alarm. Each in box................................. 1 50

"SETH THOMAS" CLOCKS.

Carefully made, nicely finished, every one adjusted and tested, 8 day, half hour cathedral gong strike. Guaranteed.

$140.00

J5237. $3.95 Each.

J5237:—Highly polished mahogany adamantine finish wood case, 10¾ in. high, 12½ in. wide at base. Fancy sash, cream colored arabic dial ornamented center. Gilt trimmed imitation onyx columns, gilt feet and side ornaments. Each in case, wt. 13 lbs. Each, **$3.95**

$145.00

J440, $4.50 Each.

J440—Gilt sash, white arabic dial. Adamantine finish trimmed with the new imitation Jersey marble. Gilt trimmed oval columns, side ornaments and feet, ht. 11 in., width 16½, wt. 16 lbs... Each, **$4.50**

$145.00

J1701, "Stanhope" Mantel Clock—One of the newest designs. *Note size and price.* Fancy gilt sash, ivory tint white dial, arabic figures, Jersey marble style ornamentations. Gilt trimmed side ornaments, feet, capitals and column base. One half round celluloid columns in any color. Adamantine finish that can be washed without injury. Width 18 in., ht. 11. Each in case, 17 lbs................... Each, **$4.50**

Rare $175.00

"Modern" KITCHEN CLOCK ASSORTMENT.

J470—Entirely new designs, 3 styles, oak finished cases, handsomely carved, 8 day, hour strike on gong, ½ hour strike on separate cup bell, 6 in. aluminum or copper dials with black figures. Ht. 16½ in., width 11½. 3 in case, asstd. Each, **$2.00**

STANDARD CLOCKS.

Keep in Mind the QUALITY of These Goods.   The Reputation of "Ansonia" Clocks is World-Wide.   They are SAFE GOODS TO OFFER.

1893 Butler Bros. New York

1905 Butler Bros. New York

WALL AND PARLOR CLOCKS.

 $295.00  $145.00 $135.00  $395.00

$3.25 Each. $3.00 Each. $3.75 Each. $5.25 Each.   Each.

Turkey Oak Clock—Eight day, half hour gong strike, 15¾ inches high and 10 inches wide, handsome antique oak case nicely finished. Each in case $3 00

"Parisian" Clock — Polished walnut case, 23½ inches high, 6-inch dial, eight-day strike. Each in strong wood case 3 25

Marbled Iron Frame Clock—Enameled iron after the style of Egyptian marble; 10½ inches high; Ansonia movement; 8 day, half-hour strike; cathedral gong. A beautiful and reliable clock. Each in case 3 75

$165.00

$250.00

$7.50 Each. $6.40 Each.

Triumph Walnut Cabinet Clock—24½ inches high, 6 inch dial, with French sash and bronze ornaments. Silver Cupid on each side. 8-day time, half hour strike. A handsome piece of furniture and an excellent time-keeper 5 25

"Cabinet A" Clock—Antique oak, highly polished, 19 inches high, 10¼ wide, gilt dial and brass trimmings. A rich and showy clock. Each in case 6 40

Bronze Figure Parlor Clock—Black enameled iron in imitation of Egyptian marble, inlaid at the side with panels of open work with bronze finish. Height of clock, 10¼ inches, surmounted by neat bronze figure. Gilt dial, hour and half-hour gong strike. Each in case 7 50

FANCY SILVERED METAL CLOCKS.

All "Ansonia" make.

 $150.00  $160.00  $160.00 $185.00  $200.00

$1.55 Each. $1.60 Each. $1.65 Each. $1.87 Each. $1.97 Each.   Each.

The "Duet" Clock—A clever design, attractively finished and handsomely silvered; 2-inch dial, 5½ inches high. Looks fine at $2.50 retail. Each in a box $1 55

The "Opera Fan" Clock—Silvered finish, one-day time, 2-inch dial, height 7¾ inches. Very showy value. 1 60

The "Cupid Wreath" Clock—*Will retail for $3.00.* Bright silvered finish, 2-inch dial, height 5 inches. Each in case 1 65

The "Florist" Clock—A 30-hour time clock, 2-inch French bevel glass, set in fancy silvered frame. 9 inches high, figure of girl on one side and potted flowers on the other. Each in wood box 1 87

The Barge Clock—Representing Cupid sailing a boat, the whole in handsome silver finish. A 30-hour time clock with 2-inch dial set in center. Each in wood box 1 97

$215.00

The "Lawn Tennis" Clock—Height 7¼ inches, plain dial, one-day time, handsomely silvered metal. Each in case 2 12

$2.12 Each.

GENUINE ONYX CLOCKS.

A line of very fine goods which have not heretofore been purchasable at moderate prices. Cases are of the finest onyx marble, beautifully finished and polished, in the most ornate designs. Solid gold bronze dials and trimmings. All Ansonia make, 8-day time, half-hour strike. Each in case.

$225.00  $220.00  $250.00

"Alvesta," $12.00 Each.   "Almont," $13.00 Each.   "Ansonia," $17.50 Each.   Each

"Alvesta" Onyx Clock—11¾ inches high by 11 wide. Each $12 00

"Almont" Onyx Clock—10¼ inches high, 12½ wide. Each 13 00

"Ansonia" Onyx Clock—11½ inches high, 14¼ wide. Each 17 50

$80.00

NOVELTY GILT CLOCK.

J1481—Very ornamental gold plated, metal frame, ht., 10¾ in. 30 hour American movement, 3 in. dial, gilt center, bevel plate glass . . . . Each, **80c**

$100.00

THE NEW "LILY" PHOTO CLOCK.

J1608: Verde bronze finish with place for photograph in lower part of clock frame. Ht. 10½ in., width of clock in widest part 6¼ in. Fitted with 30 hour American movement, fancy decorated dial. Movement guaranteed. Each, **$1.00**

NEW HIGH ART CLOCKS.

Entirely new, big show for little money.

$125.00 $125.00

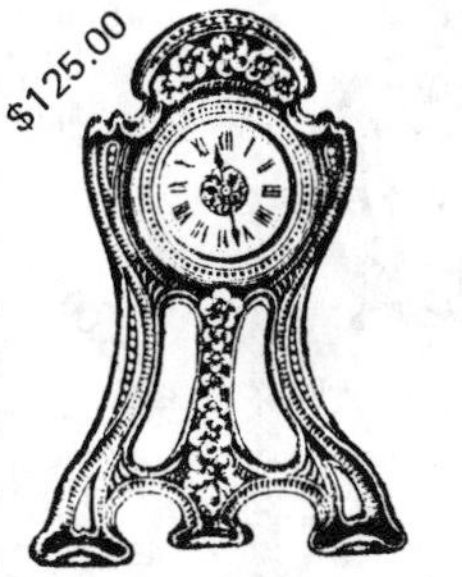

J474:—2 designs, embossed scroll openwork patterns, 2 handsome colors, gold stippled, one with art nouveau medallion center, other with profuse embossed floral decorations, enameled in natural colors. 30 hour movement, fully guaranteed, 3 in. gilt decorated center dial with beveled glass, ht. 10¼, width 6¼. Each in box. Each, **$1.25**

HIGH ART GOLD CLOCKS.

 $75.00 $85.00 $95.00 $110.00

J9203, 78c Each.   J8643, 89c Each.   J8644, 95c Each.   J8645, $1.10 Each

J9203—Ormolu gold finish, embossed design, raised parts burnished, easel back, fitted with 30 hour guaranteed movement, celluloid porcelain dial, ht. 4¾ in. Each in box . . . . Each, **78c**

J8643—Gold plated ormolu finish, embossed open work and cupid design, 30 hour American movement, guaranteed. Ht. 6¼ in., width 4½. Each in box . . . . Each, **89c**

J8644—Scroll and cupid design, gold plated ormolu finish, raised parts burnished, 30 hour American movement, ht. 6 in., width 4¾ in. . . . . Each, **95c**

J8645—Gold plated ormolu finish, embossed design, footed, porcelain dial with beveled glass, guaranteed 30 hour movement, ht., 7½ in., width 3½ in . . . . Each, **$1.10**

$80.00 $45.00

R919. Mauser-Calendar Clock. 1 day time, with alarm, calendar, nickel plated case, beaded edge, 4 inch dial..............EACH, .75

R923. Alert. Straight alarm clock, bell on back, nickel case, 1 day time, 4 inch dial, with second hand, 6¾ inches high, W. C. make. ....EACH, .78

R91. Strenuous. 5 minutes long alarm, American movement, 4½ inch dial, can be shut off at will......................EACH, .75½

$120.00 $130.00 $180.00

J8646, $1.20 Each.   J8647, $1.50 Each.   J8648, $1.80 Each.

J8646:.Gold plated, art nouveau head design, embossed cupid sides, 4 feet, bright burnished, guaranteed 30 hour movement, porcelain dial, double glass, ht. 7 in. Each in box..Each, **$1.20**

J8647—Colonial design, gold plated ormolu finish, neatly embossed, 4 burnished columns 2 in. porcelain dial, beveled glass, guaranteed 30 hour movement, ht. 4½ in., width 4½, 2¾ in. deep............Each, **$1.50**

J8648—Gold plated ormolu finish, embossed footed base holding cupid figure, clock with embossed and bow-knot frame, best 30 hour American movement, guaranteed. ht. 7 in., width 4 in.............Each, **$1.80**

$85.00 $100.00

R131   R141

R141. Guide. Oblong square base, nickel plated, with fancy embossed gilt front and handles, 2¾ - inch dial, with second hand, 30 - hour movement, with long alarm under base, has glass sides, 7 inches long. ....EACH, **1.75**

R925. Seth Thomas. Long alarm, rings 20 minutes, but can be switched off; bronzed fancy case with urn base; 4 - inch dial and second hand. ....EACH, **2.10**

$75.00 .... $100.00 $125.00

$125.00

J8651, $2.75 Each.   J8652, $3 25 Each.

J8651:.Gold plated ormolu finish, embossed openwork pattern, 4 feet, front decorated with 2 cupids, best 30 hour American movement, 2½ in., celluloid dial, beveled glass, ht. 11 in., width 6 in.............Each, **$2.75**

J8652:.Chariot design holding clock on which is a cupid driving team of mules, gold plated ormolu finish, embossed, guaranteed 30 hour American movement, 2 in. white dial, large figures, length 7½ in., ht. 6½ in.............Each, **$3.25**

Windmill   Watermill

$135.00 each

Mandolin   Flirt

R1-WINDMILL. Novelty alarm clock, 1-day time, 4-inch dial, height 5½ inches, good time piece; in the following patterns — Windmill, Watermill, Mandolin and Flirt; each packed in neat wooden box ....EACH, .95

$135.00 $135.00 $135.00

No. 12, $1 00 Each.   No. 13, $1.00 Each.   No. 14, $1.00 Each.

12, Ballet Dancer Alarm—One-day nickel alarm, colored dial showing a lady in ballet costume dancing..... 1 00

13, Tete-a-tete Alarm—One-day alarm, nickel, colored dial, gilt hands, at each tick the man salutes the lady... 1 00

14, "Bull Fight" Alarm—One-day alarm, a good time-keeper. Dial shows a Spanish bull fight, keeping motion to time of clock. Each in box....................... 1 00

$125.00

R909

MUSICAL ALARM CLOCKS.

R909. Musical alarm clocks, same style and pattern as R131 Patrol, can be made to play at will, one tune, cannot get out of order, will afford amusement to your friends, can be set as an alarm.EACH, **2.20**

MINIATURE ALARM CLOCKS.

$50.00 $55.00 $40.00

R930   R930-C   R664

R930. Wasp Alarm Clock. 1-day time; clear ringing long alarm, with shut off; nicely finished; full nickel plated; 2-inch dial. ....EACH, **1.05**

R930-C. Same clock, with leather traveling case...........................EACH, **1.72**

$85.00

R19

R664. Drone. 1-day time, long alarm, nickeled, 2¾-inch dial, height 4¾ inches; an alarm shut off; 1 in box..........EACH, **1.10**

R19. The Winner. Continuous alarm clock, very attractive, has 2-inch dial with Arabic figures, beveled glass, stands 4 inches high on fancy nickel plated base, fully nickeled with bell at base. ....EACH, **1.25**

$30.00 $30.00

R92   R921

R920. Gatling intermittent, solid nickel gong on back; has 4-inch dial with large Arabic plain figures, fully nickeled throughout; is of the N. H. make, provided with shut off to stop alarm; fully guaranteed......EACH, .90

R92. Daylight. Solid nickel gong on back of case. Can be used as an intermittent or long alarm; can be shut off by pressing button placed at top of clock; has a 4-inch dial with full nickel plated case. ....EACH, .98

R921. Champion. Long alarm, solid bell metal gong on back of case, rings continuously for 7½ minutes unless shut off at switch provided for this purpose an A1 timepiece, and the loudest alarm on the market; fine nickel plated case; fancy edge and top. ....EACH, **1.00**

$40.00

NEW LONG ALARM CLOCK.

The new long alarm with patent shut off in front.

J1680—4 in. dial, long alarm, pressing button at top in front shuts off alarm, raising button sets in. Movement made by the Parkers, makers of the well known Parker guns. Each, **76c**
(In case lots of 100, 74c.)

$40.00

"TICK TOCK" NICKEL CLOCK.

Guaranteed a reliable timekeeper. We will replace within one year any which fail to give satisfaction.

J934—High grade, 30 hour movement, 2 in. fancy dial, regular short wind, best nickel plated case. Each in tin box......................Each, **56c**

ROUND AND OCTAGON OFFICE CLOCKS.

1902

T . . $225.00
TS . . 250.00
TC . 300.00
TSC . 325.00

T . . $250.00
TS . . 275.00
TC . 300.00
TSC . 325.00

8D $225.00
8DS 250.00
8DSC 275.00

T . . $250.00
TS . . 275.00
TC . 300.00
TSC . 325.00

Waterbury Clock Co.'s 12-inch Arion.
8-day time, 12-inch dial, height 24 inches, polished oak case. Each...2 60
Arion, with calender. Each....2 80

Gilbert Clock Co.'s Admiral Octagon Office Clock. Polished oak cases, fine hand carved designs, height 26¾ inches, 12-inch dial, 8-day time. Each....2 55
Admiral, 8-day strike, wire bell. Each....................3 05
Admiral, 8-day time, calendar. Each....................2 80
Admiral, 8-day strike, wire bell, calendar. Each.......................3 25

Ansonia Clock Co.'s 12-inch Drop Octagon Extra. 8-day time, 12-inch dial, height 23½ inches, rosewood or walnut veneer, polished. Each............2 80
12-inch Drop Octagon, time with calendar. Each.........................3 05
12-inch Drop Octagon, with spring strike. Each....................3 30

New Haven Clock Co.'s Braddock Regulator. Height 27 inches, dial 12 inches. Cases are made of solid oak, nicely polished and carved.
Braddock, time. Each..........2 80
Braddock, strike. Each..........3 20
Braddock, 30-day, time. Each...3 75

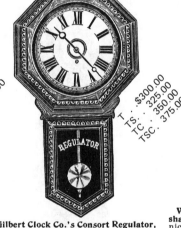

T . . $300.00
TS 350.00
TC 350.00
TSC 375.00

T . . $300.00
TS. . 325.00
TC . 350.00
TSC . 375.00

8D $335.00
8DS 360.00
8DC 360.00
8DSC 385.00

8D $275.00
8DS 300.00
8DSC 325.00

New Haven Clock Co.'s Bank Regulator. Octagon shape, oak case, nicely carved and polished, height 33 inches, width 18 inches, 12-inch dial.
Bank Regulator, time. Each....3 05
Bank Regulator, strike. Each...3 55
Bank Regulator, time, calendar. Each.........................3 30
Bank Regulator, strike, calendar. Each.........................3 80

Gilbert Clock Co.'s Consort Regulator, height 31 inches, 12-inch dial, finished in oak only, 8-day time. Each.....3 05
Consort, 8-day strike, wire bell. Each...........................3 50
Consort, 8-day time, calendar. Each. 3 25
Consort, 8-day strike, wire bell, calendar. Each.......................3 75

Waterbury Clock Co.'s Heron Octagon shape Regulator. Hand carved oak case, nicely polished, height 32 inches, 12-inch dial.
Heron, 8-day time. Each.....3 05
Heron, 8-day, half-hour strike. Each...........................3 50
Heron, 8-day time, calendar. Each...........................3 25
Heron, half-hour strike, calendar. Each...........................3 75

Seth Thomas 12-inch Drop Octagon. Height 23½ inches, dial 12 inches, finish oak, 8-day time. Each...........3 40
12-inch Drop Octagon, time with calendar. Each...................3 75

$1,050.00

$350.00
375.00
400.00
425.00

$375.00
400.00

$900.00

T
TS
TC
TSC

T
TS

Waterbury Clock Co.'s Regulator No. 20. Height 38 inches, 12-inch dial, oak finish, 8-day weight, time, dead-beat escapement, retaining power, solid movement frames. Each.........8 20

Ansonia Clock Co.'s Regulator A. Height 32 inches, 12-inch dial, can be had in ash or black walnut finish, 8-day time. Each.....................4 25
Regulator A, with calendar. Each.4 50

Seth Thomas Clock Co.'s Regulator Globe. Height 31 inches, 12-inch dial, 8-day, spring, time, can be had in rosewood or old veneer, polished. Each 4 90

Seth Thomas Clock Co.'s Regulator No. 2. Walnut, cherry, oak or old oak veneer, polished, 8-day, weight, time, height 34 inches, 12-inch dial, movement 2½x4¼ inches, lantern pinions, Graham pallets, brass covered zinc ball and wood rod, 80 beats to the minute, movement has retaining power. Each 10 65

8-DAY WOOD MANTEL CLOCKS—Continued.

$245.00

Waterbury Clock Co.'s Cato. This popular style hanging clock is 27 inches high, has a 6-inch dial, case comes in oak or walnut, thermometer and barometer, 8-day, half-hour strike. A very rich, attractive and beautifully carved frame, without alarm. Each......2 80
Cato, with alarm. Each.........3 05
Cato, with calendar. Each......3 05

$235.00
1902

Waterbury Clock Co.'s Bermuda, nicely carved oak or walnut finish, 6-inch dial, height 29¾ inches, 8-day, half-hour strike. Each..........................2 80
Bermuda, 8 day, half-hour strike with alarm. Each..........................3 05

Seth Thomas Clock Co.'s Dixie, 8-day half-hour strike, made in oak only; ornamented with metal, 28 inches high, 17½ inches wide, ½ hour gong strike. Each..........................4 00
Dixie, half-hour gong strike, with alarm. Each..........................4 30
Dixie, half-hour wire bell strike, alarm. Each..........................4 10

T $250.00
TS $275.00
TC $300.00
TSC $325.00

$395.00

Ansonia Clock Co.'s Triumph, finished in black walnut or oak, height 24½ inches, 6-inch dial, silver cupids, plate glass mirrors, bronze ornaments, 8-day strike. Each..........................4 30
Triumph, 8-day, gong. Each.....4 45
Triumph, 8-day, alarm. Each....4 55
Triumph, 8-day, alarm and gong. Each..........................4 70

OFFICE CLOCKS AND REGULATORS.

T . . . $400.00
TS . . 450.00
TC . . 500.00
TSC . 550.00

Waterbury Clock Co.'s Springfield, 8-day office clock, height 39⅜ inches, width 16¼ inches, 8-inch dial, oak finish, 8-day time. Each... ....3 75
Springfield, 8-day, half-hour strike, gong. Each..........................4 45

T . . $450.00
TS . . 550.00

Waterbury Clock Co.'s Eton. Height 39¼ inches, width 15 inches. Handsomely carved cases, can be had in oak or walnut finish; 8-day time, 8-inch dial. Each..........................3 75
Eton, half-hour strike, gong. Each 4 45

T . . $500.00
TS . . 600.00

New Haven Clock Co.'s Maywood, 8-day time office clock, height 43½ inches, width 17 inches, dial 8 inches. Cases made of polished oak, carved, 8-day time. Each..........................4 90
Maywood, with calendar. Each.,5 15

$1750.00

Gilbert Clock Co.'s Elberon Office Clock; Case in oak or walnut, nicely carved, height 28 inches, width 16 inches, 8-inch dial, 8-day, gong, calendar only, without alarm. Each..............5 40

$700.00

Waterbury Clock Co.'s Perpetual Calendar No. 44. Height 24 inches, 6-inch dial oak or walnut case, highly polished and finished, 8-day time, half-hour strike, cathedral gong. Each..............5 65
Calendar No. 44, with alarm. Each..........................5 90

$850.00

New Haven Clock Co.'s Columbia Regulator. Case of solid oak or cherry, polished and carved, height 48½ inches, 8-inch dial, 8-day time. Each......6 70
Columbia Regulator. 30-day time. Each..........................7 65

T . . $550.00
TS . . 650.00

Ansonia Clock Co.'s Queen Anne Office Clock. Height 40¼ inches, dial 8 inches, 8-day, spring, time, spiral pillars at sides and top, oak finish. Each..........6 80

$1,200.00

Seth Thomas Clock Co.'s Parlor Calendar No. 11. 8-day, strike, cathedral bell, height 30 inches, 8-inch dial, perpetual calendar, old oak finish. Each........ ....15 70

ANSONIA CLOCK CO.'S NICKEL ALARM CLOCKS.

$45.00

$35.00

$65.00

$45.00

$45.00

Ansonia Clock Co.'s Bee. 1-day time, 2-inch dial, nickel case, beveled glass, winds by turning the back. Each.............. 65

Ansonia Clock Co.'s Luminous Pirate. 1-day time and alarm, 4-inch luminous dial, can be seen in the dark, very reliable and accurate movement. Each.... 75

Ansonia Clock Co.'s Reveille. Heavy nickel finish, 1-day time, alarm, 4-inch dial. Each .85
Reveille, 5-inch dial.
Each.........................1 10

Ansonia Clock Co.'s Trolley. Heavy nickel-plated case, 5-inch dial, alarm rings 15 minutes, made with switch to stop alarm when desired. Each........1 00

Ansonia Clock Co.'s Repeater Intermitting Alarm. 1-day time and alarm, fine nickel finish, 5-inch dial, duration of alarm 25 minutes, silent, 15 seconds, alarm, 20 seconds. Each..1 00

ANSONIA CLOCK CO.'S CARRIAGE EXTRA.

$125.00

Ansonia Clock Co.'s Carriage Extra. Handsome embossed nickel-plated case. 1-day time, half-hour strike and alarm, height 6½ inches, 3-inch dial. Each.............2 20

GILBERT CLOCK CO.'S NICKEL CLOCKS.

$35.00

$35.00

$60.00

Gilbert Clock Co.'s Wake-Up Alarm. 1-day nickel alarm 4-inch dial, height 6¼ inches, made with the patent back clock movement, which can be removed and replaced in 4 seconds, no screws to lose or threads to strip.
Each 64
In case lots of 50. Each..... 61

Gilbert Clock Co.'s Buzz Alarm. 1-day time nickel clock, 4-inch dial, height 6½ inches, nickel-plated on a brass base. A thoroughly good reliable timekeeping alarm clock, made with a patent back. Each.................. 65
In case lots of 50. Each...... 62

Gilbert Clock Co.'s Pet Long Alarm. 1-day time, nickel alarm, 4½-inch dial, height 6¾ inches, fitted with second hand, alarm rings 7 minutes with one winding, can be cut off by switch, full nickel-plated. Each.............. 1 05

1-DAY PORCELAIN CLOCKS.

$75.00

$80.00

$80.00

5" high
$90.00

$90.00

Ansonia Clock Co.'s Elk. Fine porcelain hand-painted decorations, 1-day time, height 5¼ inches, 2-inch dial. Each......................85

Ansonia Clock Co.'s Expert. Handsome porcelain case, richly decorated in hand-painted floral designs, 1-day time, height 5¼ inches, 2-inch dial. Each........90

Ansonia Clock Co.'s Elm. Richly colored porcelain, hand painted floral designs, 1-day time, height 5 inches, 2-inch dial. Each....................90

Ansonia Clock Co.'s Flake. 1-day time, height 5½ inches, latest style porcelain case, richly decorated in hand painted floral and scroll designs. Each...1 00

Waterbury Clock Co.'s Boudoir No. 211. Extra fine finished porcelain, gilt and color decorations, on tinted case, 1-day time, lever, 2-inch dial, beveled glass, height 6 inches, width 4⅛ inches.
Each.........................1 00

$90.00

$90.00

$75.00

6" high
$85.00

$125.00

Ansonia Clock Co.'s Fawn, 1 day time, height 6 inches, 2 inch dial, latest style porcelain case, finely decorated in hand-painted floral designs. Each.......1 00

Ansonia Clock Co.'s Fresco, 1 day time, height 6 inches, 2-inch dial, very handsome porcelain case, hand-painted designs in assorted colors.
Each....................1 00

Waterbury Clock Co.'s Boudoir No. 209. Handsome porcelain case, gilt and color decorations, cobalt blue, 1-day lever time, 2-inch dial, beveled glass, height 5¾ inches, width 5⅛ inches.
Each.......................1 10

Waterbury Clock Co.'s Boudoir No. 213. Porcelain, gilt and color decorations, bronze green, 1 day lever time, 2-inch ornamented dial, beveled glass, height 5⅝ inches, width 4½ inches.
Each......................1 10

Ansonia Clock Co.'s Cameo No. 9. A handsome porcelain hand-painted design, height 6 inches, 2-inch dial, 1-day time.
Each....................1 35

HIGH GRADE 8 DAY PARLOR CLOCKS.

Each guaranteed; all have hour and ⅛ hour cathedral gong strike.

$130.00

J1714—10¼x12, heavy black enameled highly polished wood, gilt decorations, engraved base, 2 marbleized columns with gilt embossed capitols, gold feet, gilt rococo sash, 5 in. dial with gilt center. Cased, 13 lbs. Each, **$2.75**

$140.00

J9046—Highly polished black adamantine case, gilt scroll ornamentation, 4 dark green corrugated columns, embossed gilt capitols and feet, 5 in. dial, gilt rococo sash, gilt embossed center, embossed lion head side ornaments, 16x10½. Cased, 16 lbs.. Each, **$3.25**

$140.00

J1702—16x10⅛, best American movt., black enameled case, gilt trimmed green marbleized columns, heavy gilt side ornaments, gilt feet, openwork gilt sash. Cased, 15 lbs. Each, **$3.35**

$140.00

HIGH GRADE PARLOR CLOCK.

Compare prices with other offerings and you will realize the advantage of buying here.

J9005—Highly polished black enamel finish, 6 celluloid onyx columns, embossed gilt capitols, side ornaments and feet, marbleized moldings, gilt scrolls, rococo sash, 5 in. white dial, gilt decorated center, 18¼x10½ in. Cased, 15 lbs. Each, **$3.50**

HIGH GRADE 8 DAY PARLOR CLOCKS—Contd.

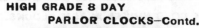

$140.00

J1703—17½x10½, black marble finish, gilt decorations, marbleized moldings, 4 celluloid onyx columns, embossed gilt capitols with feet and side ornaments, 5 in. dial with gilt center, rococo sash, Ingraham make. Cased, 16 lbs............ Each, **$3.50**

$175.00

J1720—17x16, best American movt. 5¼ in. dial, gilt feet, black marbleized enameled front, heavy green and dark marble effect side columns, genuine bell metal bell in gilt arch. Cased, 25 lbs............ Each, **$4.75**

SETH THOMAS CLOCK ASSTS.

$175.00

"Seth Thomas" 8 day mantel clocks. They have an established reputation that will find for them a ready sale.

J1747—3 styles asstd. oak and walnut cases, 8 day, ½ hour strike, wire bell, 6 in. dial, ht. 23 in., 6 clocks asstd. in case, 77 lbs. Case, **$13.87**

J1748—As above, all alarm, 6 clocks asstd. case, 77 lbs.................Case, **$15.69**

WESTERN UNION STYLE OFFICE OR WALL CLOCKS.

8DT.....$325.00
8DC.....$400.00

The best clocks for the price in the market. For schools, offices, hotels and public places.

J1756—8 day with calendar, made by Ingraham Co., 37 x 16 in., dial 12 in. Oak case, finished inside and out. Cased, 27 lbs. Each, **$2.95**

J1757—As J1756, but without calendar. Each, **$2.80**

CHINA CASE CLOCKS.

$65.00   *$235.00*

J8642, 77c Each.   J8871, $3.50 Each.

J8642: White china, colored floral and gold decorations, 30 hour New Haven movement, length 6¼ in., height 5 in. Each in box......... Each, **77c**

J8871:—Two decorations, ruby and green shade tints, gold, scroll and floral decorations, embossed case, 8 day half hour cathedral gong strike, 5 in. dial, gilt rococo sash, guaranteed Ansonia movement. Ht. 10 in., width 9½ in....Each, **$3.50**

$265.00   *$275.00*

J7448, $4.40 Each.   J8872, $4.50 Each.

J7448: Cobalt blue with wreath and floral decorations on front and sides in natural colors, gold scroll border. Gilt finished rococo sash, fine white enameled dial with gilt decoration in center. Gilbert Clock Co.'s movement, 8 day, cathedral gong strike. Width 10 in., ht. 11. Each in case. Each, **$4.40**

$300.00

J8872 — Two decorations, ruby and green tinted, handsome floral and gilt scroll decoration, fancy case, guaranteed. Ansonia half hour cathedral gong strike, 5 in. rococo porcelain sash. Size 11x11½. Each, **$4.50**

J3746, $5.00 Each.

J3746: 8 day, half hour cathedral gong strike, gold and floral decorations in asstd. tints, fine china case, ht. 11¼ in., width 11½, 5 in. gilt decorated dial. American movt. made by Gilbert Clock Co. Each in case. Each, **$5.00**

$350.00

J8873, $5.85 Each.

J8873:—Ruby or green shading, gold and floral decorations, fancy design case, visible escapement, 4 in. porcelain dial, 8 day half hour cathedral gong strike, Ansonia movement, guaranteed, width 13 in., ht. 11¼. Each, **$5.85**

MINIATURE OLD DUTCH OR MISSION CLOCK.

$75.00

J8262—Weathered oak finish, ht. 14¾ in., width 4⅜x3⅜, fitted with the best American 30 hour movement, guaranteed, same being enclosed making it perfectly dust proof. Raised gilt figures and hands, fancy medallion pendulum. Each, **$1.40**

THE WONDERFUL EVER READY
PLATO CLOCK.

"Watch the time fly." For a window attraction has no equal.
Tells time at a glance.

J1699 :. No hands or dial, upper plates show the hours, lower the minutes. Highly finished brass frame with round heavy glass globe. Twenty-four hour reliable clock movement in lower part of stand. Wound, set and regulated same as any watch or clock.............. Each, **$4.27**

J1700 :. Same as J1699, square, with French plate bevel glass on sides, front and back.......Each, **$5.22**

J1699, $4.27 Each. J1700, $5.22 Each.

HIGH GRADE NICKEL
ALARM CLOCKS.

These clocks we guarantee to be perfect in every part and reliable timekeepers, and we will replace within one year any that are not satisfactory if returned.

J1777   J1775

J1777, "Break o' Day".—The lowest priced **all brass** seamless nickel plated case clock in the world. Sold by jobbers under various names from 55c to 60c. Best American made seamless brass nickel plated case, 4½ in. arabic dial, first class American made **all brass** movement, best escapement steel, lantern pinions, runs 30 to 36 hours.........Each, **52c**

J1775, New "Signal"—30 hour, 4 in. dial shut off switch. Each in box. (No charge for special name on dials in lots of 100.) Case lots of 50.......Each, **55½c**

J1801

J1801, "Beauty"—High grade 30 hour movement, standard size, extra finish, 2½ in. dial, best nickel plated case, polished brass backs ....Each, **65c**

LONG ALARM
NICKEL CLOCKS.

J9000 and J9001.

J9000, Continuous 6 Minute Alarm— 30 hour all brass high grade American movement, etc., as J9001. Rings 6 minutes continuously. Exactly like our "Reliable," but without intermittent feature.......Each, **69c**

J9001, "Reliable" 11 Minute Repeating Alarm—30 hour, 4 in. arabic figure dial, all brass high grade American movement with steel lantern pinions. Nickel plated **all brass** seamless case (not tin), shutoff on back. Rings 15 seconds, then stops and repeats for 11 minutes or until shut off. One of the longest alarms in the market.
Each, **75c**

"ROTATOR" ALARM CLOCK.

Has all the best features of all the best alarm clocks on the market.

J9417, "Rotator"—All brass seamless nickel plated case, height 6 in., 4½ in. dial. The bell in case between the dial and movement. Perforationsencircle the case to allow the sound to escape. Dust cap between bell and movement. The alarm rings for ¼ of a minute, then silent same time, thus alternating about 12 minutes.
Each, **$1.00**

ARTISTIC
ALARM
CLOCKS.

J1789— *Practically dust proof.* Strong, untarnishable bronze case, 3 in. dial, long, very loud alarm, 5x4½. Suitable for sleeping apartment, dining room or mantel. Guaranteed. Each, **83c**

NOVELTY
ALARM CLOCK.

Each with guaranteed 30 hour movement. Each in box.

J9021, Watch Alarm—Loud ring, 8½x5¾, full polished nickel case, hinged cover back with easel, alarm shut off by pressing gold finish stem, 4½ in. white dial with alarm indicator, oval glass front.
Each, **$2.50**

"HIGH ART" ORMOLU GOLD
AND FANCY FINISH CLOCKS.

Fully guaranteed. Each in box.

J9008   J9404

J9008—3 styles, scroll, floral and art nouveau, cupid ornamentation, raised parts burnished, 30 hour time, 2 in. white dial gilt ornamented, centers, ht. 6 in. Sold only in lots of 3.
Each, **78c**

J9404—Scroll design porcelain dial with beveled glass, guaranteed 30 hr. movt., 7¼x3¼.
Each, **$1.20**

J9026   J9049

J9026—Scroll and cupid frame, 30 hr. movt., 2 in. dial, beveled glass, large embossed owl with glass eye on side, scroll embossed base, ht. 5 in., width 4.
Each, **$1.40**

J9049—New design, raised parts burnished floral and leaf scroll and fleur de lis, 30 hr. guaranteed movt., white porcelain dial, gilt center, beveled glass, ht. 7¾ in.................Each, **$1.40**

J1657   J9068

J1657—Cupid figure, embossed bow knot. New Haven 30 hr., 7x4 in.......Each, **$1.75**

J9068—Plain ormolu gold finish, 30 hour movt., 2 in. porcelain dial, beveled glass, 2 figures on side, raised parts burnished, 7⅝x6.................Each, **$3.00**

FRENCH
IVORY
CLOCKS.

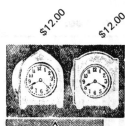

J9226—Ht. 3½ in., 2 shapes, highly glazed, guaranteed 30 hr.....Each, **65c**

J9236—4½x4¾ in., French ivory, highly polished floral and scroll gold inlay ornamentation, 30 hour guaranteed movement, 2 in. dial. Each, **72c**

J9227—Ht. 3 in., 2 styles, French ivory finish floral inlay in silver, 2 in. white dial, 30 hr. movement.
Each, **$1.00**

FRENCH IVORY
DESK TRAVELING
CLOCK OR
POCKET WATCH.

J9243—2x2x¾ in., Uncle Sam 30 hour movement nickel case open face watch, guaranteed, French white ivory box case.
Each, **75c**

LONG ALARM CLOCKS.

Showing Front and Back J2126, 68c Each.   J165, 71c Each.

J2126 Nickel plated dust proof case. Rings 8 to 12 times longer than any other low priced clock. Superior to any other make. Guaranteed perfect timekeeper....................Each, **68c**

J165, "All Day"—The lowest priced **long alarm** guaranteed nickel clock with shut off lever. Will ring over 5 minutes continuously to shut it off one must arise and shut off lever. Extra deep and large 4½ in. case............ Each, **71c**

J7459, $1.00 Each.   J4044, $1.00 Each.   J2635, $1.13 Each.

J7459—Tattoo alarm. 4½ in. nickel case. 4 in. gong on back. Long, intermitting alarm, duration 15 minutes. Made by the New Haven Clock Company. Each in box......Each, **$1.00**

J4044, "Never Stop"—Long intermitting alarm, 30 hour movt., fully guaranteed, ht. 6¾ in., 4½ in. dial, gold scroll feet, best nickel plating, 2 loud bells, sounds 30 seconds, remains silent 40 seconds, duration 12 to 15 minutes, shut off by turning switch key. Each in box................Each, **$1.00**

J2635—Loudest alarm made. With shut off. Has all high grade improvements found only in the Parker clocks. Guaranteed.
Each. **$1.13**

J170, "Junior Tattoo"—Long intermitting alarm, 2¾ in. heavy nickel case, 1¼ in. gong on back. Made by the New Haven Clock Company. Guaranteed. Each in box. Each, **$1.20**

J170, $1.20 Each.   J5235, $1.60 Each.

J5235, "Interval"—Long intermitting alarm, rings 30 seconds, is silent 30 and repeats for 15 minutes. Alarm can be switched off. High grade 30 hour movement, fully guaranteed. Frame nickel plated, glass sides and back, ht. 9 in., 2¾ in. dial. Each in box.
Each, **$1.60**

MAY, 1909.

400-DAY CLOCK.

$145.00

R202. Urania, 400-clock, movement is polished and visible from all sides, 2½-inch enamel ivory dial; has a glass shade, which protects it from dust, base is of brass; height 12 inches from base to top of glass globe, base is 7½ inches in diameter; packed 1 each in case.

EACH, 9.00

ALARM CLOCKS.

$35.00

$35.00

R500   R9

R500. Nickel alarm clocks, high grade, 30 hour, high-class movement, guaranteed, a reliable time-keeper; 4-inch dial, with second hand ....EACH, .45

R9. Dash continuous alarm, American make, guaranteed all brass movements, brass back and winding keys; has 4½-inch dial and full nickel case (under another name sells at 67c.); our price ....EACH, .53

$35.00

$35.00

R55   R915

R55. American alarm, fully guaranteed, 4 inch nickel plated case; alarm set on face of dial, has shut off which makes it an up-to-date clock; a good time piece; 50 to case. EACH, .55

R915. Rob Roy Alarm. No better timepiece made; a good strong alarm, gilt bell and enameled case; comes in 3 colors, malachite, red veined, blue veined; very plain dial, well finished, every one warranted....EACH, .60

$125.00

Seth Thomas Clock Co.'s Crystal. Gold gilt front and handle, frame nickel-plated on a brass base, with brass sides, 1-day lever time, 3-inch dial with alarm, height 7 inches. Each packed in a wooden box. Each.......1 70

CUCKOO CLOCKS.

$125.00 $135.00

J949 – Ht. 21 in., width 14, dial 5¼. Half hour strike and call, walnut or oak, with inlaid ash, ebony or mahogany ornaments.

Each, $4.35

J950 – Ht. 19 in., width 14. Carved walnut or oak with bird and oak leaves, white bone hands and figures, copper finish, iron weights, wt. 22 lbs..Each, $6.40

J949, $4.35 Each.   J950, $6.40 Each.

$85.00

GUARANTEED MINIATURE WALL CLOCK —CUCKOO DESIGN.

Strictly first quality. Each guaranteed and returnable for credit if not satisfactory. Must not be compared with similar style clocks sold for less money, but which are not accompanied by a positive returnable guarantee.

J5505: Indestructible papier mache front leaf design, fancy scroll sides, 2½ in. dial, white bands and roman figures. All parts of movement highly polished. Complete with brass winding chain and bronzed acorn weight, long pendulum. Each in box. Each, 45c

$50.00

NEW PARLOR ALARM CLOCK.

J1371 – Fancy shape, walnut case with gilt trimmings. Bell underneath and entirely hidden, thus making it possible to use as both a parlor and alarm clock. Ht. 8½ in., width 6. Ivory finish, 5 in. dial with gilt center. Imported movement of highest quality............ Each, $1.75

$60.00

'CHAMPION" NOVELTY ALARM CLOCK.

J5377 : Regular 30 hour American movement, guaranteed in every respect, beautiful openwork, metal frame, 9 in. high, ornamental feet, solid back brace. Each in strong box........... ....Each, 78c

$65.00

Waterbury Clock Co.'s Badger Alarm. This clock has a 4¼-inch dial and is 7⅜ inches high, fine nickel-plated, 1-day time, alarm. Each..................... 94

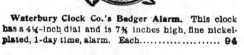

TIME CLOCKS.

$40.00 $40.00 $50.00

R54   R918   R918-C

R54. La Sallita. A small, accurate clock, 2-inch white dial, bevel plate glass, crystal; each in tin box.................EACH, .54

R918. Wasp. A small nickel clock for ladies' dresser, 2-inch dial, 1-day lever time, W. C. make, accurate.................EACH, .70

R918-C. Same clock, with leather traveling case.................EACH, 1.35

$125.00

R1510. Gold plated clock, handsome design, a good 1-day time piece, 11 inches high, 8 inches wide; packed 1 in box. EACH, 1.10

We have a large assortment of Fancy Clocks, all prices, up to $4.00 each.

R1510

$35.00

$30.00

R916   R917

R916. Beacon Continuous Alarm. Fitted with A1 American movement, full nickel case, full size, 4½ inch dial, with second hand, beaded front, very attractive, fully guaranteed; New Haven make.................EACH, .67½

R917. Sunrise Alarm. Nickel case 1 day time, 4 inch dial, height 6¼ inches W. C. make; 50 in cases.................EACH, .67½

ATTLEBORO CLOCK CO.'S NICKEL ALARM CLOCKS.

Attleboro Clock Co.'s Owl. Thirty-six-hour alarm clock, special make, the most thorough clock of its kind on the market, full nickel-plated on a brass base, sunk in back, warranted in good running order for 1 year.

Each................. 57½

In case lots of 50.

Each.................. 55

$40.00

Fine Imported Cabinet and Novelty Clocks

$375.00

No. 1541 FOUNTAIN—$12.50
Walnut case.
Height 13¾ inches.
Ivory finished dial, 1¾ inches.
One-day time.
The fountain is a very good imitation of running water and will run for about five hours with one winding.

$275.00

1915

No. 7418 ACROBAT—$10.00
Oak case
Height 14½ inches.
The acrobat performs various stunts in very liftlike manner. One of the best window attractions ever made.
Clock movement, twenty-four-hour time
Acrobat runs three hours with one winding.

$135.00

MINIATURE CLOCK WITH BAROMETER
No. 113 ....$1.20
Height 11 inches. Width 5½ inches.
Made of fancy wood, nicely carved
One-day time
The barometer indicates the weather six to eight hours ahead
In good weather lady appears
In bad weather man appears.

$375.00

No. 7640 DELPHIN—$8.50
Swing clock, gilt.
Suspended on jeweled bar
Excellent timekeeper
The clock having no pendulum spring, it is absolutely insensible to atmospheric influence and will run in any position
Gold Delphin figure on ebonized wooden base
Height 10 inches.
Two-inch porcelain dial
Eight-day time

$125.00

No. 4277 NEGRESS ALARM CLOCK—$1.70
Nickel case.
4-inch Roman or Arabic dial with negress face and moving eyes.
One-day time and alarm.
A good show-window attraction.

$375.00

No. 7127 KOLONNA—$8.00
Swing clock, gilt.
Suspended on jeweled bar
Excellent timekeeper
The clock having no pendulum spring, it is absolutely insensible to atmospheric influence.
Wood column and base
Height 12 inches.
Two-inch porcelain dial
Eight-day time

HIGH GRADE AMERICAN ALARMS

$35.00

$35.00

"Sentinel"—Long alarm, 30 to 36 hr. brass movement, steel lantern pinions, nickel plated, nickeloid case, 4½ in. dial, shutoff switch.
J9430A—1 in box. Each. **98c**
Lots of 50. **97c**

"Indian"—Long alarm, ball stem shut off 30 hr. brass movement, polished nickeloid case, bell enclosed, 3⅞ in. dial.
J9206A—1 in box. Ea. **$1.12**
J9206B—50 in case " **1.10**

$55.00

$65.00

"Ace"—Thin model, 8 day brass movement, ball stem shut off, steel, lantern pinions, seamless polished and beaded nickeled case, 5 in. dial. Ea.
J9249A—1 in box..... **$2.15**
J9249B—12 in carton.. 2.12
J9249C—24 in case.... 2.10

"Simplex"—8 day time and alarm, brass movement, 4½ in. dial, full nickeled thin model case, 24 hr. alarm dial, can be set for A. M. or P. M., resets itself and rings same time 24 hours later.
J9274A—1 in bx. Temp. Out

"AUTOCRAT" LARGE SIZE ALARM CLOCKS

55 hr. all brass movement, thin model seamless case, 7¾ in. high, 4¾ in. dial, rings every 15 seconds for 12 min., stem shutoff, concealed bell, collapsible tripod. Can be hung on wall. Guaranteed. 1 in box.

J9186 — Brass nickel plated finish.........Each, **$2.15**
J9187A—Brush brass finished.
Each, **$2.15**
Lots of 24...... Each, **$2.10**

Nickel $45.00
Brass 50.00

$135.00

J9172

J9172, Mechanical Alarm—4 in. white dial negro head with moving eyes, set in motion by ticking, ht. 6½ in., 30 hour movement, nickel plated case, brass finish back, shutoff switch, fully guaranteed.......Each, **85c**

RADIUM DIAL ALARM CLOCKS
Tell Time in the Dark

$30.00

$30.00 CONVEX GLASS

"X-Ray"—Radium dial, 4½ in. nickeled case, 30 hr. all brass movement, steel pinions, black dial with **radium numerals and hands**, back bell alarm, ball shutoff stem.
J9442—1 in box. Each. **$2.00**

"Slumber Stopper"—New Haven make, 4½x4, seamless, nickel plated solid brass case, full size alarm bell back with shutoff switch, 30 hr. movement, intermittent alarm, black dial, white figures, convex glass, **radium hands and triangle dots** over numbers.
J9440—1 in box. Each, **$2.85**
Lots of 50. Each, **$2.75**

STAR VALUE

$30.00

"Flash"—Ansonia make, 4x2¾, long alarm, white dial, highest quality **radium hands and dots** over numerals.
J9444—1 in box. Each, **$2.25**

$30.00

"Diamond" — 8 day, seamless nickeled case, brass movement, steel lantern pinions, ball shutoff stem, 4 in. black radium arabic dial and hands.
J9443—1 in box. Each, **$2.95**

$30.00

"Clatter" — Ansonia make, 4½x2¾, **intermittent** alarm, white dial, highest quality **radium hands and dots** over numerals.
J9446—1 in box. Each, **$2.75**

$25.00

"TATOO JR." ALARM CLOCK
Radium Dial

$45.00

J9441—New Haven make, 2¼ x2¾, seamless nickel plated solid brass case, alarm bell back with shut-off switch, 30 hr. movement, intermittent alarm, rings and stops for 20 seconds at intervals, for 5 minutes, black dial, convex glass, **radium hands and figures.**
1 in box...... Each, **$3.15**

"COLONIAL" 8-DAY TIME AND 8-DAY ALARM

$60.00

J9202—Full nickeled case, thin model, ht. 6¾x5¼, ivoroid, 2½ in. dial, 8 day brass movement, cut steel pinions, 12 min. loud alarm with shutoff. 1 in box.
Each, **$2.50**

WHITE FRENCH IVORY ALARM CLOCK

J9353—4¾x2¾, long alarm, 30 hr. brass American movement, highly finished case, 3¼ in. dial, back bell alarm and shut-off. 1 in box...... Each, **$2.50**

NOVELTY AND FANCY ALARM CLOCKS.

Fully guaranteed both in material and workmanship.

NOTE—As the dials on clocks Nos. J9128, J9108 and J9445 are metal, we cannot print on them, but we can furnish on ordinary white dial as used on clocks of other makes, your name and address for advertising purposes **without** extra charge on orders for 50 clocks.

$25.00 $50.00

J9128   J9139

J9128, "Never Late"—Long alarm (4 min.), ball stem shutoff. Bell within, brass case, glass over silver finish dial, 30 hr...Ea. **68c**

J9139 — Double bell nickeled brass seamless case, shut off switch, ht. 7 in., 4 in. bell, 30 hr.....................Each, **75c**

ADVERTISED ALARM CLOCKS

$30.00

"Lookout" — 30 hr. movement, brass case, 6 in. high, 3 in. dial, alarm shutoff, polished brass back. "Westclox" trademark and guarantee.
J9205A—Nickeled case. 1 in box........ Each, **$1.15**

ALARM CLOCKS

INGRAHAM

1925
Butler Bros.
New York

$22.00

$17.00 $20.00

Z9146X. Z9147X.

$20.00

J9426 J9384

$25.00

$20.00

Z9145X — Tom Tom radium dial alarm; radium compound on numerals and hands; which makes it easy to read in dark, otherwise as Z9144X. Ea. **2.85**

Z9146X — Tidy Tot; small size; height 3 inches; width 2¾ inches; dial 2¼ inches. Convex glass; heavy nickel plated seamless brass octagon case; back bell; intermittent alarm. Each **2.20**

Z9147X — Tidy Tot radium dial alarm; radium compound on numerals and hands; otherwise as Z9146X Tidy Tot alarm. Each **2.85**

J9426 — "Tidy Tot," 2¾ in. face, 40 hour movement, nickel plated octagon case, thin model, convex glass, loud long intermittent alarm.

1 in box, Each **$2.22**
24 or more, Each **2.12**

J9384 — "Tip Top," octagon shape, nickel plated, 1¼ in. silvered dial, luminous numerals and hands, stem wind, pendant set, 30 hr. movement, 1 in box.
Each **$2.95**

Z9140X — Tell Tale alarm; height 5 inches; width 3¾ inches, easy to read dial with convex glass; heavy nickel plated seamless brass case; back bell; 40 hour steel cut pinion movements. Each **1.30**

NEW MODEL "BREAK O' DAY" ALARM CLOCKS

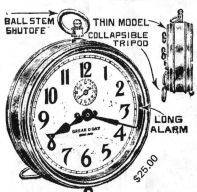

BALL STEM SHUTOFF — THIN MODEL COLLAPSIBLE TRIPOD — BALL SHUTOFF STEM — THIN MODEL SOLID BRASS SEAMLESS CASE

LONG ALARM

BRASS MOVEMENT

$25.00

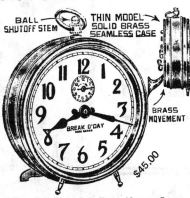

$45.00

Thin Model Large Size—7¼x5½, 2⅛ in. thick 4¼ in. dial, 30 hr. solid brass movement, steel lantern pinions, rings for 5 min., collapsible tripod, can be hung on wall.
J9434A—1 in box,..... Each, **$2.15**
J9434B—12 in shpg. carton. " **2.10**
J9434C—24 in case....... " **2.07**

8 Day Time and 8 Day Alarm—Large size, 7¼x4½, width 2⅛ in. extra thin model, solid brass, solid brass movements, steel lantern pinions, large concealed ball, ball stem shutoff
J9435A—1 in box..... Each, ★**2.48**
J9435B—24 in case,.... " **2.58**

INGRAHAM

$22.00

$20.00

Z9141X — Tell Tale radium dial alarm, height 5 inches; width 3¾ inches; otherwise as Z9140X—Tell Tale. Ea. **1.95**

Z9144X — Tom Tom alarm; height 5½ inches; width 4⅞ inches; large 4½ inch dial; convex glass; improved 40 hour movement; heavy nickel plated seamless brass, octagon case; back bell; loud intermittent alarm; dependable and good looking. Each **2.20**

FANCY HIGH GRADE METAL CLOCKS.

All are fitted with guaranteed "Westclox" 1 day movement; ideal gift clocks.

$40.00 $40.00

Z5080X. Z5082X.

$75.00

Z5080X—Grey silver finish; embossed front of Dutch figures; height 4½ ins.; width 3¾ ins.; 2-in. dial. Each **2.25**

Z5082X—Ormolu gold clock; a beautiful clock for the desk or dresser; length 7 ins.; height 4 ins.; 2 in. dial; raised floral decorations. Each **3.15**

Z5084X—Cupid clock; ormolu gold; height 9½ ins. width of base 4 ins.; a most attractive clock. Each **3.50**

Z5084X.

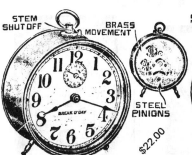

STEM SHUT OFF — BRASS MOVEMENT

STEEL PINIONS

$22.00

Long Alarm—4½ in., nickeled case, 4 in. full size nickeled bell back, long loud alarm, 30 hr. all brass movement, steel pinions, lever stem shutoff, white arabic dial.
J9431—1 in box....... Each, **$1.25**
J9431C—50 in case.... " **1.20**

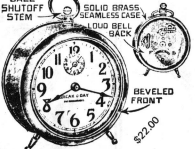

BALL SHUTOFF STEM — SOLID BRASS SEAMLESS CASE — LOUD BELL BACK

BEVELED FRONT

$22.00

Intermittent Alarm—1½ in., 30 hr. all brass movement, steel lantern pinions, 9 minute intermitting loud bell back.
J9433A—1 in box..... Each, **$1.88**
J9433C—50 in case.... " **1.85**

"GIANT"

America's Biggest Alarm Clock Value

1925

$40.00

4¾ IN. FACE

30 HOUR MOVEMENT WITH STEEL PINIONS

SLIDING SHUT-OFF

GILT REFLECTOR

FLUSH BACK

SEAMLESS BRASS CASE NICKEL PLATED

CONCEALED LOUD ALARM

Made exclusively for and distributed exclusively by Butler Brothers. American made, fully guaranteed. On no other clock at this price will you find features such as these.

"Giant," 4¾ in. face, highly polished nickel plated seamless brass case, flush back, **30 hour brass movement** with steel lantern pinions, arabic dial, polished gilt reflector, concealed loud alarm, sliding hexagon shut-off, fancy scroll handle. 1 in box.

Box - $5.00

J9500—WHITE DIAL

87c

6 or more, EACH

50 or more, EACH **85c**

J9503—BLACK DIAL, luminous numerals and hands.   Each **$1.45**

GILBERT THINALARM CLOCKS

Just as "Turnip" watches have given away to modern very thin models, so are the clumsy old-fashioned thick alarms clocks of yesterday fast giving away before the graceful slenderness and beauty of Gilbert Thinalarms.

7" high . . . . $27.00 — 32.00

White . . . .
Luminous

7" high . . . . $35.00 — 40.00

White . . . .
Luminous

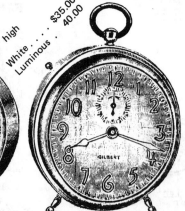

Z9160X—Height 6 ins.; diameter 4½ ins.; 30 hr. time; seamless brass case nickel plated; large easy to read numerals; bowed glass.
Each **1.95**

Z9161X—As above with luminous dial.
Each **2.75**

Z9162X—To those who prefer a clock of generous size, this model will make an instant appeal; height 7 ins.; diameter 5¼ ins.; 30 hr. time; seamless brass case nickel plated; large numerals; bowed glass. Each **2.15**

Z9163X—As above with luminous dial.
Each **2.95**

MAHOGANY FINISH WALL CLOCK

$80.00

J9416—"Ingraham," 16 in. high, mahogany finish, hand rubbed effect, 5½ in. silvered dial, gilt sash, convex glass. 8-day movement.
1 in box . . . . . Each **$4.25**

WALNUT FINISH CUCKOO CLOCK

$125.00

J9450—18x13 in., walnut finish, hand carved, 30-hour pendulum movement, 4 in. dial, cuckoo hour and half hour chime, fancy bronze weights. 1 in case 14 lbs. . . Each **$9.50**

DUTCH DESIGN KITCHEN CLOCK

$65.00

★ STAR VALUE

J9452 — 8½x8½, semi-porcelain, square panel with delft blue Dutch scenes, 8-day pendulum movement. 1 in box.

Each **$2.25**

$50.00

$55.00

Compare Prices!

8¾ in. square, paneled effect, enameled delft blue & white Dutch figures and scenes, American movement. Each in box.

J9410—30 hour movement.
Each **$1.45**

J9411—8-day movement.
Each **$2.20**

J9413—8½ in. octagon paneled, white enameled wood, blue border, silvered dial, gilt sash, 8-day American movement. 1 in box . . . . Each **$4.0**

$50.00

$65.00

J9412—10¾x6¾ in., white enameled wood, 5½ in. white dial, black numerals and hands. 1 in box . . . . Each **$3.50**

J9414—11½x7¼ in., white enameled wood, blue line decoration, 5 in. silvered dial, gilt sash, 8-day American pendulum movement. 1 in box . . . . . Each **$7.50**

Every Month We Buy and Sell More

ALARM CLOCKS

Than Any Other Jobber In America

1927

Add $5.00 for Black Dial

White — $35.00

J9425—"Gem," 4 in. face, highly polished nickel plated case, flush back, 30 hour brass movement with steel pinions, **concealed loud alarm**, side shutoff.

1 in box, Each **69c**
50 or more, Each **67c**

J9300—"Flyer", 4 in. face, nickeled case, loud clear top bell alarm, handy shut off switch, 30 hour all brass movement. 1 in box.

1 in box, Each **67c**
Doz **$7.80**

Guard

5¼ in. face, nickel plated, highly polished seamless case, **thin model**, loud alarm with front shut-off, 8-day solid brass movement with steel lantern pinions, gilt reflector.

J9525—White dial.
1 in box, Each **$2.50**
12 or more, Each **$2.40**

J9526—Black dial, luminous numerals and hands.
1 in box, Each **$3.00**
12 or more, Each **$2.90**

Pirate.... $30.00
Pirate.... 35.00
Rascal.... 35.00
Simplex... 75.00
Racket.... 125.00
1DSA

"ANSONIA" SQUARE ALARMS

Square shape, platinum finish case, 30 hour brass movement, concealed alarm, back shutoff switch. 1 in box.

J9475—"Pirate," 4¼x3½, 3 in. dial, continuous alarm. Each **$1.35**

J9488—"Pirate," 4¼x3½, 3 in. dial, continuous alarm, black dial with luminous numerals and hands. Each **$1.95**

J9476—"Rascal," 3x2½, 1⅞ in. dial, intermittent alarm. Each **$1.90**

J9489—"Simplex," 4½x5¼, 3¾ in. dial, 10 day time and 10 day alarm, new 24 hour alarm dial can be set for A. M. or P. M. Resets itself and rings at the same time 24 hours later without readjusting. Each **$3.25**

"WESTCLOX" ALARMS

6 in. high, 3½ in. dial, double dome bell, seamless nickel plated case, 30 hour movement, steady alarm, shut off. 1 in box.

J9428—"Blue Bird," white dial, black hands and numerals....Each **$1.22**
12 or more, Each 1.19
24 or more, Each 1.15

J9424—"Black Bird,"black dial, luminous hands and numerals....Each **$1.76**
12 or more, Each 1.70
24 or more, Each 1.65

5 in. high, 3½ in. dial, back bell, seamless brass case, nickel plated, roll front, 32 hour movement, shut off. 1 in box.

J9440 — "Sleep Meter," white dial, black hands and numerals....Each **$1.40**
12 or more, Each 1.36
24 or more, Each 1.32

J9441—"Jack-O-Lantern," black dial, black hands and numerals. Each **$2.10**
12 or more, Each 2.04
24 or more, Each 1.98

4½ in. high, 3½ in. Arabic dial, back bell, nickeled case, 32 hour movement, steady alarm. 1 in box.

J9457—"Ben Hur," white dial, black hands and numerals....Each **$1.76**
12 or more, Each 1.70
24 or more, Each 1.65

J9458—"Ben Hur Luminous," black dial, luminous hands and numerals. Each **$2.46**
12 or more, Each 2.38
24 or more, Each 2.32

7 in. high, 4½ in. dial, back bell, dustproof, seamless brass case, nickel plated, 30 hour movement, steady and repeat alarm, shut off. 1 in box.

J9442—"Big Ben," white dial, black hands and numerals....Each **$2.29**
12 or more, Each 2.21
24 or more, Each 2.15

J9443—"Big Ben Luminous," black dial, luminous hands and numerals. Each **$3.16**
12 or more, Each 3.06
24 or more, Each 2.97

5¾ in. high, 4½ in. dial, back gong, dustproof nickeled case, 32 hour movement, steady and repeat alarm. 1 in box.

J9459—"Big Ben De Luxe," white dial, black hands and numerals. Each **$2.64**
12 or more, Each 2.55
24 or more, Each 2.47

J9460—"Big Ben De Luxe" Luminous, black dial, luminous hands and numerals........Each **$3.52**
12 or more, Each 3.40
24 or more, Each 3.32

3¾ in. high, 2½ in. dial, back bell, steady and repeat alarm, 32 hour movement, shut off. 1 in box.

J9444—"Baby Ben," white dial, black hands and numerals....Each **$2.29**
12 or more, Each 2.21
24 or more, Each 2.15

J9445—"Baby Ben Luminous," black dial, luminous hands and numerals....Each **$3.16**
12 or more, Each 3.06
24 or more, Each 2.97

3½ in. high, 2½ in. dial, back gong, dustproof nickeled case, 32 hour movement, steady and repeat alarm. 1 in box.

J9461 — "Baby Ben De Luxe," white dial, black hands and numerals. Each **$2.64**
12 or more, Each 2.55
24 or more, Each 2.49

J9462—"Baby Ben De Luxe" Luminous, black dial, luminous hands and numerals. Each **$3.52**
12 or more, Each 3.40
24 or more, Each 3.32

J9422—"America," 3½ in. dial, dome bell, nickeled case, 36 hour movement, steady alarm, shut off.

1 in box, Each **$1.05**
12 in case, Each 1.02
24 in case, Each .99

Westclox

A Nationally Advertised Line

QUANTITY PRICES Apply On All Orders For The Quantity—One Kind or Assorted

$8.00

"BANTAM"
J-3765—1 in box. **Each 70c**
Lots of 24, **Each** 68c
Lots of 72, **Each** 67c
4½ in. **green** seamless case, 30-hour movement.

$8.00

"AMERICA"
J-3769.—1 in box. ......**Each $1.05**
Lots of 24, **Each** 1.02
Lots of 72, **Each** 1.00
4 in. nickeled seamless case, 30-hour movement.

$17.00

"Big Ben" Chime Alarm

First it WHISPERS—then it SHOUTS!
No other name in the Alarm Clock industry ranks so high in public opinion.

Plain Dial —Retails $3.50
J-3754—1 in box.
Each $2.46
Lots of 24, **Each** $2.40
Lots of 72, **Each** 2.34

Luminous Dial—Retails $4.50
J-3755—1 in box.
Each $3.16
Lots of 24, **Each** $3.08
Lots of 72, **Each** 3.00

5⅝ in. high, **black & nickeled** seamless case. **2-VOICE** chime alarm... first it whispers, then it shouts. You don't hear it tick. Guaranteed for 2 years.

$15.00

"SLEEP-METER"
J-3767—1 in box.
Each $1.40
Lots of 24, **Each** 1.37
Lots of 72, **Each** 1.33
4¾ in. high, nickeled seamless case, **black base**, 32-hour movement.

$15.00

"BEN HUR"
J-3768—1 in box.
Each $1.76
Lots of 24, **Each** 1.72
Lots of 72, **Each** 1.67
5⅝ in. high, nickeled case, **black base.**

BUTLER BROTHERS 1932

$10.00

ELECTRIC WALL CLOCK
J-3771—1 in box.
Each $2.97
Lots of 24, **Each** 2.90
Lots of 72, **Each** 2.82
6¾ in. **green** metal case, front setting knob and starting lever. 8-ft. cord and plug.

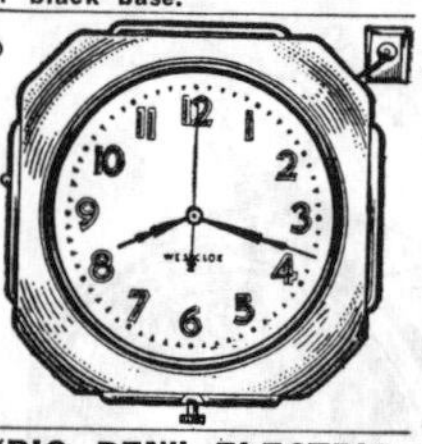

$20.00

"BABY BEN"
J-3766—1 in box.
Each $2.06
Lots of 24, **Each** 2.01
Lots of 72, **Each** 1.96
3⅜ in. high, **black & nickeled case**, 32-hour movement.

$25.00

"BIG BEN"
J-3756 – 1 in box. .....**Each $2.29**
Lots of 24, **Each** 2.23
Lots of 72, **Each** 2.18
7 in. high, nickeled seamless case, 30-hour movement. Guaranteed 2 years.

$10.00

"BIG BEN" ELECTRIC
J-3762—Plain dial. Retails for $8.75.
Each $5.25
Lots of 24, **Each** 5.12
Lots of 72, **Each** 4.99
J-3763—**Luminous dial.** Retails for $10.00.
Each $6.00
Lots of 24, **Each** 5.85
Lots of 72, **Each** 5.70
5¼ in. high, **black & chromium case**, sweep second hand, bell alarm, 6-ft. cord and plug. A. C. current only.

POPULAR PRICE QUALITY ALARM CLOCKS

$20.00

J-3709—1 in box. **Each 59c**
Lots of 24, **Each** 57c
"SIGNAL"—4 in. face, nickeled seamless case, 30-hour movement.

$25.00

J-3703—Nickeled **Each 67c**
Lots of 24, **Each** 65c
J-3704—Green
J-3705—Blue
J-3706—Rose
} **Each 69c**
Lots of 24, **Each** 67c
"LORD BALTIMORE"—4¾ in. face, seamless case, 30-hour movement.

$22.00

J-3737—Rose
J-3738—Green
Each 69c
Lots of 24, **Each** 67c
3⅛ in. face, colored metal case, **convex crystal**, 30-hour Gilbert movement. **Excellent $1.00 value!**

$25.00

J-3733—Green
J-3734—Rose
J-3735—Blue
Each ★▲78c
Lots of 24, **Each** 75c
"RIO RITA"—3¼ in. face, colored metal case, embossed cast front, gold decorations, 30-hour movement.

$20.00

J-3736—Each in box.
Each ★▲ 84c
Lots of 24, **Each** 80c
4½ in. face, **black & nickeled** seamless case, silvered shadow striped dial, 30-hour movement.

$30.00

J-3718—Ebony black
J-3719—Chinese red
J-3720—Sage green
Each $1.05
1 in box
"CORIL MODERNNE"—4½ in. high, silver finish dial, **lacquered satin finish case, convex unbreakable** celluloid crystal, Gilbert **40-hour movement, guaranteed** for one year.

A SELECT LINE OF ELECTRIC CLOCKS

The Electric Clocks you must have to get volume at a profit. BIG VALUES! Each with 6 ft. cord and plug. 60-cycle motor, for 115 volt, alternating current only.

Art Deco $15.00

Low Price ALARM!
J-3993—1 in carton. ☆**Each 87c**
Lots of 24, **Each** 84c
5⅝ in. high, genuine **bakelite case**, flasher disc, metal back plate, lever alarm control, single coil motor.

Art Deco $15.00

Knockout Value Alarm!
J-3992—1 in carton. **Each $1.15**
Lots of 12, **Each** 1.10
5½ in. high, felt cushion base, diecast green metal case, flasher disc, metal back plate, double coil motor, lever alarm control, Tungsten contact points.

$10.00

"Paris" ALARM
J-3994—1 in box.
Each $1.45
4½ in. high, black bakelite case, silvered dial, sweep second hand, convex crystal.

$12.00

"Hammond" Alarm with Illuminated Dial
J-3996—1 in box.
Each $2.85
"Fire Fly," 5 in. high, black bakelite case, rubber cushioned base, **electrically lighted dial,** sweep second hand, buzzer alarm. Retails for $4.75.

$75.00

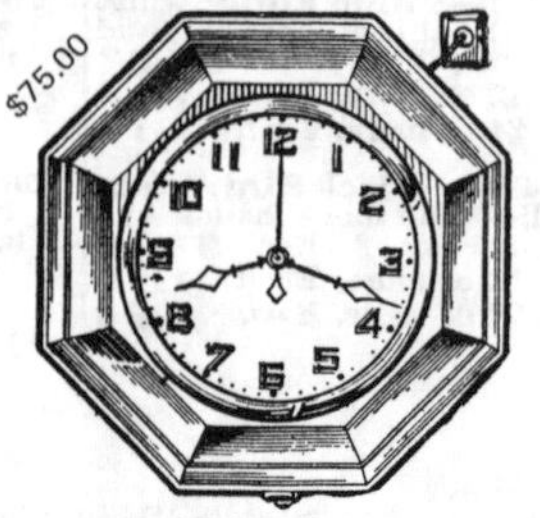

Kitchen Model
J-3997—1 in box.... **Each $1.95**
8½ in. **green** metal case, silvered dial, raised gold numerals, black hands, sweep second hand. **Licensed by "Telechron."**

Art Deco $40.00

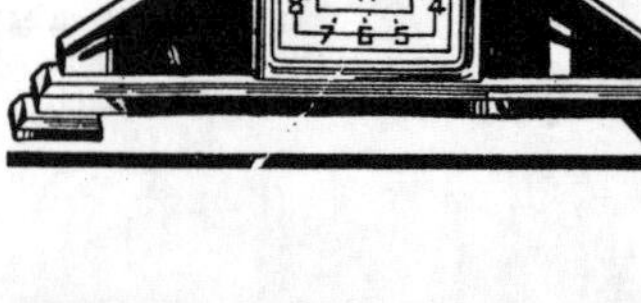

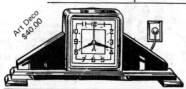

Modern Tambour Model
J-3998—1 in box.
Each $3.25
14⅜ in. long, 3⅛ in. deep, 4½ in. nickeled metal front, black wood case, silvered dial, black hands and raised numerals, sweep second hand. **Licensed by "Telechron."**

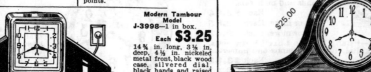

$25.00

"Paris" Mantel Model
J-3995—1 in carton. **Each $4.15**
19 in. long, 4 in. deep, 7¾ in. high, "Tambour" 5½ in. dial, mahogany case, inlay panel effect, convex crystal, black hands and numerals.

8-DAY ALARMS
Wind them once a Week

- **Ingraham Made for Reliability**
- **Graceful Scrolled Base Design**
- **Chromium Plated Front and Base**

$2.55

Stunning looking—and you'll appreciate the convenience of winding it just once every eight days! Clear bell alarm has shut-off at top. Height, 5½ inches, width at base 5 in. Dial 4½ inches in diameter. Convex glass. Shipping weight 2 pounds.

Lacquered finish green or black. State color wanted. Chromium-plated front and base.
45 A 954—Two-tone silver color metal dial. $2.55
45 A 955—Same as above but with luminous hands and numerals. $3.35
Similar to above but black lacquered finish, nickel-plated front and base. Attractive paper dial.
45 A 956 .... $2.39
45 A 957—Same as 45 A 956 with luminous numerals and hands. $2.98

Recommended by WARD'S BUREAU OF STANDARDS MONTGOMERY WARD & CO.

The SMARTEST LOOKING CLOCKS
We've Ever Seen at These Low Prices

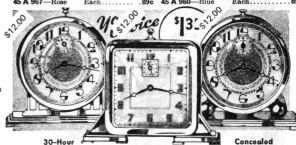

Your Choice
89c
Choice of 3 Colors

Famous Gilbert Movement
This dainty little Gilbert alarm has dependable concealed alarm and 40-hour movement that keeps accurate time; 3-inch cream color dial has attractive black numerals. Non-breakable crystal. Height to top of alarm shut-off, 4¼ in. Width, 3¾ in. your choice of three smart colors. Ship. wt. 1 lb. 8 oz.
45 A 965—Green 45 A 966—Blue
45 A 967—Rose Each........ .89c

Thin, Graceful Model
An inexpensive alarm with the neat, slim lines of a higher priced clock.
Made in a choice of three smart colors with opaline finish. 3½-in.-convex glass. Dependable, concealed alarm has shut-off stem at top of clock. Accurate one-day movement. Ship. wt. 1 pound 8 ounces.
45 A 959—Green 45 A 961—Rose
45 A 960—Blue Each.......... .89c

REGULAR STYLE
8 DAY ALARM $2.29

Nickel Plated—Large Numerals
Popular with Ward customers for many years! You can rely on it to wake you on the dot in the morning ... to keep time faithfully ... to run along steadily for years with no more attention than a weekly winding.

You'll like its generous size too—7 inches from foot to ring with a 4½ inch dial printed in big, plain numerals. Nickel-plated case, feet and back rest. Alarm has handy shut-off at top.
45 A 1262—Plain dial. Ship. wt. 2 lbs. 8 oz.... $2.29
45 A 1263—Luminous dial that shows time in the dark. Ship. wt. 2 lbs. 8 oz. $2.98

ULTRA MODERN THIN MODEL 8-Day
$2.59

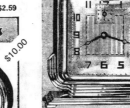

1934

- Black and Chromium
- Alarm Shut Off at Top
- 8-Day Movement

NEW DESIGN—SMART HEAVY BASE
The nice thing about this alarm clock is that it doesn't look like one! Its handsome modern lines and shining black and chromium finish make it an ornament for your nicest room ... yet it gets you up in the morning with a good loud ring. Another convenience—it runs for 8 days on one winding. Its reliable movement keeps excellent time. Two-tone silver color metal dial has modernistic black numerals ... slender metal hands. Convex glass. Height, 5¾ in.; width 6⅝ in. 4-in. dial and a pedestal base to add a smart finishing touch. Shipping weight 2 pounds 8 ounces.
45 A 916 .... $2.59

30-Hour Movements
NEW DESIGNS
Concealed Alarms

CONTRASTING COLORED METAL CASES

Concealed bell alarm. Shut off at top. 3½-in. gray and white dial; pierced hands; convex glass. Ht. 5 in.; base, 5 in. wide.
45 A 988—Black and nickel. Ship. wt. 2 lbs... $1.35
45 A 922—Brown and copper. Ship. wt. 2 lbs. $1.35

3½ in. cream color square dial. Convex glass. Concealed alarm shut-off at top. Ht. 4¾ in. Base 6¼ in. Ship. wt. 2 lbs.
45 A 987—Black and nickel............ $1.35
45 A 921—Brown and copper........... $1.35

3½-inch dial. Shut-off on top. Ht. 5 in., base 5 in. Convex glass. Wt. 2 lbs.
45 A 951—Black with nickel trim........ $1.35
45 A 908—Green with nickel trim....... $1.35
45 A 909—Brown, with Copper trim...... $1.35

Your Choice
$1.75

Black and Chromium
It's a beauty—square and slim, in silvery chromium and rich black. Tucked away inside is a reliable alarm that shuts off conveniently at the top. 30-hour movement keeps excellent time. Black lacquer case has shiny chromium-plated bezel and base. Silver color metal dial is 3½ in. square. Convex glass. 5¼ in. high. Width at base 5 in.
45 A 952—Ship. wt. 2 lbs.......... $1.75

Unusual Diamond Shape
An exquisite little mantel or bedroom clock with concealed alarm. 30-hour movement keeps excellent time. Black enameled case, chromium-plated base and bezel. Two-tone silver color metal dial ... 3½ in. square ... convex glass. Pierced hands. Ht. 6¼ in. Width at base 5 in. Alarm shut-off at top.
45 A 953—Ship. wt. 2 lbs.......... $1.75

Famous WESTCLOX in Smart New Cases

- Black and Nickel **$1.45**
- Smart Square Case

All of Westclox' famous time-keeping features in a stunning new black and nickel case with square, modern lines and non-tip pedestal base. Dependable alarm is concealed inside—convenient shut-off on back. One-day movement. Attractive, easy-to-read dial has convex glass. Height, 4½ inches.
45 PA 949—Postpaid.$1.45

A NEW ALARM
First Warns You Then Wakes You
First a few taps—then, ten minutes later, a steady ring. Black and nickel case, non-breakable crystal.
One-day movement Alarm shut-off on back.
45 PA 950—Postpaid.$2.95
45 PA 958—Similar to 45 PA 950 but with electric movement, steady alarm, 2-tone dial with black numerals on light color circle. For 110-120 volts, 60 cycle A. C. Postpaid.............$2.95
The Siesta

Famous BIG BEN $3.50
First He Whispers Then He Shouts

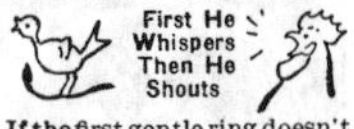

If the first gentle ring doesn't wake you, it goes into a loud, steady alarm. Pedestal base. Lustrous black-nickel trim. Pierced hands. 5¼ in. high. One day movement.
45 PA 1176—Plain dial. Postpaid............$3.50
45 PA 1177—With luminous hands and numerals. Postpaid............$4.50

New Style BABY BEN $2.95
Adjustable loud or soft Alarm. 3¼ in. high. 2⅝ in. dial. Pierced hands. Postpaid.
45 PA 989—With Plain Dial. Black and nickel............$2.95
45 PA 990—With Plain Dial. Brown and copper.....$2.95
45 PA 991—With Luminous Dial. Black and nickel.
45 PA 992—With Luminous Dial. Brown and copper............$3.95

SPRING WOUND or ELECTRIC

8-Day Lever Style $2.79
Choice of ivory or green finish. Dependable 8-day lever movement. New style case. 7½ by 7½ in. Large 5-in. dial with large figures. Convex glass. Ship. wt. 3 lbs.
45 A 986—Green............$2.79
45 A 993—Ivory............ 2.79
Same as above for electric current, 110-120 volts. 60 cycle A.C. Ship. wt. 3 lbs.
45 A 963—Green............$2.79
45 A 964—Ivory............ 2.79

- Two-Tone Alarm
- Spring Wound
- 30 Hour Movement
- Metal Case Nickel Trim

First, a soft ting-ting, then a loud alarm. 3½ in. dial. 6¼ in. high. Ship. wt. each 2 lbs. 8 oz.
45 A 999—Black
45 A 985—Green............ $1.98
Same but Electric with single tone alarm. 110-120 volts, 60 cycle, A.C.
45 A 983—Black. Wt. 2 lbs. 8 oz.. 1.98
45 A 984—Green. Wt. 2 lbs. 8 oz. 1.98

SETH THOMAS CLOCK
8-Day PENDULUM MOVEMENT $6.98

Cathedral Gong
Mahogany veneer case, 20 in. wide by 9¼ in. high. Large 5½-in. silver color metal dial with raised gilt figures. Pierced hands. Strikes hours and half hours.
445 A 1332—Ship. wt. 11 pounds............. $6.98

Mahogany Veneer Case Ash Burl Panels Westminster Chimes
8-Day
Sessions Movement 6-Inch Metal Dial—Raised Gilt Figures

... four notes on the quarter-hour; eight on the half-hour; twelve on the three-quarter hour; and sixteen on the hour, followed by striking of the hour. Length 21½ in., height 10¼ in., depth 5¼ in.
45 A 1245—Ship. wt. 12 pounds........ $19.98

GILBERT 8-Day MANTEL CLOCK

2-TONE NORMANDY CHIMES
CHIMES STRIKE HOUR AND HALF HOURS

- Beautiful Mahogany Finish **$7.79**
- Veneered Panels
- Up-to-Date Pedestal Design

An amazingly low price for this famous Gilbert clock! Mellow Old World chimes strike the hours and half-hours. Pendulum movement runs for eight days on one winding. And it will keep excellent time for years and years.

The beautifully designed pedestal case is finished in rich mahogany color with burl veneer panels ... just the right finish for a living room clock because it blends so well with other furnishings.

Large 6½-inch silver color metal dial has raised bronzed numerals and hands. Convex glass. Height, 9 inches by 21 inches wide.
445 A 1309—Shipping weight, 10 pounds....... $7.79

ELECTRIC MANTEL CLOCK
- Walnut Veneer Case
$4.98

Now—the convenience of a clock that never needs winding—electrically operated so that it can't gain or lose a fraction of a minute. New, perfected Ingraham movement is enclosed in a beautifully shaped case of rich, light brown Walnut Veneer. 9½ in. high; 7 in. wide—the ideal proportion for a mantel clock. Silver color metal 5 in. dial. 110-120 volt. 60 cycle A. C. Shipping weight 4 pounds.
45 A 1334 .... $4.98

MONTGOMERY WARD

$30.00

All Star Eight - Day Alarm Clock. Beautifully designed case, guaranteed Ingraham eight-day movement, concealed mellow sounding alarm, with handy top shut-off switch. Black metal case with nickel trimming.

Fancy Dial With Black Numerals

No. 60W951. Each......... 1.75

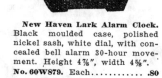

$20.00

New Haven Lark Alarm Clock. Black moulded case, polished nickel sash, white dial, with concealed bell alarm 30-hour movement. Height 4⅞", width 4⅝".

No. 60W879. Each........... .80

$20.00

Gilbert Duval Alarm Clock. Mahogany finish case, 3-inch metal dial with ornamental hands, 40-hour lever movement with concealed bell alarm, convenient top shut-off switch. Height, 5⅝ inches; width, 5¾ inehes.

No. 60W931. Each 1.33

$8.00

Eltime Electric Alarm Clock. Moulded Durez case, walnut finish, buffed dial with black numerals, flasher indicator, buzzer alarm, synchronous type manual starting motor, height 4½ inches, width 4 inches.

No. 60W846. Each......... .85

$15.00

Ingraham Mystic Alarm Clock. A distinctive new design, metal case, lacquered enamel finish, 3½" fancy silver finish dial, chromium finish bezel, 30-hour concealed bell alarm movement with shut-off switch on top. Height 6¼", width 5¼".

No. 60W831. Black. Ea. .87

No. 60W832. Green. Ea. .87

$7.00

New Haven Octet Electric Alarm Clock. A modernistic style clock in black metal with nickel trimming, metal dial, heavy cast base with metal rests, full tone alarm bell, guaranteed synchronous type manual starting motor. Height, 4¼ inches; width, 4 inches.

No. 60W857. Each........... 1.70

$45.00

Ingraham Bates Eight-Day Alarm Clock. Walnut case, striped maple and walnut inlay, ebonized feet. Height, 7 in.; width, 6 in. An unusual attractive eight-day alarm clock which can be used anywhere in the home.

No. 60W953. Each 3.15

$12.00

White House Alarm Clock. Made with 30-hour American movement with alarm. Celluloid case, with front finished in pearl effect. Can be had in Rose, Blue or Green front. Length 9 inches, height 6 inches. 3½-inch colored dial to match case. Each in box.

No. 60W463. Each........... 1.75

$7.00

Gilbert Alarm Clock. Metal case, black lacquered enamel finish with wood side brackets, chromium finish bezel, 3" dial, 40-hour concealed bell alarm movement with stem shut-off switch. Width 5½", height 4¼".

No. 60W880. Each........... .79

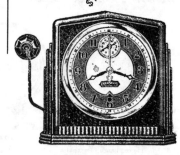

$10.00

Ingraham Electric Alarm Clock. Genuine solid mahogany case, 3½-inch silver plated dial, gold sash, guaranteed synchronous self-starting motor, bell alarm. Height, 5¾ inches; width, 5¾ inches.

No. 60W834. Each........... 3.00

$50.00

Session Sparta 8-Day Alarm Clock. Nickel finish case, 4½-inch dial, convex glass, eight-day movement. Top shut-off switch. Height, 6½ inches; width, 5½ inches.

Metal Dial With Raised Numerals.

No. 60W865. Each......... 2.60

Radium Dial.

No. 60W866. Each......... 3.00

$7.00

Gilbert Alarm Clock. Metal case in assorted colors of ivory, blue and green. Fancy dial and unbreakable crystal. 40-hour lever movement with concealed alarm.

No. 60W697. Each........... .65

$10.00

Fashion Novelty Easel Alarm Clock. Concealed bell type, patented pull-ball shut-off switch on back. Height, 5½ inches. Accurate time-keeper, carefully tested and fully guaranteed. Assorted colors: Green, blue and rose.

No. 60W680. Each........... .92

$12.00

Ingraham. Gable Eight-Day Alarm Clock. Seamless drawn metal case, black lacquer finish, chromium plated bezel, metal dial, attractive die cast base. 8-day movement, inside alarm with stem shut-off. Height, 5½ inches, width, 4½ inches.

No. 60W845. Each........... 1.65

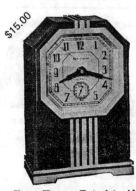

$15.00

New Haven Futurist Alarm Clock. Black metal case, silvered trim, unusual dial design, with cubist numerals, and attractive hands. One day movement with duo-chime alarm. Height, 6 inches; width, 4 inches.

No. 60W950. Each........... 1.65

$8.00

Gilbert Mineola Electric Alarm Clock. A miniature tambour clock of unusual graceful design in a new modern finish. Jet black base and side brackets are in pleasing contrast to the chromium finish case, attractive buff dial, modernistic hands, unbreakable convex glass, guaranteed synchronous type manual starting motor. Height, 4½ inches; width, 10 inches.
No. 60W856. Each 1.67

$35.00

New Haven Chime-Call Alarm Clock. A mild staccato call as musical as a chime and then a vigorous, business-like ring that demands immediate attention. The case is a handsome design in cast metal with a color selection of green or black, with nickel trim. Concealed alarm bell and 30-hour movement. Height, 6¼ inches; width, 5 inches.
No. 60W893. Black. Each... 1.60
No. 60W894. Green. Each... 1.60

German
$45.00

1934

Reflector Alarm Clock. Height 9½ inches, width 7½ inches, fancy nickel case, beaded edge, one-day lever movement, 5-inch dial. Arabic figures, enameled black, 2 extra large dome shaped bells. Alarm equipped with a shut-off switch on top.
No. 60W158. Each.......... 1.35

New 8-Day Gilbert Alarm Clock. A distinctive modernistic design case, chromium plated with base and sides in black finish, two-tone metal dial and embossed numerals and modernistic hands; 8-day movement with inside alarm. Convenient silent switch. Height, 5¼ inches; width at base, 6½ inches.
No. 60W755. Each............................. 2.60

$7.00

$8.00

Classic Alarm Clock. A new design for desk or boudoir, metal case, opaline finish in green, 30-hour concealed bell alarm movement, oval shaped metal dial, length 6¼", height 4¾".
No. 60W878. Each.............................. .92

German
Wood Dial
$20.00
Porcelain Dial
$40.00

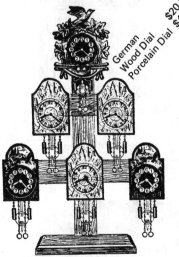

Miniature Pendulum Clock Assortment. Six clocks on a stained wood stand consisting of one miniature Cuckoo style clock, walnut finish, black dial, and gilt hands. Three two-tone Pyralin miniature clocks in assorted colors, green on amber, pink on amber, lavender on amber, with silver finish dials. Two black wood miniature Pendulum clocks with painted landscape scenes in bright colors. Average height 3½ inches. Fitted with 30-hour lever spring wind movements. Keep the clocks running on your showcase and they will attract attention and sell quickly.
No. 60W634. Per asst. 6.25

© 1978 RADEN C, INCORPORATED

$8.00

A New Alarm Clock, Waterbury-Winner with Base. Metal case, black finish, nickel trim. Height, 4¾ inches. Cream tinted dial, inside bell with strong and clear ring, high convex crystal, shut-off switch on top.
No. 60W753. Each........... .70

$15.00

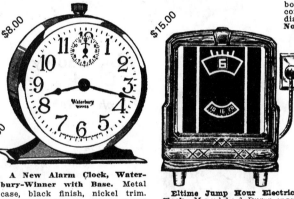

Eltime Jump Hour Electric Clock. Moulded Durez case with feet, walnut finish. Black and white dial. A modern system of time telling. Synchronous type manual starting motor. Height 5½ inches, width 4 inches.
Electric Time Clock.
No. 60W847. Each......... 1.75
Electric Alarm Clock.
No. 60W848. Each......... 2.05

$7.00

Ingraham Magic Electric Alarm Clock. Die cast case, lacquered black enamel finish, 3½-inch silver finish metal dial, stem shut-off, reliable synchronous manual starting motor with sweep second hand. Height, 6¼ inches; width, 5¼ inches.
No. 60W833. Each........... 1.25

Musical Clock
An Exclusive Creation

The very latest idea. Originated, designed and manufactured by us. Not only is this clock ornamental in appearance but it is useful as a timepiece and each has the added feature of playing two different tunes. Simple and compact, the music apparatus is so arranged that by lifting the clock up, the strains of sweet music are immediately heard and when the clock is put down the music stops. This music arrangement is independent of the clock and can be wound and played whenever desired. The 30-hour clock movement is the best American manufacture.

The case is moulded of metal in shape of a radio console showing on front below clock dial, a panel with radio dials, etc. Lower part of front representing the doors is engraved with lifelike portraits in relief of Wagner and Schubert, the noted composers, embellished with musical instruments. Each side of case is engraved with musical notes and instruments. Case is 8 inches high and 5½ inches wide. Weighs about 5 pounds.

We recommend this article, as all who have seen it have been enthusiastic about it. Order a sample and see for yourself.
No. 60W460. Oxidized Silver Finish.....................
No. 60W461. Gilt Finish............................
No. 60W462. Antique Mahogany Finish................

Each 5.50

$125.00

$10.00

Eltime Electric Clock. Walnut finish case, 3-inch white dial with black numerals, flasher type indicator, synchronous manual starting motor, height 6 inches, width 7 inches.

No. 60W849. Each.................. .85

Same as above with buzzer type alarm.
No. 60W850. Each.............. 1.05

PRINTED IN U.S.A.

1934

Novelty Clocks
For Library—Boudoir or Office—For Premiums and Special Sales

Miniature Novelty Banjo Clock. Metal case, fancy design, fine quality thin guaranteed 30-hour lever movement, with metallic dial. Assorted colors, gold, antique silver, blue or green. Length, 6 inches; width, 2¾ inches.

$40.00

No. 60W927. Each......... 1.25

$40.00

Miniature Colonial Banjo Clock. Metal case, handsomely designed showing Marine scene, fine quality thin guaranteed 30-hour lever movement, with metallic dial. Assorted colors, gold, antique silver, blue or green. Length, 6½ inches; width, 2¼ inches.

No. 60W928. Each......... 1.40

$50.00

Miniature Grandfather Clock. Metal case, artistically designed, with fine quality thin guaranteed 30-hour lever movement, with metallic dial. Assorted colors, gold, antique silver, blue or green. Height, 6 inches; width, 3⅛ inches.

No. 60W929. Each......... 1.45

$15.00

American Made Desk Watches. Nickel silver, assorted fancy engine turned designs, easel back, fitted with a reliable American made Columbia jeweled movement with white enameled dial. Each in box with retail price, 6.50.

No. 7W9. Each.............. 1.50

$45.00

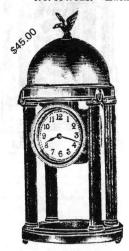

A Big Showy Clock

17 Inches High

CAPITOL DOME CLOCK

Handsome mantel clock in rich two-tone bronze finish. Good looking and an unusual value. Dependable 30-hour movement.

No. 60W311.
Each..... 2.75

$25.00

Novelty Clock, gilt finish, fancy bezel, fancy etched effect dial with black figures on gilt. Size 3⅛ in. square, assorted colored dials fitted with dependable 30-hour lever spring wind movement. An attractive clock suitable for library, boudoir or office.

No. 60W404. Each......... 1.60

$20.00

$20.00

Novelty Barrel Electric Clock. Cast metal case in exact representation of barrel showing staves and hoops and mounted on fancy decorated base. Quiet, dependable electric motor with sweep second hand. Four-inch silvered raised numeral dial. Width at base 5¼ inches. Height 8½ inches. Finished in silver or bronze.
No. 60W820. Silver finish. Each.............. 1.85
No. 60W819. Bronze finish. Each.............. 1.85

Dice Clock. Made of composition with number of dice on the outside; fitted with a 30-hour movement, gilt hands. Height, 2⅞ inches. A ready seller for premium purposes. Each in box.

No. 60W154.
Each .... .75

$75.00

Auto Electric Clock. An exact reproduction of a 1933 model automobile, cast metal case, synchronous type manual starting motor, 2-inch dial, sweep second hand, chromium finish bezel. Length 13½ inches, height 6 inches.
No. 60W837. Bronze. Each 1.85
No. 60W838. Copper. Each 1.85
No. 60W839. Green. Each 1.85

Electric Clocks

Cast metal cases. Beautifully finished. Correct time is assured by dependable motors. Big showy clocks that can be used for premiums and special sales.

1934

$80.00

Spirit Electric Clock with Bulbs. Thousands of people have reason to be grateful to this trio of administrators—Roosevelt, Johnson and Perkins. Their efforts inspired this attractive clock-lamp. Height, 10½ inches; width, 9½ inches. Antique silver finish. Synchronous type 60 cycle electric motor. 3½-inch dial. Sweep second hand.

No. 60W938. Each............................ **2.50**

$40.00

Knight Clock

A fine clock for the mantelpiece of a boy's bedroom. Heavy bronze or silver finish to represent a knight in full regalia. Fitted with a high grade 30 hour movement with artistically designed dial. Height 6¼ inches width 3 inches. Shipped postpaid. **No. 8173. Miniature Knight Clock. Price.. $2.75**

$35.00

Ku-Ku Electric Clock. New and novel. Cast metal walnut finish. Height, 12¾ inches; width, 7 inches. Synchronous type 60 cycle electric motor; 3½-inch dial. Very striking in appearance.

No. 60W935. Each.................. **2.50**

$35.00

Unique Figured Design Novelty Electric Lamp Clock With Two Candle Light Bulbs. In composition metal case. Height, 10½ inches; width of clock 9 inches. Synchronous type 60 cycle electric motor. Attractive silver spun finished dial with two-tone gold and black finished figures, black hands, red sweep second hand, convex crystal. Oxidized Bronze finish.

No. 60W937. Each........................... **2.35**

$35.00

Banjo Electric Clock in composition metal case. Height, 19½ inches; width, 7 inches. Synchronous type electric motor with silver dial, black and gold figures. Black hands, red sweep second hand, convex crystal.

No. 60W936. Oxidized Bronze Finish. Each **2.00**

$75.00

Roosevelt At The Wheel for a New Deal new novelty electric clock. Cast metal case. Height, 13 inches; width, 9 inches. Synchronous type 60 cycle alternating current motor. 3½-inch dial.

No. 60W919. Bronze Finish } Each
No. 60W920. Silver Finish } **2.00**

$30.00

Electric Clocks

1934

SAILING SHIP CLOCK

Electric Movement

Ideal sportsman's clock. Makes fine decoration for mantel, den, office or bedroom clock. Modeled in white china after a smart sailing boat, it stands nearly 12-inches high. Face of clock is set in pilot's wheel design with handles hand decorated in 22 kt. gold. Accurate self-starting electric movement never needs winding. Sweep second hand. 110 volts, 60 cycle. **$5.95**

No. 8718. Sailing Ship Clock. Postpaid.

Windsor $40.00

The New Coach Model Electric Clock. Made of cast metal, beautifully finished in two color gilt and English silver, fitted with 60 cycle synchronous alternating current, motor of dependable quality, four-inch silver finished raised figure dial. Length 17 inches, height 7½ inches.

No. 60W824. Gilt }
No. 60W825. Silver } Each................................... 1.85

Windsor $20.00

40 Hr. $50.00
Electric 20.00

Windsor $50.00

Novelty Electric Clock. Cast metal case finished in burnished bronze. Dependable quiet running electric motor. Four-inch silvered dial with raised numerals and sweep second hand. Width 6 inches, height 7¼ inches.

No. 60W816.
Each.................... 1.40

Ukulele Clock

Handsomely designed so as to make a pleasing decoration to any room. Combined with each clock in addition is the dependable room thermometer. Gold, walnut and ivory finishes.

No. 8172. 40 Hour Spring Movement. Price **$3.80**
No. 8171. Electric Model. 60 cycle, 110 volts **$3.95**

Combination Pagoda and Rickshaw Electric Clock. Made of cast metal, beautifully finished in gilt and English silver, fitted with synchronous type 60 cycle alternating current motor, 3½-inch silver finished dial. Length 12½ inches, height 10 inches.

No. 60W826. Gilt finish. }
No. 60W827. Silver finish. } Each........ 1.85

Windsor $40.00

Windsor $40.00

"The Storm." The latest model in Electric Clocks. English Silver finish, cast metal case, fitted with synchronous type 60 cycle alternating motor of dependable quality, 4¼-inch silver finished dial with raised numerals. Length 10 inches, height 11¼ inches.

No. 60W828.
Each... 1.85

Electric Coach Clock. Case of cast metal with a good, quiet motor. Dial is 4-inch diameter with raised numerals and sweep second hand. Choice of three finishes.

No. 60W788. Gilt finish. }
No. 60W789. Bronze finish. } Each........................1.85
No. 60W809. Silver finish. }

1934

Novelty Clocks With Animated Dials

$85.00

Dutch Arch Clock with animated dial. Metal case finished in antique brass. The animated feature on the dial shows the pilot working at the helm. 30-hour movements. Height 9½ inches, width 4½ inches, length 8½ inches.

No. 60W892. Each..........................2.15

$10.00

Paper Clip and Desk Clock. High grade mahogany finish, length, 4½ inches; width, 3½ inches. Made as a paper clip, equipped with a good strong spring; 30-hour lever time, 2-inch movement, white dial. Each in box.

No. 60W174. Each...........1.25

$85.00

Animated Marine Clock. 30-hour movement. Metal case, finished in antique silver. Animation on dial shows pilot at the wheel. Height 12 inches, length 10 inches.

No. 60W891. Each..........................2.15

$135.00

Barrel Clock finished in Statuary bronze. 30-hour movement. The ball room animated scene on the dial shows the waiter shaking a beverage. Height 8¼ inches, length 6 inches.

No. 60W890. Each..........................2.15

$85.00

Roosevelt Clock

For all those admirers of Roosevelt here is a specially designed clock that will forever be popular. Movement either electric model or key wind. Height designed dial. Height 6¼ inches.

No. 8170. 30 Hour Spring. Price Postpaid.....**$3.80**

No. 8169. Electric Model. Price Postpaid.....**$3.95**

$125.00

F.D.R. The Man of the Hour Novelty Clock. Animated dial, 30-hour movement, cast metal case. Height, 13½ inches; width, 9 inches. Bronze finish.

No. 60W934. Each..........................2.15

$225.00

CARTHAGE — NO. 224

Imitation Marble. Height, 12 inches.
Visible Escapement. 8 day, ½ hour strike, gong.
Porcelain Dial. French Sash.

$190.00

SOUDAN — NO. 221

Imitation Marble and Red Marble. Height, 15 inches.
8 day, ½ hour strike, gong. Porcelain Dial, French Sash.

$200.00

TUNIS — NO. 225 B

Imitation Marble and Red and Black Marble.
Height, 10¾ inches. 8 day, ½ hour strike.
Visible Escapement, French Sash and Dial.

Marble . . . $225.00
Plush 250.00

ROYAL — NO. 235

Imitation Red Marble and Plush Body.
Height, 12½ inches. 8 day, ½ hour strike.
Porcelain Dial, French Sash.

$175.00

SUEZ — NO. 227 B

Imitation Marble. Height, 11 inches.
9 day, ½ hour strike. Visible Escapement.
Patent Regulating Attachment.
French Sash and Dial.

$240.00

ANTIQUE — NO. 239

Height, 11¼ inches.
8 day, ½ hour strike.
Porcelain Dial, French Sash.

MULLER ADVERTISMENTS
CA 1886 to 1888

$175.00

CORINTH — NO. 196

Imitation Marble. Height, 11½ inches.
8 day, ½ hour strike. Visible Escapement.
French Sash and Dial.

$190.00

THEBES — NO. 243

Imitation Marble. Width, 18 inches. 8 day, ½ hour strike, gong.
Visible Escapement, Regulating Attachment.
Porcelain Dial, French Sash.

$225.00

PLACQUE CLOCK — NO. 254

Height, 14 inches.

$185.00

CRETE — NO. 243 B
In Black Marble.
CRETE — NO. 243 C
Black & Colored Marble.

Imitation Marble. Width, 18 inches. 8 day, ½ hour strike.
Visible Escapement, Patent Regulating Attachment.
French Sash & Dial.

CAIRO — NO. 197

Imitation Marble — Height, 12 inches.
8 day, ½ hour strike.
French Sash and Dial.

$150.00

NUBIA — NO. 195

Imitation Marble — Height, 12 inches.
8 day, ½ hour strike, gong.
Porcelain Dial, French Sash

$150.00

ALEXANDRIA — NO. 194

Imitation Marble — Height, 11½ inches.
Made also in red marble.
8 day, ½ hour strike, gong.
Visible Escapement, Porcelain Dial.
French Sash.

$175.00

MULLER ADVERTISMENTS
CA 1886 to 1888

Marble.... $225.00
Plush.... 250.00

PALLAS — NO. 228

With Imitation Marble or Plush Body.
Height, 11¾ inches — 8 day, ½ hour strike
Porcelain Dial, French Sash.

$175.00

SPARTA — NO. 222

Imitation Marble, Height, 11 inches.
Made also in red, black & colored marble.
8 day, ½ hour strike, gong.
Porcelain Dial, French Sash.

Marble.... $210.00
Bronze.... 225.00

CABINET — NO. 234
Imitation Marble.
CABINET — NO. 234 C
Real Bronze.

Height, 14½ inches
8 day, ½ hour strike. Visible Escapement.
Patent Regulating Attachment.
French Sash and Dial.

$155.00

ATHENS D. — NO. 220 D
Black, Imitation Marble.
ATHENS B. — NO. 220 B
Red, Imitation Marble Body.

Height, 10¼ inches.
8 day, ½ hour strike. Visible Escapement.
French Sash and Dial.

PYRAMID — NO. 198

Front Bronze, Ornaments Omitted.
Imitation Marble - Height, 13½ inches.
8 day, ½ hour strike. Visible Escapement.
French Sash and Dial.

$200.00

$165.00

SYRIA — NO. 223

Imitation Black and Red Marble.
Height, 11 inches. Visible Escapement.
8 day, ½ hour strike, gong.
Porcelain Dial, French Sash

$175.00

CHAPEL — NO. 162

Bronze. Height, 13 inches .
8 day, ½ hour strike.
Black or White American Dial.

Call $250.00
Without 200.00

VESTA — NO. 218

With or Without Call Bell.
1 day Calendar Inkstand Clock.
Height, 10 inches, with Call Bell, as illustrated.

T $160.00
TC 235.00

URANUS — NO. 202

Nickel and Bronze, Cut Glass Ink Bottles.
1 day lever time. 1 day lever time Calendar.
Height, 6½ inches.

With $185.00
Without 135.00
If Brass, add 40.00

ELEPHANT — NO. 248
With Top Figure, No. 248 B.

Height, No. 248, 10½ inches., No. 248 B, 21 inches.
8 day, ½ hour strike.

$125.00

**WHEELBARROW CLOCK
NO. 668 F**

1 day Time, Small Movement.
Height, 6½ inches.

MULLER ADVERTISMENTS
CA 1886 to 1888

MARS — NO. 207

With or Without Call Bell.
Bronze Calendar Inkstand Clock, Cut Glass Bottles
Height, 8 inches. Without Call Bell.
Height, 10 inches. With Call Bell.

With $275.00
Without 225.00

8DT $250.00
8DTC 350.00

NEPTUNE — NO. 208

Nickel and Bronze. Height, 9 inches.
8 day lever time. 8 day lever time Calendar.

PHANTOM — NO. 204

Bronze Thermometer Clock.
1 day Calendar, Time, Alarm
Height, 10 inches.

T $175.00
TC 225.00
TA 185.00

$400.00

HARVEST — NO. 240 B

Height, 17 inches.
Porcelain Dial and French Sash.
8 day, ½ hour strike.

$135.00

ZULU — NO. 199

Bronze, with Imitation Marble Base,
or with Plush and Satin.
1 day Alarm. Height, 7½ inches.

$350.00

PANDORA — NO. 240

Height, 12½ inches. 8 day, ½ hour strike.
Porcelain Dial and French Sash.
Brass or Bronze Finish.

$185.00

DEXTER — NO. 161 B

Bronze. Black or White American Dial.
Height, 19¼ inches. 8 day, ½ hour strike.

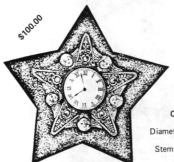

$100.00

CHERUB — NO. 245

Diameter of Plush Star, 9 inches.
1 day time clock.
Stem Winder, Cast metal dial.

With $230.00
Without . . 180.00

AUGUR — NO. 247
With Top Figure, No. 247 C

Height, No. 247, 10¼ inches, 247 C, 18 inches.
8 day, ½ hour strike.

MULLER ADVERTISMENTS
CA 1886 to 1888

$250.00

BEE — NO. 241

Porcelain Dial, French Sash. Height, 11½ inches.
8 day, Visible Escapement, Patent Regulator, ½ hour strike.
The Top Ornament to match the set is No. 724 Urn.

1DT $200.00
1DTC 250.00

JUPITER — NO. 201

Nickel and Bronze, Cut Glass Ink Bottles.
1 day lever time. 1 day lever time Calendar.
Height, 8½ inches.

$110.00

AUTUMN — NO. 244

Hammered Placque on Plush Panel.
Square, 10½ inches.
1 day time clock, to stand or hang.
Winds from back, cast dial.

E. N. Welch Manufacturing Co. AND Welch, Spring & Co.

MANUFACTURERS OF

Fine American Clocks and Regulators,

IN GREAT VARIETY.

Also Importers of French Marble Cathedral Gong Clocks,

158 AND 160 STATE ST., CHICAGO.

FACTORIES: Forestville, Conn. | F. E. MORSE, Agent and Atty.

DOLARO.
Black Walnut.

$225.00

August 1884

Height, 23½ Inches. Dial, 6 Inches. Wire Bell.
8 Day Strike. 8 Day Strike, Alarm. Fitted
also with Gong Bell.

SCALCHI.
Polished Black Walnut, with
"Patti" Movement.

$900.00

E.N. Welch Mfg. Co. sold out
to Sessions in 1903. The
Welch clocks will bring $50
to $100 more.

Height, 19½ Inches. Dial, 5 Inches. 8 Day
Cathedral Gong.

NILSSON.
Polished Black Walnut, with "Patti"
Movement.

$950.00

Height, 22 Inches. Dial, 6 Inches. 8 Day Strike, with
Cathedral Gong. Glass Side.

REGULATOR No. 8.
Polished Black Walnut.
EXTRA FINE FINISH. HANGING.

$1,400.00

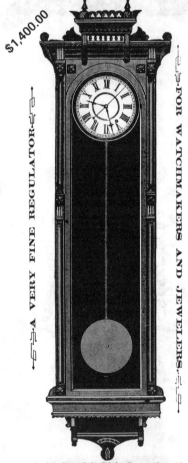

A VERY FINE REGULATOR

FOR WATCHMAKERS AND JEWELERS.

9 Inch. Porcelain Dial. Sweep Second.
Seconds Pendulum. Dead Beat Es
capement. 8 Day. Weight, Time.
Height, 66 Ins. Width, 19 Ins.

SEMBRICH.
Walnut.

$700.00

Height, 39 Inches. Dial, 8 Inches. Eight Day,
Gong Strike.

JEWEL.

$150.00

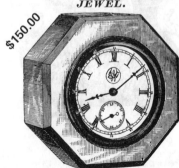

Height, 3¾ Inches. Dial, 2½ Inches.
One Day. Lever. Time.
Porcelain Dial.

NEW HAVEN CLOCK COMPANY.

31 Washington Street, Chicago. ✳ 16-18 Park Place, New York.

August 1884

$145.00

CABINET NO. 7.
Height, 16 Inches. 8 Day, Strike.

The Latest ⸸ Most Popular Novelties

⸻ IN ⸻

EBONY & MAHOGANY

CABINET CLOCKS

VISIBLE PENDULUM

WALNUT CLOCKS,

$165.00

NO. 500. WALNUT.
8 Day, Striking on Gong or Wire Bell.
Height, 22 Inches.

$1,100.00

REGULATOR NO. 00. OAK OR MAHOGANY.
Weight or Spring. 8 Day Time Movement.

$170.00

NO. 502. WALNUT.
8 Day, Striking on Gong or Wire Bell. Height,
20 Inches.

French Clocks & Bronzes,

JEWELERS' REGULATORS.

Our Eight Day, Half Hour, Slow-Striking
Movements are furnished with our
Patent Pendulum and Patented
Cathedral Gongs.

$180.00

NO. 501. WALNUT.
8 Day, Striking on Gong or Wire Bell. Height,
22 Inches.

*Illustrations of New Designs for Fall Trade in Wood and Metal Cased Clocks, in addition to above,
will soon be ready.*

New Haven Clock Company,

31 Washington Street, Chicago.

16-18 Park Place, New York.

1885

No. 1004.
ROYAL COPPER, WITH SOLID SILVER ORNAMENTS.

1D $125.00
1DA . . 135.00
8D . . . 140.00

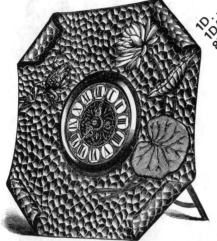

Height, 8½ Inches.　Dial, 3 Inches.　1 Day Time.
1 Day Time Alarm.

No. 1004 Extra.
Height, 10 Inches.　Dial, 3½ Inches.　8 Day Time.

$140.00

CABINET, No. 5.
OAK OR MAHOGANY, POLISHED FINISH.
White, Black or Red Dials.

Height, 13¾ In.　Dial, 5 Inches.　8 Day Striking and Alarm.
Also with Hour and Half-hour Strike on Cathedral Gong.

According to a Jewelers' Journal article dated August 1884, Mr. J. C. Slafter of Minneapolis brought out and patented October 9, 1882 this unique little timepiece. The New Haven Clock Co. took control, perfected its mechanism and improved the design, until they produced one of the most attractive and funny clocks ever. The value given here is for an old clock. This flying pendulum clock has been reproduced from time to time.

$350.00

No. 1002.
CAST BRASS, HAND FINISHED.
Height, 14 Inches.　Dial, 6 Inches.
Length over all, 21 Inches.
8 Day Time.

OUR

COMPLETE × PRICE × LIST

AND

Supplementary Catalogue

Has recently been mailed to the Trade.

Dealers who have not received this will confer a favor
by notifying us immediately.

FLYING PENDULUM CLOCK.
Patented Oct. 9, 1882.

$500.00

1 Day Time.
The Latest Novelty in Clock Escapement.　The Flying Ball takes the place of the Pendulum, and keeps good time.　The best show window attraction ever made.　Will draw a crowd wherever exhibited.
Cases are finished in Oak or Mahogany and Ebony.

No. 1009.
CAST BRASS, HAND FINISHED.

$225.00

Height, 13 Inches.　8 Day Time.

NEW HAVEN CLOCK COMPANY,

NEW HAVEN, CONN

1888

General Salesroom: 29 Murray and 33 Warren Sts., New York.

$165.00

No. 550.

$175.00

No. 557.

$175.00

No 553.

$175.00

No. 554.

$185.00

No. 555.

$180.00

No. 556.

THE ABOVE NEW PATTERNS WILL BE READY FOR THE SPRING TRADE.

Offices and Salesrooms: 7 Franklin Street, Boston. 315 to 321 Wabash Ave., Chicago.

WATERBURY CLOCK CO.

MANUFACTURERS OF AMERICAN CLOCKS.

Factories, Waterbury, Conn.

 1885

NEW YORK OFFICE: CHICAGO OFFICE:

10 CORTLANDT ST., NEW YORK. 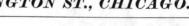 **63 WASHINGTON ST., CHICAGO.**

SELBORNE.
WALNUT.

$200.00

Eight Day — Spring — Strike.
With or Without Alarm. 6 Inch Dial.
Height, 22⅞ Inches.

ELBERON.
WALNUT.

$650.00

Eight Day — Weight.
Height, 33 Inches. Gong Bell. List Price, $20.00.

CATALOGUES AND PRICE LIST

Furnished on Application.

H. S. PECK, Western Agent.

ELMWOOD.
BLACK WALNUT OR CHERRY.

$175.00

Eight Day — Spring — Strike.
Height, 18½ Inches. 6 Inch Dial.

COBALT.
BLACK WALNUT OR CHERRY.

$175.00

Eight Day — Spring — Strike.
Height, 18½ Inches. 6 Inch Dial.

RAPIDAN.
WALNUT.

$200.00

Eight Day — Spring — Strike.
With or Without Alarm. 6 Inch Dial.
Height, 23 Inches.

TERRY CLOCK COMPANY, ⁷¹

Manufacturers of CLOCKS. Sole Manufacturers of Luminous

→•→ Factories, Pittsfield, Mass. ←•←

$165.00

STANLEY.
WALNUT.

Eight Day. Spring Strike, with or without Cathedral Gong. Strikes Half Hours. 6 Inch Dial. Height, 21½ Inches.

NEW YORK OFFICE:

8 Thomas Street.

CHICAGO OFFICE:

65 Washington St.

A FINE LINE OF

Luminous Clocks,
Nickel Clocks,
Walnut Clocks,
Mahogany Clocks,
Cabinet Clocks,
Plush Clocks,
Enameled Iron Clocks.

PLUSH No. I.
COLORS, CARDINAL AND DARK BLUE.

April 1885

$145.00

One Day Time. One Day Time, Alarm. With or without Luminous Dial. 3 Inch Dial. Height, 6½ Inches.

ENVOY LUMINOUS.
Time distinctly visible in the dark. NICKEL.

Chapman & Bloomer, N.Y.

Alarm. 3 Inch Dial. Height, 6 Inches.

$165.00

$145.00

CABINET No. I.
MAHOGANY, ASH, CHERRY. OIL FINISH.

Eight Day. Spring Strike. Strikes Half Hours. Cathedral Gong. 4 Inch French Sash and Dial, with Patent Regulating Attachment. Height, 18 In.

≡ CATALOGUES AND DISCOUNTS ≡

Furnished upon Application.

$135.00

No. 1300.
ENAMELED IRON.

Eight Day. Spring Strike. Strikes Half Hours. Cathedral Gong. 4 Inch French Sash and Dial, with Patent Regulating Attachment. Height, 10 Inches.

ANSONIA

The "Easy-Going" Clock Assortment

ALL OAK
ALL 8=DAY
ALL MADE GONG STRIKE

The Finest Ever Offered. Every Clock Guaranteed.

THIS ASSORTMENT, COMPLETE, $12.⁶⁰ NET CASH.

Nov. 1897

$185.00

GALLATIN. Oak.
Dial, 6 inches. Height, 23½ inches.

$185.00

ECHO. Oak.
Height, 24½ inches. Width, 15¼ inches. Dial, 6 inches.

$185.00

GRISWOLD. Oak.
Dial, 6 inches. Height, 23½ inches.

THIS ASSORTMENT, ALL GONG STRIKE, AND ALL WITH ALARMS, $13.⁷⁰ NET CASH.

$190.00

EOLA. Oak.
Height, 24½ inches. Width, 15¼ inches. Dial, 6 inches.

$185.00

GIRARD. Walnut.
Dial, 6 inches. Height, 23½ inches.

$190.00

ELBA. Oak.
Height, 24½ inches. Width, 15¼ inches. Dial, 6 inches.

Sure Sellers, Big Money-Makers. The best assortment of Clocks ever put up. Sold only by us.

By Red Rabeneck

KROEBER'S CLOCKS FOR THE COLLECTOR AND THEIR PRICES

Florence Kroeber's clocks have long been recognized by the collectors to have that something special that sets them apart from the run-of-the-mill and makes them desirable. Usually at the Marts you will find their prices are 10% to 20% above those for comparable clocks made by the major companies. Those that are priced the same as the major company clocks usually sell quickly. Yet, in discussing prices with dealers, some dealers say that Kroeber clocks will bring no more than other comparable clocks. This brings up three possibilities: (1) One or both of the parties involved in a sale are not knowledgeable; (2) The dealer is being out-manuevered by his customers; (3) There are no Kroeber collectors among the dealer's customers.

This situation, whether one or all of the three possibilities apply, leads to wide fluctuations in the prices reported, with little or no standardization. And some of Kroeber's clocks are so rare that sales rarely occur and become like the sales on old museum pieces—each one a matter of individual negotiation.

Compounding the situation is the evidence pointing to the probability that Kroeber sometimes put his labels on standard mass-produced American and imported clocks. This seems to be particularly true with regard to the labels that said: "F. Kroeber, Agent for the New Haven, Gilbert, Jerome, Atkins, Seth Thomas, and other companies." It is not known whether Kroeber put his labels on all clocks that he sold, or only those that he modified in some way. Regardless, the more information the collector has, the more the prices will tend to standardize and stabilize.

The true Kroeber collector will certainly try to complete his collection to have examples of all the patents and trademarks used by Kroeber. This could lead to a lifetime of searching, as we have no idea how many examples of each might still survive. You can be certain that any museum would welcome a chance to display a collection showing these American patents on actual products.

The collector who looks at a Kroeber clock should look for the features that distinguish it as a Kroeber. If the clock appears identical to a mass-produced model, it should have three items to bring maximum price: A Kroeber label, a Kroeber dial, and a marked Kroeber movement. If any of these are missing, be wary and realize that it probably will not bring the top price listed.

And now the final mystery——three clocks have turned up with the label of "Fuller & Kroeber" with the address of "25 John Street", which was the address given for Kroeber's business in the earliest listing in the city directory. One of these used the George Owen case patent. Fuller has not yet been identified but these are undoubtedly some of the earliest clocks made by Kroeber in the 1863—68 period when it was thought he was merely importing clocks.

DATING F. KROEBER CLOCKS

Therefore, on the labels, if they are "Fuller & Kroeber, 25 John Street" it is an early clock, probably between 1863 and 1868. If they are "F. Kroeber" or "F. Kroeber & Co." with an "8 or 14 Cortlandt Street" address, the clock can most likely be dated before the incorporation in 1887. "F. Kroeber Clock Co., 360 Broadway" probably dates the clock between 1887 and 1899, while a label with "F. Kroeber" or "F. Kroeber & Co." with a "14 Maiden Lane" or "45 Maiden Lane" address probably dates the clock between 1899 and 1904. We say probably because there may be some overlap due to using up supplies of labels.

The catalog reprint shows the dials used. It is doubtful that any mint rubber dials survive. The porcelain dials with visible escapement are the most desirable; the paper "American dials" the least desirable. But the most desirable dial to a collector is the one marked with Kroeber's name or monogram.

The movement should have Kroeber's name stamped on a plate. Everyone knows that Seth Thomas Clock Co. made the No. 89 movement especially for Kroeber. The movement lists put out by Seth Thomas shows other movements listed for Kroeber. It is suspected that Kroeber bought movements from still other companies, but if he did he probably had them stamp his name on the plate.

Most new collectors receive their first introduction to Florence Kroeber when they are in a mart or clock shop looking at clocks, and, like most people, noting the type or style of clock, then looking at the price before they look at the clock. A low whistle, pursed lip, or shocked expression at the high price will lead the seller to say, "It's a Kroeber". This is the normal welcome to the world of Kroeber clocks, and the astute collector will soon realize that his collection will not be complete without a Kroeber clock, and it makes no difference if the collector collects only a certain type of clock, as Kroeber put his touch on most types of clocks. So, find your Kroeber before the price goes higher, for the name of Florence T. Kroeber will live for many years to come on his clocks and in the minds of many clock collectors who will be proud to own a clock that is distinctively "Kroeber".

The above articles represents all of the information that I have at my disposal at this time. Anyone with additional information as to original factory catalogs, advertisements in trade magazines of the day, or small articles and bits and pieces, I would appreciate your letting me know about them in some way. Any new information submitted will be used in a future article. Send to me at P.O. Box 11097, Kansas City, Missouri 64119.

F. KROEBER CLOCK CO. IDENTIFICATION & PRICE GUIDE
ROY EHRHARDT AND RED RABENECK, 1983
36, 8½x11 pages. $10.00. Order No. 10497

A very important book for F. Kroeber collectors and dealers. Information has heretofore been rare and vague on Florence Kroeber and his clocks. Contains 292 actual clock illustrations from two rare, original F. Kroeber factory sales catalogs, one dated 1888 and one dated 1893, and pictures from factory advertisements and sale flyers from the 1888-1895 era. The same format and style as **Clock Identification & Price Guide, Books 1, 2 and 3.** The following information is given for each clock: One of the years it was offered for sale; The factory description; The present retail value. After reading the special article by Red, titled "Florence T. Kroeber, The Mysterious Clockmaker", you will have a much better understanding of the man and his clocks, as well as a market advantage.

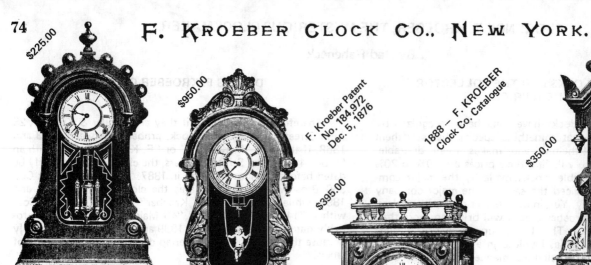

$225.00

$950.00

F. Kroeber Patent
No. 184,972
Dec. 5, 1876

1888 — F. KROEBER
Clock Co. Catalogue

$395.00

$350.00

FULTON.

Walnut. 8 Day Gong Strike.
5 inch Dial. Height, 20 inches.

ANGEL SWING, No. 2.

Walnut. 8 Day Gong Strike. 5 inch Dial.
Height, 19 inches.

CONGRESS.

Walnut. 8 Day Gong Strike.
6 inch Dial. Height, 24 inches.

$400.00

"MARIPOSA"
F. Kroeber Patent
No. 5,409
Dec. 11, 1877

$445.00

CORINTH.

Mahogany. 8 Day Strike Gong. 6 inch Porcelain Dial.
Height, 18 inches.

CLOCKS IN THIS BOOK
ARE VALUED AS IF THEY
ARE IN MINT ORIGINAL
OR COMPLETELY
RESTORED CONDITION.

MARIPOSA—Gilt.

Walnut. 8 Day Gong Strike. 6 inch Dial.
Height, 21½ inches.

ALEXANDRIA.

Mahogany. 8 Day Strike Gong. 5 inch Porcelain Dial.
Height, 18½ inches.

$225.00

$225.00

$340.00

$220.00

LEGHORN.

Walnut. 8 Day Gong Strike.
5 inch Dial. Height, 20 inches.

JEFFERSON.

Walnut. 8 Day Gong Strike.
5 inch Dial. Height, 20 inches.

FLORETTA.

Walnut. 8 Day Gong Strike.
5 inch Dial. Height, 20 inches.

ESSEX.

Walnut. 8 Day Gong Strike.
5 inch Dial. Height, 21½ inches.

$340.00

VIRGIL.

Walnut. 8 Day Gong Strike. 6 inch Dial.
Height, 24½ inches.

$475.00

PYRAMID.

Mahogany. 8 Day Strike Gong. 5 inch Porcelain Dial.
Height, 18 inches.

$275.00

WANDERER.

Walnut. 8 Day Gong Strike.
6 inch Fancy Dial. Height, 23 inches.

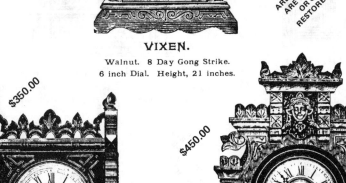

$255.00

1888 — F. KROEBER
Clock Co. Catalogue

CLOCKS IN THIS BOOK
ARE VALUED AS IF THEY
ARE IN MINT ORIGINAL
OR COMPLETELY
RESTORED CONDITION.

$265.00

VIXEN.

Walnut. 8 Day Gong Strike.
6 inch Dial. Height, 21 inches.

THUNDERER.

Walnut. 8 Day Gong Strike.
6 inch Dial. Height, 21 inches.

$350.00

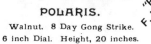

POLARIS.

Walnut. 8 Day Gong Strike.
6 inch Dial. Height, 20 inches.

"POLARIS"
F. Kroeber Patent
No. 2,236
Feb. 16, 1875

$450.00

ARTIC.

Walnut. 8 Day Gong Strike. 6 inch Dial. Height, 25 inches.

$490.00

LANGTRY.

Walnut. 8 Day Gong Strike. 6 inch White Dial.
Height, 23 inches.

Mirror . $300.00

$280.00

Mirror . $300.00

CABINET, No. 60.

Walnut. 8 Day Gong Strike. 5 inch American Dial.
Height, 14½ inches.

CABINET, No. 53.

Walnut. Bronze Columns. 8 Day Strike.
4½ inch Black Dial. Height, 14 inches.

CABINET, NO. 59.

Walnut. 8 Day Gong Strike. 5 inch American Dial.
Height, 16½ inches.

$240.00

$200.00

$240.00

CABINET, No. 50.

Walnut. 8 Day Strike. 4½ inch Black Dial.
Height, 13 inches.

DELTA.

Ash. Cabinet Finish. 8 Day Gong Strike.
5 inch American or Porcelain Dial.
Height, 14 inches.

CABINET, No. 13.

Mahogany. Polished Brass Panel. 8 Day Strike Gong.
5 inch Black Dial. Height, 14½ inches.

1888 — F. KROEBER Clock Co. Catalogue

$280.00

$550.00

$290.00

CABINET, No. 4.

Ebony.
8 Day Strike. 5 inch Black Dial.
Height, 12½ inches.

CABINET, No. 51.

Walnut. 8 Day Strike. 4½ inch Black Dial.
Height, 13½ inches.

MUSICAL, No. 4.

Enameled Iron. 8 Day, 5 inch American Dial.
Height, 12½ inches.

8D........ $450.00
8DS....... 500.00
8DC....... 500.00
8DSC...... 550.00

$300.00

1888 — F. KROEBER
Clock Co. Catalogue

8D........ $400.00
8DS....... 450.00
8DC....... 450.00
8DSC...... 550.00

PET.

Walnut. 8 Day Gong Strike.
5 inch Dial. Height, 16½ inches.

MALTESE GALLERY.

Spring. Pendulum.
14 inch Dial. Height, 27½ inches.
8 Day Time. 8 Day Strike.

1D... $120.00
1DS.. 145.00

Walnut. $275.00
Ash ... 300.00

CLOCKS IN THIS BOOK
ARE VALUED AS IF THEY
ARE IN MINT ORIGINAL
OR COMPLETELY
RESTORED CONDITION.

CABINET GALLERY—Calendar.

Walnut or Mahogany.
Spring. Pendulum.
14 inch Dial. Height, 35 inches.
8 Day Time. 8 Day Strike Gong.

COTTAGE, No. 2.

1 Day Time. 1 Day Strike.
5 inch Dial. Height, 12 inches.

CABINET, No. 57.

Walnut. 8 Day Gong Strike. 5 inch American Dial.
Height, 18 inches.

Ash ... $300.00
Walnut. 275.00

$150.00

"ECLIPSE"
F. Kroeber Patent
No. 28,793
Aug. 18, 1896

$395.00

CABINET, No. 58.

Walnut. 8 Day Gong Strike. 5 inch American Dial.
Height, 16 inches.

ECLIPSE—Alarm.

Mahogany. Height, 7½ inches.

ARABIA, No. 2—With Figure.

Brass Finish. 8 Day Strike Gong. 5 inch Porcelain Dial,
Visible Escapement. Height, 20½ inches.
Also furnished with Porcelain Dial.

8D.....$400.00
8DS.....450.00

REGULATOR—Spring.

Spring. 12 in. Dial. Height, 32 ins. 8 Day Time. 8 Day Strike.

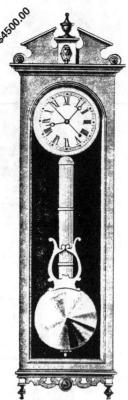

$4500.00

SWISS REGULATOR,
No. 21.

Walnut. Best Quality Movement.
Dead-beat, Pin Escapement.
12 inch Porcelain Dial.
Length, 6 feet 5 inches.

8D....$1,400.00
8DS....1,500.00

REGULATOR, No. 42.

Walnut,
12 inch Dial. Height, 50½ inches.
8 Day Time. 8 Day Strike Gong.

Warranted to run within half a minute in a week.

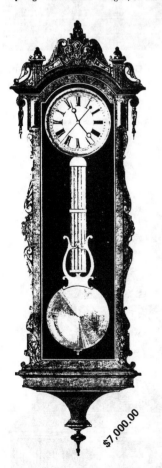

CLOCKS IN THIS BOOK
ARE VALUED AS IF THEY
ARE IN MINT ORIGINAL
OR COMPLETELY
RESTORED CONDITION.

$7,000.00

SWISS REGULATOR,
No. 24.

Walnut. Best Quality Movement.
Dead-beat, Pin Escapement.
12 inch Porcelain Dial.
Length, 7 feet 5 inches.

8D....$1,350.00
8DS....1,450.00

REGULATOR, No. 41.

Walnut.
14 inch Dial. Height, 44½ inches.
8 Day Time. 8 Day Strike Gong.

Warranted to run within half a minute in a week.

1888 – F. KROEBER
Clock Co. Catalogue

8D....$300.00
8DS... 325.00
8DC... 325.00
8DSC. 350.00

DROP OCTAGON, R. C.

Spring.
12 inch Dial. Height, 24 inches.
8 Day Time.   8 Day Strike.
8 Day Time Calendar.   8 Day Strike Calendar.

REGULATOR, No. 44.
6 inch Dial. Height, 30 inches.
8 Day Time. 8 Day Strike Gong.

8D... $500.00
8DS.. 550.00

8D... $550.00
8DS.. 600.00

REGULATOR, No. 31.
Walnut or Mahogany.
6 inch Dial. Height, 34 inches.
8 Day Time. 8 Day Strike Gong.

REGULATOR, No. 45.
Walnut or Ash or Mahogany.
6 inch Dial. Height, 33 inches.
8 Day Time. 8 Day Strike Gong.

8D... $500.00
8DS.. 550.00

8D... $850.00
8DS.. 900.00

REGULATOR, No. 46.
Walnut or Ash or Mahogany.
6 inch Dial. Height, 33½ inches.
8 Day Time. 8 Day Strike Gong.

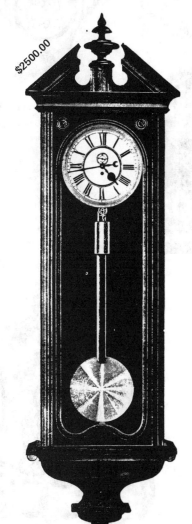

$2500.00

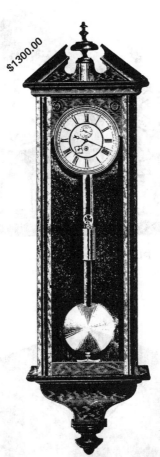

$1300.00

1888 – F. KROEBER Clock Co. Catalogue

CLOCKS IN THIS BOOK ARE VALUED AS IF THEY ARE IN MINT ORIGINAL OR COMPLETELY RESTORED CONDITION.

$1,500.00

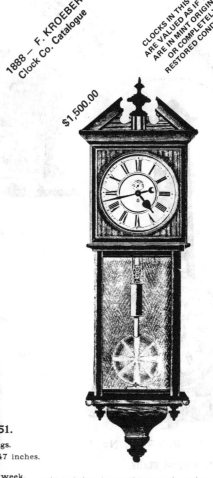

VIENNA REGULATOR, No. 51.
Polished Walnut, with Ebony Trimmings.
8 Day Time. 7 inch Porcelain Dial. Length, 47 inches.

Warranted to run within five seconds in a week.

VIENNA REGULATOR, No. 84.
Polished Walnut, with Ebony Trimmings.
8 Day Time. 9 inch Porcelain Dial. Length, 47 inches.

Warranted to run within five seconds in a week.

VIENNA REGULATOR, No. 19.
Polished Ebony. 8 Day Time. 10 inch Dial. Length, 6 feet.
Warranted to run within five seconds in a week.

$900.00

MANTEL TRUMPETER, No. 9.

I DAY, BRASS MOVEMENT.

Height, 25½ inches.

$700.00

TRUMPETER, No. 1.

I DAY, BRASS MOVEMENT, WITH WEIGHTS.

Height, 24 inches.

$900.00

MANTEL CUCKOO, No. 5029.

I DAY, BRASS MOVEMENT.

Height, 23½ inches.

1888 — F. KROEBER
Clock Co. Catalogue

CLOCKS IN THIS BOOK
ARE VALUED AS IF THEY
ARE IN MINT ORIGINAL
OR COMPLETELY
RESTORED CONDITION.

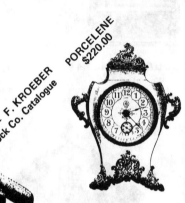

PORCELENE
$220.00

JOSEPHINE ALARM.

Height, 8¼ inches.　　　Width, 6¼ inches.

Lever Movement.

$2300.00

NOISELESS ROTARY, No. 1.

WITH GLASS SHADE.

Totally Noiseless in the Escapement.
6 inch Dial. Total Height, 20½ inches.
8 Day Strike.

$340.00

PLUSH HOUSE, No. 3 A.

Silk Plush. With Assorted Decorated Bisque Figures.

Height, 6½ inches.

$250.00

SWISS COTTAGE.—Alarm.

Natural Walnut. Height, 8¼ inches. Decorated Bisque Figure.

PORCELENE
$565.00

POMPADOUR-EMPIRE.

Height, 18¼ inches.　　　Width, 9¼ inches.

Eight Day, Gong Strike.

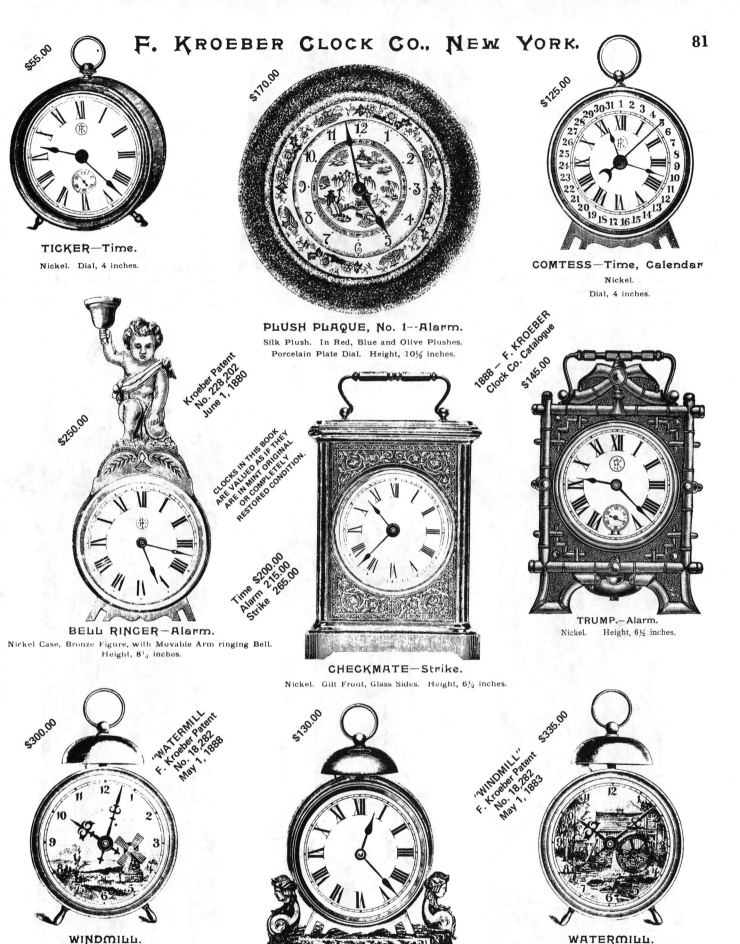

$55.00

TICKER—Time.

Nickel. Dial, 4 inches.

$170.00

PLUSH PLAQUE, No. 1--Alarm.

Silk Plush. In Red, Blue and Olive Plushes.
Porcelain Plate Dial. Height, 10½ inches.

$125.00

COMTESS—Time, Calendar

Nickel.
Dial, 4 inches.

$250.00

Kroeber Patent
No. 228,202
June 1, 1880

BELL RINGER—Alarm.

Nickel Case, Bronze Figure, with Movable Arm ringing Bell.
Height, 8½ inches.

CLOCKS IN THIS BOOK
ARE VALUED AS IF THEY
ARE IN MINT ORIGINAL
OR COMPLETELY
RESTORED CONDITION.

Time $200.00
Alarm 215.00
Strike 265.00

CHECKMATE—Strike.

Nickel. Gilt Front, Glass Sides. Height, 6½ inches.

1888 – F. KROEBER
Clock Co. Catalogue

$145.00

TRUMP.—Alarm.

Nickel. Height, 6½ inches.

$300.00

"WATERMILL"
F. Kroeber Patent
No. 18,282
May 1, 1888

WINDMILL.

Nickel.

Time.   Alarm.
Dial, 4 inches.   Dial, 4 inches.

With Movable Wings.

$130.00

BRILLIANT Alarm.

Nickel. Marbleized Iron Base. Height, 6 inches.

"WINDMILL"
F. Kroeber Patent
No. 18,282
May 1, 1883

$335.00

WATERMILL.

Nickel.

Time.   Alarm.
Dial, 4 inches.   Dial, 4 inches.

With Movable Waterwheel.

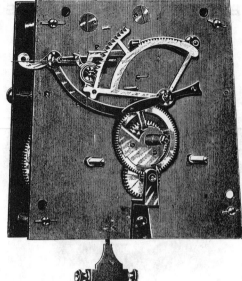

This movement is being used for our weight regulators.

Polished plates and wheels, solid steel cut pinions.

No. 389
Walnut, polished case, 52 inches long, 8 day, hour and half strike, 7 inch enamelled dial, (two weights).
List each $27.00

No. 390
Walnut polished case, 52 inches long, 8 day, time only, 7 inch enamelled dial (one weight).
List each $22.00

1911 Imported Clock Catalog
THEODORE SCHISGALL
118 Chambers St.
New York

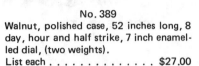

$950.00

$500.00

$950.00

No. 2501
Walnut polished case, 41 inches high, 5½ inch dial.
List each, $16.00

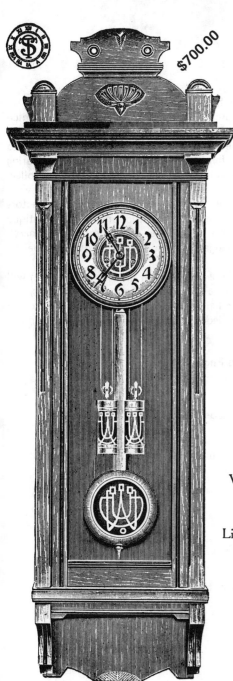

$700.00

$500.00

$950.00

$600.00

No. 350

Walnut, 49 inches high, half hour strike, richly ornamented 7 inch dial, weights and pendulum.

List each $30.00

No. 2500
Walnut polished case, 42 inches high, 5½ inch dial.
List each, $16.00

No. 2601

Walnut, 36 inches high, 14 day strike, (spring wind), without weights.

List each $16.00

No. 2504

Walnut polished case, mirror side brackets for ornaments, 41 inches long, 25 inches wide, 5½ inch enamelled dial and pendulum ball, 14 day half hour strike on beautifully sounding gong.

List each $21.00

1911 Imported Clock Catalog
THEODORE SCHISGALL
118 Chambers St.
New York

FRENCH CLOCKS
EXPLANATION OF PRICING

By Roy Ehrhardt and Red Rabeneck

The next few pages of French clocks were taken from a 1913 general merchandise catalog entitled, **Manufacture Francaise D'Armes et Cycles de Saint—Etienne (Lorie) France.**

We had more trouble trying to figure out acceptable retail collector prices for these few pages than anything else we have attempted before, partly because the lack of knowledge in the United States about French clocks has caused an extreme spread of prices, sometimes with no apparent rhyme or reason.

French clocks have a good reputation among collectors, repairment, etc. as being fine, accurate clocks. This is generally true but as is evident from these pages the French produced low quality as well as high quality clocks. This is easily determined by the number of years for which each clock was guaranteed. We cannot recall any other clocks that have been advertised as being guaranteed for as much as 20 years.

Generally, French clocks are priced and prized highly. When an antique store or dealer acquires a French clock, his first move is to put a high price on it. Then, he proceeds to do practical market research by attempting to sell the clock, which may take years, during which he will probably reduce the price a number of times before it is sold. Interior decorators love to include all types of fancy French clocks in their decorating schemes and can and will pay many dollars more than a collector will pay.

We have priced these clocks according to what collectors are willing to pay for them. The transactions involving antique dealers, interior decorators, and other non-collectors are generally not between knowledgeable persons and do not fit our definition of retail value.

It is hoped that the information given in this section will lead to a desire for more knowledge about these clocks by the collectors involved and thus give more price standardization in the future. More knowledge leads to greater satisfaction and fair deals for all parties involved.

Listed below are some of the French words translated into English.

aiguilles: hands
ancre: anchor escapement; recoil escapement
an: year

basse avec: low; deep; bottom
biscuit: bisque
bois: wood
bureaux: office

carillon: chimes
cartel: wall clocks
codran: face
cheininee: chimney or mantle
colosse: giant
cuisines: kitchen
cuivre nickele: nickeled copper

decoupe: carved
deur reprises: repeating rings
diametre: diameter
dite: called
dore: gilded
dorure: gilding

epingle: pin
existants: existing

fantaisie: extravagant
forte: strong

garantie: guarantee
garnitures: decoratives
grandes pendules: large clocks

habitacle: binnacle, abode
haut: height
hauteur: height
heures: hours
horloge: clock

marbre: marble
meilleurs: best
meme modele: small model
modeles: models
monture: mounting
movement tres soigne a ancre: movement is very precise (to) the recoil escapement
mural: wall clocks

nouveaute: novelty
noyer: walnut

oeils-de-boeuf: ox eyes

pendule: clock
pendulettes: small alarm clocks
petits: small
poids: weights
prix: price

reglable: adjustable
remontage: rewinding
renforce: reinforced
reveil: alarm clock
reveils de voyage: travel clocks
robuste: sturdy

socle: pedestal
soigne: meticulous
sonnerie: ringing
sonnerie sur timbre: ringing on bell tone

timbre: tone

utilement: profitably; usefully

varni: varnished
volonte: will or wish
vrai: true

PENDULERIE

NOS RÉVEILS ET PENDULES FORMENT UNE SÉLECTION DES MEILLEURS MODÈLES EXISTANTS

Chaque pièce est soigneusement CONTRÔLÉE et mise en OBSERVATION avant le départ, ce qui nous permet d'en GARANTIR la bonne marche.

UN CADEAU A NOS CLIENTS : A tout envoi d'un réveil ou d'une pendule, nous joignons, à titre gracieux, un exemplaire de notre brochure illustrée " **Nos Montres et nos Pendules** ".

Cette brochure explique d'une façon très claire et compréhensible à tous, avec de nombreuses gravures le détail d'un mouvement d'horlogerie. Elle donne, de plus, tous les renseignements désirables pour la **mise en marche** à réception, le **remontage**, la **mise à l'heure**, et les **quelques précautions** à prendre pour en assurer le bon fonctionnement.

NOUS NE SAURIONS TROP ENGAGER NOS CLIENTS à lire attentivement cette brochure, car ils y trouveront presque toujours la solution facile à toutes les causes d'arrêt ou irrégularité de marche, ce qui leur évitera, dans la plupart des cas, des correspondances ou envois inutiles.

RÉVEILS MODÈLES CLASSIQUES

$35.00
$45.00

$40.00
$50.00

$50.00

$65.00

$65.00

8DT. . . . 100.00
(Beveled glass)

6320. Réveil, en métal nickelé, sonnerie sur timbre, haut. 18 c/m, pds 450 grs. *Garantie 1 an.*
Prix **2.45**
6320 bis. Même modèle, mouvement soigné, cadran à secondes. *Garantie 5 ans.*
Prix **3.50**

6325. Réveil en métal nickelé, mouvement très soigné à ancre, sonnerie sur timbre, cadran secondes, haut. 18 c/m, pds 500 grs. *Garantie 5 ans.* . . . **4.75**
6325 bis. Même mod., mouv.t de précision, boite décorée. *Garantie 8 ans.* **6. »**

6350. Réveil en métal nickelé, mouvement de précision à ancre, forte sonnerie sur timbre, hauteur 18 c/m, pds 750 grammes. *Fabrication extra-robuste.*
Garantie 5 ans.
Prix **7.25**

6360. Réveil en cuivre nickelé, emboitage et mouvement extra robuste, échappement à ancre, visible sur le cadran, forte sonnerie sur timbre. Haut. 18 c/m, pds 750 grs. *Garantie 8 ans.*
Prix . . . . **9. »**

6365. Réveil, cuivre massif nickelé, mouvement de précision extra-robuste à ancre, monture renforcée, très forte sonnerie sur timbre intérieur, hauteur 15 c/m, pds 700 grs. *Fabrication parfaite.* *Garantie 10 ans.* **10.75**

6368. Réveil dit "Phare", cuivre nickelé, g.d cadran, glace bombée, mouv.t très soigné à ancre, forte sonnerie sur timbre invisible, monture genre phare d'auto, arrêt automatique de la sonnerie par simple inclinaison du réveil. H.r 17 c/m, pds 690 grs. *Garantie 10 ans.* . . **13.25**

RÉVEIL-MONTRE

$45.00

6372. Réveil-montre, en cuivre nickelé, mouvement très soigné à ancre, forte sonnerie sur timbre intérieur, dispositif chevalet. Hauteur 20 c/m, pds 750 grs. **8.75**

┌─────────────────────────┐
│ **RÉPARATIONS** │
│ **D'HORLOGERIE** │
│ voir page 801. │
└─────────────────────────┘

NOUVEAUTÉ
RÉVEIL COLOSSE

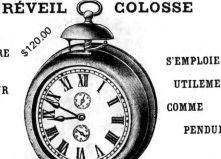

$120.00

DIAMÈTRE
17 c m

HAUTEUR
26 c/m

POIDS
780 grs.

S'EMPLOIE

UTILEMENT

COMME

PENDULE

6376. Grand Réveil "Colosse", en métal nickelé, mouvement soigné, forte sonnerie sur timbre. Haut.r 26 c/m, pds 780 grs. *Garantie 3 ans.* . . **5.50**
6376 bis. Même modèle, mouv.t de précision extra soigné, monture fantaisie. *Garantie 6 ans.* **7.90**

RÉVEIL-CARILLON

$150.00

6379. Réveil dit " carillon ", en cuivre nickelé, socle bois, mouvement très soigné à ancre, sonnerie puissante sur double timbre (*genre sonnerie électrique*).
Prix **12.75**

Pour l'entretien et le réglage des réveils et des pendules, consulter la brochure " **Nos Montres et nos Pendules** "

RÉVEILS SPÉCIAUX — COMPTEURS DE MINUTES

$40.00

$40.00

$50.00

$55.00

$35.00

6383. Réveil à répétition, métal nickelé, mouvement soigné à ancre, forte sonnerie sur timbre, se produisant à deux reprises et à quelques minutes d'intervalle. Hauteur 19 c/m, pds 500 grs.
Garantie 3 ans.
Prix **4.75**

6386. Réveil à répétition, en cuivre nickelé, mouvement de précision à ancre, forte sonnerie sur timbre, se produisant à deux reprises, à quelques minutes d'intervalle, monture renforcée. Haut. 15 c/m, pds 700 grs.
Garantie 5 ans.
Prix **7.50**

6387. Réveil Universel à répétition, modèle américain en cuivre nickelé extra renforcé, mouv.t de précision avec dispositif permettant de faire fonctionner ou non le réveil ou la répétition, forte sonnerie intérieure, fabr. mécanique extrem.t robuste, haut.r 18 c/m, pds 920 g. *Gar. 6 ans.* **14.75**

6388. Réveil lumineux à répétition, monture bois verni, mouv.t très soigné, sonnerie intr.e se produisant à deux reprises et à quelques minutes d'intervalle, cadran et aiguilles lumineux par l'application d'un composé de radium, mouv.t extr.t robuste, haut.r 18 c/m, pds 825 grs. *Garantie 5 ans.* **15.50**

6389. Réveil dit " compteur de minutes ", métal nickelé, mouv.t soigné, forte sonnerie sur timbre, réglable à volonté à 1 minute près. Très pratique p.r contrôles divers. Remplace les sabliers d'autrefois p.r vérifier la durée de cuisson des œufs, etc. Haut. 18 c/m, pds 450 grs. **5.75**

PENDULETTES-RÉVEILS ET PENDULETTES-RÉVEILS A SONNERIE DES HEURES

$90.00

$100.00

$135.00

$140.00

$155.00

6391. Grand réveil forme pendulette, en métal nickelé, ornementé de dorures sur reliefs, glaces sur 3 faces, mouvt soigné à ancre, forte sonnerie réveil sur timbre placé dans la monture. Haut. 18 c/m, poids 700 grs. *Garantie 5 ans* **7.50**

6392. Réveil grand modèle forme pendulette, en cuivre nickelé, mouvement soigné à ancre, forte sonnerie sur grand timbre, cadran métal patiné mat. Haut. 18 c m, poids 750 grs. *Garantie 5 ans.* Prix **10.50**

6393. Réveil-pendule à sonnerie à répétition, cuivre nickelé, mouvt de précis., sonnt au réveil à 2 reprises, frappant aussi les demies, les heures et répét. celles-ci à volonté par simple pression du doigt sur un levier spécial. Haut. 18 c/m, poids 700 grs. *Gar. 5 ans.* **11.75**

6396. Grand réveil-pendule à sonnerie en métal nickelé, ornementé de dorures sur reliefs, glaces sur 3 faces, mouvt très soigné, sonnerie-réveil et sonnerie des demies et des heures sur timbre placé sous la monture. Ht 18 c/m, pds 1 kg. *Garantie 5 ans.* **12.50**

6398. Grand réveil-pendule de précision, à sonnerie, en métal nickelé massif, glace protégeant le cadran, mouvt extra soigné, sonnant au réveil à 2 reprises et frappant aussi les demies et les heures sur timbre placé sous la mont. Ht 24 c/m, pds 950 grs. *Gar. 5 ans.* **15.**

RÉVEILS DITS "A MUSIQUE" ET RÉVEILS ÉLECTRIQUES

$130.00

$140.00

$160.00

$75.00

$120.00

6399. Grand réveil à musique forme pendulette en métal nickelé et doré, glaces sur 3 faces, mouvement soigné à ancre, sonnerie du réveil jouant un air de jolie musique. Haut. 18 c/m, poids 800 grs. *Gar. 3 ans.* **11.75**

6401. Réveil "Géant à musique" forme ronde (diam. 17 c/m) en métal nickelé et cadran doré sur relief au centre, mouvt à ancre, sonnerie du réveil jouant un air de jolie musique. Ht 24 c/m, poids 910 grs. *Gar. 5 ans* **12.50**

6402. Grand réveil à musique forme pendulette fantaisie en métal nickelé massif et doré sur reliefs, mouvt très soigné à ancre, sonnerie du réveil jouant un air de jolie musique. Haut. 21 c/m, pds 1 kg. *Gar. 5 ans.* **14.25**

6403. Réveil électrique cuivre verni, mouvt à sonnerie mue à l'heure du réveil par un dispositif électrique placé dans le circuit de n'importe quelle pile ou sonnerie électrique. Ht 17 c/m, pds 500 grs. *Gar. 5 ans.* .... **21.**

6404. Réveil électrique portatif mouvt logé avec 2 piles dans un coffret noyer verni. Déclanchement électrique de la sonnerie fixée pour le réveil. Ht 19 c/m, pds 2 kgs. 250. .... **24.**

THERMO — RÉVEIL

$125.00

3407. Thermoréveil, en beau bois sculpté (*sculpture très en relief*) et découpé à jour. Emboitage bois entourant le réveil, mouvement soigné à ancre, forte sonnerie sur timbre, applique thermomètre centigrade sur plaquette métal mat, fabrication très soignée. Ht 50 c/m, pds 1 k. *Garantie 5 ans.* **8.25**

RÉVEIL "TYPE"

$125.00

6410. Réveil "Type" en métal fortement nickelé, sujets chasse, pêche et faisceaux d'attributs spéciaux à ces sports, mouvement à ancre de précision soigneusement repassé. *Fab. spéciale pour la Manufre Fçe d'Armes et Cycles de St-Etienne.* Ht 34 c/m, pds 5 kgs. *Gar. 10 ans.* **13.75**

RÉVEIL AVERTISSEUR

$250.00

6415. Réveil-pendule avertisseur, monture bois, mouvt robuste à poids, sonnerie s'effectuant à volonté à des intervalles de temps que l'on détermine aisément au moyen d'un système spécial de goupilles. Parfait pour veilleurs de nuits, garde-barrière, portiers. Convient aussi aux industries exigeant une surveillance particulière des fours, machines, etc., diam. 33 c/m, pds 6 k. **22.50**

PENDULES-RÉVEILS ET GRANDS RÉVEILS A MUSIQUE AVEC MONTURE BOIS

$125.00

$140.00

$170.00

$185.00

$200.00

6420. Grand réveil forme pendule à poser, façade chêne, découpé, sculpté et verni, mouvement soigné, forte sonnerie sur timbre, grand cadran métal. Haut. 26 c/m, poids 1 kg. 250. *Garantie 5 ans* .... **11.**

6425. Grand réveil forme pendule à poser, en beau bois mouluré et verni, ornements en cuivre doré, mouvement très soigné, forte sonnerie sur timbre, cadran fantaisie. Hauteur 35 c/m, poids 1 kg. 500. *Garantie 5 ans.* **12.75**

6430. Grand réveil "Forteresse" forme pendule à poser, modèle gracieux, reproduisant un petit fort, beau bois sculpté et verni, ornements cuivre doré, mouvement de précision, forte sonnerie sur timbre. Ht 27 c/m, pds 1 k. *Gar. 5 ans.* **18.**

6435. Grand réveil "à musique" forme pendule à poser, façon noyer verni et sculpté, appliques cuivre doré, mouvement très soigné, sonnerie du réveil signalée par 1 air de jolie musique. Ht 38 c/m, pds 1 k. 780. *Garantie 5 ans.* **19.**

6440. Grand réveil "à musique" forme pendule à poser, en beau bois découpé et verni, appliques cuivre doré, mouvement très soigné, sonnerie du réveil signalée par 2 airs de jolie musique. Ht 50 c/m, pds 2 k. 100. *Garantie 5 ans.* **21.**

PETITS RÉVEILS ET PENDULETTES PRESSE-PAPIERS

$50.00
$60.00
$80.00
$100.00
$50.00
$35.00
$60.00

6444, Petit réveil dit " de sous-officier ", métal nickelé, mouvᵗ soigné, sonnerie sur timbre. Hᵗ 11 ᶜ/ᵐ, pᵈˢ 180 gr. *Gar. 3 ans*. **4.75**
6444 bis. Même modèle dit " d'officier ", extrêmement réduit, mouvᵗ de précision. Hᵗ 7ᶜ/ᵐ ½. *Gar. 5 ans.* **8. »**

6447. Petit réveil "Phono", métal nickelé, mouvᵗ très soigné, sonnerie très bruyante obtenue par le battement rapide d'un pᵗ marteau sur un diaphragme et renforcé par un cornet métallique. Hᵗ 12 ᶜ/ᵐ, pᵈˢ 250 grs. *Garantie 5 ans.* **9.75**

6451. Petit réveil "Carillon", en métal nickelé, socle bois verni, mouvᵗ très soigné à ancre, forte sonnerie sur 2 timbres accouplés. Hauteur totale 9ᶜ/ᵐ, poids 190 grs. *Garantie 5 ans.*
Prix.......... **13. »**

6453. Petite pendulette " presse-papiers ", en métal argenté et patiné, inaltérable, socle massif ciselé, piliers tournés, mouvᵗ très soigné. Haut. 11 c.m, poids 435 grs. *Garantie 3 ans.*
Prix **5.25**

6456. Petite pendulette " presse-papiers ", en métal argenté et patiné, inaltérable, forme "borne", décors ciselés Louis XVI, mouvᵗ très soigné. Haut. 12 c.m, poids 470 grs. *Garantie 3 ans.*
Prix.......... **5.75**

6459. Petite pendulette-réveil " presse-papiers ", en métal nickelé, socle massif formant porte-épingles, piliers tournés, mouvᵗ très soigné, forte sonnerie sur timbre. Haut. 11 c/m, poids 350 grs. *Garantie 3 ans*... **7.25**

PETITS RÉVEILS DE VOYAGE

$70.00
$75.00
$100.00
$100.00

6461. Réveil "Tambour", en cuivre nickelé, forme ronde, mouvᵗ très soigné, forte sonnerie sur timbre extérieur. Livré en écrin, façon maroquin, intérieur fantaisie de 11 c/m de haut, poids 435 grs. *Garantie 3 ans.*
Prix.......... **7.75**

6463. Réveil "Lilliput", en fort cuivre doré mat, forme carrée, mouvᵗ très soigné, sonnerie puissante par le choc d'un marteau spécial sur la paroi de la boite formant résonnateur. Livré en écrin "Chapelle", façon maroquin, intᵗ fantaisie. Parfait pʳ le voyage. Haut. 7 ᶜ/ᵐ, pᵈˢ 235 grs. *Gar. 3 ans* **8.75**

6467. Réveil "Ecolier", en fort cuivre nickelé, modèle extra-robuste, forme carrée, mouvᵗ très soigné, sonnerie puissante par le choc d'un marteau spécial sur la paroi de la boite formant résonnateur. Livré en écrin, façon maroquin, intᵗ fantaisie de 9 c/m de haut, poids 500 grs. *Garantie 3 ans*...... **13. »**

6469. Réveil " de poche " en acier bronzé extra, forme carrée, poignée et pieds dorés, mouvᵗ très soigné, sonnerie puissante par le choc d'un marteau spécial sur la paroi de la boite formant résonnateur. Livré en écrin façon maroquin de 8ᶜ/ᵐ de haut, épais. 4 ᶜ/ᵐ, poids 250 grs. *Garantie 3 ans.* **13.50**

RÉVEILS DE VOYAGE ET RÉVEILS "RADIUM"

RÉVEILS "RADIUM"

L'emploi des cadrans avec application de sels radifères permettant la lecture des heures la nuit, se généralise chaque jour davantage. Rien de plus pratique que les 2 genres de réveils de dimensions réduites et de fabrication très soignée que nous présentons ci-dessous. Ils donnent toute satisfaction.

$100.00

$125.00

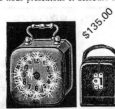

$135.00
$150.00

$150.00

$175.00

6474. Réveil de voyage, en cuivre verni et poli, forme pendulette, mouvᵗ à ancre soigné, forte sonnerie sur timbre placé dessous la monture. Livré en écrin "Chapelle" façon maroquin, intᵗ fantaisie de 12 c/m de haut, poids 420 grs. *Garantie 3 ans*.... **12. »**

6479. Réveil de voyage " Bijou ", en cuivre doré, mouvement de précision, renfermé dans un emboitage robuste en forme de coffret noyer verni avec porte s'ouvrant automatiquement, poignée pliante. Hᵗ 10 c/m, pds 420 grs. *Gar. 5 ans*..... **15. »**

6481. Réveil de voyage "Radium", très petit modèle, en fort cuivre doré mat, forme carrée, mouvement très soigné, à ancre, sonnerie puissante par le choc d'un marteau spécial sur la paroi de la boite formant résonnateur. Cadran émail fin et aiguilles imprégnés d'un composé de radium lumineux, permettant la lecture de l'heure la nuit. Livré en écrin spécial de 7 ᶜ/ᵐ de haut, poids 325 grs. **16.25**

6484. Réveil de voyage "Radium", modèle carré en métal argenté mat, forme plate, boite à charnière, mouvement très soigné, à ancre, façon ivoire et aiguilles imprégnés d'un composé de radium permettant la lecture aisée de l'heure la nuit. Livré en écrin cuir de 85 m/m de hauteur, épaisseur 40 m/m, poids tot. 340 grs.
Prix .... **22. »**

RÉPARATIONS D'HORLOGERIE
Voir page

6489. Réveil de voyage "Mignonnette", en cuivre patiné mat, forme carrée, mouvᵗ très soigné, sonnerie puissante par le choc d'un marteau sur la paroi de la boite formant résonnateur. Livré en écrin "Chapelle", façon maroquin, intᵗ riche de 9ᶜ/ᵐ de hᵗ, pᵈˢ 275grs. *Gar. 3 ans.* **18.»**

6493. Réveil de voyage " Niel ", en métal poli, bandes brunes, genre "niel", mouvement très soigné, forte sonnerie sur timbre dans la boite résonnatrice. Livré en écrin "Chapelle", façon maroquin, intérieur riche. Hᵗ 10ᶜ/ᵐ, pᵈˢ 325 grs. *Gar. 5 ans*......... **19.90**

PENDULETTES-RÉVEILS DE VOYAGE

$150.00
$175.00
$160.00
$250.00

$175.00
$180.00
$250.00
$185.00

6497. Pendule-réveil en cuivre finement poli, glaces biseautées sur les quatre faces, mouvement soigné, forte sonnerie de réveil sur timbre logé sous la monture. Livrée en gainerie grenat, intérieur doublé à rideau rigide. Haut. 12 c/m, poids 700 grs. *Garantie 3 ans*............ **17. »**
6497 bis. Même modèle, avec mouvᵗ marchant 8 jours, poids 1 kg. *Garantie 5 ans*.............. **27. »**

6499. Pendule-réveil en bronze finement doré et glace biseautée sur trois faces, mouvement très soigné, sonnerie au réveil et aux heures et demies par un poussoir spécial sous la monture. Poussoir spécial permettant la répétition à volonté de la sonnerie des heures. Livrée en écrin gainerie grenat, intᵗ doublé à rideau rigide. Haut. 15 c/m, pᵈˢ 1 kg. 100. *Gar. 5 ans.* **23. »**
6499 bis. Même modèle mais avec mouvᵗ huitaine (sᵗ répét.). *Gar. 10 ans.* **65. »**

6503. Pendule-réveil en cuivre découpé, poli et finement doré, glace biseautée sur les 4 faces, mouvᵗ très soigné, à ancre, marchant 8 jours, forte sonnerie-réveil sur timbre logé sous la monture. Livrée en écrin gainerie grenat, intᵗ doublé à rideau rigide. Hᵗ 15 ᶜ/ᵐ, pᵈˢ 1 kg. 500. *Gar. 10 ans.* **28.75**
6503 bis. Même modèle, mais avec cadran et aiguilles lumineux par application d'un composé de radium. *Garantie 10 ans*...... **39.50**

6507. Pendule-réveil en bronze doré riche, glaces biseautées, mouvᵗ de précision marchant 8 jours, sonnerie au réveil et aux heures et demies sur timbre logé sous la monture ; poussoir spécial permettant la répétition à volonté de la sonnerie des heures. Livrée en écrin gainerie grenat, intᵗ doublé à rideau rigide. Haut. 16 ᶜ/ᵐ, pᵈˢ 1 kg. 500. *Garantie 10 ans*... **89. »**
6509. Même mˡᵉ dit "Mignonnette", mouvᵗ huitaine (sans sonnerie des heures). Hᵗ en écrin 9 ᶜ/ᵐ ¼. pᵈˢ 495 grs. **49. »**

GARNITURES ET PENDULETTES FANTAISIE EN CÉRAMIQUE ET BISCUIT

$100.00 $130.00

Clock Set.... $195.00 225.00

$175.00

$185.00

Clock Set.... $225.00 275.00

6534. Petite garniture fantaisie, céramique décorée. Motifs divers, paysages, etc., en couleur, soigné. *Livrée avec vases assortis.* H.r 13 c/m, p.ds 1 kg. **4.90**
6534 bis. **Même modèle**, avec réveil.............. **7.50**

6540. Petite Garniture fantaisie "Renommée", céramique décorée, nuance vieux vert, mouv.t soigné. *Livrée avec 2 vases assortis.* H.r 48 c/m, p.ds 765 g. G.ie 2 ans. **8.25**
6540 bis. **Même modèle**, avec réveil.............. **9.50**

6545. Pendulette fantaisie "Savoyard", genre porcelaine de Saxe, fabrication et mouvement très soignés, haut. totale 18 c/m, poids 695 grs. *Garantie 2 ans.*
Prix **8.50**

6550. Pendulette fantaisie "Taquinerie", genre porcelaine de Saxe, fabrication et mouvement très soignés, haut. totale 20 c/m, poids 665 grs. *Garantie 2 ans.*
Prix **9.25**

6555. Garniture fantaisie "Delft", forme Louis XV, céramique, nuan.ces genre hollandais, mouv.t soigné, grand cadran, lunette dorée, h.r tot. 24 c/m. *Livrée avec 2 vases assortis.* Haut. 21 c/m, p.ds 1 kg 610. *Garantie 2 ans.* **10.**

PENDULETTES ET RÉVEILS FANTAISIE

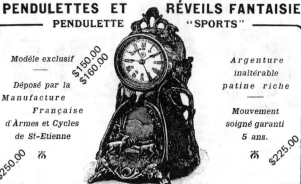

$100.00

6560. Petite pendulette "Obus", métal verni, forme originale, mouvement à ancre soigné, convient comme presse-papier pour bureaux, magasins, etc., hauteur totale 16 c/m ½, poids 700 grs.
Garantie 5 ans.
Prix............. **7.75**

6565. Pendulette sans aiguilles, cuivre nickelé, glace circulaire, mouvement à cylindre soigné (*marche 30 heures*). Petites plaquettes ivoire montées à jour qui se déclenchent automatiquement et donnent l'heure à 1 minute près. Hauteur 16 c/m, poids 450 grs.
Garantie 5 ans............. **28.**

PENDULETTE "SPORTS"

Modèle exclusif
$150.00 $160.00
Déposé par la Manufacture Française d'Armes et Cycles de St-Etienne
$250.00

Argenture inaltérable patine riche

Mouvement soigné garanti 5 ans
$225.00

6570. Pendulette fantaisie "Sports", métal argenté et patiné, socle de forme gracieuse, décorée sur chacune des faces de ciselures artistiques (*scènes de Chasse, Cyclisme, Pêche et Voyage*), guirlande de feuillages. Mouv.t très soigné, 30 heures, cadran argenté. Haut. 18 c/m, p.ds 650 grs. *Garantie 5 ans. Prix exceptionnel* **7.25**
6570 bis. **Même modèle**, mais avec mouvement à réveil et forte sonnerie.
Garantie 5 ans .... *Prix exceptionnel* **8.75**

$75.00

6573. Pendulette cuivre nickelé, très stable, montre-boule.t de précision, échappement à ancre, cadran diam. 42 m/m. Convient comme presse-papier, etc. Haut. tot. 12 c/m ½, p.ds 340 grs. Gar. 8 ans....... **34.**

6576. Pendulette "Universelle", bronze massif doré, forme cubique avec, sur chaque face, un cadran spécial indiquant : 1° l'heure, mouv.t de précision huitaine; 2° la température centigrade; 3° la température Fahrenheit; 4° la pression barométrique et le temps probable (*baromètre anéroïde*); 5° le Nord (*boussole aimantée*). Parfaite pour bureaux et pour le voyage. *Livrée en écrin de* 10×10×10, p.ds 975 grs. **125.**

PETITES PENDULETTES AVEC SUJETS BRONZE IMITATION

$120.00

$130.00

$175.00

$175.00

$130.00

6577. Pendulette "Epagneul", en bronze imitation, patine, mouv.t soigné marchant 30 heures. Haut. 19 c/m, long. 29 c/m, poids 1 kg 340.
6578. **Chien épagneul seul**, conv.t comme porte-montre. **4.50**

6579. Pendulette "Gavroche", métal argenté, patine, mouvement soigné. Hauteur totale 17 c/m, poids 790 grs.
Garantie 2 ans....... **14.**
Ne se fait pas avec réveil.

6580. Pendulette fantaisie "Eléphant", métal argenté, patiné, mouvement très soigné à réveil, hauteur totale 15 c/m, poids 1 kg.
Garantie 2 ans....... **15.**

6582. Pendulette "Lion", en bronze imitation, patiné, mouvement très soigné à réveil. Hauteur 13 c/m, long. 17 c/m, poids 1 kg. 275.
Garantie 3 ans...... **19.**

6584. Pendulette "Napoléon" en bronze imitation, socle marbre, roc doré et statuette patinée bronze ancien finement ciselée, mouv.t soigné 8 jours. Hauteur 22 c/m, larg. 14 c/m, p.ds 1 k. 550.
Garantie 5 ans....... **27.**

PENDULES LUMINEUSES ET PENDULES AVEC SUJETS BRONZE IMITATION

$350.00

Set.. $250.00

$200.00

$225.00

$425.00

6585. Pendule veilleuse Louis XVI, bronze imitation doré, mouv.t soigné, 30 heures, globe mobile verre opale, portant les chiffres des heures, aiguille fixe, veilleuse dans le globe pour le rendre lumineux la nuit, h.r 33 c/m, p.ds 1 kg. 250.
Garantie 3 ans...... **36.**

6590. Pendule "Mutine", sujet fillette, bronze imitation, patiné, mouv.t soigné, 30 heures, cadran diam. 6 c/m, haut. tot. 32 c/m, poids 2 kgs.
Garantie 3 ans....... **19.**
6590 bis. **Même modèle** mais avec sujet garçonnet "Espiègle"............. **19.**

6595. Pendulette "Aigle", bronze imitation, socle marbre, montre boulet cristal, diam. 55 m/m, mouvement à ancre, haut. 22 c/m, poids 2 kgs 250.
Garantie 3 ans...... **26.**

6600. Pendulette "Aigle sur Forum", bronze imitation patiné, socle marbre, montre boulet cristal, diam. 55 m/m, mouv.t ancre, p.ds 3 kgs 500. Gar. 3 ans. **32.**

6605. Pendulette "Mystérieuse", bronze imitation, mouvement à ancre marchant 8 jours, balancier compensateur métal doré, oscillant régulièrement sur 2 pivots acier, hauteur 38 c/m, poids 1 kg. 600.
Garantie 3 ans...... **33.**

TOUT CE QUE VOUS POUVEZ DÉSIRER SE TROUVE DANS CE TARIF — VOIR LA TABLE DES MATIÈRES

PENDULES POUR CUISINES ET BUREAUX

$85.00

$100.00
$125.00

$130.00

$125.00

$175.00

6610. Pendule de cuisine en métal verni, bordure faux-bois, nuance acajou, filet or, lunette dorée, mouvement 8 jours à balancier compensateur, diam. 30 c/m, poids 900 grs. *Bonne fabrication. Garantie 5 ans.*
Modèle exclusif spécialement fabriqué pour la Manufacture Française d'Armes et Cycles de Saint-Etienne.
Prix exceptionnel...... 5.95

6615. Pendule de cuisine en métal façon faïence, motifs damier simple ou fantaisie, nuances claires ; mouvement 8 jours, à balancier compensateur, diam. 33 c/m, poids 1 kg. Ces pendules d'une apparence coquette sont parfaites pour bureau, cuisine, etc.
Garantie 5 ans........ 7.50
6615 bis. Même modèle, sonnerie.
Garantie 5 ans ...... 14.

6620. Pendule de cuisine en bois verni, large bordure en cuivre nickelé, mouvement 8 jours à ancre, système Roskopf. cadran de 19 c/m de diamètre, diamètre total 29 c/m, poids 1 kg. 250. Convient aussi pour bureau, magasin, atelier, etc.
Garantie 5 ans 14.50

┌─────────────────────────┐
│ Ameublement de cuisine │
│ voir pages 1042 et 1043.│
└─────────────────────────┘

6625. Pendule dite " d'atelier " en métal verni, très grand cadran avec aiguilles et heures très apparentes afin de permettre une lecture aisée de l'heure à grande distance, dans un hall, un atelier, un vestibule, une serre, etc., mouvement à ancre, marchant 8 jours, balancier compensateur, convient aussi pour bureau, magasin, poids 1 kg. 300, diam. 45 c/m.
Garantie 8 ans 10.75

6630. Pendule dite " d'atelier " bois verni, grand cadran, heures et aiguilles très apparentes permettant la lecture aisée de l'heure à grande distance, dans un hall, un atelier, un vestibule, etc., mouvement 8 jours, sonnerie sur gong, convient également pour bureau, magasin, cuisine, écoles, administration, mairies, etc., diam. 46 c/m, poids 3 kgs 500.
Garantie 20 ans.
Prix .... 25. »

HORLOGES COMTOISES DITES " ŒILS-DE-BŒUF "

$150.00
$175.00

$175.00
$200.00

$225.00
$275.00

$235.00
$280.00

6635. Pendule ronde, dite *"Œil-de-bœuf"*, modèle classique, en beau bois façon chêne verni, lunette dorée, mouvement soigné, balancier compensateur, marche 8 jours, pour tous usages, appartements, magasins, écoles administrations, ateliers, etc., diam. 37 c/m, poids 2 kgs 750.
Garantie 10 ans.......... 15. »

6635 bis. Même modèle, mais avec forte sonnerie dite *"Gong"*, mouvement de précision, marchant 8 jours. Livrée façon chêne verni ou avec incrustations nacre (*ind. ce que l'on désire*), diam. 37 c/m. poids 3 kgs 600.
Garantie 15 ans .... 25. »

6640. Horloge ronde, dite *"Œil-de-bœuf"*, bordure chêne massif ciré, à moulures, grand cadran émail de 26 c/m de diam., mouvement huitaine, sonnerie sur ressort, très soigné, cabinet de forme octogonale, pour appartements, magasins, hôtels, ateliers, écoles, administrations, etc., diam. total 50 c/m, poids 4 kgs.
Garantie 10 ans .... 22. »

6640 bis. Même modèle, mais avec mouvement comtois, marchant 8 jours, platines acier, forte sonnerie (répétition aux heures) dite *"indécomptable"*, cadran émail, avec écussons des chiffres en relief, poids 5 kgs 500. *Garantie 25 ans* .... 28. »

6645. Horloge ronde, dite *"Œil-de-bœuf"*, bordure ondulée vernie noir, avec moulures, grand cadran émail de 26 c/m de diam., avec entourage incrusté nacre, mouvement quinzaine, sonnerie sur ressort, très soigné, pour appartements, magasins, cafés, ateliers, écoles, administrations, etc., diamètre total 50 c/m, poids 5 kgs.
Garantie 10 ans............ 25. »

6645 bis. Même modèle, mais avec mouvement comtois, marchant 8 jours, à platines acier, forte sonnerie (répétition aux heures) dite *"indécomptable"*, cadran émail, avec écussons des chiffres en relief, poids 6 kgs 500. *Garantie 25 ans* .... 32. »

6650. Horloge ovale dite *"Œil-de-bœuf"*, bordure ondulée, vernie noir, avec moulures, grand cadran émail de 26 c/m de diam., avec entourage incrusté nacre, mouvement quinzaine à sonnerie sur ressort, très soigné, pour appartements, magasins, cafés, ateliers, écoles, administrations, etc., haut. tot. 60 c/m, poids 5 kgs.
Garantie 10 ans............ 25. »

6650 bis. Même modèle, mais avec mouvement comtois, marchant 8 jours, à platines acier, forte sonnerie (répétition aux heures) dite *"indécomptable"*, cadran émail, avec écussons des chiffres en relief, poids 6 kgs 500. *Garantie 25 ans*.......... 32. »

┌──┐
│ Pour la mise en place des pendules   │
│ consulter la brochure "NOS MONTRES" et   │
│ "NOS PENDULES"   │
└──┘

┌──┐
│ RÉPARATIONS D'HORLOGERIE.   │
│ Voir page 801.   │
└──┘

CARTELS DE STYLE

$350.00

$375.00

$400.00

$600.00

$625.00

6655. Cartel mural tout en chêne poncé et ciré avec colonnettes et ornements sculptés, fronton balustre, mouvement huitaine sans sonnerie, cadran fantaisie, aiguilles dorées, hauteur totale 55 c/m, poids 3 kgs. *Garantie 5 ans.*
Prix exceptionnel..... 17.50

6660. Cartel mural tout en noyer ciré, colonnettes, fronton et ornements sculptés, mouvement huitaine à sonnerie, cadran à moulures avec chiffres émail, aiguilles dorées, hauteur totale 60 centimètres, poids 5 kgs.
Garantie 10 ans ...... 24. »

6665. Cartel mural Henri II, en noyer ciré, avec colonnes cannelées, galerie et moulures, mouvement huitaine très soigné à moulures avec chiffres émail, aiguilles dorées, hauteur totale 65 c/m, poids 5 kgs. *Fabrication supérieure.*
Garantie 10 ans ...... 29. »

6670. Cartel mural Louis XVI, en noyer ciré, colonnes cannelées, moulures riches et sculptures : attributs, carquois et flèches ; mouvement soigné à sonnerie, huitaine, cadran avec chiffres émail, hauteur totale 77 c/m, poids 6 kgs 500.
Garantie 10 ans ...... 56. »

6675. Cartel mural Louis XV, en noyer ciré, colonnes cannelées, superbes moulures et sculptures : motifs coquilles, appliques et écusson, mouvement huitaine à sonnerie, soigné, cadran avec chiffres émail, haut. tot. 82 c/m, pds 6 kgs 500.
Garantie 10 ans ...... 68. »

HORLOGES, CARTELS ET RÉGULATEURS SPÉCIAUX

PENDULES "ÉCOSSAISES"

$200.00

$475.00

$550.00

$500.00

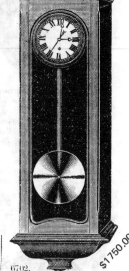

$1750.00

6680. Horloge applique à poids dite "Ecossaise", en chène clair massif, mouvement très soigné, à sonnerie avec chaine et poids; cadran cuivre poli, poids et balancier garni cuivre décoré, haut. tot. 48 c/m, pds 4 kgs 300. *Modèle simple et parfait p^r salle à manger, bureau, etc. Gar. 5 ans.* **25. »**

6690. Pendule baromètre-thermomètre, noyer ciré avec colonnes cannelées, petite galerie et moulures, mouvement huitaine très soigné, à forte sonnerie sur timbre, cadran noyer moulure, chiffres émail sur fond blanc, thermomètre à alcool sur plaque ivoirine et baromètre anéroïde de 11 c/m de diam, haut. tot. 92 c/m, poids 5 kgs 600. *Mod. très décoratif pour bureau, salle à manger, etc. Gar. 10 ans.* **53. »**

6693. Grande pendule-baromètre-thermomètre, noyer ciré sculpté avec colonnettes cannelées, galerie, balustres et fronton Renaissance, mouvement de précision huitaine avec forte sonnerie sur "gong", cadran noyer, artistement sculpté, chiffres émail sur fond blanc, thermomètre à alcool, baromètre anéroïde de 13 c/m de diam, haut. tot. 104 c/m, pds 11 kgs. *Modèle très artistique, Garantie 10 ans.....* **115. »**

6700. Régulateur "Calendrier", style moderne en beau bois façon noyer verni, moulures et appliques soignées, mouvement de précision marchant 8 jours, avec balancier compensateur, sonnerie sur "gong" aux heures et demies. Un ingénieux dispositif déclanche chaque jour à minuit un rouleau spécial où est inscrit le quantième du mois, haut. 85 c/m, pds 8 kgs. *Parfait p^r bureau, cabinets de travail. Gar. 10 ans.* **55. »**

6702. Grand régulateur-chronomètre, de précision, tout chène massif, avec glace, mouvement huitaine spécial à poids, sans sonnerie, avec échappement battant la seconde, grande aiguille trotteuse au centre du cadran, balancier tige bois avec lentille montée cuivre de 30 c/m de diam, réglage parfait Convient comme pendule étalon pour magasins, bureaux, usines, chemins de fer, etc. Haut. tot. 1m92, pds 29 kgs. *Gar. 25 ans. Prix..........* **235. »**

> Pour la mise en place et le réglage des régulateurs, consulter la
> Brochure "NOS MONTRES ET NOS PENDULES" jointe à tout envoi.

PETITES PENDULES HOLLANDAISES ET PENDULES RÉGULATEURS

PETITES HORLOGES REGULATEURS POUR OFFICES, MAISONS, VESTIBULES, ETC.

$135.00
$160.00

$200.00

$225.00

$250.00

$325.00

6704. Horloge-régulateur, bois verni nuance claire, avec glaces, balancier visible, grand cadran (genre céramique), mouvement soigné huitaine sans sonnerie, haut. totale 44 c/m, poids 2 kgs 500. *Convient pour cuisines, offices, etc. Garantie 3 ans. Prix..............* **15. »**

6704 bis. Même modèle, avec cadran et appliques finement émaillés au four, mouvement avec sonnerie aux heures et demies, haut. totale 53 c/m, pds 4 kgs. *Garantie 5 ans. Prix..............* **21.75**

6705. Régulateur mural, en beau bois finement verni, mouvement huitaine à sonnerie sur timbre, balancier compensateur visible, cadran émail, glaces sur 3 faces. Hauteur totale 90 c/m, poids 5 kgs.

Bonne fabrication.

Garantie 5 ans...... **22. »**

6710. Régulateur mural, en beau bois verni, mouvement huitaine à sonnerie sur timbre, balancier compensateur visible, fronton balustre genre Henri II, glaces sur 3 faces, hauteur totale 85 c/m, pds 6 kgs. *Fabrication garantie 8 ans. Prix..............* **26. »**

6715. Régulateur mural Henri II, en beau bois verni avec belles colonnettes moulurées, mouvement huitaine à sonnerie sur "gong", façade à 3 glaces dont 2 bisautées montrant le balancier compensateur visible, glaces latérales. Haut. 78 c/m, pds 7 kgs. *Fabrication garantie 10 ans. Prix..............* **32. »**

6720. Régulateur mural Charles IX, en beau bois ciré, façade avec belles moulures et appliques noyer, colonnettes cannelées, fronton balustre et fond genre console du plus bel effet, mouvement très soigné huitaine, balancier compensateur, sonnerie bourdon, glaces sur 3 faces, haut. totale 93 c/m, poids 7 kgs 500. *Fabrication supérieure. Garantie 10 ans. Prix..............* **36. »**

> **RÉPARATIONS D'HORLOGERIE**
> voir page

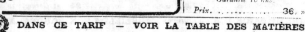 

GRANDES PENDULES — RÉGULATEURS DE PRECISION

GRANDES HORLOGES FRANÇAISES

Ces horloges, établies d'après les anciens et excellents modèles de fabrication bien connue, ont été très heureusement adaptées au style de l'ameublement moderne, qu'elles complètent de la manière la plus agréable et la plus décorative.

6725. Grand régulateur en beau bois verni avec colonnettes, moulures et fronton sculptés, glaces sur 3 faces. Mouvement très soigné marchant 8 jours, avec balancier tige bois et grande lentille compensatrice en cuivre c'menté. Sonnerie carillon aux quarts et demies sur double tige. bourdon aux heures. Cadran diam. 18 c/m. Hauteur tot. 1 m. 15, poids 9 kgs 500. *Garantie 10 ans.*
Prix .... **43.**

6735. Grand régulateur de précision en beau bois ciré avec colonnettes, moulures et fronton Renaissance sculptés, façade noyer, glaces sur 3 faces, mouvement, dit "*comtois*", monté sur fortes platines acier. marchant 8 jours, avec balancier tige bois et grande lentille compensatrice en cuivre poli. Forte sonnerie sur tige. bourdon aux heures et demies. Cadran diam. 18 c/m. Hauteur 120 c/m, poids 10 kgs 800.
Garantie 15 ans. ..... **53.** »

6747. Grand régulateur de précision en beau noyer ciré, colonnettes et fronton cannelés, moulurés et sculptés. Grandes glaces sur 3 faces. Mouvement à poids gainés cuivre marchant 8 jours, échappement de précision avec très grand balancier compensateur à tige bois, forte sonnerie aux heures et demies sur "gong". Grand cadran argenté de 18 c/m ½ de côté. Haut. 1 m. 25, poids 12 kgs. *Garantie 20 ans.* **76.** »

6755. Grand régulateur de précision Renaissance en beau noyer massif finement poli et ciré, façade, colonnettes et fronton moulurés et sculptés. Grandes glaces sur 3 faces, mouvement de précision huitaine, balancier à tige bois avec lentille compensatrice cuivre poli, forte sonnerie sur "gong". Cadran diam. 18 c/m ½. Haut. 1 m. 25, poids 12 kgs. *Gar.* 20 ans. **105** »

6730. Grand régulateur de précision en beau bois ciré avec colonnettes, moulures et fronton tournés et sculptés. Façade noyer, glaces sur 3 faces, mouvement dit "*comtois*". monté sur fortes platines acier. marchant 8 jours, avec balancier tige bois et grande lentille compensatrice en cuivre poli. Forte sonnerie sur tige, bourdon aux heures et demies. Grand cadran de 18 c/m de diamètre. Hauteur 120 c/m, poids 10 kgs 500.
Garantie 15 ans. ..... **48.** »

6740. Grand régulateur "Moderne" en beau bois, façon chêne verni, fines moulures et cannelures. fronton sculpté, façade à 4 glaces dont 3 biscautées, mouvement de précision, marchant 8 jours, balancier tige bois et lentille compensatrice en cuivre poli et orné. Forte sonnerie sur tige bourdon aux heures et demies à ressort circulaire formant "gong". Grand cadran argenté de 19 c/m de diam. Haut. 83 c/m, poids 7 kgs 500. *Gar.* 20 ans. **69.** »

6752. Grand régulateur "Moderne" de précision en beau chêne clair g^re Hollandais, très finement mouluré avec appliques, façade à 4 glaces biscautées, mouv^t de précision marchant 8 jours, balancier tige bois et lentille compensatrice en cuivre poli et orné. Sonnerie sur "gong". Cadran argenté de 19 c/m de côté. Modèle riche p^r salles à manger meublées chêne ou noyer clairs. Haut. 81 c/m, poids 8 kgs.
Garantie 20 ans
Prix .... **93.** »

6760, Grand régulateur de précision en noyer ciré, supports, façade et fronton entièrement sculptés à jour style gothique très pur, grande glace, mouvement huitaine très soigné, balancier compensateur tige bois, forte sonnerie sur tige bourdon aux heures et demies. Grand cadran émail nuance ivoire, hauteur totale 123 c/m, poids 11 kgs 500, *Modèle très riche, recommandé.*
Prix .... **195.** »

6770. Grande horloge Henri II, en noyer massif poli et ciré. avec colonnes cannelées, moulures fines, fronton balustre et panneau richement sculpté; mouvement régulateur quinzaine dit "*comtois*", à poids, très forte sonnerie sur double gong à ressort aux heures et demies, grand cadran de 30 c/m de diamètre en métal argenté et doré, lentille réglable, grande porte avec glace unie. hauteur totale 2^m35.
Garantie 20 ans.
Prix .... **180.** »

6770 bis. Même modèle, ébénisterie de luxe avec moulures extrêmement soignées et panneaux assortis, mouvement régulateur quinzaine de grande précision, cadran et montures très riches, hauteur totale 2 m. 25.
Garantie 25 ans.
Prix .... **350.** »

6773. Même modèle, ébénisterie de luxe (*comme le n° 6770 bis*), mais avec mouvement de grande précision et sonnerie produisant aux heures, demies et quarts, une mélodie semblable à celle du carillon de l'Abbaye de Westminster.
Garantie 25 ans.
Prix .... **485.** »

Pour la mise en place et le réglage des pendules, consulter la brochure "Nos Montres et nos Pendules" jointe à tout envoi.
RÉPARATIONS D'HORLOGERIE, voir page

PENDULES-RÉGULATEURS A SONNERIE DITE "CARILLON"

Tous les régulateurs ci-dessous sont de fabrication supérieure, les cages sont en ébénisterie de luxe et les mouvements d'extrême précision. Ils s'assortissent parfaitement avec les ameublements modernes de salles à manger, bureaux, etc..., dont ils forment le complément indispensable.

Ces pendules murales ont une sonnerie spéciale dite « carillon », mue par le mouvement. Elle s'effectue au moyen de tiges métalliques d'une grande résonance, produisant, sous le choc de marteaux disposés à cet effet, un ensemble de notes harmoniques, formant un accord sonore, bien rythmé et très juste. Les différents modèles sont à 3 tubes avec sonnerie dite « angelus » ou « cathédrale » et 4 tubes produisant aux quarts, aux demies et aux heures, une mélodie agréable rappelant très exactement le carillon célèbre de l'Abbaye anglaise de **Westminster**. Les heures sont décomptées sur un ressort dit « bourdon », donnant la note bien timbrée et très grave des grosses cloches. Ces régulateurs sont absolument garantis.

GRANDS RÉGULATEURS A CARILLON. STYLE MODERNE ET FANTAISIE

RÉGULATEUR A SONNERIE CARILLON dit "CATHÉDRALE

$250.00 $300.00 $350.00 $300.00 $425.00 $435.00

6775. Régulateur à carillon dit « cathédrale », en bois verni façon noyer, avec moulures et appliques cuivre, mouvem.t soigné, marche 8 jours avec sonnerie carillon aux heures, demies et quarts, balancier compensé à tige bois, 4 glaces devant, fronton à moulures, h.r totale 75 c/m, poids 6 kgs. *Garantie 5 ans.*
Prix .... **52.** »
Nota. — *Ameublement de salles à manger, voir pages 1044 et 1045.*

6780. Régulateur mural à carillon, en beau bois poli et verni façon noyer mouluré, mouv.t huitaine très soigné, avec sonnerie carillon aux heures, demies et quarts, mélodie de Westminster, balancier compensé à tige bois, glaces biseautées devant, hauteur tot. 78 c/m, poids 4 kgs 900. *Garantie 10 ans.* **65.** »
6782. Même modèle, boiserie finement moulurée, carillon sur 8 gongs accordés.
Prix .... **92.** »

6785. Régulateur mural à carillon, en beau chêne verni, nuance "fumée", mouluré, avec fronton sculpté, belles glaces, ornements bronze, mouvem.t de précision huitaine, sonnerie carillon aux quarts, mélodie de Westminster, bourdon aux heures sur double gong, balancier compensé à tige bois, h.r 76 c/m, p.ds 8 kgs. *Gar. 15 ans.* **157.** »

> Réparations d'horlogerie, voir page 801.

6787. Régulateur mural "Byzantin" à carillon, vieux-chêne fumé, colonnettes, moulures et fronton artistement sculptés, glaces biseautées, ornements bronze, mouvem.t de haute précision huitaine, sonnerie carillon aux quarts, mélodie de Westminster, bourdon aux heures sur double gong, balancier compensé à tige bois, haut. tot 96 c/m, poids 13 kgs. *Garantie 20 ans.....* **210.** »

6789. Régulateur mural "Acanthe" à carillon, noyer massif ciré, co, lonnettes cannelées, moulures et fronton ébénisterie riche, fines sculptures, glaces biseautées, ornements bronze, mouvem.t de précision huitaine, sonnerie carillon aux demies et aux quarts, mélodie de Westminster, bourdon aux heures, balancier compensé, h.t 115 c/m, pds 13 kgs. *Garantie 20 ans......* **219.** »

GRANDS RÉGULATEURS A CARILLON "WESTMINSTER" DITS DE STYLE

$325.00 $375.00 $400.00 $425.00 $450.00

6790. Grand régulateur mural à carillon, en acajou finement verni et mouluré, colonnettes appliques en bronze doré, style "*Empire*", riches glaces biseautées, ornements bronze, mouvem.t de précision huitaine, sonnerie carillon aux quarts, mélodie de Westminster, bourdon aux heures, hauteur totale 86 c/m, poids 11 kgs. *Garantie 15 ans.....* **139.** «

6795. Grand régulateur mural "Sully" à carillon, en noyer ciré, moulures appliques et fronton artistement sculptés, glaces sur 3 faces, mouvement de précision huitaine, sonnerie carillon aux quarts, mélodie de Westminster, bourdon aux heures, sur double gong, balancier compensé à tige bois, haut. tot. 105 c/m, poids 10 kgs 500. *Garantie 20 ans.....* **183.** »

6800. Grand régulateur mural style Louis XVI à carillon, noyer ciré, moulures et cannelures sculptées, glaces biseautées, mouvem.t de haute précision huitaine, sonnerie carillon aux quarts, mélodie de Westminster, bourdon aux heures sur double gong, balancier compensé à tige bois, hauteur tot. 103 c/m, poids 10 kgs 500. *Garantie 20 ans.....* **199.** »

6805. G.d régulateur mural style Louis XVI à carillon, noyer ciré, moulures et cannelures, fronton sculpté, glaces biseautées, mouvem.t de haute précision huitaine, sonnerie carillon aux quarts, mélodie de Westminster, bourdon aux heures sur double gong, balancier compensé tige bois, haut. tot 90 c/m, poids 8 kgs 500. *Garantie 20 ans.....* **214.** »

6820. Grand régulateur mural "Valois" à carillon, noyer ciré, moulures, colonnettes appliques et fronton balustre de pur style XVI.e siècle, sculptures d'art, glaces biseautées, mouv.t huitaine, sonnerie carillon aux quarts, mélodie de Westminster, bourdon aux heures, balancier compensé à tige bois, hauteur tot. 109 c/m, poids 13 kgs 200. *Garantie 20 ans.....* **248.** »

> Pour la mise en place et le réglage des carillons dits "de Westminster" consulter la brochure "NOS MONTRES ET NOS PENDULES", jointe à tout envoi.

TOUT CE QUE VOUS POUVEZ DÉSIRER SE TROUVE DANS CE TARIF — VOIR LA TABLE DES MATIÈRES

HORLOGES-COUCOUS

 $125.00
 $160.00
 $225.00
 $225.00
 $350.00

6825. Coucou-horloge, chêne sculpté, feuillage et sujet oiseau, mouvement soigné, sonnerie et coucou chantant aux heures et aux demies, poids (*pommes de pin*) sur chaînettes cuivre, haut. tot. (*sans le balancier*) 40 c/m, poids complet 4 kgs. *Garantie 5 ans.* Prix............ **19.** »

6830. Coucou-horloge, noyer ou chêne sculpté, feuillage et tête de cerf, mouvement soigné à *ressort sans poids*, sonnerie sur gong et coucou chantant aux heures et demies, hauteur totale (*sans le balancier*) 49 c/m, poids 3 kgs. *Garantie 5 ans. Recommandé.* Prix............ **23.** »

6835. Coucou-horloge, chêne sculpté, feuillage et sujets oiseaux, mouvement très soigné, sonnerie sur gong et coucou chantant aux heures et demies, poids (*pommes de pin*) sur chaînettes cuivre, hauteur totale (*sans le balancier*), 50 c/m, poids 5 kgs. *Garantie 5 ans......* **31.** »

6840. Coucou-horloge, noyer ou chêne clair, sculpté, feuillages, s'assortissant aux ameublements anglais, hollandais, etc., sujet "*cerfs*", mouvement soigné, sonnerie sur gong et coucou chantant aux heures et aux demies, poids (*pommes de pins*) sur chaînettes cuivre, haut. tot. (*sans le balancier*), 57 c/m, poids 5 kgs. *Gar. 10 ans.* **39.** »

6845. Coucou-horloge, à chant double (*coucou et caille*), chêne sculpté, feuillage et sujet oiseaux, mouvt soigné, sonnant les heures sur gong avec coucou ; les demies et les quarts au timbre et chant de caille, poids (*pommes de pin*), sur chaînettes cuivre, haut. tot. (*sans le balancier*) 58 c/m, poids complet 7 kgs 500. *Gar. 10 ans.* **46.** »

CARTELS ET GRANDS COUCOUS

 $675.00
 $750.00
 $900.00
$1,200.00

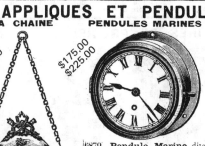
Pour la mise en place des cartels, consulter la brochure : "Nos montres et nos pendules".

6850. Grand cartel régulateur de chasse, noyer ciré, sculptures artistiques massives représentant un lièvre, un faisan et une tête de cerf ; ornements, feuillages et trophées de chasse, grand cadran avec chiffres émail, mouvement quinzaine à ressort, forte sonnerie bourdon, haut. tot. 75 c/m, poids 8 kgs. *Garantie 20 ans..........* **69.** »

6855. Coucou-horloge, chêne sculpté, feuillage et sujets oiseau et cerfs, mouvemt soigné, sonnerie sur gong et coucou chantant aux heures et demies, poids (*pommes de pin*) sur chaînettes cuivre, haut. totale (*sans le balancier*) 60 c/m, poids complet 6 kgs 300. *Garantie 10 ans.* Prix.................... **52.** »

6860. Coucou-horloge, chêne sculpté, feuillage et 3 têtes de cerf, gibier et trophée de chasse, mouvt soigné, sonnerie sur gong et coucou chantant aux heures et demies, poids (*pommes de pin*) montés sur chaînettes cuivre, haut. tot. (*sans le balancier*), 90 c/m, pds 8 kgs. *Garantie 10 ans.............* **65.** »

6865. Grand coucou-horloge, chêne sculpté, feuillage, tête de cerf, lièvre, perdrix, faisceau de fusils, cor de chasse et trophées, mouvt soigné à sonnerie sur gong et coucou chantant aux heures et demies, pds (*pommes de pin*) sur chaînettes cuivre, haut. tot. (*sans le balancier*) 105 c/m, pds 12 kgs. *Gar. 12 ans..* **95.** »

CARTELS APPLIQUES ET PENDULES "HABITACLES"

CARTELS APPLIQUES A CHAINE — **PENDULES MARINES** — **CARTELS APPLIQUES en BRONZE MASSIF**

 $250.00 $300.00
 $300.00 $325.00
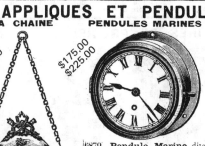 $175.00 $225.00
 $325.00
 $350.00

6867. Cartel applique, monture métal émaillé, avec décors "Bouquets" en couleurs, ornements et chaîne en bronze doré, mouvement très soigné à cylindre, haut. totale 55 c/m, pds 2 kgs. *Garantie 5 ans.....* **21.** »
6867 bis. Même modèle, à sonnerie......... **29.** »

6871. Cartel applique, style Louis XVI, monture fine porcelaine décorée, sous émail, de bouquets en couleurs, ornements et chaîne en bronze doré riche, mouvt très soigné, hauteur totale 58 c/m, poids 2 kgs 500. *Gar. 10 ans.* **36.** »
6871 bis. Même modèle, à sonnerie......... **51.** »

6879. Pendule Marine dite "Habitacle", pour canots-automobiles, bateaux de pêche, yachts, etc., forme ronde hermétique, tout en cuivre poli, mouvt huitaine, à ancre, marchant dans toutes les positions, diam. 20 c/m, pds 1 k. 850. Cette pendule se visse au mur ou sur une boiserie et convient aussi pour bureaux, magasins, administrations, etc.. *Garantie 10 ans.....* **27.** »
6879 bis. Même modèle, gaine massive, mouvt de grande précision, diam. 14 c/m, pds 1 k.750. *Garantie 20 ans.....* **39.** »

Réparations d'horlogerie voir page

6885. Cartel applique "Fantaisie" tout en vrai bronze massif, ornementé et ciselé, décors Louis XV, mouvement de précision quinzaine à sonnerie, hauteur totale du cartel 52 c/m, poids 4 kgs. *Garantie 10 ans.* Prix............. **38.** »

6890. Grand cartel applique, tout en vrai bronze massif doré, style Louis XVI, décors guirlandes, palmes et écusson, mouvement de précision quinzaine, à sonnerie, hauteur totale du cartel 53 c/m, poids 5 kgs. *Garantie 10 ans.* Prix............. **55.** »

Maisons PARIS (42, R. du Louvre). MARSEILLE, LYON, BORDEAUX, LILLE, TOULOUSE, NANTES, ROUEN, NANCY, TOURS.

PENDULES EN BOIS SCULPTÉ

$165.00 $200.00 $300.00 $290.00 $350.00

6895. Pendule bois, genre noyer sculpté et verni, avec moulures et fronton balustre, mouv* 30 heures soigné, à forte sonnerie, balancier compensateur visible, grand cadran fantaisie, porte vitrée montrant le balancier, haut. tot. 35 c/m, poids 2 kgs. *Bon modèle. Gar. 3 ans. Prix exceptionnel.* **10.50**

6899. Pendule bois sculpté, poli et verni, avec moulures et fronton ornementé, mouv* huitaine, très soigné, à sonnerie des heures et demies, échappement à ancre, balancier compensateur, cadran fantaisie, porte vitrée, haut. totale 50 c/m, pds 2 kgs 500. *Garantie 4 ans.* **24.50**

6940. Pendule Suisse, en noyer massif poli et ciré, moulures et ornements très gracieux, mouv* huitaine, à ancre, très soigné, sonnerie bourdon, balancier compensateur, cadran nuance ivoire, haut. tot. 42 c/m, poids 2 kgs. *Gar. 10 ans. Prix* **33.**

6913. Pendule Henri III, en beau bois finement poli et ciré, genre noyer, colonnettes, moulures et fronton balustre, mouvement huitaine à ancre très soigné, forte sonnerie, balancier compensateur, cadran nuance ivoire, haut. 48 c/m, poids 1 kg 900. *Gar. 10 ans. Prix* **35.**

6915. Pendule Châtelaine, noyer massif poli et ciré, moulures et ornements rappelant très originalement la façade d'un château, mouvement huitaine soigné à ancre, sonnerie bourdon, balancier compensateur, haut. tot. 48 c/m, poids 3 kgs. *Gar. 25 ans. Prix* **42.**

Vases d'accompagnement p' pendules, voir page 845.

Ameublements de style, voir pages 1044 et suivantes.

PENDULES DE STYLE ET PENDULES A CARILLON EN BOIS SCULPTÉ

$200.00 $450.00 $395.00 $475.00 $450.00

1913 French Catalog

6920. Pendulette "Empire", acajou poli et verni, socle et fronton moulurés, colonnettes avec monture cuivre verni, mouv* huitaine sans sonnerie, haut. tot. 28 c/m, poids 1 kg 200. *Garantie 5 ans.* **18.50**

6930. Pendule Empire, acajou poli et verni, socle à moulures surmonté de 4 colonnes avec chapiteaux cuivre doré, mouvement huitaine, à forte sonnerie, échappement à ancre, balancier compensateur visible, cadran émail avec ornements dorés et glace biseautée, haut. 36 c/m, pds 2 kgs 650. *Garantie 15 ans.* **38.**

6935. Pendule Empire, noyer ou acajou massif (*ind. laquelle*) poli et ciré, colonnes cannelées, guirlandes et belles moulures, appliques cuivre, glace à biseau, mouvement quinzaine soigné, sonnerie -bourdon, échappement à ancre et balancier compensateur visible, cadran à glace, haut, 38 c/m, pds 3 kgs 700. *Gar. 15 ans.* **45.**

6940. Grande. Pendule de style, tout en noyer, avec sculptures et moulures riches, fronton guirlandes et colonnes cannelées, mouvement de précision, quinzaine, avec sonnerie carillon dite "*de Westminster*" sur 5 tubes, grand cadran métal décoré, haut. 46 c/m, poids 7 kgs 800. *Garantie 15 ans.* **98.**

6945. Grande pendule "Moderne", tout en noyer massif ciré, ébénisterie de luxe, mouvement de grande précision quinzaine, avec sonnerie carillon dite "*de Westminster*", sur 5 tubes, grand cadran métal argenté, haut. tot. 42 c/m, pds 8 kgs. *Garantie 15 ans. Prix* **145.**

Voir page 837, la description de nos pendules avec mouvement à carillon dit "de Wesminster".

Pour la mise en place et le réglage des pendules, consulter la Brochure "Nos Montres et nos Pendules" jointe à tous nos envois d'horlogerie.

PENDULES ET GARNITURES DE PRÉCISION EN VRAI BRONZE

$125.00 $325.00 $375.00 Clock .... $700.00 Set .... 800.00 Clock $1,000.00 Set 1,200.00

6947. **6950.**

6947. Pendule dite 400 jours, se remontant chaque année environ, socle cuivre, mouvement très soigné avec balancier spécial compensateur. Livré avec globe verre protecteur, haut. tot. 31 c/m, poids 1 kg 850. *Gar. 5 ans.* **39.**

6950. Pendule régulateur, bronze doré, 4 glaces biseautées, mouvement quinzaine, sonnerie de précision, balancier compensateur à mercure, haut. 25 c/m, poids 3 kgs 500. **59.**

6950 bis. Même modèle, échappement visible sur le cadran, haut. 25 c/m, poids 4 kgs. **75.**

6959. Garniture régulateur riche, en vrai bronze massif doré avec moulures et ciselures de luxe, forme ovale avec glaces biseautées sur toutes les faces, mouvement de précision quinzaine à sonnerie, balancier mercure, convient pour salons, cabinets de travail, etc. Haut. 27 c/m. Livrée avec 2 vases assortis également en bronze doré, haut. 23 c/m, pds tot. 5 kgs. *Gar. 15 ans. La garniture.* **195.**

6961. Vases seuls. *La paire* **69.**

6964. Grande garniture "Carthage", tout en vrai bronze massif doré et enrichi de décors en émaux de couleurs cloisonnés, richement moulurée avec fronton et glaces biseautées, mouvement de très grande précision quinzaine à sonnerie, balancier mercure, modèle de luxe pour salons, cabinets de travail, etc. Haut. 33 c/m. Livrée avec vases assortis onyx et bronze, haut. 32 c/m, pds total 16 kgs. *Garantie 5 ans. La garniture complète* **250.**

6967. Vases seuls. *La paire* **75.**

Réparations d'Horlogerie, voir page

 TOUT CE QUE VOUS POUVEZ DÉSIRER SE TROUVE DANS CE TARIF — VOIR LA TABLE DES MATIÈRES

GARNITURES DE CHEMINÉES FANTAISIE EN MÉTAL BRONZÉ

Clock . . $150.00 / Set . . . 350.00
Clock . . $275.00 / Set . . . 325.00
Clock . . $300.00 / Set . . . 350.00

6975. Petite Garniture fantaisie, bronze imitation patiné dorée, ciselé, mouvᵗ soigné 30 heures, cadran émail, haut. tot. 26 c/m. Livrée avec 2 candélabres assortis à 2 lumières, haut. 18 c/m, poids tot. 2 kgs 200. Gar. 3 ans. *La garniture complète.* **17.** »
6975 bis. Même modèle dit "Coquille", style Louis XV, patiné vieux cuivre, haut. 40 c/m, avec candélabres 3 lumières, haut. 36 c/m, pds 9 kgs 450, mouvᵗ huitaine, très soigné. *La garniture compl.* **39.50**
Nota. — *Ces garnitures ne sont livrées que complètes.*

6980. Garniture "Art Nouveau" en métal bronzé patiné, moulé et ornementé en relief, pendule huitaine, mouvement soigné sans sonnerie, cadran émail, haut. 39 c/m. Livrée avec 2 candélabres 3 lumières, assortis, de 37 c/m de haut, poids total 6 kgs. *Garantie 5 ans.* *La garniture complète.* **23.90**
6980 bis. Même modèle, avec glace, mouvement quinzaine à sonnerie. *Garantie 10 ans.* *La garniture complète.* **34.** »
6985. Candélabres seuls. *La paire* **9.50**

6990. Garniture "Sully" en métal bronzé patiné, moulé et ornementé en relief, pendule huitaine, mouvement soigné sans sonnerie, cadran émail, haut. 40 c/m. Livrée avec 2 candélabres à 3 lumières, assortis de 43 c/m de haut, poids total 6 kgs 300. *Garantie 5 ans.* **29.50**
6990 bis. Même modèle, avec glace, mouvement quinzaine à sonnerie. *Garantie 10 ans.* *La garniture complète.* **39.** »
6995. Candélabres seuls. *La paire* **16.** »

GARNITURES DE CHEMINÉES DITES "BORNES" EN VRAI BRONZE

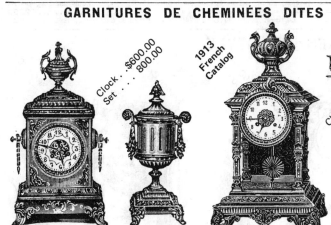

1913 French Catalog
Clock . . $600.00 / Set . . . 800.00
Clock . $1,200.00 / Set . . $1,500.00
Clock . $1,400.00 / Set . . . 1,700.00

7000. Garniture "Renaissance" en bronze massif patiné vieux cuivre et parties polies, appliques pieds et anses également en bronze massif patiné, mouvement quinzaine, à sonnerie, très soigné, cadran nuance ivoire, glace à biseau, haut. 43 c/m, larg. 22 c/m, poids 4 kgs 500. Livrée avec 2 vases assortis, haut. 29 c/m, poids 9 kgs. *Garantie 10 ans. La garniture complète* **69.50**
7005. Pendule seule **44.** »
7007. Vases seuls. *La paire* **27.** »

7010. Garniture "François Iᵉʳ", en bronze massif patiné vieux cuivre et parties polies, appliques, pieds et anses également en bronze massif patiné, mouvement quinzaine à sonnerie, très soigné, cadran émail fin, balancier visible, glace à biseau, haut. 49 c/m, poids 9 kgs. Livrée avec candélabres 5 lumières, assortis, haut. 61 c/m, poids 3 kgs 500. *Garantie 15 ans. La garniture complète* **125.** »
7015. Pendule seule **79.** »
7020. Candélabres seuls **47.** »

7025. Garniture "Chimères" en bronze massif patiné vieux cuivre, parties polies, pieds chimères et ornements également en bronze massif patiné et ciselé, mouvement quinzaine à sonnerie, très soigné, cadran émail fin avec ornements en bronze, glace à biseau, haut. 56 c/m, poids 10 kgs 500. Livrée avec candélabres 5 lumières, assortis, haut. 62 c/m, pᵈˢ 9 kgs. *Garantie 20 ans. La garniture complète.* **165.** »
7030. Pendule seule **95.** »
7035. Candélabres seuls **75.** »

GARNITURES DE CHEMINÉES DE STYLE EN VRAI BRONZE

Clock . $450.00 / Set . . . 600.00
Clock . . $900.00 / Set . . . 1,100.00
Clock $1,000.00 / Set . . . 1,300.00

7040. Garniture Louis XV bronze massif patiné vieux cuivre entièrement ciselé, mouvement quinzaine soigné, à sonnerie, cadran nuance ivoire, pur style, haut. 42 c/m. Livrée avec candélabres 5 lumières, assortis à la pendule, haut 41 c/m, pᵈˢ tot. 6 kgs 500. Gar. 10 ans. *La garniture complète.* **94.** »
7045. Pendule seule **59.** »
7050. Candélabres seuls. *La paire* **36.** »

7070. Garniture "Marie-Antoinette" bronze massif patiné vieux cuivre, entièrement ciselé, mouvement quinzaine soigné, à sonnerie, cadran nuance ivoire, haut. 45 c/m. Livrée avec candélabres 5 lumières, assortis à la pendule, haut. 50 c/m, poids 7 kgs 600. Gar. 10 ans. *La garniture complète.* **115.** »
7075. Pendule seule **70.** »
7080. Candélabres seuls. *La paire* **45.** »

7081. Garniture "Régence" bronze massif finement ciselé et doré, fonds mats et godrons brunis, du plus bel effet artistique. Modˡᵉ reproduit des musées nationaux. Mouvᵗ quinzaine de précision, à sonnerie. Haut. 30 c/m. Livrée avec flambeaux assortis, haut. 21 c/m, pᵈˢ tot. 8 kgs 400. *Garantie 15 ans.* **169.** »
7083. Pendule seule **105.** »
7084. Flambeaux seuls **66.** »

 RÉPARATIONS D'HORLOGERIE, *Voir page*

GARNITURES DE CHEMINÉES FANTAISIE "BORNES"

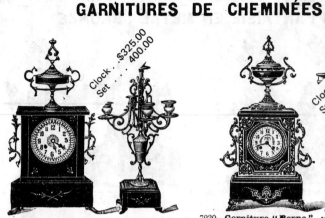

Clock .. $325.00
Set 400.00

Clock .. $475.00
Set 575.00

Clock .. $525.00
Set 625.00

7220. Garniture "Borne" en beau marbre noir et appliques griotte, pieds et ornements cuivre doré, mouvement quinzaine à sonnerie, soigné, cadran fantaisie, haut. 43 c/m. Livrée avec candélabres 5 lumières, assortis à la pendule, haut. 40 c/m, poids total 9 kgs. *Garantie 10 ans.*
La garniture complète................. **37.50**

7225. Candélabres seuls. *La paire.*...... **12. »**

7230. Garniture "Borne", tout en beau marbre noir, moulures et appliques onyx vert du Brésil, ornements en vrai bronze doré, ornementé et ciselé en relief, mouvement quinzaine à sonnerie, échappement à ancre, très soigné, grand cadran fantaisie, avec appliques bronze doré et glace à biseau, haut. 48 c/m. Livrée avec 2 candélabres à 5 lumières, assortis à la pendule, haut. 52 c/m, poids total 13 kgs.
Garantie 10 ans. La garniture complète.... **77. »**

7235. Candélabres seuls. *La paire.*..... **27.50**

7237. Garniture "Borne" dite "Japonaise", tout en beau marbre noir avec riches incrustations or et couleurs, superbes appliques, moulures fines et galbées, socle, décors "dragon" et poignées en vrai bronze patine vieillie, mouvement de précision quinzaine, sonnerie, grand cadran fantaisie. Haut. 53 c/m. Livrée avec vases assortis, marbre et bronze. Haut. 37 c/m. Poids total 45 kgs 200.
La garniture complète................. **225. »**

7239. Vases seuls. *La paire*........... **82. »**

GARNITURES DE STYLE

Clock .. $495.00
Set 595.00

-E
EXCLUSIF

Clock .. $600.00
Set 700.00

1913
French Catalog

Clock .. $650.00
Set 750.00

7240. Garniture "Bergère" à colonnes, en beau marbre blanc avec ornements et appliques en vrai bronze massif ciselé, modèle de style, mouvement quinzaine à sonnerie, hauteur 43 c/m. Livrée avec 2 flambeaux bouts de table assortis, hauteur 30 c/m, poids total 7 kgs. *Garantie 10 ans. Prix exceptionnel.*
La garniture complète............. **135. »**

7245. Candélabres seuls. *La paire*..... **45. »**

7250. Garniture "Bergère" à colonnes, en beau marbre blanc avec ornements et appliques en vrai bronze massif, ciselé en relief, mouvement quinzaine, sonnerie, cadran fantaisie, aiguilles de style, haut. 43 c/m. Livrée avec 2 vases assortis à la pendule, haut. 28 c/m, pds 6 kgs 800. *Garantie 10 ans.*
La garniture complète............. **150. »**

7255. Vases seuls. *La paire*........... **52. »**

7280. Garniture "Lion" en beau marbre skyros, style Empire, 4 colonnes, pieds et appliques en bronze doré massif, ciselé en relief, sujet "Lion" en bronze imitation également ciselé, mouvement soigné, quinzaine, à sonnerie, cadran genre émail, haut. 40 c/m. Livrée avec 2 vases assortis à la pendule, haut. 24 c/m, Pds 9 kgs. *Garantie 10 ans. La garnit. complète* **152. »**

7285. Vases seuls. *La paire*.... ...... **47. »**

GARNITURES RICHES ET RÉGULATEURS

Clock .. $750.00
Set 850.00

Clock .. $800.00
Set 900.00

Clock -$1,000.00
Set ... 1,100.00

7287. Garniture "Versailles" à 6 colonnes, en beau marbre skyros, appliques et sujet en vrai bronze et ciselé, décor de pur style, mouvᵗ quinzaine sonnerie, cadran fantaisie, haut. 46 c/m. Livrée avec 2 candélabres 3 lumières, assortis, haut. 39 c/m, pds tot. 18 kgs. *Gar. 10 ans. La garniture complète.* **259. »**

7289. Candélabres seuls. *La paire* ...... **95. »**

7290. Garniture "Régulateur", socle et fronton en beau marbre skyros, pieds, cadran et sujet "Aigle" en vrai bronze ciselé, cage glaces biseautées, bombées, mouvᵗ de précision à sonnerie, haut. 43 c/m. Livrée avec 2 vases assortis, haut. 36 c/m, pds tot. 14 kgs 500. *Gar. 10 ans. La garniture complète.* **275. »**

7295. Vases seuls. *La paire*........... **90. »**

7300. Garniture "Empire" en beau marbre skyros, avec pieds, appliqués et sujet "Lion" en vrai bronze ciselé, mouvᵗ de précision dit "Régulateur" à sonnerie, cage glaces biseautées, haut. tot. 47 c/m. Livrée avec 2 vases assortis, haut. 36 c/m, pds tot. 30 kgs. *Gar. 10 ans. La garniture complète.* **350. »**

7305. Vases seuls. *La paire*........... **110. »**

 RÉPARATIONS D'HORLOGERIE, *Voir page*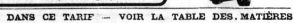

TOUT CE QUE VOUS POUVEZ DÉSIRER SE TROUVE [NF] DANS CE TARIF — VOIR LA TABLE DES MATIÈRES

GARNITURES DE CHEMINÉES AVEC SUJETS BRONZE IMITATION

1913 French Catalog

Clock ..$300.00
Set 400.00

Clock $450.00
Set 600.00

Clock ..$400.00
Set 590.00

7307. Garniture sujet " *Le Travail* " tout en bronze imitation, socle, pieds et lunette genre ciselé décors de style, mouvement huitaine très soigné, cadran fantaisie. Haut. 60 c/m. Livrée avec deux vases assorti, haut. 33 c/m, p^ds tot. 10 k.730. *Gar. 4 ans. Prix exceptionnel*..................... **33.50**

7310. Garniture sujet " *Brise d'Avril* ", par PALADINE, en bronze imitation, socle marbre rose, pieds et appliques dorés, mouv. quinzaine sonnerie, très soigné, cadran émail, haut. 60 c/m. Livrée avec 2 candélabres à 5 lumières, assortis, haut. 59 c/m, poids total 13 kgs. *Gar. 5 ans. La garniture complète*. **63.** »

7315. Garniture sujet "*Maraudeuse*", par F. MOREAU, en bronze imitation, socle marbre griotte, pieds et appliques dorés, mouv. quinzaine sonnerie, très soigné, cadran émail, haut. 61 c/m. Livrée avec 2 vases assortis, haut. 38 c/m, poids total 13 kgs 500. *Gar. 5 ans. La garniture complète*....... **79.** »

Clock ..$450.00
Set 550.00

Clock ..$450.00
Set 550.00

Clock ..$475.00
Set 575.00

7316. Garniture sujet " *Messagère* ", par A. MOREAU, en bronze imitation, socle marbre rose, pieds et appliques dorés, mouv. quinzaine sonnerie, très soigné, cadran émail, haut. 64 c/m. Livrée avec 2 candélabres à 5 lumières assortis. Haut. 67 c/m, poids tot. 19 kgs 500. *Gar. 5 ans. La garniture complète*..... **85.** »

7318. Garniture sujet " *Renommée* ", par BRUCHON. en bronze imitation, socle marbre griotte, pieds et appliques dorés, mouv. quinzaine sonnerie, très soigné, cadran émail, haut. 73 c/m. Livrée avec 2 candélabres à 5 lumières assortis, haut. 74 c/m, pds tot. 18 kgs. *Gar. 5 ans. La garniture complète*.. **88.** »

7320. Grande garniture sujet "*Retour des Bois*", par RANCOULET, en bronze imitation, socle marbre skyros, pieds et appliques dorés, mouv. quinzaine sonnerie, très soigné, cadran émail, h. 66 c/m. Livrée avec 2 candélabres à 5 lumières assortis h. 61 c/m, pds tot. 20 kgs. *Gar. 10 ans. La garniture complète*.... **92.** »

Clock ..$500.00
Set 600.00

Clock ..$475.00
Set 575.00

Clock ..$550.00
Set 650.00

7325. Garniture sujet " *La Victoire* ", par A. MOREAU, en bronze imitation, socle marbre grenat, pieds et appliques dorés, mouv. quinzaine sonnerie, très soigné, cadran émail, haut. 58 c/m. Livrée avec 2 candélabres à 5 lumières assortis, haut. 67 c/m, poids total 17 kgs 500. *Gar. 10 ans. La garniture complète*........ **95.** »

7327. Garniture sujet " *La Source* ", par A. et F. MOREAU, en bronze imitation, socle marbre griotte, pieds et appliques dorés, mouv. quinzaine sonnerie, très soigné, cadran émail, haut. 60 c/m. Livrée avec 2 candélabres assortis, haut. 47 c/m, poids total 17 kgs 500. *Garantie 10 ans. La garniture complète*........................... **105.** »

7330. Grande garniture sujet "*Jeanne d'Arc*", par L. MOREAU, en bronze imitation, socle marbre blanc, pieds et appliques dorés, mouv. quinzaine sonnerie, très soigné, cadran émail, haut. 78 c/m. Livrée avec 2 candélabres à 5 lumières assortis, hauteur 68 c/m, poids total 22 kgs 500. *Garantie 10 ans. La garniture complète*.......... **125.** »

 RÉPARATIONS D'HORLOGERIE, *Voir page*

GRANDES GARNITURES DE CHEMINÉES, SUJETS BRONZE IMITATION

Clock... $500.00
Set.... 600.00

Clock... $500.00
Set.... 600.00

1913 French Catalog

Clock... $525.00
Set.... 625.00

7335. Grande Garniture sujet "*Printemps*", par L. Moreau, en bronze imitation, socle onyx vert du Brésil, pieds et appliques dorés et ciselés, mouvement quinzaine à sonnerie très soigné, cadran émail, hauteur 72 c/m. Livrée avec 2 vases assortis à la pendule, hauteur 53 c/m, poids total 25 kgs.
Garantie 20 ans... La garniture complète. **155.**

7340. Grande Garniture sujet "*La Corde brisée*", par A. Moreau, en bronze imitation patiné et décoré, socle massif, marbre grenat (dit *griotte*), pieds et appliques ornementés et dorés, mouv^t quinzaine sonnerie, cadran fantaisie avec glace à biseau, haut. 74 c/m. Livrée avec 2 candélabres à 6 lumières assortis à la pendule, haut. 82 c/m, poids tot. 36 kgs 500.
Garantie 20 ans.. La garniture complète. **175.** »

7350. Grande Garniture sujet "*Les Cerises*", par Carra, en bronze imitation, patiné et décoré genre Barbedienne, socle massif marbre skyros, pieds et appliques ornementés et dorés, mouv^t quinzaine sonnerie, cadran fantaisie avec glace à biseau, haut. tot. 82 c/m. Livrée avec 2 candélabres à 6 lumières assortis à la pendule, haut. tot. 93 c/m, poids total 38 kgs.
Garantie 20 ans.. La garniture complète. **189.** »

GARNITURES FORME BASSE AVEC SUJETS BRONZE IMITATION

Clock... $400.00
Set.... 500.00

Clock... $500.00
Set.... 700.00

Clock... $400.00
Set.... 500.00

7357. Garniture "Chantilly" tout en bronze imitation, socle, pieds et lunette entièrement découpés et ciselés à jour, décors de style, mouvement huitaine très soigné, cadran fantaisie. Haut. 42 c/m. Livrée avec 2 flambeaux assortis à la pendule. Haut. 54 c/m, poids total 10 kgs 850.
La garniture complète .... **39.** »

7371. Garniture "Porteurs", socle beau marbre blanc, supportée par 2 jolies statuettes en bronze imitation, finement dorées. Mouvement à balancier compensateur visible, haut. totale 36 c/m, poids 6 kgs. Livrée avec 2 superbes vases assortis à la pendule, haut. 32 c/m, poids 4 kgs. *Garantie 5 ans.*
La garniture complète .... **110.** »

7381. Garniture "Coquille" style Louis XV, socle en beau marbre blanc supportant une monture finement ciselée en bronze imitation doré et patiné vieil or, motifs et guirlandes également dorés, mouv^t soigné quinzaine sonnerie, haut. 43 c/m. Livrée avec 2 flambeaux assortis, haut. 46 c/m, poids 9 kgs.
Garantie 5 ans. La garniture complète... **117.** »

Clock... $400.00
Set.... 500.00

Clock... $350.00
Set.... 500.00

Clock... $800.00
Set.... 1,000.00

7363. Garniture sujet "*Semeuse*" en bronze imitation, socle en beau marbre couleur, grand cadran fantaisie, pieds et appliques bronze doré, mouvement soigné quinzaine à sonnerie. Haut. 46 c/m. Livrée avec 2 candélabres assortis à la pendule, haut. 58 c/m, poids 17 kgs. *Garantie 10 ans.*
La garniture complète .... **85.** »

7377. Garniture "Vocation" en bronze imitation, socle en vrai marbre skiros, grand cadran fantaisie, pieds et appliques bronze doré ; mouvement soigné quinzaine à sonnerie. Haut. 35 c/m. Livrée avec 2 vases assortis à la pendule. Haut. 32 c/m, poids total 17 kgs. *Garantie 10 ans.*
La garniture complète .... **115.** »

7389. Garniture "Triomphe de l'Amour", de pur style, superbe socle en marbre vert de mer supportant une colonne antique avec guirlandes, attributs et statuettes, patiné vieux cuivre (*reproduction d'une œuvre ancienne*), mouv^t quinzaine sonnerie, haut. 44 c/m. Livrée avec vases cassolettes genre brûle-parfums, haut. 38 c/m, poids total 18 kgs. *Garantie 10 ans.*
La garniture complète .... **150.** »

  RÉPARATIONS D'HORLOGERIE, *Voir page*

GARNITURES DE CHEMINÉES DITES " BORNES "

Clock.. $150.00
Set 200.00

Clock.. $275.00
Set 350.00

Clock.. $200.00
Set 300.00

7396. Garniture " Borne ", forme carrée, marbre noir avec moulures et colonnettes incrustées en marbre vert de mer, filets dorés, glace biscautée, mouvement quinzaine à sonnerie sur timbre, cadran émail avec garniture cuivre doré. Haut. 25 c/m, poids 5 kgs. Livrée avec 2 vases d'accompagnement assortis, en marbre. Haut. 19 c/m, poids 4 kgs 600. *Garantie 10 ans*.................... **42.** »
7398. Pendule seule................... **29.** »
7402. Vases seuls. *La paire*.......... **15.** »

7404. Garniture " Borne ", marbre noir incrusté, modèle à tambour surélevé, colonnettes moulurées et appliques en marbre vert de mer, glace biscautée, mouvement de précision quinzaine à sonnerie, échappement à ancre visible sur le cadran, balancier compensateur à mercure, cadran ornementé. Haut. 39 c/m, poids 11 kgs. Livrée avec coupes assorties. Haut. 23 c/m, pds 5 kgs 300. *Gar. 15 ans*. **73.** »
7406. Pendule seule................... **58.** »
7408. Coupes seules. *La paire*.......... **16.** »

7409. Garniture " Borne " fantaisie, forme haute, tout en marbre noir avec moulures et colonnettes bronze patiné et sculpté avec appliques bronze ciselé, glace biscautée, mouvement quinzaine, à sonnerie sur timbre, cadran émail avec garniture cuivre doré. Haut. 33 c/m, poids 8 kgs 400. Livrée avec 2 vases d'accompagnement assortis. Hauteur 21 c/m, poids 3 kgs 600. *Garantie 15 ans*.. **75.** »
7411. Pendule seule................... **51.** »
7413. Vases seuls. *La paire*.............. **26.** »

GRANDES GARNITURES DE CHEMINÉES DITES " BORNES "

Clock.. $325.00
Set 425.00

Clock.. $400.00
Set 500.00

Clock.. $500.00
Set 600.00

7414. Garniture " Borne " marbre noir, modèle à tambour surélevé, colonnettes rosaces et appliques en marbre vert de mer, glace biscautée, mouvement de précision quinzaine à sonnerie, échappement à ancre visible sur le cadran, balancier compensateur à mercure, cadran ornementé. Haut. 47 c/m, long. à la base 38 c/m, poids 20 kgs. Livrée avec coupes assorties, haut. 28 c/m, long. à la base 17 c/m, pds 10 kgs. *Garantie 20 ans*.............. **103.** »
7416. Pendule seule.............. **78.** »
7418. Coupes seules. *La paire*......... **29.** »

7419. Garniture " Borne " marbre noir, modèle à tambour surélevé, fines moulures et sculptures galbées, colonnettes torses et appliques massives en bronze ciselé et patiné vert antique, incrustations marbre vert de mer, glace biscautée, mouvement de précision quinzaine, à sonnerie, échappement à ancre visible sur le cadran, balancier compensateur à mercure. Hr 52 c/m, pds 25 kgs. Livrée avec coupes assorties, hr 28 c/m, pds 10 kgs. *Gar. 20 ans*. **165.** »
7421. Pendule seule.............. **115.** »
7423. Coupes seules. *La paire*........... **53.** »

7424. Garniture " Borne " marbre noir, modèle à tambour surélevé, fines moulures et sculptures galbées, socle arrondi, colonnettes, incrustations en marbre vert de mer, 6 colonnes à jour en vieux bronze patiné avec chapiteaux dorés, appliques artistiques en bronze ciselé, glace biscautée, mouvement de précision quinzaine à sonnerie, échappement à ancre visible sur le cadran, balancier compensateur à mercure. Hr 48 c/m, pds 21 kgs 300. Livrée avec coupes assorties. *Gar. 20 ans*. **195.** »
7426. Pendule seule. **133.** » |**7428. Coupes** seules. *La p[re*. **64.** »

GRANDES GARNITURES DE CHEMINÉES MODÈLES RICHES

1913 French Catalog

Clock.. $225.00
Set 300.00

Clock.. $300.00
Set 400.00

Clock.. $300.00
Set 400.00

7429. Grande garniture " Parthenon " marbre noir, modèle riche, fines moulures et sculptures de style, socle massif, 6 colonnes à jour en bronze patiné avec chapiteaux dorés, appliques artistiques au fronton en vieux bronze ciselé, glace biscautée, mouvement quinzaine à sonnerie sur timbre, cadran émail avec garniture cuivre doré. Hauteur 31 c/m, poids 15 kgs 500. Livrée avec 2 vases assortis, marbre. Hauteur 23 c/m, poids 5 kgs 500. *Garantie 20 ans*...................... **105.** »
7431. Pendule seule.............. **71.** »
7433. Vases seuls. *La paire*........... **36.** »

7434. Grande garniture " Aigle " marbre noir, modèle très riche, fines moulures et sculptures de style, socle massif, 4 colonnes à jour en bronze patiné avec chapiteaux dorés, appliques artistiques au fronton découpé avec, au milieu, un aigle aux ailes déployées, en bronze massif ciselé et patiné à la main, glace biscautée, mouvement quinzaine à sonnerie sur timbre, cadran avec garniture cuivre doré. Haut. 45 c/m, pds 23 kgs 900. Livrée avec 2 vases assortis. Hr 31 c/m, pds 10 kgs. *Gar. 20 ans*. **199.** »
7436. Pendule seule.............. **132.** »
7438. Vases seuls. *La paire*.............. **72.** »

7439. Grande garniture " Thèbes " en beau marbre noir, fines moulures et sculptures de style, socle massif avec décors et incrustations marbre vert de mer, 6 colonnes à jours avec chapiteaux dorés, fronton massif avec, au milieu, un Sphinx en vrai bronze massif ciselé et patiné à la main, glace biscautée, mouvement quinzaine à sonnerie sur timbre, cadran avec garnitures cuivre doré. Haut. 43 c/m, poids 20 kgs 800. Livrée avec 2 vases assortis. Haut. 30 c/m, pds 7 kgs. *Garantie 20 ans*............. **269.** »
7441. Pendule seule.............. **182.** »
7443. Vases seuls. *La paire*............. **90.** »

 RÉPARATIONS D'HORLOGERIE, *Voir page*

STATUETTES EN BRONZE IMITATION

$75.00 $75.00 $100.00 $125.00 $80.00 $80.00 $80.00 / $125.00

7601. " **Siffleur** ", bronze imitation, par H. VIENIS, hʳ 50 ᶜ/ᵐ, pds 2 kgs 700.
Prix...... **11.50**

7604. " **Mozart** ", bronze imitation, par RUCHON, hʳ 54 ᶜ/ᵐ, pds 5 kgs.
Prix...... **12.75**

7607, "**Faneuse**", bronze imitation, par A. MO-REAU, hʳ 40 ᶜ/ᵐ, pds 2 kgs 700.... **15.** »
Ce bronze fait pendant au nᵒ 7611.

7609. "**La Victoire**", bronze imitation, par A. MOREAU, hʳ 51 ᶜ/ᵐ, pds 3 kgs 500.
Prix........ **19.** »

7611. " **Faucheur** ", bronze imitation, par VIENIS, hʳ 40 ᶜ/ᵐ, pds 2 kgs 300.... **15.** »
Ce bronze fait pendant au nᵒ 7607.

7614. " **Enfant à la mouche** ", bronze imitation, par A. Mo-REAU, hʳ 34 ᶜ/ᵐ, pds 3 kgs 500.
Prix **20.** »

" **L'Amour mouillé** ", bronze imitation, par H. MOREAU.
Nᵒˢ Haut. Pds *Prix*
7617. 30ᶜ/ᵐ 1 kg. **21.** »
7617 A. 50ᶜ/ᵐ 5 kgs. **48.** »

$100.00 / $150.00 $125.00 $125.00 $125.00 / $200.00 $100.00 $100.00 $100.00

"**La Semeuse**", bronze imitation, pr A. MOREAU. Nᵒˢ Haut. Pds *Prix* 7619. 50ᶜ/ᵐ 3k250. **20.** » 7619 A. 65ᶜ/ᵐ 5k750. **36.** »

7623. " **Tambour** ", bronze imitation, par PICAULT, hʳ 54 ᶜ/ᵐ, pds 2 kgs 600.
Prix ..... **31.** »

7626. " **Achetez-moi** ", bronze imitation, par SCOTTE, hʳ 40 ᶜ/ᵐ, pds 3 kgs
Prix........ **22.** »

" **Mutualité** ", bronze imitation, par L. MOREAU. Nᵒˢ Haut. Pds *Prix* 7629. 52ᶜ/ᵐ 3 kgs. **21.** » 7629 A. 70ᶜ/ᵐ 7k200. **36.** »

7632. " **Petite fermière** ", bronze imitation, par H. MOREAU, hʳ 47 ᶜ/ᵐ, pds 4 kgs 500.... **27.** »

7637. " **Enfant à la toupie** ", bronze imitation, par LA-VERGNE, hʳ 63 ᶜ/ᵐ, pds 5 kgs... **24.** »

7641. " **La Science** ", bronze imitation, par LÉVY, hʳ 61 ᶜ/ᵐ, pds 3 kgs 200
Prix....... **22.** »

$100.00 $100.00 / $150.00 $100.00 / $135.00 $85.00 $80.00 / $125.00 $100.00 $80.00 / $125.00

7644. "**Porte-drapeau**", bronze imitation, par A. MOREAU, hʳ 73 ᶜ/ᵐ, pds 3 kgs 550.
Prix... **20.** »

" **Victoire** ", bronze imitation pr C. PICAULT. Nᵒˢ Haut. Pds *Prix* 7647. 35 ᶜ/ᵐ 4k700. **22.** » 7647 A. 58ᶜ/ᵐ 7k700. **42.** »

" **Jamais** ", bronze imitation, pr H. MOREAU. Nᵒˢ Haut. Pds *Prix* 7651. 45ᶜ/ᵐ 3k100. **23.75** 7651 A. 70ᶜ/ᵐ 8k100. **60.** »

7654. " **Jeanne-d'Arc au combat** ", bronze imitation, pds 2 k 500. Ne se fait qu'en une seule taille.
Prix... **15.50**

" **Dévouement** ", bronze imitation, pr H.MOREAU. Nᵒˢ Haut. Pds *Prix* 7657. 40ᶜ/ᵐ 3 kgs. **27.** » 7657 A. 62ᶜ/ᵐ 7k500. **60.** »

7661. " **Méléagre** ", bronze imitation, par BRUCHON, hʳ 60 ᶜ/ᵐ, poids 8 kgs 500.
Prix........ **24.** »

" **Patria** ", bronze imitation, pʳ BRUCHON. Nᵒˢ Haut. Pds *Prix* 7664. 50ᶜ/ᵐ 3 kgs. **24.** » 7664 A. 75ᶜ/ᵐ 7k150. **48.** »

$75.00 / $100.00 $100.00 $100.00 $100.00 $80.00 / $125.00

" **Le Fer** ", bronze imitation, par PICAULT. Nᵒˢ Haut. Pds *Prix* 7667. 34ᶜ/ᵐ 2 k 600. **29.** » 7667 A. 60ᶜ/ᵐ 8 kgs. **67.** »

7671. " **Napoléon à cheval** ", bronze imitation, haut. 47 ᶜ/ᵐ, poids 11 kgs.......... **45.** »

7674. " **Jeanne-d'Arc à cheval** ", bronze imitaiton (*une seule taille*), haut. 66 ᶜ/ᵐ, pds 4 kgs. **24.** »

7679. " **En reconnaissance** ", bronze imitation, socle bois peint, haut. 58 ᶜ/ᵐ, pds 4 kgs... **24.** »

" **Le Mineur** ", bronze imitation, par PICAULT. Nᵒˢ Haut. Pds *Prix* 7681. 34ᶜ/ᵐ 2 k 400. **29.** » 7681 A. 60ᶜ/ᵐ 8 kgs... **67.** »

Consoles, appliques pour pendules et statuettes, voir page

TOUT CE QUE VOUS POUVEZ DÉSIRER SE TROUVE DANS CE TARIF — VOIR LA TABLE DES MATIÈRES

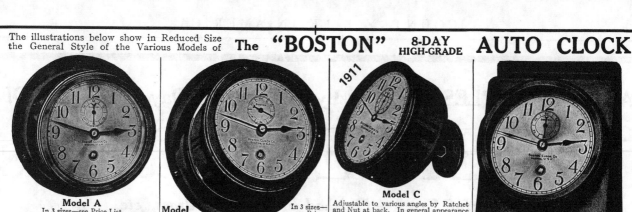

Geo. Borgfeldt & Co., New York

1922 Imported Clock Catalog
GEO. BORGFELDT & CO.
16th St. and Irving Place
New York

DOMESTIC CABINET WORK

SOLID MAHOGANY

$1,500.00

(COPYRIGHT)

No. 3687

Height 36 in.   Width 13¼ in.
Mahogany Sash
Convex Glass

Special "Chateau-Thierry"
scene illustrated above

IMPORTED MOVEMENTS

Eight day time.   Solid Pinion

Best quality weight movement

Dial 7½ in.

Chateau-Thierry, 1922 Cost . . . $130.00 No. 3687

Willard clock, 1922 Cost . . . . . $105.00 No. 192

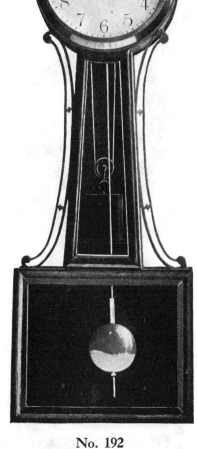

$1,400.00

No. 192

Height 32½ in.   Width 10½ in.
Cast Brass Sash
Eagle and Side Mounts
Convex Glass

Fitted with hand painted glass panels, copies of original motives:

"Mill and Stream"—"Hull"—"Mount Vernon"

Williard Banjo Clocks

HARRIS & HARRINGTON
Fine Imported Clocks
12 West 45th Street
New York, N.Y.

Williard Sconces

Sconces

1915 Cost $39.50

$1,500.00

12¾ in. high
9½ in. wide

No. 5
Plain Mahogany, 1915 Cost $68.50
Gold Front, Mahogany sides 79.00
All Gold $82.00

$1,800.00

No. 5. 38 in. high, 10¾ in. wide, 7 in. dial

No. 6
Plain Mahogany, 1915 Cost $75.00
Gold Front, Mahogany sides 86.00

No. 7
Plain Mahogany, 1915 Cost $83.50
Gold Front, Mahogany sides 94.50
All Gold 96.00
H & H note to dealers: Special glasses
painted to order.

$1,800.00

No. 6. 38 in. high, 10¾ in. wide, 7 in. dial

No. 7. 41½ in. high, 10¾ in. wide, 7 in. dial

H & H Cases

Willard Banjo Clocks

Fitted with Chelsea 8 day time
Weight Movements.

After reading the catalog, Red Rabeneck &
Roy Ehrhardt think the cases and glass
panels are imported.

For assortment of Glass Panels
see Pages 106 and 107.

No. 3. 38 in. high,

11 in. wide, 7 in. dial

$1,800.00

No. 3
Plain Mahogany $85.00
1915 Cost . . . .

HARRIS & HARRINGTON

Fine Imported Clocks
12 West 45th Street
New York, N.Y.

American Agents for
Elliott
English Chime Clocks
on the front of their catalog
September 1915

105

$1,500.00

Gold Front, Mahogany Sides
1915 Cost $64.00
All Gold – 1915 Cost . . . $70.00

No. 2

No. 2
34 in. high, 10 in. wide, 7 in. dial

Nos. 3 and 4 are only fitted
with the glass panels
as illustrated.

No. 1
Plain Mahogany . . . $56.00
1915 Cost . . . . . .
Gold front, Mahogany sides
1915 Cost $60.00

$1,500.00

No. 1
34 in. high, 10 in. wide, 7 in. dial

$150.00

No. 4 French CT
Plain Mahogany, 1915 Cost . $20.00
movement.
Plain Mahogany, French LS
movement. 1915 Cost . $30.75

No. 4. 21 in. high,

6 in. wide, 3½ in. dial

This clock is fitted with French
movement only.

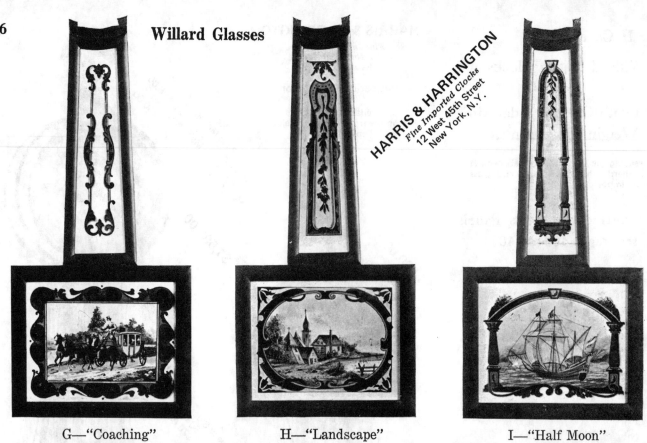

G—"Coaching"   H—"Landscape"   I—"Half Moon"

The following glasses are for cases No. 5 No. 6 and No. 7 only.

J—"Hull Victory"   K—"Mt. Vernon"   L—"Paul Revere"

M—"Boston Tea Party"   N—"Old Mill"   O—"Molly Pitcher"

P—"Coaching"   Q—"Landscape"   R—"Half Moon"

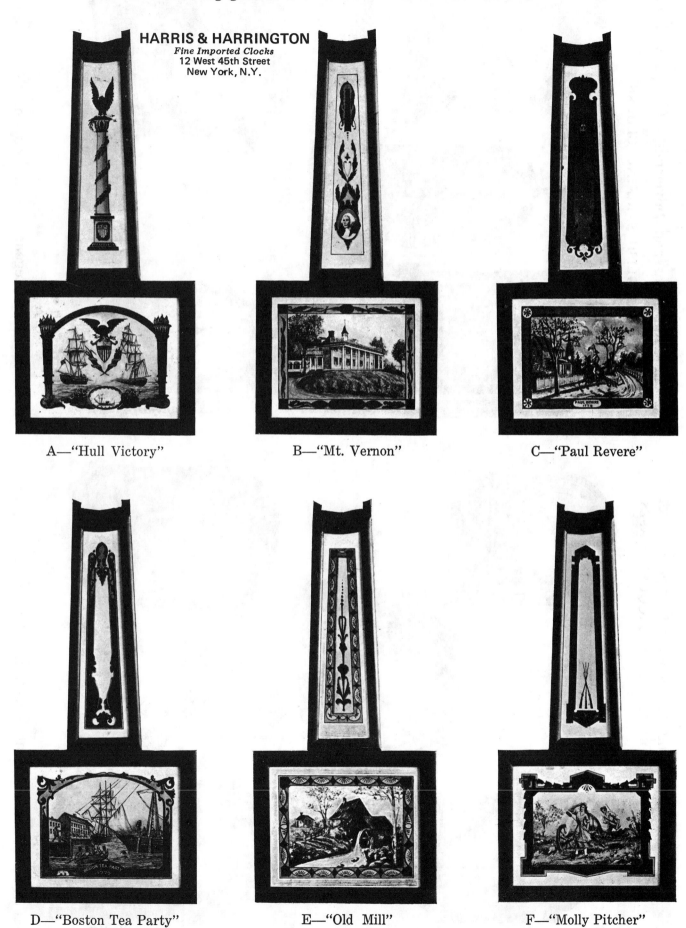

HARRIS & HARRINGTON
Fine Imported Clocks
12 West 45th Street
New York, N.Y.

A—"Hull Victory"

B—"Mt. Vernon"

C—"Paul Revere"

D—"Boston Tea Party"

E—"Old Mill"

F—"Molly Pitcher"

The Goldsmiths and Silversmiths Company, Ltd.

ENGLISH STRIKING CLOCKS

London Made
Eight-Day

1915

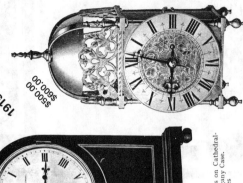

$450.00

S735
Striking hours and half-hours on Cathedral-toned Gong. In Polished Oak, Walnut, or Mahogany Case, Oxydised Engraved Dial. Height 12 inches.
£22 0 0

$500.00 $600.00

S734
"Lantern" or "Cromwellian" Clock in Brass Case. Height 15 inches. Striking hours and half-hours
£25 0 0

Chiming quarters on two Fine-toned Bells.
£30 0 0

$400.00

S737
Striking hours on Cathedral-toned Gong in Mahogany or Oak Cases. Height 12 inches
£25 0 0

$375.00

S733
Striking hours and half hours on Cathedral-toned Gong. In Mahogany Case. Height 14 inches
£25 0 0

$525.00

S736
Striking hours and half-hours on Cathedral-toned Gong. In Inlaid Mahogany Case Height 14 inches
£30 0 0

ONLY ONE ADDRESS   112 Regent Street, London, W.1   NO BRANCHES

The Goldsmiths and Silversmiths Company, Ltd.

CLOCKS IN MAHOGANY AND LACQUER CASES

1915

Selections forwarded
On Approval
Carriage Paid

$275.00

S743
8-day Lever Clock in Inlaid Mahogany Case. Height 8 inches.
£5 0 0

$400.00

S746
Striking hours and half-hours on richly-toned Gong. Height 13 inches.
£14 0 0

$300.00

S744
8-day Lever Clock in Red, Green, or Black Lacquer Case. Height 6½ inches.
£6 0 0

$290.00

S742
8-day Lever Clock in Inlaid Mahogany Case. Height 8 inches.
£5 0 0

$365.00

S745
Striking hours and half-hours on richly-toned Gong. In Inlaid Mahogany Case. Height 9½ inches.
£12 10 0

Collectors not shown much interest in these clocks. Mostly sold for decoration. Decorator prices shown. Collector prices may be about 50%.

ONLY ONE ADDRESS   112 Regent Street, London, W.1   NO BRANCHES

The Goldsmiths and Silversmiths Company, Ltd.

DRAWING-ROOM CLOCKS

1915

$600.00

$950.00

$400.00

S740. Lever Movement. Striking hours and half-hours on richly-toned Gong. In Ormolu-mounted Red Shell Case. Height 11 inches.
£21 0 0

S739. Fine White Marble and Ormolu Clock. Striking hours and half-hours.
£30 0 0

S738. Striking hours and half-hours on richly-toned Gong, in Ormolu-mounted Red Shell Case. Height 12 inches.
£12 10 0

Set — $1,450.00

S741. Fine White Marble and Ormolu Clock. Striking hours and half-hours with Pair Candelabra to match.
£45 0 0

ONLY ONE ADDRESS 112 Regent Street, London, W.1   NO BRANCHES

The Goldsmiths and Silversmiths Company, Ltd.

8-DAY CARRIAGE CLOCKS

Complete in Cases for Travelling

$150.00

$165.00 / $175.00

$175.00

$165.00 / $200.00

S725. Timepiece in Gilt Case.
£2 15 0
Lever Timepiece in Gilt Case.
£4 0 0

S726. Timepiece in Gilt Case, fitted with Alarm.
£5 0 0

S727. Timepiece in Gilt Case, fitted with Alarm. Gilt surrounds Dial.
£6 0 0

S728. Timepiece in Gilt Case.
£5 10 0
Striking hours and half-hours on fine-toned Gong.
£7 10 0

Carriage Clocks in bright polished Bronze Cases, Heavily Gilt, Extra Fine Quality 8-Day Lever Movements, with Compensation Balance, and fully Jewelled Escapements, fitted in Leather Cases for Travelling

$400.00

$425.00

$400.00

$375.00

S729. Striking hours and repeating same on richly-toned Gongs.
£18 10 0

S730. Striking hours and half-hours, and repeating hours on richly-toned Gong.
£20 0 0

S731. Striking hours and half-hours, and repeating hours on richly-toned Gong.
£18 10 0

S732. Striking hours and half-hours, and repeating hours on richly-toned Gong.
£17 10 0

ONLY ONE ADDRESS 112 Regent Street, London, W.1   NO BRANCHES

The Goldsmiths and Silversmiths Company, Ltd.

TRAVELLING WATCHES AND CLOCKS

Foreign Grandfather clocks and other decorator clocks bring much higher prices in antique stores than they do in the collector market. However, the buyers in the antique stores are one-time buyers and thus do not establish a stable market price. The clocks on this page are not old enough to elicit collector interest. The prices shown are between decorator and collector prices and it is hard to predict an actual sale price.

1915

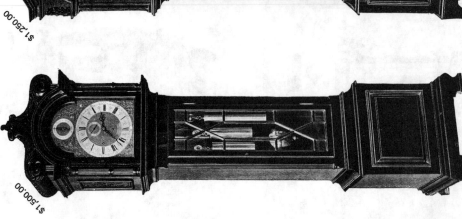
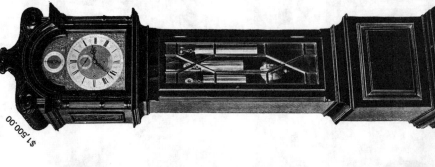
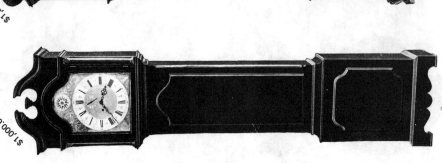

$1,250.00

$1,500.00

$1,000.00

S749

Fine quality 8-Day English Grandfather Clock, with Ornamental Gilt and Silvered Dial, striking the hours and half-hours on Cathedral-toned Gong. In Fumed Oak Case.

Height 7 feet 8 inches

£50 0 0

S748

Fine quality 8-Day English Grandfather Clock, with Ornamental Gilt and Silvered Dial, striking the Westminster Chimes on Four richly-toned Gongs and the hours on deep-toned Gong. In Polished Mahogany "Chippendale" Case.

Height 7 feet 6 inches

£87 10 0

S747

Fine quality 8-day English Grandfather Clock, striking hours and half-hours on Cathedral-toned Gong. In Oak or Polished Mahogany Case. Brass Dial.

Height 7 feet 2 inches

£35 0 0

ONLY ONE ADDRESS 112 Regent Street, London, W.1 NO BRANCHES

$100.00

$140.00

S717

Large Nickel 8-Day Lever Watch, fitted in Fine Tortoiseshell-Fronted Case.

£8 15 0

$150.00

S720

Large Nickel 8-Day Lever Watch in Case, with Extra Heavy Solid Silver Engine-turned Front.

£6 15 0

$75.00

S724

8-Day Clock, in Fine Tortoiseshell Case, with plain Silver Mounts.

£15 10 0

$125.00

$100.00

S716

8-Day Lever Watch in Fold up Leather Case.

£4 0 0

With Luminous Dial, £4 5 0

Watches must have Bow & Crown

$40.00

S719

8-Day Motor Clock, in Brass or Nickel, flat or wedge-shape Cases.

£5 0 0

$35.00

S723

8-Day Gilt Boudoir Clock.

£5 15 0

$100.00

S715

Large Nickel 8-Day Lever Watch, fitted in best Morocco Case.

£4 10 0

$175.00

S718

Large Nickel 8-Day Lever Watch in Case, with extra heavy plain Silver Front.

£6 5 0

$35.00

S722

8-Day Gilt Boudoir Clock.

£5 15 0

$175.00

S721

8-Day Lever Clock. In heavy plain Solid Silver Case.

£10 0 0

ONLY ONE ADDRESS 112 Regent Street, London, W.1 NO BRANCHES

ANSONIA DROPS AND REGULATORS

Pendulum Movements

1928

8" $175.00 / 200.00 — 8D / 8DS
10" $200.00 / 225.00 — 8D / 8DS
12" $225.00 / 250.00 — 8D / 8DS

DIAMOND A MOVEMENTS
THIRTY DAY MOVEMENTS
WEIGHT DRIVEN MOVEMENTS

All of the clocks described on this page are furnished in solid mahogany or solid oak, and packed in individual boxes. Dials are mounted on heavy metal plates. Specify Roman or Arabic Dials as wanted.

$225.00 / 250.00 / 275.00 / 300.00 — 8D / 8DS / 8DC / 8DSC

12" DROP OCTAGON
24½"x16¾"x3¾" 12"dial. Diamond A Movement
8 Day Time.....$22.02   8 Day Strike....$24.08

10" DROP OCTAGON
21½"x14"x3¾" 10" dial. Diamond A Movement
8 Day Time.....$19.38   8 Day Strike....$21.68

8" DROP OCTAGON
19½"x12"x3¾" 8" dial. Diamond A Movement
8 Day Time.....$18.57   8 Day Strike....$20.63

12" ROUND DROP
Diamond "A" Movement
25" x 16⅜" x 4¾" 12" dial
8 Day Time..$24.76   *8 Day Strike*..$26.82

Calendar Dial and attachment as illustrated above, $1.38 extra. This calendar attachment may be specified with Roman Dials on all 8 day clocks illustrated on this page except Standard Regulator.

$800.00

$350.00 / 375.00 / 375.00 / 400.00 — 8D / 8DS / 8DC / 8DSC

$300.00 / 325.00 / 325.00 / 350.00 / 375.00 — 8D / 8DS / 8DC / 8DSC / 30D

STANDARD REGULATOR
Weight driven movement with solid plates, cut wheels, cut and hardened steel pinions and verge, deadbeat escapement, 78-beat.
37" x 15⅝" x 5⅝"   12" dial
8 Day Time..................$68.80

REGULATOR "A"
Diamond "A" Long Pendulum Movement
32" x 17" x 4" 12" dial
8 Day Time....$28.89
8 Day Strike...$30.95

REGULATOR "M"
32" x 16¾" x 4⅞" 12"dial
30 Day Time.....$35.08
8 Day Strike....$30.95
8 Day Time.....$28.89

Publication No. 82091.   Printed in U. S. A.

1928 *Modern Clocks for Modern Buildings*

$650.00

$200.00

"Ben Franklin" No. 1
$54.21

Height, 22½"; width, 15½";
depth, 4¾".
93 Beat Pendulum Movement.
Solid Mahogany Cabinet Work,
Finished Brown.
Operates on either 50 or 60 cycle
alternating current; also on any
direct current. Momentary interruptions of current do not inter-
rupt time keeping.

$200.00

"Ben Franklin" No. 2
$54.21

This clock is of the same general
description as the "Ben Franklin"
No. 1, except its design is different, as shown in the illustrations.

"Lord Kelvin"..$101.63

Height, 48"; width, 15¾".
60 Beat Pendulum, Dead Beat
Movement with Sweep
Second Hand.
12" Dial.
Solid Mahogany Case.
This model is designed for use
where great accuracy is required.

$125.00

"James Watt"....$54.21

18¾" Square.
100 Beat Pendulum.
Solid Mahogany Case.

$200.00

"Faraday" No. 2..$33.89

Height, 24¾"; width, 17".
93 Beat Pendulum.
12" Dial.
Mahogany Finish Case.

PRICES SHOWN ON THIS PAGE ARE KEYSTONE

WALTHAM
PICTURE CLOCKS

1928

$125.00

No. 1821
Price $62.50
A modernistic design in Gilt. 6 inches high.

$185.00

No. 1871—*Oval Easel*
Price $62.50

The design above shows the application of an Easel to Picture Clocks. In addition to the Oval Model shown, these Easel Clocks are available in Cut Corner, Cushion, Rectangular, and Rectangular Curved Ends — 5 inches high. They are graceful in design and beautifully Inlaid with Enamel.

$200.00

No. 1821
Price $62.50
Gilt Frame. Dial Hand-Painted. 4½ inches high.

No. 1821
Price $62.50
Gilt Frame with Green Numeral Track.

$125.00

Waltham Picture Clocks have 8-day 7-jewel Movement
15-Jewel Movement, extra............... 7.50

No. 1821
Price $62.50
Gilt Frame. Enamel Inlay Numerals. Dial Center Hand-Painted. 4⅝ inches high.

$175.00

No. 1821
Price $62.50
Gilt Frame and Dial. 5¼ inches high.

$200.00

PRICES SHOWN ON THIS PAGE ARE KEYSTONE LESS 6%
WALTHAM WATCH COMPANY ~ WALTHAM ~ MASSACHUSETTS

WALTHAM
PICTURE CLOCKS

1928

$200.00

$150.00

WALTHAM presents in these exquisite Picture Clocks that which has long been amongst Europe's famous creations.

In fascinating and charming variety of design and color, Waltham Picture Clocks have either bronze or silvered frames and exquisite dials. The pictures are hand painted on a base of synthetic ivory.

These clocks, combining as they do the rare artistry of the Old World blended with the watch-like precision developed by the maker of America's most distinguished timepieces, make unforgetable gifts that will be treasured for a lifetime.

$185.00

$150.00

Waltham Picture Clocks have 8-day 7-jewel Movement
15-Jewel Movement, extra............... 7.50

No. 1801
Price $44.40

All Clocks illustrated on this page are No. 1801, 3 to 4 inches high.

$150.00

$200.00

$135.00

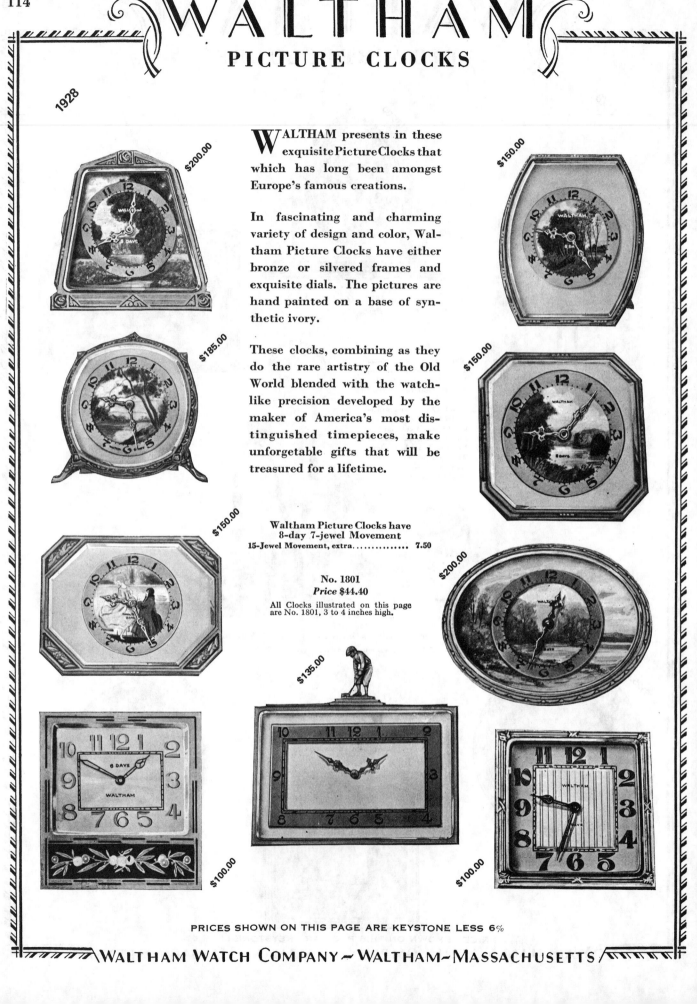

$100.00

$100.00

PRICES SHOWN ON THIS PAGE ARE KEYSTONE LESS 6%

WALTHAM
PICTURE CLOCKS

1928

$175.00

No. 1831
Price $95.10

A magnificent Gilt Clock with contrasting Pattern and Numerals of Enamel Inlay. 6¾ inches high.

Illustrated below is a beautiful Waltham design in Gilt with Green Enamel Inlay. Chiseled Base. 7⅞ inches high.

$275.00

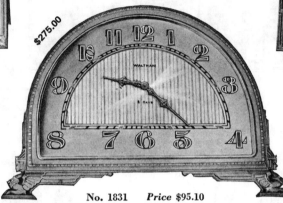

No. 1831   Price $95.10

$175.00

No. 1831
Price $95.10

Beautifully finished in Silver with Blue Enamel Inlay in Frame and Numerals. Very decorative. 8¼ inches high.

$140.00

No. 1851
Price $44.40

A dainty Cabinet Model Boudoir Clock that will appeal to the woman of discrimination and taste. It is Line Engine Turned, Enamel Inlay. 2½ inches high.

IF you love beautiful and unusual designs, you will find these new Waltham Picture Clocks beyond compare. The Clock illustrated below is a magnificent example of the line. The colorful Dial is hand-painted. The side Panels carry out the general color-scheme of gold, green, and blue, the graceful inlaid enamel patterns contrasting pleasingly with the background. The Case is symmetrical and dignified, the Clock a masterpiece of harmony in color and design that will adorn any setting. 8½ inches high.

15-Jewel Movement, extra.............. 7.50

No. 1841   Price $126.80

$175.00

No. 1861
Price $76.10

An exquisite Cabinet Clock of obvious distinction. It is Hand-Carved and set with Semi-Precious Stones or Hand-Painted Crystals. 3 inches high.

$225.00

Waltham Picture Clocks have 8-day 7-jewel Movement

Waltham Picture Clocks make unforgetable Gifts

PRICES SHOWN ON THIS PAGE ARE KEYSTONE LESS 6%

WALTHAM WATCH COMPANY ~ WALTHAM ~ MASSACHUSETTS

WALTHAM
LIBRARY CLOCKS

1928

Waltham Library Clocks have the famous Waltham 8-day 7-jewel Lever Escapement Movement with Temperature Compensating Balance, assuring those dependable time-keeping qualities that have made Waltham respected the world over.

$125.00

A well-chosen Waltham Library Clock becomes the center of interest for the whole room, the design reflecting the spirit of the setting, the color harmonizing with the dominant motif of the room.

$125.00

No. 1238   *Price $44.40*

Easel Type. Mahogany, Walnut, or Crackle Finish in Color. 11¼ inches high, 14¼ inches wide, 1¼ inches deep.

15-jewel Movement, extra	$7.50
Luminous Dots and Hands, extra	9.40
Luminous Figures and Hands, extra	19.00

$100.00

No. 1239   *Price $44.40*

Easel Type. Mahogany, Walnut, or Chinese Red. 11⅛ inches high, 14 inches wide, 1⅜ inches deep.

No. 1215   *Price $44.40*

Easel Model. Mahogany, Walnut, Antique Gilt, or Crackle in Ivory, Red, or Green. 7¾ inches high, 13 inches wide, 1¼ inches deep.

$325.00

$700.00

$325.00

No. 1270   *Price $62.50*

Mahogany only. Brass Trimmings, Hand-Painted Panel Glasses. 12 inches high, 5¾ inches wide.

No. 1702   *Solid Bronze*
Price $95.10

Natural or Verde Finish. 11¾ inches high, 11½ inches wide, 1½ inches deep.

No. 1701   *Solid Bronze*
Price $95.10

Natural or Verde Finish. 11 inches high, 11½ inches wide, 1⅝ inches deep.

Nos. 1701, 1702, and 1750 are three notable examples of Waltham thin-model 8-day clock designs in Solid Bronze.

$150.00

No. 1750
Solid Bronze
Price $38.00

Natural Finish. A handsome Clock for desk, table, or mantel. 6½ inches high, 3⅜ inches wide, ¾ inch deep. 7 Jewels.

WALTHAM WATCH COMPANY ~ WALTHAM ~ MASSACHUSETTS

WALTHAM
LIBRARY CLOCKS

1928

Add $25 for 15-jewel.

$40.00

No. 1264
Price $44.40

Mahogany or Walnut. 9¼ inches high, 16¼ inches long, 1⅛ inches deep.

$45.00

No. 1262
Price $44.40

Mahogany or Walnut. 9 inches high, 19¾ inches long, 1⅛ inches deep.

THIN-MODEL

Only Waltham makes these modern thin-model Library Clocks. The models illustrated on this page are no thicker than your two fingers. Backs are attractively panelled, a feature that will be appreciated when used as table clocks. They keep accurate time whether or not the support is level. Waltham Library Clocks are fitted with the 8-day 7-jewel Waltham Movement.

15-jewel Movement, extra.........$7.50
Luminous Dots and Hands, extra.....9.40
Luminous Figures and Hands, extra..19.00

$45.00

No. 1241
Price $44.40

Mahogany, Walnut, and Red, Green, or Ivory Crackle. 10½ inches high, 10¼ inches long, 1⅛ inches deep.

$45.00

No. 1263
Price $44.40

Mahogany or Walnut. 7⅛ inches high, 20¾ inches long, 1⅛ inches deep.

$40.00

No. 1261
Price $44.40

Mahogany or Walnut. 7¾ inches high, 18½ inches wide, 1⅛ inches deep.

$40.00

No. 1233
Price $44.40

Mahogany, Walnut, or in Green, Red, or Ivory Crackle. 13⅛ inches high, 11¼ inches wide, 1⅛ inches deep.

$75.00

No. 1207
Price $44.40

Solid Mahogany or Walnut. 11⅛ inches high, 13¼ inches wide, 1¼ inches deep.

$75.00

No. 1240
Price $44.40

Inlaid Mahogany or Walnut, or finished in Color, Old Ivory, Red, or Green Crackle. 11½ inches high, 15 inches wide, 1⅛ inches deep.

PRICES SHOWN ON THIS PAGE ARE KEYSTONE LESS 6%

WALTHAM
BOUDOIR CLOCKS

1928

In refreshing originality of design, Waltham Boudoir Clocks bring a new note of life and color to the home. Their rich beauty, fashioned in the smartest models, is combined with the famous Waltham 8-day 7-jewel Lever Escapement Movement, insuring superlative grace combined with exceptional timekeeping qualities.

$125.00

No. 1605
Price $38.00

An unusual and appealing model available in Mahogany or Red and Green Crackle Finish. 7⅝ inches wide, 9⅛ inches high.

$75.00

No. 1607
Price $38.00

A charming design in the Colonial spirit. In Mahogany, Walnut, or Gilt Bronze Finish. 6¾ inches wide, 9 inches high.

Dials are Tinted and Gilded. Luminous Figures and Hands

15-jewel movement extra, $7.50

$70.00

No. 1601
Price $31.70

A graceful design of the Easel Type. Finished in Mahogany, Walnut, Gilt Bronze, Green Bronze, or Pastel Shades. 7¾ inches wide, 8½ inches high.

These are Waltham's newest designs; smart, colorful Clocks for the Modern Boudoir.

$95.00

No. 1609
Price $38.00

This colorful model will grace any setting where it is placed. Available in Mahogany only. 7⅛ inches wide, 9¾ inches high.

PRICES SHOWN ON THIS PAGE ARE KEYSTONE LESS 6%

WALTHAM WATCH COMPANY ~ WALTHAM ~ MASSACHUSETTS

WALTHAM
WALL CLOCKS

1928

THIS happy adaptation of a quaint Colonial Clock is an exclusive Waltham design (No. 1470). The gilded eagle, hand-painted glasses, and carved base are reminiscent of the early American period. Especially pleasing is the brilliant contrast of brass ornaments and gilt rope against the rich lustre of solid mahogany. Furnished in ivory dial with black figures. 14½ inches high, 5¼ inches wide.

$100.00

No. 1421
Price $44.40

Simplicity marks this Clock, useful alike in Home, Bank, or Office. Case furnished in Solid Mahogany or Walnut. 13 inches in diameter, 1⅜ inches deep.

$1,000.00

No. 1470   **Price $62.50**

This design is also equipped with a base for use as a mantel or table clock and available at the same price. (Waltham Library Clock No. 1270.)

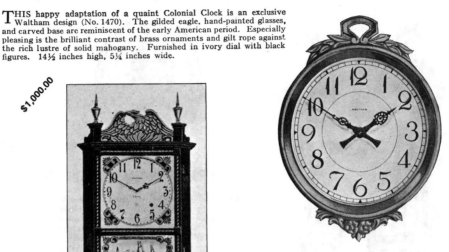

No. 1455
Price $44.40

Handsome Hand-carved Case Finished in Antique Gilt. 15½ inches high, 12 inches wide, 1⅛ inches deep.

$100.00

No. 1425
Price $44.40

Decorative as well as practical. 13 inches in width, 1⅜ inches deep. Available in Mahogany and Walnut.

THE unusual assortment of thin-model designs shown proves that a Wall Clock can be charming as well as useful. Waltham offers in these new and distinctive models Wall Clocks that add a touch of beauty to the home, office, bank, or public building.

Waltham Wall Clocks are fitted with 8-day 7-jewel Lever Escapement Movements. The Cases are solid Mahogany or Walnut in Rubbed Natural Finish or Hand Carved with Antique Gilt Finish. The Dials are of Metal, and harmonize or contrast with finish of Frame. The Hands are slender, graceful and perfectly balanced.

Luminous Dots and Hands, extra......$12.50
Full Figures and Hands Luminous, extra 31.70
15-Jewel Movement, extra............. 7.50

$100.00

No. 1429
Price $44.40
With Raised Numerals, $56.90

This dignified Square Model lends itself to Homes as well as Public Buildings. Mahogany or Walnut Case. 13 inches high, 1⅜ inches deep.

$75.00

No. 1460
Price $44.40

This Hand-Carved Clock finished in Antique Gilt is a center of interest for any Hallway or Room. 15 inches high, 10¾ inches wide, 1⅛ inches deep.

No. 1465
Price $56.50

A New Waltham Wall Clock Design with Carved Panels. Mahogany only. Graceful Ball Ornaments. 16⅛ inches high, 13⅛ inches wide, 2¼ inches deep.

$200.00

PRICES SHOWN ON THIS PAGE ARE KEYSTONE LESS 6%

WALTHAM
WILLARD BANJO CLOCKS

$2,500.00

$350.00

No. 1553
Price $50.70

No. 1500   *Price $95.10*

1928

WILLARD REPRODUCTIONS

In these beautiful designs the makers of America's most distinguished Timepieces present reproductions of Simon Willard's famous creations combined with the finest modern Movements. Offering Willard charm with Waltham accuracy, they are worthy successors to those masterpieces of America's Colonial Period.

Luminous Dots and Hands on large
  models, extra..................................$6.50
  Small models, extra....................4.50
Dial with Luminous Figures and Hands
  on half-size models only, extra.............9.00
  Gold-leafed Base (full size), extra...19.00
  (half size), extra.............12.50
  Models 1525 and 1555 excepted.
15-jewel Movement for half-size model,
  extra 7.50

CHOICE OF GLASS SUBJECTS

Hand Painted

WASHINGTON-
MT. VERNON
CONSTITUTION
AND GUERRIERE
WALTHAM DESIGN
LONE SHIP
ENGLISH CASTLE
BOSTON STATE HOUSE
MONTICELLO-
JEFFERSON
PERRY'S VICTORY
WAYSIDE INN
INDEPENDENCE HALL-
LIBERTY BELL
OLD IRONSIDES

$4,000.00

No. 1505   *Price $126.80*

CASES AND DIALS
Cases are Solid Mahogany, Walnut, Gilt, or Crackle finish in Color on No. 1500 and No. 1554. Dials on both sizes are Ivory Enamel with either Arabic or Roman figures.

MOVEMENTS
The large clocks have 8-day weight-driven Movements and Pendulums with heavy Brass Plates. The half-size Models have the famous Waltham 8-day 7-jewel Movements.

$3,000.00

$375.00

$2,750.00

$2,500.00

$2,500.00

No. 1525
Price $158.50
24K Gold Leaf Front

No. 1554   *Price $50.70*

SIZES
The large-size Waltham Banjo Clocks are 42 inches high, 10½ inches wide, 4 inches deep. Half sizes are 21 inches high, 5¼ inches wide, 2 inches deep.

No. 1543
Price $107.80

No. 1555   *Price $95.10*
24K Gold Leaf Front

ORNAMENTS
Choice of Brass Eagle or Carved Acorn Top Ornament. Solid Brass Side Rails.

No. 1546
Price $95.10

PRICES SHOWN ON THIS PAGE ARE KEYSTONE LESS 6%

(left)

WALTHAM
Curtis
Girandole

Only four clocks of this beautiful banjo design were made by Lemuel Curtis, of Concord, Massachusetts, during the period 1810 to 1818. The clock at the left is now classified as a museum piece with a reported value of $7000. Waltham has reproduced this famous clock so carefully that none of its original color, style, or charm is lost. The time-keeping accuracy of this reproduction is guaranteed by Waltham's dead-beat escapement pendulum movement.

#1510
Actual Height 49 Inches
$350.00

Keystone
$420.00

(center)

WALTHAM
Abbot Lyre

The original of this remarkable Waltham copy of a banjo lyre clock is reported to be 104 years old, and is now in the possession of a well-known Massachusetts family. The original dial bears the inscription S. Abbot, Boston, and no more than a dozen copies were ever offered by the maker. Here, again, Waltham has reproduced this famous clock with absolute fidelity. The accuracy of this beautiful clock is guaranteed by Waltham's finest pendulum movement.

#1515
Actual Height 43 Inches
$225.00

Keystone
$270.00

(left)

WILLARD
BANJO
CLOCKS

Mahogany case; choice of hand-painted glasses; weight-driven pendulum movement. 42″ high; 10½″ wide; 4″ deep.

. . . . $75.00

Keystone 90.00

Glass illustrated Mount Vernon and Washington.

#1500

$6,000.00

1939

$2,500.00

(right)

WILLARD
BANJO
CLOCKS

Bridal model; Mahogany case; 23K gold leaf front, base and cone; hand-painted glasses; weight-driven pendulum movement. 42″ high; 10½″ wide; 4″ deep.

. . . . $125.00

Keystone . . $150.00

Glass illustrated Waltham design.

#1525

$3,000.00

WALTHAM CHRONOMETER

8-Day, Lever Escapement, Winding Indicator Movement Adjusted to Changes in Temperature and Isochronism, enclosed in a Dust and Weather Proof Solid Mahogany Box.

#8725 — 15 Jewels $60.00

Keystone 72.00

$400.00

The Waltham 8-Day Lever Escapement Chronometer has established its absolute reliability under the most exacting tests and conditions. It is accurate to a degree not exceeded by the highest-priced imported ship's chronometers. Wherever time precision is demanded the Waltham Chronometer is the final word in accurate time keeping. *Now in use by Radio Broadcasting Stations for announcing correct time.*

On top of the Mahogany Box there is a jet black plate which has been especially treated to retain its luster. It is also easily cleaned by wiping with a dry cloth. The upper brass strip, held down by two bolts, may be engraved with customer's name. Winding and setting is done from the back. The dial has heavy plain figures and graduations, with heavy hands to correspond. Winding Indicator shows number of days the Chronometer has run.

WALTHAM
AUTOMOBILE CLOCKS

1928

Model FF
Price $24.00

$35.00

This Model is adaptable to any car where a flush-fitting Clock is desired. It is easily installed in metal or wood dash and swings out from the cowl board to wind. Case is finished in Bright Nickel or Black with Corresponding Dials. 4 inches outside diameter (over all). 2¾ Bezel opening.

THE Waltham Automobile Clock has stood the test of time. Since 1910 it has been used on America's finest cars. More recently its accuracy and dependability have made Waltham standard equipment for airplanes. Government aircraft, and the "Spirit of St. Louis," now resting in its place of honor at the Smithsonian Institute, are Waltham-equipped.

The 8-day 7-jewel movement is specially designed to withstand vibrations and road shocks. Cases are finished in nickel, bronze, black, and colors, with harmonizing dials to match the upholstery. They are easily mounted on any make of car.

Radium Dials and Hands Extra, $4.80
(Except on Model XA)

$35.00

Model R-5 Round
Price $24.00

Usually mounted above the windshield. Raised Numeral Track. Dials in a wide range of attractive colors. Case finished in Light Bronze, Dark Bronze, or Gun Metal.

This same Clock is available at additional cost in Square, Barrel, Cushion, and Cut-Corner Cases. Square Case illustrated below.

$35.00

Model R-1
Price $27.60

For mounting above the windshield. The Face of the Clock being on an angle can be seen easily from any part of the car. The Movement turns one-quarter way around, making it convenient to wind and set the Clock. Case finished in Bright Nickel.

In addition to the Automobile and Airplane Clocks illustrated, Waltham offers Automobile Panel Clocks, Speedometers, and Clocks for Telephone Switchboards, Radios and special purposes.

$30.00

WALTHAM AIRPLANE CLOCK
Model XA   **Price $54.00**

This Waltham Model, used by leading aviators, keeps accurate time in spite of extreme vibration and exposure. Model XA is built to meet the rigid U.S. Government Aeronautical Specifications. Each Clock must pass the Government Test before leaving the factory. For 22 days it is tested for accuracy under conditions of continuous vibrations and temperature changes similar to those experienced in actual service. Radium Dial and Hands.

$35.00

Model R-5 Square
Price $27.00

Model XX
Price $30.00

Similar to Model XA, illustrated at the left, with Waltham standard 8-day 7-jewel Movement and regulation Automobile Clock Dial.

PRICES SHOWN ON THIS PAGE ARE KEYSTONE LESS 6%

WALTHAM WATCH COMPANY ~ WALTHAM ~ MASSACHUSETTS

THE WALTHAM AUTOMOBILE CLOCK has stood the test of time. Since 1910 it has been used on America's finest cars. More recently its accuracy and dependability have made WALTHAM standard equipment for airplanes. Government aircraft, and the "Spirit of St. Louis," now resting in its place of honor at the Smithsonian Institute, are Waltham-equipped.

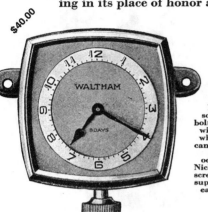

$40.00

1932

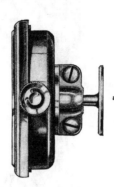

Side view showing ball type attachment with pendant winding at 3.

Readily screwed or bolted above windshield, where clock can be seen by all car occupants. Nickel plated screws or bolts supplied with each clock.

$40.00

"CUSHION"
8703 — Butler Nickel with Butler Silver Dial, White Ring, Black Hands . **Price $20.12**
These clocks can be supplied in the following combinations and shapes:

CUT CORNER
8707 — Bright Nickel with Green Dial White Ring, Black Hands . **Price $20.12**

BARREL
8711 — Bright Nickel with Butler Silver Dial, White Ring, Black Hands . **Price $20.12**

SQUARE
8719 — Butler Nickel with Butler Silver Dial, White Ring, Black Hands . **Price $20.12**

RECTANGULAR
8706 — Bright Nickel with Gray Dial, White Ring, White Hands . . **Price $20.12**

"SQUARE"
8731 — Bright Nickel, Butler Silver Full Figured Dial **Price $20.12**
These clocks can be supplied in the following combinations and shapes.

CUSHION
8732 — Bright Nickel, Butler Silver Full Figured Dial . . . **Price $20.12**

CUT CORNER
8734 — Butler Silver, Butler Silver Full Figured Dial . . . **Price $20.12**

BARREL
8736 — Butler Silver, Butler Silver Full Figured Dial . . . **Price $20.12**

RECTANGULAR
8738 — Butler Silver, Butler Silver Full Figured Dial . . . **Price $20.12**

$30.00

ELECTRIC
8720 — Mounting above Windshield . **Price $24.00**
8722 — Mounting for Dash or Panel . **Price $24.00**

Bright Nickel, Butler Silver Dial, Black Figures and Hands

$70.00

$45.00

$70.00

$45.00

WALTHAM AIRPLANE CLOCK, Model XA
8715 — 15 Jewels . . . . **Price $60.00**
Constructed and tested in accordance with the rigid U. S. Government Aeronautical Specifications.

WALTHAM AIRPLANE CLOCK, Model XX
8716 — 7 Jewels . . . **Price $28.80**

WALTHAM AIRPLANE CLOCK, Model XP
8729 — 15 Jewels, Flush Fitting Type **Price $60.00**
Constructed to Government Specifications

WALTHAM AIRPLANE CLOCK, Model XZ
8730 — 7 Jewels, Flush Fitting Type **Price $28.80**

$30.00

ELECTRIC
8719 — Mounting above Windshield . **Price $24.00**
8721 — Mounting for Dash or Panel . **Price $24.00**

Bright Nickel, Butler Silver Dial, Black Figures and Hands

Side View 8721-8722 For Attachment on Dash

Diameter of Hole Necessary in Instrument Board 1¾ Inches

WALTHAM ELECTRIC AUTOMOBILE CLOCKS

THESE automobile clocks have a 7-jewel watch movement with compensating balance, designed to run on a 6-volt battery. When connected to the battery in your car, they are wound automatically by an electromagnetic device. They are constructed to perform accurately under varying temperatures and vibrations experienced in actual service.

Side View 8719-8720 For Attachment Above Windshield

$300.00

1932

Small Banjo
21 inches high, 5¼ inches wide,
2½ inches deep. Seconds
Indicator
9015 — Mahogany, Mt. Vernon
Washington Panels,
Price $24.00

$2,000.00

Large Banjo
42 inches high, 10½ inches wide
4 inches deep.
9010 — Mahogany, Mt. Vernon
Washington Panels.
Price $54.00

$600.00

Medium Banjo
30 inches high, 7¾ inches wide,
3 inches deep
9012 — Mahogany, Mt. Vernon
Washington Panels.
Price $36.00

$125.00

Station Clock
20 inches wide, 4 inches deep. Dial 13½ ches in
Diameter

9030 — Oak	. . . . .	**Price $36.00**
9031 — Mahogany	: : : : :	**Price $36.00**
9033 — White Enamel	: : :	**Price $36.00**

Waltham Self-Starting Synchronous Movement

Overall size of movement — Diameter
3¹¹⁄₁₆ inches, thickness 1⅝ inches.
9000 — Movement only   Price **$9.60**
9001 — Movement in con-
tainer—no Dial   Price **$10.20**
9002 — Movement in Spider Price **$10.20**
9003 — Movement in Con-
tainer: — complete
with Bezel, Dial, and
Hands . . . Price **$11.40**

Side View

$80.00

Commercial Clock
Diameter of case, 17½ inches. Diameter of dial, 15 inches
9032 — Round Metal, Bronze Finish . **Price $18.00**

Waltham Conversion Kit
Waltham Kit for converting spring-wound and pendulum clocks into
the modern electric clock. Instructions for assembling are furnished
with each kit.
9004 — Kit Complete . . . . **Price $11.40**
Consists of the following:

Kit...$35.00

1 — Movement complete without dial	6 — Key hole plugs, 2 sizes
3 — Pair hands, assorted sizes	2 — Rubber Grommets
1 — Top plate, 2 metal mounting strips with 6 bolts and nuts	1 — 8-foot cord with plug
	1 — Name plate with pins
	6 — Lock Washers

WALTHAM ELECTRIC CLOCKS

1932   WALTHAM

NEW ELECTRIC SELF-STARTING SYNCHRONOUS MOTOR CLOCKS

MATERIAL and Workmanship guaranteed to be of the usual WALTHAM quality. Made by manufacturers who know how to make clock trains (wheels and pinions) that will last. We invite comparison.

$40.00

Small Tambour
5¼ inches high, 12½ inches wide, 3½ inches deep
Seconds Indicator

9021 — Mahogany . . . . . **Price $15.00**

$23.00

Cushion Wall
7½ inches wide, 2¼ inches deep, 5-inch Dial

9035 — Ivory . . . . **Price $12.00**
9036 — Green . . . . **Price $12.00**
9037 — Blue . . . . **Price $12.00**
9038 — Grey . . . . **Price $12.00**

$200.00

Gothic
12 inches high, 8½ inches wide, 5 inches deep
9022 — Mahogany . . . . . **Price $30.00**

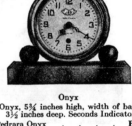

$60.00

Onyx
Genuine Onyx, 5¾ inches high, width of base 7 inches,
3½ inches deep. Seconds Indicator

9025 — Pedrara Onyx . . . . **Price $30.00**
9026 — Green Onyx . . . . **Price $30.00**

Cubical
7½ inches high, 5¾ inches wide, 3½ inches deep.
Seconds Indicator

9024 — Mahogany . . . . . **Price $18.00**

$40.00

$85.00

Large Tambour
8½ inches high, 19½ inches wide, 5 inches deep.
Applied Figure Dial

9020 — Mahogany . . . . . **Price $30.00**

$40.00

Round Top
6½ inches high, 5½ inches wide, 3½ inches deep.
Seconds Indicator

9023 — Mahogany . . . . . **Price $15.00**

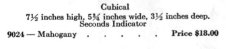

Leather Traveling and Desk Clocks

1936

•• THESE DESK AND TRAVELING CLOCKS are all good time keepers —Finished in a first class manner—Particularly desirable for boudoir or office.

Make Choice Gifts

$30.00

CW920—Waltham—$29.00
(Suggested retail price $22.50)
Folding leather clock, square case in ecrase leather, luminous figured dial and hands, 4½" high, 4⅛" wide, 4¼" deep. Available in colors, brown, black, blue and green.

$40.00

CW922—Boudoir Clock—$22.00
(Suggested retail price $25.00)
An unusually beautiful boudoir clock, case in chrome finish on a swivel green onyx base. Raised figured dial, 3½" high by 5½" wide. Eight day *Mauthe* guaranteed movement.

$30.00

CW921—Waltham—$34.00
(Suggested retail price $25.00)
Folding leather clock, square case in ecrase leather, square luminous figured dial and hands, 4" high, 4⅛" wide, 4¼" deep. Supplied in colors, brown, black, blue and green.

$40.00

$60.00

CW923—Boudoir Alarm—$14.00
(Suggested retail price $10.00)
Mauthe alarm movement in a fine chrome finished case; swivel standard. 5½" wide by 4½" high.

CW924—Waltham—$24.50
(Suggested retail price $20.00)
An eight day Waltham in a chrome finished case, size 5½" wide, 4" high. Beautiful, luminous figured dial. Suitable for any place. Good timekeeper.
(Limited quantity)

$35.00

CW925—Waltham—$21.00
(Suggested retail price $20.00)
Waltham movement with luminous hands and dial; black figures. Hinged easel back, chromium finished case.
(Limited Quantity)

All Clocks Are Fully Guaranteed

List Prices subject to Catalog Discounts

$35.00

CW926—Easel Clock—$19.50
(Suggested retail price $16.50)
The original Mauthe; an eight day clock to be depended upon. Case in chrome finish. Raised figured dial. Size 5" x 3¾".

$50.00

CW927—Boudoir Clock—$18.00
(Suggested retail price $15.00)
Highly finished chrome case on swivel base. 8 day Mauthe movement. Handsome raised figured dial. Size 8½" wide, 4½" high.

1939

$120.00

#8085

Rectangular, double-face clear glass model; all metal parts gold plated; winds and sets at top; regulator at bottom; 9 jewel movement; 2 tone dial; black hands.

7¼″ wide; 5¾″ high; 2⅞″ deep..........**$40.00**

Keystone.... 48.00

$125.00

#8088

Combination metal and colored glass base, with matching glass side-posts; satin finished gold plated metal parts; silver lacquered dial; black hands; 9 jewel backwind movement. Choice of dark blue, peach, or smoke glass.

11¾″ wide; 6″ high; 2⅜″ deep...........**$25.00**

Keystone.... 30.00

$100.00

Add $25 for 15-jewel.

#8087

Double-face stirrup clock; regulation stirrup in silver steel set on black onyx base, or gilt stirrup on mottled green onyx base; 9 jewel movement; 2 tone dial; black hands.

6¼″ wide; 7⅜″ high; 1¼″ deep..........**$40.00**

Keystone.... 48.00

$80.00

#8089

5″ round swivel glass model; 9 jewel backwind movement; all metal parts gold plated with satin finish; perforated dial; black hands. Available with light blue, dark blue, green, or smoke colored glass.

8″ wide; 5¾″ high; 2¼″ deep.............**$25.00**

Keystone.... 30.00

$100.00

#8094

Twin-face 9J and 15J movement. Chrome and Gilt.
4⁹⁄₁₆″ wide; 1½″ deep; 4″ high.

#8094 — 9 jewel; chromium finish case.....**$27.50**

Keystone....33.00

#8095 — 15 jewel; chromium finish case..... 30.00

Keystone....36.00

#8096 — 9 jewel; gold plated case........ 27.50

Keystone....33.00

#8097 — 15 jewel; gold plated case......... 30.00

Keystone....36.00

$160.00

#8081

8″ round glass dial in light blue, dark blue, green, peach; gilt applied stick figures; gold plated case; 9 jewel backwind movement.

9¾″ wide; 10½″ high; 2″ deep, Colored Glass **$25.00**

Keystone....30.00

WALTHAM Electric Clocks

1939

#9097

$15.00

Bedroom alarm; bakelite case in black with white line. Dial 3¾"; black figures and hands; rubber cord and plug.

5⅝" wide; 6¼" high; 2⅝" deep......**$3.95**
Keystone.... 4.84

With radium figures and hands........ 4.95
Keystone.... 5.94

#9094

$15.00

Living room alarm; case obtainable in Ebony and Walnut or Satin and Mahogany. Square dial 3½"; metal feet; hand rubbed finish; rubber cord and plug.

7⅛" wide; 5⅜" high; 2½" deep....**$6.95**
Keystone.... 8.34

#9096

$30.00

"The Skipper." Solid mahogany case in shape of ship's capstan; quartermaster's wheel fitted with bezel and dial to represent compass. Sweep second hand polished on one end, blued on other, representing compass needle. Hands resemble belaying pins.

7¾" wide; 7¾" high; 4¾" deep..... $ 9.95
Keystone....11.94

...Eight Day Jeweled Clocks...

#8075

$70.00

Rectangular swivel chromium or gold plated case; 9 jewel backwind movement; embossed figure dial; black hands.

9" wide; 4" high; 2⅝" deep........$22.50
Keystone....27.00

#8093

$50.00

Square bezel, 8-day glass clock; metal parts gilded; dial silver white with black figures.

7¼" wide; 1¾" deep; 5" high....**$25.00**
Keystone....30.00

#8084

$70.00

Rectangular glass model; gilt frame; combination glass and gilt base; 9 jewel backwind movement; 2 tone dial; black hands; choice of light blue, dark blue, green, peach, or clear glass.

7½" wide; 5¼" high; 2½" deep **$30.00**
Keystone....36.00

#8086

$70.00

Add $25.00
for 15D

5" square glass model; 9 jewel backwind movement; frame and base of gold plated metal with satin finish; dial is perforated metal; black hands. Glass furnished in light blue, dark blue, green, peach, or clear.

6¾" wide; 5¾" high; 2⅛" deep....**$25.00**
Keystone....30.00

$30.00

Square genuine leather case, natural grain; round dial; 9 jewel pendant movement. Cases available in brown Ostrich, laced Hornback, tooled Pigskin, Pinseal, and light blue, dark blue, brown, dark green, jade, rose tooled Ecrase. 4¼" wide; 4" high; 4¼" deep.

#8001 Radium figures and hands; 9 jewel movement.......................$22.50
Keystone.... 27.00

#8002 Radium figures and hands; 15 jewel movement................... 25.00
Keystone.... 30.00

#8003 Gilt raised figures and hands; radium dots; 9 jewel movement........... 22.50
Keystone.... 27.00

#8004 Gilt raised figures and hands; radium dots; 15 jewel movement.......... 25.00
Keystone.... 30.00

#8092

$80.00

Mirror glass model; frame is colored glass of light blue, dark blue, peach, or green; rod at bottom is clear glass; gold plated base; 9 jewel backwind movement; black hands.

9¾" wide; 7" high; 3" deep........**$30.00**
Keystone....36.00

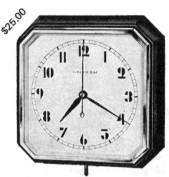

$25.00

Cut-Corner wall model; available in chromium or gilt trim. 7″ wide; 7″ high; 2¼″ deep. Choice of following colors with harmonizing color dial and hands:
#9050 — Green; #9051 — Ivory; #9052 — Blue; — #9053 — Black; #9054 — Red; #9055 — Yellow....................$3.50
Keystone....4.20

$20.00

1939

Round wall model; 5″ dial with black figures and hands; moulded ring in color; chromium finished bezel. Overall diameter 7½″; 2″ deep.
#9080 — Green; #9081 — Ivory; #9083 — Black; #9084 — Dubonnet; #9085 — Yellow....................$4.75
Keystone....5.70

$20.00

#9071

Small round top model; Mahogany veneer case with Maple overlay and holly inlay.
5¾″ wide; 6¾″ high; 2¾″ deep.....$4.95
Keystone....5.94

$15.00

#9095

Tambour; hand rubbed in Mahogany or Walnut case; dial opening . 4¾″; raised gilt numerals.
13¼″ wide; 6″ high; 2½″ deep.......$7.95
Keystone....9.54

$40.00

#9086

Case in Mahogany, Maple, or Walnut veneer, with black beading; silvered dial; gold plated bezel; black hands and figures; base is gold plated rod extending back in semi-circle.
6⅞″ wide; 5¾″ high; 3½″ deep $7.95
Keystone....9.54

$30.00

#9087

Furnished with Mahogany, or Walnut veneer case; semi-circular chromium plated base; silver finished dial track and hands; black figures.
6¾″ wide; 5¾″ high; 3⅝″ deep.....$7.95
Keystone....9.54

15″ $150.00
16″ $170.00

Square office model; regularly stocked with Mahogany finish frame; Oak or white enamel frame available on special order. 15″ wide; 15″ high; 2¾″ deep.
#9029............................$9.95
Keystone....11.94

Same as above with 16½″ square case, 3¾″ deep; hinged cover; illuminated with four lamps at corners and six extra bulbs included.
#9075............................$12.50
Keystone....15.00

$150.00

12″ round office model; drawn steel case finished in black; white dial with black hands and figures. Overall diameter 16¾″; 3⅜″ deep.
#9040............................$8.95
Keystone....10.74

Same as above with weather-proof case for outside installation.
#9073............................$8.95
Keystone....10.74

$30.00

#9093

Square bezel wood case in Walnut and Mahogany with gilt dial and black numerals. In Maple case with black dial and white numerals.
9″ wide; 2½″ deep; 6⅛″ high.......$7.95
Keystone....9.54

WALTHAM
GRANDMOTHER CLOCKS

1928

In these beautiful models, Waltham has adapted the stately Hall Clock of Colonial times to modern requirements. Under six feet in height, Waltham Grandmother Clocks are admirably suited to the hall, living-room, or dining-room. In even the smallest home or apartment an appropriate setting can be found for these slender, graceful designs that combine the charm of the Grandfather Clock with the exceptional time-keeping qualities assured by the Waltham Movement.

Waltham Grandmother Clocks are fitted with 8-day 7-jewel Lever Escapement Movement with Compensating Balance. Dials have Roman Numerals. Cases are Mahogany. The hinged front when opened reveals a compartment with shelf typical of the hiding-places built into Period Furniture. The Door is opened by a concealed latch.

$500.00

No. 703
Price $158.50
This Grandmother Clock is characterized by the exceptionally beautiful grain of the Mahogany Case, the graceful Top Ornament, and Hand-Painted Dial. 5 feet 7 inches high, 9½ inches wide, 7½ inches deep.

$500.00

$500.00

No. 701
Price $158.50
A magnificent gift that will be cherished for a lifetime. 5 feet 3 inches high, 10 inches wide, 7½ inches deep.

No. 702
Price $158.50
The Hand-Decorated Dial adds to the charm of this appealing Clock. 5 feet 5 inches high, 10 inches wide, 7¼ inches deep.

PRICES SHOWN ON THIS PAGE ARE KEYSTONE LESS 6%

WALTHAM WATCH COMPANY ~ WALTHAM ~ MASSACHUSETTS

Stunning New Models for Desk or Boudoir

JOHN PLAIN CO . - 1928
NEW HAVEN CLOCK CO.

$75.00

$100.00

$100.00

$40.00

8-DAY ABBEY CLOCK
JEWELED MOVEMENT

A most delightful new Easel clock fitted with a dependable New Haven 8-day jeweled movement. The beautiful case is in Mahogany finish. Has 2¼-inch silvered dial with raised numerals. Measures 4½ inches high. A boudoir clock of unusual charm.

2E25070 PRICE.................... **$17.50**

8-DAY JEWELED MOVEMENT
HAND CARVED CASE

A handsome clock fitted with a dependable 8-day jeweled movement. The hand carved case is in a beautiful pastel red shade, hand colored with a handsome decoration. Fitted with 3½ inch solarchrome dial and convex crystal. Measures 8¼ inches high by 8 inches wide.

2E25071 PRICE.................... **$27.50**

GOTHIC BOUDOIR CLOCK

A delightful new Gothic Boudoir clock made of antique solid Mahogany with black panels. Has accurate 8-day jeweled movement and 3½ inch dial with raised gold numerals. Height 7¾ inches. Width 7½ inches.

2E25072 PRICE.................... **$25.00**

INLAID MAHOGANY

Beautiful inlaid antique Mahogany case fitted with an accurate 8-day jewel movement. Has a 3¾ inch square dial with raised gold numerals. Measures 5¼ inches high x 5⅜ inches wide. A charming desk or boudoir clock.

2E25073 PRICE.................... **$17.50**

The Electric Clock the World Has Been Waiting For

Accurate Timekeepers That Will Run on Battery or Light Circuit

IMPERIAL CLOCK CO.

NO WINDING

The movements in all of these 3 new electric clocks are made without springs or other delicate mechanism; without platinum tips to adjust, contacts or switches to cause trouble. Truly a movement with all electrical problems solved. The two models to the right operate on batteries only. The model illustrated just below may be operated from any 110 volt A. C. or D. C. circuit. The driving mechanism consists of a weighted lever, and a simple armature arm, controlled by magnets. The lever descends by gravity and runs the movement; when it reaches its lowest point, it comes in contact with the armature arm, which in turn, is instantly attracted by the magnets, causing the weighted lever to be thrown to the highest point. Batteries will last 12 to 30 months depending on their quality. The two battery models shown here come complete with two batteries already for use.

NO SPRINGS

The movements used in these clocks are made of the very highest quality of materials obtainable. Being without springs, the greatest accuracy has been obtained. The movement plates are all of heavy brass on cast iron brackets insuring greater rigidity. The wheels are all milled, not stamped. The dial is fastened to the movement by means of machine screws so that it will under all circumstances have the proper relation to the movement. Perfect interchangeability of all parts is the result of precision in manufacture. Each and every movement is tested at the factory insuring the proper operation when it is delivered to you. The cases are all finished in a beautiful Duco which is the best lacquer finish obtainable. Not susceptible to heat or cold and will not check. These clocks are all guaranteed high grade in every respect. They are offered at the prices of ordinary key wind clocks although they are far superior.

$135.00

$300.00

$135.00

PLUG IN ON LIGHT CIRCUIT

This high grade electric clock contains the guaranteed movement which is described above. Comes already for use, just plug in on the regular 110 volt electric light circuit. The movement is high grade in every respect and is made without springs or other delicate mechanism. Has spun brass pendulum and 12-inch metal dial. The case is in brown Mahogany Duco finish. Measures 17 inches square by 5½ inches deep.

2E25074 PRICE **$40.00**

BATTERIES LAST TWO YEARS

The extra long pendulum on this high grade electric clock makes for greater accuracy. Has the same guaranteed high grade movement as described above. The case is especially well constructed and measures 33 inches high, 17¾ inches wide and 4½ inches deep. Has 12-inch dial and spun brass pendulum 14½ inches long. The battery receptacle is at the top of case. Comes complete with batteries ready for use. Batteries last about two years. Case is in brown Mahogany Duco finish.

2E25075 PRICE **$30.00**

ELECTRIC WALL CLOCK

One of the most accurate and dependable electric wall clocks ever made. Hast the same standard guaranteed movement as described above. Case is in a beautiful Mahogany Duco finish. Has brass bezel, 12-inch metal dial, and mat with convex glass. Case measures 15 inches square by 4½ inches deep. Entire front of case opens forward with battery receptacle on either side, facilitating installing new batteries. Comes complete with two batteries ready for operation.

2E25076 PRICE **$30.00**

SILVERCRAFT EASEL CLOCKS OF RARE INDIVIDUALITY

1932

These clocks combine practical utility with distinction. Accurate timepieces of character that have won immediate favor everywhere. Guaranteed American movements. Their distinctive dials and general high grade workmanship, accuracy and dependability, make instant appeal to people of distinctive taste.

Chromium finish. Jade Karolith base. Height, 4¼ inches. Base, 6¼ by 2¼ inches.
A505H01. Each...................$12.00

Chromium finish. Black Karolith base. Height, 4¾ inches. Base, 6¼ by 2¼ inches.
A505H02. Each...................$12.00

English finish. Maize Karolith base. Width, 4¾ inches; height, 4 inches.
A505H03. Each...$9.00

Alarm, 22 karat rose gold plated finish. Height, 4½ inches. Base, 6¼ by 2¼ inches.
A505H04. Each...$16.50

English finish. Maize Karolith base. Height, 5½ inches. Base, 6¼ by 2¼ inches.
A505H05. Each...$12.00

Chromium finish. Jade Karolith base. Width, 5¾ inches; height, 4¾ inches.
A505H06. Each...$9.00

$25.00

Capitol, 8-day lever, 8½x9 inches.
R14562   Apple green.   Each, $6.80

Similar style
R15510   Naples blue.   Each, 6.50
R15511   Rose.   Each, 6.50

$25.00

Wakemaster electric alarm clock, complete with cord and plug for 100 to 130 volts, alternating current, 60 cycle. Size 4½x3¾ inches.

R14630   Green.   Each, $6.50
R14631   Rose.   Each, 6.50
R14632   Champagne.   Each, 6.50

R14633   Same size as above, silver finish. Black trim with radium dial.   Each, $9.00

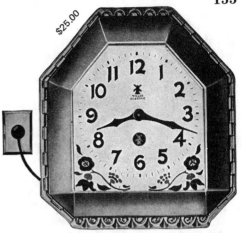

$25.00

Revere.   Sealed synchronous motor complete with cord and plug for 100 to 130 volts alternating current, 60 cycle lines. Fits flush to wall. Size 8x8⅝ inches.

R14551   Blue on ivory.   Each, $10.00
R14552   Green on ivory.   Each, 10.00
R14553   Yellow on ivory.   Each, 10.00

$25.00

A very neat all electric kitchen clock. All metal heavy enameled case. Size 7½x7½ inches.
R14634   Green.   Each, $5.00
R14635   Blue.   Each, 5.00
R14636   Ivory.   Each, 5.00

$20.00

R14637   Gothic style electric clock that can be placed anywhere in the home. Walnut finish bakelite case. Complete with cord and plug for 100 to 130 volts alternating current, 60 cycles. Height 5½ inches, width 4 inches.   Each, $2.70

$35.00

WATERBURY ALARM

This modernistic all electric clock comes in "mahogany" with gilt trimming and black with chromium. Moulded case. Self-starting, harmonic electric bell, sweep second hand. 7 inches high.
R14638   Mahogany.   Each, $15.00
R14639   Black.   Each, 15.00

$20.00

R14640   A beautiful Tambour mantel clock. All electric. Rubbed mahogany finish case with walnut inlays. Gold dial with ebonized black numerals, convex crystal with gold finish bezel. Complete with cord and plug for 100 to 130 volt alternating current, 60 cycle. Width 19 inches, height 8 inches.   Each, $13.00

$25.00

R14641   Mahogany finish Tambour. All electric clock. Complete with cord and plug, for 100 to 130 volts alternating current. Width 14 inches, height 5½ inches.   Each, $6.50

Marble, Onyx and Novelty Electric Clocks

E LEGANCE and accuracy combine to make these high grade clocks really appreciated. The Hammond all-electric movement will maintain exact to the second accuracy without winding, oiling, or even regulating on your part. It has no springs but instead a small electric motor that registers the time impulses sent to it by the electricity from the light socket. Electrically regulated time brings observatory time to your home or office.

Merely insert the plug into the light socket, set the hands, start, and thereafter receive correct time. Regularly made for 110 to 120 volt and 60 cycle.

$40.00

R14566 Made of genuine Arizona onyx and inset with genuine Italian black and gold marble. Height 7 inches, width 5 inches.
Each, $24.00

$50.00

R14567 Made of genuine Italian black and gold marble with two side pieces of green onyx. Height 6 inches, width 7 inches.
Each, $29.00

$40.00

R1456S Distinction marks every line of this genuine Argentine green onyx case. Height 7 inches, width 7 inches. **Each, $40.00**

$100.00

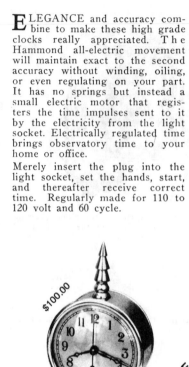

CARSON, PIRIE, SCOTT & CO. — Chicago Catalog

R14577 Black enamel trim. chromium plated clock. Rich in any surrounding. Height 10½ inches. Base 6⅞ inches. **Each, $19.00**

$50.00

R14569 All the charm of modern times is combined in this case of Arizona onyx and black and gold marble inset with Argentine green onyx. Height 8 inches, width 7½ inches. **Each, $41.00**

$100.00

R14578 Black enamel trim chromium plated case. Charm in every line of this exquisite model. Width 10 inches, height 8 inches.
Each, $30.00

$75.00

R14575 Black enamel trim, chromium plated case. A charming model for any home. Height 6¼ inches, width 5⅞ inches. **Each, $18.00**

$75.00

R14576 Black enamel trim, chromium plated case. A radio or end table the logical home for this delightful model. Height 6½ inches.
Each, $23.50

AN ENTIRELY NEW IDEA IN COMPACT TIMEPIECES AND ALARMS

These unusually smart alarms and timepieces are fitted with an ultra-thin movement made exclusively for Silvercraft by one of America's foremost factories. Entirely different pedestal clocks from the Silvercraft workshop, that express the highest ideals of conscientious Craftsmanship. Artistically original metal dial designs with fascinating numerals. Movements guaranteed dependable and accurate.

1932

Alarm, rose gold plated finish. Easel back. Width, 5 inches; height, 3 inches.
A504H01. Each...................$12.00

Alarm, antique green gold plated finish. Easel back. Width, 4¼ inches; height, 3¼ inches.
A504H02. Each..................$12.00

English finish. Easel back. Etched dial. Width, 5 inches; height, 3 inches.
A504H03. Each......................$7.50

English finish. Easel back. Etched dial. Width, 3¼ inches; height, 4¼ inches.
A504H04. Each...................$7.50

Chromium finish. Easel back. Width, 3¼ inches; height, 4¼ inches.
A504H05. Each...................$7.50

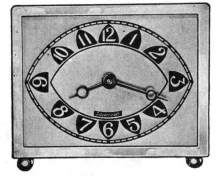

Chromium finish. Easel back. Width, 5 inches; height, 3 inches.
A504H06. Each......................$7.50

English finish. Easel back. Width, 4¼ inches; height, 3¼ inches.
A504H07. Each...................$7.50

Chromium finish. Easel back. Etched dial. Width, 4 inches; height, 4 inches.
A504H08. Each...................$7.50

MAY & MALONE, INC.

EXQUISITELY SHAPED AND COLORED CLOCKS FOR THE HOME

1932

$40.00

$65.00

$30.00

LATTICE PATTERN

Size of plate 10 by 10 inches. Porcelain Wall Clock fitted with guaranteed American Eight Day Lever movement—no pendulum required. Case flares back toward wall, partially hiding the movement. Plate is handsomely decorated with a floral pattern. It is washable and appears new for a lifetime. An attractive decoration for any home and a perfect timekeeper.

Furnished only in apple green finish.

A503H01. Price...................................$5.40

OLD DUTCH DELF PATTERN

Size of Porcelain plate 8½ by 8½ inches.

Again we bring out the clock that seems to please a large majority of the housewives.

In accord with the modern trend an inversion of design has been made and now flares back toward the wall. A necessity that should not conflict with any color scheme. Can be obtained only in white with blue figures.

A503H02. Price.......................$4.20

CONSOLE PATTERN

Size of plate 8¼ by 9¼ inches. Depth 2¼ inches.

Porcelain Wall Clock fitted with guaranteed American Eight Day Lever Movement—no pendulum required. A startling new shape, the most distinctive kitchen clock to date. The bracket effect used cleverly, conveys the impression that the clock is setting on its own shelf. The sunken dial and floral decoration on ivory background, appear framed within the beautiful two-toned border. An attractive decoration for any home and a perfect timekeeper.

Furnished only in popular green on ivory finish.

A503H03. Price...................................$7.70

$10.00

TRIANGLES PATTERN

Size of plate 8½ by 8½ inches.

Porcelain Wall Clock fitted with guaranteed American Eight Day Lever Movement—no pendulum required. Case flares back toward wall; washable; appears new for a lifetime. A decorative necessity for any home.

Obtainable only in two-tone Naples blue or two tone sunshine yellow finish.

A503H06. Price.......................$5.00

$25.00

$60.00

$50.00

ELF ELECTRIC PATTERN

Diameter 8½ inches, 5-inch Metal Dial with Raised Numerals. Polished Brass Sash. Operates on alternating current 110-120 volts, 60 cycle. Clocks for 50 cycle current are furnished only on special order, without an extra charge. Can be obtained only in Walnut or Green crackle finish.

A503H04. Price...................................$12.80

SALON PATTERN

Same dimensions and specifications as the ELF ELECTRIC, except 8 day lever, spring wind, movement. Can be obtained in Green or Old Ivory Crackle finish.

A503H05. Price...................................$8.09

$30.00

SESSIONS ALARM

Size 6½ inches high, 5½ inches wide. Metal dial 4½ inches with raised numeral. Convex glass, 8-day movement. Sessions have taken the alarm clock, and made it a thing of charm and beauty. A unique refinement is the convenient alarm shut-off, merely tap the button at the top. The bottom of base is cushioned to prevent scratching of polished surfaces. Can be obtained in Green or Rose Crackle finish.

A503H08. Price, Plain Dial.............$7.06
A503H09. Radium Dial.................8.52

MANSION PATTERN

Size of plate 9¾ by 9 inches, re-supporting shelf. Porcelain Electric Wall Clock. Operates from ordinary outlet without winding. (A. C. Current 100-130 volts, 60 cycle only.)

A gracious design with flowing lines; the solid pastel border is set off by the gaily colored floral sprays. "Evernu" porcelain case fits flush to wall.

Furnished only in popular green on ivory finish.

A503H07. Price...................................$14.30

CHRONART ELECTRIC WINDMILL PATTERN

Size of plate 10½ inches long, 9 inches wide; 2½ inches deep. Dial 5¾ inches. Arms of windmill serve as front starter and indicator. Modern housewives have been quick to show their appreciation for this electric clock that requires no winding or regulating, and gives exact—to the second time at a low price. Comes only in one style, but so designed as to harmonize with the decorative scheme of any kitchen. Will operate on 80-135 volt, 50 or 60 cycle alternating current, where the frequency is regulated. 60 cycle furnished unless otherwise authorized.

A503H10. Price...................................$10.85

1931

Clock . . . $40.00
Set . . . 75.00

Clock . . . $30.00
Set . . . 60.00

Clock Set: Made of composition white metal, finished in antique silver, equipped with fully guaranteed, American made 8 day movement, etched metal dial and convexed glass, 7¼″ high x 6″ wide. Candlesticks 3″ high.
K394+1 .... **$16.50**

Clock Set: Base made of composition white metal, finished in imperial bronze, bottom covered with felt, equipped with silk cord, socket and plug, has parchment shade. Size of lamp from base to top of socket 5¾″ x 11½″. Guaranteed 30 hour American made movement.
K394+2 .... **$16.50**

$125.00

Clock Set: Made of composition white metal, finished in antique gold, equipped with fully guaranteed 30 hour American made movement, etched metal dial and beveled glass. 6¼″ high x 4¼″ wide. Candlesticks 3″ high.
K394+3 .... **$12.00**

Clock . . . $30.00
Set . . . 60.00

Clock Set: Made of composition white metal, finished in Imperial bronze, equipped with a 30 hour fully guaranteed American made movement, etched metal dial, convexed glass. 9⅛″ high x 7¼″ wide. Candlesticks 6¼″ high.
K394+4 .... **$15.00**

Clock . . . $30.00
Set . . . 60.00

Clock Set: Made of composition white metal, finished in antique silver, equipped with a 30 hour fully guaranteed American made movement. Gold colored dial. 7″ high x 5″ wide. Candlesticks 5″ high.
K394+5 .... **$7.50**

Clock . . . $40.00
Set . . . 80.00

Clock Set: Made of composition white metal, finished in imperial bronze, equipped with a 30 hour American movement fully guaranteed, etched metal dial with beveled edge glass. 8½″ high x 5¾″ wide. Candlesticks 3″ high. Same as shown under No. K394+1.
K394+6 .... **$13.50**

$85.00

400 DAY CLOCK
White or green alabaster base, satin silver finish pendulum balls and stand a very high grade movement, hardened steel pinions, patented new pendulum spring guard. 4″ silver dial with sun ray effect, raised gold numerals. Height 12¼″, diameter 7½″.
K394+7 .... **$38.25**

Clock . . . $30.00
Set . . . 60.00

Clock Set: Made of composition white metal, finished in Nile green, equipped with a 30 hour American made fully guaranteed movement, etched metal dial with beveled edge glass. 8″ high x 5½″ wide. Candlesticks 3″ high. Same as shown under No. K394+1.
K394+8 .... **$13.50**

THE FINEST OF ELECTRIC CLOCKS

Suitable for any room in the home, highest grade cases obtainable, with HAMMOND movements in the onyx and marble cases. MANNING AND BOWMAN movements in the other styles. An accurate time-piece that will add beauty and refinement to the finest of home decoration.

1931

$75.00

$70.00

$75.00

$75.00

$72.00

Distinction marks every line of this entrancing time-piece of imported Argentine onyx in a symphony of green colors. An efficient movement in keeping with the beauty of the case will eliminate eternally the uncertainty of telling correct time. Manufactured under HAMMOND patents. Height 8", base 6", dial 3½".
K393+1..................................**$57.00**
Equipped with the same movement and of the same onyx. Just a little smaller. Height 7", base 6", dial 3½".
K393+2..................................**$51.00**

Here is a design that is most unusual. It is modern, but conservative enough to harmonize with other home-furnishings. The metal work is all finished in aranium, the beautiful plate that does not tarnish. In contrast, the base and inlay are of genuine ebony Catalin. Width 11⅛", height 9⅞", depth 3¾".
..................................**$83.20**

Imported green Argentine onyx is used in this modern timepiece which will enchant your guests with its beauty and impress them with its accurate timekeeping. The movement is manufactured under the HAMMOND patents, will bring correct time to the second. Height 8", base 7", dial 3½".
K393+4..................................**$72.00**
For the small apartment, this clock of same design and onyx as that above. Height 7", base 6", dial 3½".
K393+5..................................**$51.00**

$75.00

$40.00

$40.00

One of the most attractive boudoir clocks you can buy. The cloisonne enamel finish comes in any one of three pastel shades of Rose, green or turquoise. Width 6¼", height 4¾", depth 3".
K393+6 Rose.........................**$28.80**
K393+7 Green.........................**28.80**
K393+8 Turquoise.....................**28.80**

"Chic" is the word to describe this modern case of unusually fine black and gold marble with inlays of imported Argentine onyx and contrasting Arizona white. Height 8", width 7¾", dial 3½".
K393+9..................................**$67.50**

An unusual boudoir clock. The edges of these clocks are silver plated outlined with a black stripe. The dials are beautifully etched in two tones of silver and the second is gold finished. Width 5", height 5½", depth 3".
K393+10 Rose.........................**$25.60**
K393+11 Green.........................**25.60**
K393+12 Turquoise....................**25.60**

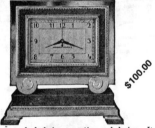

$100.00

$150.00

$85.00

A very unusual clock in conception and design. It is entirely different from anything that has ever been produced. Frankly, it will appeal to those people who have unusual decorative schemes and want clocks for particular settings and purposes. The metal work is finished in aranium, the plate that does not tarnish. The beauty of this clock is enhanced by trimmings of genuine catalin in either jade or onyx. Height 9¾", depth 3½", width 9¾" dial 5½"x3¾".
K393+13 Jade catalin...............**$73.50**
K393+14 Onyx catalin...............**73.50**

Without a doubt, this is one of the most handsome clocks on the market today. It makes an ideal mantel clock or it can be used on a table or in many other places. The case is of mahogany with a beautiful inlay of curly maple. There is an aranium bezel and the dial is silvered. Width 17", height 9", depth 5¼".
K393+17..................................**$44.80**

$40.00

$85.00

This clock appeals because of its dignified simplicity of design. It can be used in nearly any setting in the living room or library. The case is finished in mahogany. The bezel is aranium and the dial is silvered. Height 6½", depth 4⅛".
K393+18..................................**$38.40**

This clock is made so that it is not necessary to remove it from the wall to either set or start off. No. K393+15 has panels of ebony catalin above and below the dial, the same material is also used for the pendant. The metal parts are aranium plated, the plate that does not tarnish. No. K393+16 is finished in antique gold and is a very beautiful clock for either the dining room or living room. Height 19¼", depth 2¾", width 6", dial 4".
K393+15 Ebony Catalin...**$63.80**
K393+16 Antique Gold....**63.80**

A very distinctive design. The case is of mahogany with an inlay of curly maple. Solid cast brass bezel. Silver plated dial. Height 8", width 14¾", depth 4¾", dial 4¾".
K393+19..................................**$48.35**

Highly polished enamel cases in Rose, Green, Blue and Maise, encased either in gold or silver frames. 30-hour American movements.

ENAMELED SESSIONS

1928

$70.00

$50.00

$50.00

GOTHIC ON SWINGING EASEL
Size 6¼"x6"
No. 106. Silver.............$8.00
No. 206. Gold..............$8.00

GOTHIC
Size 5½"x4" White Enamel Frame.
No. 10. Gold Border...........$6.00
No. 20. Enamel Border.........$6.00

GOTHIC
Size 5½"x4"
No. 101. Silver.............$6.00
No. 201. Gold..............$6.00

$50.00

$70.00

$50.00

OCTAGON
Size 4½"x4½"
No. 103. Silver.............$6.00
No. 203. Gold..............$6.00

OCTAGON ON SWINGING EASEL
Size 5¾"x6"
No. 104. Silver.............$8.00
No. 204. Gold..............$8.00

OVAL
Size 3¾"x5"
No. 100. Silver.............$6.00
No. 200. Gold..............$6.00

"CAP-MAID" ASSORTMENT

ases furnished in Red, Green, Gray, Tan and Mottled Ivory. Movements 1-day. Silver Dial.

$35.00

$35.00

$35.00

No. 95. CUT CORNERS
Size 4¼"x6"
Price.........................$8.00

No. 95. OCTAGON
Size 4¼"x6"
Price.........................$8.00

No. 95. GOTHIC
Size 4¼"x6"
Price.........................$8.00

PRICES SHOWN ON THIS PAGE ARE KEYSTONE

$120.00

1928

High Grade Imported Clocks in French Cloisonne Enamel Cases. These Clocks represent the finest movements and best workmanship. They are truly works of art.

No. 8630......................$90.00
Size, 4⅜"x4½".
8 Day, 15 Jewel Movement.
Gilt Radium Dial.
Delicate Light Blue Cloisonne Enamel Frame with White Enamel Lined Border.
Floral Decorated.

$75.00

No. 8710......................$72.00
Size, 3¾"x3¾".
8 Day, 15 Jewel. Gilt Radium Dial.
Furnished in either delicate rose pink or light blue Cloisonne Enamel Frame.

$25.00

No. 5133.
8 Day, 6 Jewel..........$20.00
8 Day, 15 Jewel.......... 24.00
Size, 2¾"x2¾".
Gilt Luminous Dial and Frame.
Can be furnished in octagon, square, up tonneau or down tonneau.

$75.00

No. 8707......................$72.00
8 Day, 15 Jewel. Gilt Radium Dial.
Furnished in either delicate rose pink or light blue Cloisonne Enamel Frame.

HIGH GRADE IMPORTED CLOCKS WITH ALARMS

Jeweled Movements

$55.00

No. 180..............$15.00
Size, 3⅞"x4⅝".
1 Day Alarm Movement.
Square Gilt Dial. Inlaid French Briar Case.

$65.00

No. 164..................$19.80
Size, 3⅞"x7½".
1 Day Alarm Movement.
Square Dial. Inlaid French Briar Case.

$25.00

No. 168..........$17.20
Size, 3"x4⅜".
1 Day Alarm Movement.
Square Dial. French Grey Marble Case.

Jeweled Movements. Radium Dials

1928

No. 7/700. 1 Day Alarm........$9.00
Size, 2¾"x2½".
Jeweled Movements.
Furnished in Black, Copper, Green, Peach,
White, Violet and Gilt Cases.

No. 7/97. 1 Day Alarm........$8.40
Size, 3½"x2½".
Jeweled Movements.
Furnished in Green, Peach, Violet and
Burgundy and Copper Cases.

No. 4/114. 1 Day Alarm......$12.50
Size, 3½"x2¼".
Jeweled Movements.
Furnished in Royal Copper Case only.

No. 4/75. 1 Day Alarm........$11.40
Size, 2"x4".
Furnished in Black or Royal Copper Cases.

No. 7608.............$24.00
Height, 2⅞"; width, 2½".
A beautifully enameled boudoir clock fitted with
alarm. Furnished in Green, Blue, Black and
White color combinations. Two-inch gilt radium
dial and hands.

No. 4274.............$15.70
Height, 3"; width, 3½".
Made of a composition metal gilded and inlaid
in delicate combinations of enamel—Green
and Black, Blue and Black, Rose and Gold,
Black and White. Oval embossed dial with
radium numerals and hands, with enclosed
alarm.

HIGH GRADE IMPORTED
TRAVELING CLOCKS
IN FINE LEATHER FOLDING CASES.

Six and Fifteen Jewel Movements.

Gold Finish Screw Bezel. Bevel Glass, 2⅛" diameter.

Gold Radium Dials and Hands.

No. 4122. SQUARE

	1 Day 6 Jewel Movement	8 Day 6 Jewel Movement	8 Day 15 Jewel Movement
Black Sheepskin...................	$16.00	$18.90	$34.00
Colored Sheepskin, tooled border Rose, Blue, Helio, Tan, Brown and Green.	16.80	19.70	35.00
Colored Ecrase, tooled border, above colors	20.70	23.50	39.00

SAME CASES AS ABOVE WITH ALARM
1 Day Six Jewel Alarm Movement, add $6.20 list
to 1 Day Six Jewel Prices.
8 Day Fifteen Jewel Movement, add $27.00 list
to 1 Day Six Jewel Prices.

No. 4293. CUT CORNER
(Also made Cushion and Tonneau Shape)

	1 Day 6 Jewel Movement	8 Day 6 Jewel Movement Engine Turned Dial with Raised Minute Circle	8 Day 15 Jewel Octavia Movement
Colored Sheepskin, tooled border Rose Blue, Helio, Tan, Brown and Green.	$18.00	$23.50	$36.00
High Grade Ecrase Case, tooled border in above colors..................	24.00	29.50	42.00
Genuine Ostrich, Pinseal, or Tapir Cases	31.00	36.50	49.50

8 Day Fifteen Jewel Alarm Movement fitted to above cases,
add $27.00 list to 1 Day Six Jewel Price.

PRICES SHOWN ON THIS PAGE ARE KEYSTONE

High Grade Imperial Electric Clocks
Salient Features

24 hours reserve power in case of current interruption. Will operate on any alternating current from 40 to 70 cycles, 110 volts, Will operate equally well on either synchronized current or current that is not synchronized. Full jeweled compensated escapement, exceptionally accurate in time keeping. Escapement has micrometric adjustment. This provides for accurate and definite adjustment if necessary. Clock will run equally well in any position.

ALL OF THESE CLOCKS ALSO MADE FOR DIRECT CURRENT WITHOUT STRIKING MECHANISM

Movement consists of highest grade compensated marine escapement, milled wheels throughout, burnished and polished pivots, cut pinions with polished leaves, extra heavy plates, entire movement accurately made.

STRIKING ALTERNATING CURRENT CLOCKS

Strikes the hours and half hours on two chime rods. Hands can be moved backward or forward without getting the striking mechanism out of order. Movement decidedly simple in construction, consisting of 2 small motors, one of which controls time indicating mechanism, and the other controlling the striking mechanism. Very simple to install by attaching to any light socket and set the hands.

$175.00

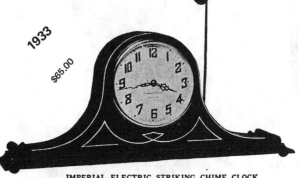

1933

$65.00

$60.00

$275.00

IMPERIAL ELECTRIC STRIKING CHIME CLOCK
Mahogany Cabinet—Ivoroid Inlaid

Width 22 inches, height 9¾ inches, depth 4 inches. 7 inch silvered dial convexed with raised bronze numerals, convex glass, serpentine hands. Case constructed of mahogany, finished with lacquer and rubbed. Inlay of ivoroid in front panel and along edge of the contour of front of case. Movement consists of high grade full jeweled marine escapement, compensated for temperature changes and other technical errors. All wheels are milled, all pivots are burnished and polished, all pinions are cut and pinion leaves polished, heavy brass plates. Strikes the hours and half hours on 2 chime rods. 24 hours reserve power, hands can be turned back or forward.

No. K8K200 Each **$45.00**

IMPERIAL ELECTRIC STRIKING CHIME CLOCK
Gothic Design Nicaraguan Mahogany Cabinet

15½ inches high, 11½ inches wide, 4 inches deep. 7 inch silvered dial, convexed with raised bronze numerals, convex glass, serpentine hands. Case constructed of Nicaraguan mahogany, finished with lacquer, rubbed and polished. Movement consists of high grade, full jeweled marine escapement, compensated for temperature changes and other technical errors. All wheels are milled, all pivots are burnished and polished, all pinions are cut and pinion leaves polished, heavy brass plates. Strikes the hours and half hours on 2 chime rods. 24 hours reserve power. Hands can be turned back or forward.

No. K8K204 Each.....................**$40.00**

IMPERIAL ELECTRIC STRIKING CHIME CLOCK
Banjo Mahogany Cabinet

Height 37 inches. 7 inch silvered dial, convexed, raised bronze numerals, serpentine hands, convexed glass. Case finished in Mahogany, trimmings of polished brass. Lacquer finish and rubbed. Movement consists of high grade, full jeweled marine escapement, compensated for temperature changes and other technical errors. All wheels are milled, all pivots are burnished and polished, cut pinions and pinion leaves, polished, heavy brass plates. Strikes the hours and half hours on 2 chime rods. 24 hours reserve power, hands can be turned back or forward.

No. K8K206 Each....................**$50.00**

IMPERIAL ELECTRIC STRIKING CHIME CLOCK
Mahogany Cabinet—Lacquered and Rubbed

Width 22 inches, height 9¾ inches, depth 4 inches, 7 inch silvered dial convexed with raised bronze numerals, convex glass, serpentine hands. Case constructed of mahogany, finished with lacquer and rubbed. Movement consists of high grade, full jeweled marine escapement, compensated for temperature changes and other technical errors. All wheels are milled, all pivots are burnished and polished, cut pinions and pinion leaves, polished heavy brass plates. Strikes the hours and half hours on 2 chime rods. 24 hours reserve power. Hands can be turned back or forward.

No. K8K202 Each...**$40.00**

Walnut . . $75.00
White . . 60.00

Walnut . $85.00
White . . 60.00

Walnut . . $75.00
White . . 60.00

IMPERIAL ELECTRIC WALL CLOCK
Specify Alternating or Direct Current
Choice of Walnut or White Enameled Octagon Cabinets

14¾ inches in diameter, 3¾ inches deep. White zinc dial 12 inches in diameter. Black Arabic numerals, new principles of case construction, finished in Walnut or White **convex glass.** Hinged door opens from front, not necessary to take clock from wall to get at hands. Movement consists of highest grade, full jeweled escapement, compensated against temperature changes and other technical errors. Milled wheels, burnished and polished pivots and pinion leaves, extra heavy brass plates. Clock has 24 hours reserve power. Escapement has micrometric adjustment. A well balanced design and a very accurate clock.

No. K8K58WF Walnut, Each **$38.80**
No. K8K58EF White Enamel, Each...........**38.80**

IMPERIAL ELECTRIC WALL CLOCK
Specify Alternating or Direct Current
Choice of Walnut or White Enameled Square Cabinets

16½ inches square, 3¾ inches deep. 14 inches square white zinc dial, black Arabic numerals. Case especially well constructed, finished in Walnut or White. Hinged door opens from front, not necessary to take clock from wall to get at hands. Movement consists of highest grade, full jeweled escapement. Compensated against temperature changes and other technical errors. Escapement equipped with micrometric adjustment. Movement has all milled wheels, burnished and polished pivots and pinion leaves, extra heavy brass plates. Clock has 24 hours reserve power. New detail in design and a very accurate time keeper.

No. K8K59WF Walnut, Each **$35.45**
No. K8K59EF White Enamel, Each...........**35.45**

IMPERIAL ELECTRIC WALL CLOCK
Specify Alternating or Direct Current
Choice of Walnut or White Enameled Square Cabinets

14¾ inches square, 3¾ inches deep. White zinc dial, 12 inches in diameter. Black Arabic numerals. Case is well constructed, mitred door finished in Walnut or White. Walnut cases have three slightly varying shades of color, **convex glass.** Hinged door opens from front, not necessary to take clock from wall to get at hands. Movement consists of highest grade, full jeweled escapement, compensated against temperature changes and other technical errors. Milled wheels, burnished and polished pivots and pinion leaves, extra heavy brass plates. Clock has reserve power of 24 hours. Escapement has micrometric adjustment. A well appointed design and a very accurate clock.

No. K8K57WF Walnut, Each.................**$35.45**
No. K8K57EF White Enamel, Each...........**35.45**

Low Priced Quality "USA-LITE" Electric Clocks

Every "Usalite" model is a fast selling original design which cannot be compared with anything on the market. The cases of these clocks are made of heavy sculptor's Duralloy metal. This extraordinary durable alloy prepared according to a special formulae is chip, crack and break resisting throughout the years and retains its fine firm texture and luster and is not to be confused with cheap substitutes which soon disintegrate. The original of every Duralloy case is sculptored by hand. Every duplicate, thereafter is actually hand finished which is why the cheap mechanical appearance is entirely absent.

"Usalite" electric clocks have low speed motors, about one half the speed of the average motor assuring about triple the average life. Full floating, jar-proof suspension; triple-life lubrication; multi-test inspection.

All "Usalite" clocks are fully guaranteed by the manufacturer, back of which stands 25 years of unquestionable reliability.

USALITE TRADE MARK

1933

$40.00

"HAMPTON" ELECTRIC ALARM

Modernized Gothic type, finished in jeweled Gold, with touches of ruby, turquoise and similar colors at appropriately ornamental points. Fitted with re-call alarm, a pleasant, cheery, melodious, wake-up note. Satin silver finished dial 3⅜ inches. Height 5¾ inches; width 6⅜ inches.

No. K705A With Alarm, Each................**$4.40**

$15.00

"WALDORF" ELECTRIC KITCHEN OR WALL CLOCK

(Choice of Ivory or Jade Green Colors)

Here is a real departure in wall clock silhouettes. This clock has a closed back and is notched for electric cord and has invisible wall hanger. Beetle case finished in Ivory or Jade Green. Height 7 inches. Width 7 inches. White dial 4½ inches, with light blue minute circle, convex glass. The breakfast nook or kitchen needs a practical dirt resisting easily readable timepiece. Priced very low.

No. K720V Ivory, Each **$3.95**
No. K720G Jade Green, Each.. **3.95**

$40.00

"MALBOURNE" ELECTRIC ALARM

Modernized Roman type, heavy sculptor's duralloy metal case. Finished in jeweled Gold with touches of ruby, turquoise and other attractive colors at appropriately ornamental points. Height 6⅝ inches; width 5½ inches. Satin silver finished 3⅜-inch dial. Fitted with re-call alarm, which rings intermittently, until shut off.

No. K707A With Alarm, Each................**$4.40**

$100.00

"TOWER" ELECTRIC TIME

Modernistic type, heavy sculptor's duralloy metal case. Finished in frosted silver with panels of solid black with inlay effect. Height 9 inches; width 5 inches. Satin silver finished 3⅜-inch dial. An ideal gift, prize or trophy.

No. K704 Electric Time only, Each..**$5.00**

$100.00

"BEN HUR" CHARIOT ELECTRIC TIME

Mantel type, heavy sculptor's duralloy metal case finished in jeweled gold. Height 8¼ inches; length 16 inches; depth 2¼ inches. Dial 3⅜ inches. The Historic Ben Hur and His Chariot are the inspiration for this authentic reproduction in the form of an artistic and useful electric clock. Beautifully finished in jeweled Gold, it is truly a model which will enhance the appearance of any room. It is an exceptional value at this low price.

No. K740 Electric Time Only, Each....................................**$5.25**

$100.00

"ATLAS" ELECTRIC TIME

Art object type, heavy sculptor's duralloy metal case, finished in moss bronze (bronze with a deposit of moss green). Height 9⅜ inches; width 4¾ inches. Satin silver finished 3⅜-inch dial. An artistically rendered replica of the original classic statue of Atlas supporting the earth on his neck and shoulders. Appropriate in any room, particularly suited to the den or library.

No. K700 Electric Time Only, Each..**$5.25**

$150.00

"ART-GLO" ELECTRIC TIME

Indirect lighting type. Rose floodlight behind figure. White light illuminating dial. Heavy sculptor's duralloy metal case, finished in antique and hammered silver with pearl jade figure. Height 10⅜ inches; width 5¼ inches. A genuine work of art with an added lighting function. A switch operates a soft white light which makes the dial visible in a dark room, also floods supporting panel and figure with a diffused rose colored light. Satin silver finished 3⅜-inch dial.

No. K716 Electric Time Only, Each..**$8.90**

$40.00

"MANTELA" ELECTRIC TIME

Modern Gothic mantel type, heavy sculptor's duralloy metal case, finished in moss bronze. Height 6⅝ inches; width 12⅜ inches; depth 3⅜ inches. Rich brushed silver finished dial, 4⅛ inches with etched frosted center. A genteel adaption of the gothic motif with a touch of the modern. A real household clock of impressive dignity and imposing beauty.

No. K701 Electric Time, only, Each....................................**$5.90**

$40.00

"NITE-GLO" ELECTRIC TIME

Boudoir Night Lamp Clock, heavy sculptor's duralloy metal case, finished in turquoise blue with decorative engravings in silver. White glass lamp bed. Height 6 inches; width 5½ inches; depth 5½ inches. Satin silver finished 3¾ inch dial. Domed crystal. The very essence of modernism is this space-saving, simple and compelling model, which not only tells time but tells it in a dark room. The lamp, which can be switched on or off, shines through the white glass-top base, bathing the face of clock with a soft light with sufficient diffusion to serve as a night light.

No. K715 Electric Time Only, Each..**$6.75**

Guaranteed U.S.A. Gov't. Time from your LITE socket

Electric Clocks in Marble and Onyx

Electric clock with beautiful marble cases. All marble and onyx used on these clocks is of the finest grade, is highly polished and perfectly fitte. They create the impression of stability and permanence and their beauty leaves nothing to be desired. They will grace any room and can be used any modern home. Fitted with Hammond electric movements which are nationally advertised, are thoroughly dependable and will furnish the accura time to the second.

$100.00

1933

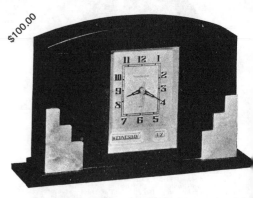

$100.00

A beautiful case of modern design of delicately grained imported onyx trimmed with Italian black and gold marble. Beautifully polished and perfectly matched. Diameter 9 inches, height 7½ inches. Fitted with electric calendar movement, silver dial, plain center with sun-ray edges and raised black enameled figures. In addition to the time, it gives you the day and date.

No. F61W59. Each $31.90

> *The clock units are of the synchronous electric type, manufactured and guaranteed by the Hammond Clock Company.*
>
> **Models are designed to operate on 60 cycle alternating current,** where such current is regulated by a master clock. If in doubt whether or not your power company supplies time service for synchronous clocks, phone them. Special models can be supplied for 50 cycle current without additional cost. Unless specified 60 cycle will be furnished.

A modern design in perfect proportion. Made of hig ly polished jet black Belguim marble with front orn ment of delicately veined white onyx. Diameter of ba 11¾ inches, height 7½ inches. Fitted with the celebrate Hammond calendar movement, silver dial, plain cent with sun-ray edges and raised black figures.

No. F61W63. Each $31.4

$125.00

$120.00

An unusually modern design beautifully executed. A combination of Italian black and gold marble with highly polished delicately veined white onyx. An artist's conception of a beautiful case perfectly matched and fitted. Diameter of base 8 inches, height 7¾ inches. Fitted with a Hammond calendar movement with buff colored dial, plain center, Sun Ray edges and raised black figures.

No. F61W60. Each $35.65

Marble Desk Set. A modern design case of fine Italian black and gold marble beautifully polished with white onyx trimming. The large base with space fo pens, pen holders, pins, etc., is also of Italian black and gold marble and figure on the front are in gilt finish. Fitted with Hammond electric calendar movemen buff dial, plain center with Sun Ray edges and raised black enamel figures. Diam eter of base 11 inches, width 7 inches, height 7 inches.

No. F61W61. As illustrated. Each $47.8

Same as above but fitted with two Wahl Lifetime pens in sockets with ba attachments permitting them to be placed in any position.

No. F61W62. Each $60.6

A black and white marble case, the simplicity and beauty of which has an almost irresistible appeal and will keep the pride of ownership fresh for years. Case is made of highly polished Belgium jet black marble with four bars of delicately veined white onyx. Width 12 inches, depth, 3¾ inches, height 7¼ inches. Fitted with Hammond electric movement, silver dial, raised gold figures, convex glass with gilt sash.

No. F61W57. Each $30.85

$125.00

$100.00

A massive case of pleasing design, highly polished gold and black Italian marbl with two white bars of delicately veined white onyx on front. Width 18½ inches, depth, 3¾ inches, height, 8¾ inches. Fitted with Hammond electri movement, silver dial, raised gold figures, convex glass with gilt sash.

No. F61W58. Each $41.50

Electric clock sets with cabinets of fine selected imported marble and onyx. Beautifully matched sets, perfectly fitted which are gorgeous in appearance and besides beauty the pride of ownership is permanent and the clocks with the dependable Hammond electric motors will deliver accurate time to the second, leaving nothing to be desired.

The clock units are of the synchronous electric type, manufactured and guaranteed by the Hammond Clock Company. All models are designed to operate on 60 cycle alternating current, where such current is regulated by a master clock. If in doubt whether or not your power company supplies time service for synchronous clocks phone them. Special models can be supplied for 50 cycle current without additional cost. Unless specified 60 cycle will be furnished.

1933

Clock .. $125.00
Set 150.00

No. F61W51 Clock Set

A combination of highly polished Italian black and gold marble and onyx. Base of selected green and white onyx, center of clock case Italian black and gold marble with side ornaments of alternate white delicately veined onyx and gold Italian marble. Hammond electric movement, dial silver, gold figures, convex glass with gilt sash. Two beautiful side ornaments to match. Diameter of clock base 11 inches, height 6½ inches. Height of ornaments 5¾ inches.

No. F61W51. 3-piece Set as Illustrated $44.70

No. F61W52. Clock only (without side ornaments). Each........ 30.85

An artistic production of a modern design made of a combination of Italian black and gold and selected white and green onyx. Base of black and gold Italian marble, center of beautiful veined white onyx sides of onyx to match center with panels of deep sea green onyx and black and gold Italian marble. Width of base 9 inches. Height 6¼ inches. Two side ornaments to match. Height 5¾ inches. Hammond electric movements, silver dial, raised gold figures, convex glass with gilt sash.

No. F61W55. 3-piece Set as Illustrated $47.85

No. F61W56. Clock only (without side ornaments). Each........ 35.10

Clock .. $125.00
Set 150.00

No. F61W55 Clock Set.

Clock .. $125.00
Set 150.00

No. F61W53 Clock Set.

A new design combining the always popular Doric in subdued pattern with modern trimmings. The center of delicately veined highly polished white onyx. Larger side pieces and front center ornaments of beautifully selected green finely figured onyx with end pieces and small front ornament of black and gold Italian marble. The movement is of the dependable Hammond make with silver dial, raised gold figures, convex glass and gilt sash. Width of base 8¾ inches, height 8½ inches. Height of side ornaments 6½ inches.

No. F61W53. 3-piece Set as Illustrated $51.05

No. F61W54. Clock only (without side ornaments). Each........ 37.25

$75.00

Bring higher price as decorator.

$75.00

Like fleecy clouds lazily floating over mirrored waters of cool sea green, such is the picture reflected in the genuine green Brazilian onyx of this all-electric clock. Its center layer and side ornaments are of black and gold marble. Unconsciously all eyes will be turned to this clock wherever it is placed. It brings accurate, split second time over the wires from the observatory. Height, 6¼ inches; width, 12¾ inches.

No. F60W640. Each..................................$44.70

Some mantle or executive office will be made more beautiful with the addition of this remarkably accurate, all electric clock to the room. Misty waves of white seem to float in sea green waters, for such is the color of the Brazilian onyx of which this clock is so exquisitely adorned. Genuine black and gold marble adds its beauty to the piece. Height, 6¾ inches; width, 13⅜ inches.

No. F60W641. Each..................................$58.50

Clocks

Presenting Crystal Vue and Mirror Vue Clocks that are keyed to the 1936 fashion trend. Movements are made by the New Haven Clock Company—fine timepieces which will keep excellent time with reasonable care.

Prices subject to Catalog Discount

Prices subject to change without notice

1936

30-Hr. Mirror Clock

CC600 - - - - - $12.00

Crystal Glass Base and Dial with circle mirror in center and straight modernistic engraved mirror stick numerals. Chromium finished hands and housing. Height, 5¾" Diameter of Dial, 4¾", Base, 4¾" x 2½".

40-Hr. Mirror Clock

CC601 - - - - - $9.50

Crystal Glass Base and Dial with circle mirror in center; twelve mirrored modernistic time numerals. Chromium finished hands and housing. Height, 4½"; Diameter of Dial, 4"; Base, 4¼" x 2½".

30-Hr. Mirror Clock

CC602 - - - - - $12.00

Circle mirror in center and twelve blue time numerals on flat mirrored circles; oval ½" blue mirrored crystal plate glass base with felt protection. Chromium finished hands and housing. Height, 5¼"; Diameter of Dial, 4¾"; Base, 4¾" x 3⅜".

30-Hr. Mirror Clock

CC603 - - - - - $11.40

Crystal Glass Base and Dial with circle mirror in center and twelve blue time numerals on flat mirrored circles. Chromium finished hands and housing. Height, 5¾"; Diameter of Dial, 4¾"; Base 5" x 2½".

30-Hr. Mirror Clock

CC604 - - - - - $7.50

Square Crystal Glass Clock with easel back; square silver center mirror and modernistic silver mirrored time numerals. Chromium finished easel-back, hands and housing. Size 5" x 5".

30-Hr. Mirror Clock

CC605 - - - - - $10.70

Crystal Glass Base and Dial with circle mirror in center and twelve mirrored, modernistic time numerals. Chromium finished hands and housing. Height, 5½"; Diameter of Dial, 4¾"; Base, 5" x 2⅜".

Sessions

"Nevel" Electric Alarm Clock

CC230 - - - - - $5.90

Mahogany or Maple Finish Case with metal band trimming; 3½ inch Raised Numeral Dial; Height, 5"; Width, 6". Manual starting alarm movement.

"Maxwell" Electric Time Clock

CC230½ - - - - - $3.70

Same case as above, with electric time movement.

"Sandra" Desk Clock

CC249 - - - - - $3.40

Wood Case with metal band trimming; 30-hour movement; 3½ inch Raised Numeral Dial. Height, 4¼"; Width, 5". Choice of Green, Ivory or Blue. May be used in the boudoir.

"Morgan" Electric Clock

CC250 - - - - - $3.70

Mahogany Finish Case with black moulding; 3½ inch Raised Numeral Dial; Height, 5¾"; Width, 5¾".

"Suffield" 8-Day Clock

CC251 - - - - - $5.40

Mahogany Finish Case with black moulding; 4 inch Raised Numeral Dial; Height, 5¼"; Width, 6¼".

"Sonus" Alarm Clock

CC252 - - - - - $4.30

Mahogany Finish Case with black moulding; 3½ inch Silvered Dial; 30-hour lever alarm; Height, 5¼"; Width, 6¼".

SMARTLY STYLED MIRROR CLOCKS

1938

The newest vogue in fine clocks. Beautifully polished plate glass with blue mirror finish. Accurate and dependable movements made by leading American manufacturers. Fully guaranteed. Electric movements for use on alternating current only. 60 cycles. 110 to 120 volts.

$50.00

$75.00

$60.00

GC7748 Electric Movement....... **$9.40**
The popular square shape with a New Haven electric movement. Blue mirror glass with a bevelled edge securely held to rectangular base by 2 chromium plated fittings. Numeral dial. Height 5 inches. Base 2½ x 5½ inches.

GC7749 New Haven Electric Movement....................... **$17.50**
A handsome new style in the popular mirror clock. Square blue mirror glass center securely attached to base by two chromium plated fittings. Heavy rectangular glass base with bevelled edge. Chromium plated posts with ball tops. Height 4¾ inches. Length of base 7½ inches, width, 2½ inches.

GC7750 Electric Alarm........... **$14.20**
A distinctive clock equipped with an alarm which increases its usefulness. Open dial with a combination of numeral and hour indicators on a frosted circle. Hammond electric alarm movement. Blue mirror glass. Height 6¼ inches. Oval base 3⅞ x 5⅜ inches.

$30.00

$50.00

$30.00

GC7751 Carrara Glass Electric Clock........... **$21.00**
The latest style in a fine clock. An attractive combination of heavy black and white Carrara glass. Beautiful highly polished finish. Effective gold and white colored dial, diameter 4 inches. Hammond electric movement. Height 6⅝ inches. Length of base 7¾ inches, width 3 inches.

GC7752 Waltham Electric Movement....... **$28.30**
One of the prettiest clocks we have seen. Heavy crystal clear glass with bevelled edge. Effective recessed center, open face, with modern numerals on a frosted circle. Upper part securely attached to base by two chromium plated fittings. Waltham electric self-starting movement. Height 5¼ inches. Size of base 5½ x 2½ inches.

GC7753 Carrara Glass Electric Clock.... **$18.00**
Another style in the modern Carrara glass clocks. Beautiful highly polished combination of black and ivory. Effective gold and white colored dial, diameter 3¾ inches. Hammond self-starting electric movement. Height 6⅛ inches. Length of base 6¼ inches, width 3 inches.

$65.00

$50.00

GC7754 Spring Wound.. **$16.30**
Accurate 8 day spring movement, made by Lux.
GC7755 Electric.................................... **17.20**
Waltham self-starting electric movement.
A smartly designed clock of unusual shape. Open dial with a combination of numeral and hour indicators on a frosted circle. Substantial blue mirror glass securely held by 2 chromium plated fittings. Bevelled edge blue glass base, 2½ x 7 inches. Height 6 inches.

GC7756 New Haven Electric Movement....................... **$12.80**
An effective combination of blue mirror glass and crystal. The open faced dial, diameter 4 inches, has white numerals and the frame has an etched line design. The upper part is securely attached to the step design base by two chromium fittings. Height 5½ inches. Length of base 8 inches. Width 2½ inches.

L.&C.MAYERS CO. FIFTH AVE., NEW YORK

EC616—Mirror Clock—$9.40

Simple and distinctive in design, this 4" Sq. Open Face Mirror Clock with its Modernistic Lettering will add an attractive note to any room. Eight-day Lux movement. Easel-back. Key Wind. Colors—blue, and Champagne.

$35.00

1938

$50.00

EC617—Elec. Mirror Clock—$8.70

Very new! Very modern! This Round Easel-back Clock has a 6" diameter and comes in Blue and Green. Hammond Movement.

$40.00

EC618—Electric Crystal Clock—$14.90

This handsome Electric Clock mounted on a heavy crystal block has a sturdy appearance, particularly pleasing to men. Size—4½" high by 5½" long. New Haven movement. Available in Crystal with Chromium Numerals.

EC626—Phantom Clock—$7.50

Made in a distinctive style of die-cast Chrome combined with a plated dial. Size is 10" x 10¼". Dial plate available in Black or Blue. 8 day wind movement.

$50.00

EC1014—Elec. Mirror Clock—$15.90

An unusually handsome model with its Open Glass Face and Glass Base. Self-starting Electric Waltham movement. Diameter 6", Height 6¼", Length of Base, 5¼". Choice of Champagne or Blue with White Enamel Numeral Band and Hands, Chromium Sweep Minute Hand.

$50.00

$45.00

EC625—Stirrup Clock—$5.50

Chrome plated wind clock with solid walnut case and base. Height overall 6", width 4½". A beautifully styled timekeeper for the home and office.

$75.00

Send for Special
Literature on
Prize & Premium
Contest

EC620—Open-Face Glass Clock—$12.80

This unusual and handsome Clock has a Mirror Face and Base—available in Green and Champagne—in a Crystal Setting with Chromium Trimming. Measurements 6" high, 8" long. New Haven Electric Movement.

$50.00

EC619—Electric Crystal Clock—$28.40

The face of this Clock is sunken in a heavy Crystal Block, making an unusual and attractive design. Electric Waltham Movement. 5¼" high by 6" long. Available in Crystal.

1938

Styled for the best modern homes by outstanding artists. Fitted with fine electric movements by Waltham and Hammond. Use only on alternating current 110-120 volts, 60 cycle.

$60.00

$60.00

GC7768 Desk Set $34.00
Fine self-starting electric movement encased in gleaming chromium flanked by two fine Wahl fountain pens in chromium holders. Base is rare grained natural brown Macassar Ebony with gray Harewood inlay. Silver dial, black numerals. Height 5½ inches. Width 14 inches. Depth 6 inches. Retails for $25.00.

GC7769 Desk Set $48.00
Clock Case and Base of rare Macassar Ebony. Fine electric clock, thermometer and hygrometer. Automatic cigarette lighter, modern ash tray and fine Wahl fountain pen. Self-starting electric movement. Dials are silver with black numerals. Length 16 inches. Width 14 inches. Height 7 inches. Retails for $35.00.

$20.00

$200.00

$20.00

GC7770 Electric Alarm.......... $9.40
Case is knotty pine, antique finish. Silver dial with gold bezel. Combines beautifully with pine or maple furniture. Height 5 inches. Width 5 inches. Retails for $6.95.

GC7771 Westminster Chime Clock.................................. $54.00
This unusually beautiful clock has a maple burl base with natural finished mahogany and chrome composing the bezel surrounding the dial. Chrome ornaments. Silver dial, black numerals. Chimes each quarter hour. Height 9¼ inches. Width 17 inches. Depth 6 inches. Retails for $40.00.

GC7772 Electric Alarm.......... $8.10
Unique case of white holly and walnut woods. Silver dial, black numerals. Height 4¾ inches. Width 4¾ inches. Retails for $5.95.

$40.00

$20.00

$35.00

GC7773 Curved Desk Clock..................... $17.00
Macassar Ebony case. Sand color Micarta face. Self-starting electric movement. Silver dial, black numerals. Height 3¾ inches. Width 8¼ inches. Depth 4 inches. Retails for $12.50.

GC7774 Electric Alarm............. $10.20
Gleaming chrome frame, black base. Dial has black center, cream background. Height 6¼ inches. Width 6 inches. Depth 3 inches. Retails for $7.50.

GC7775 Fine Desk Clock..................... $13.50
East Indian Laurel wood, walnut color, case resting on chrome base. Self-starting electric movement. Silver dial, black numerals. Height 4¼ inches. Width 7¼ inches. Depth 2 inches. Retails for $10.00.

MODERN ELECTRIC CLOCKS

ONYX CLOCKS   NUMERAL CLOCKS   MIRROR CLOCKS

Smart up-to-the-minute clocks with movements from such reliable manufacturers as Waltham, New Haven, Sessions and Pennwood. Fully guaranteed. Electric clocks can be used on alternating current only, 60 cycles, 110 to 120 volts.

1938

GC7757 Pennwood Numeral Clock, without pens..................... $19.90
GC7757A Two 14 Kt. Green Pearl Moore Pens, as illustrated........ 6.00
A modernly styled clock that will add a note of distinction to any desk. Black finished plastic case and base with crystal clear Lucite vanes. Equipped with Parkette pen holders. Self-starting electric movement. Height 4¼ inches. Length of base 14½ inches, depth 4½ inches.

GC7758 New Haven Numeral Clock.................. $13.30
Smart—modern—practical. The large legible numerals fall in place automatically. Beautiful case of genuine natural mahogany with white holly trim. Ivory colored tabs with brown numerals. A handsome addition to the home or office. Length 7¾ inches. Height 3¾ inches. Depth 3¾ inches. Quiet self-starting electric motor.

GC7759 Pennwood Numeral Clock....... $29.00
The latest addition to the Pennwood line. A beautiful clock cased in mirror finished crystal plate glass with bevelled edges. Self-starting electric movement. Height 4 inches. Length 7 inches. Depth 3½ inches.

GC7760 Pennwood Numeral Clock....... $13.10
This handsome case of solid walnut, rubbed to a glossy finish, is very effective. This clock will add charm to any surroundings. Self-starting electric movement. Height 4 inches. Length 7¾ inches. Depth 3½ inches.

GC7761 Pennwood Numeral Clock........ $8.60
A smart low priced clock in the famous Pennwood line. Attractive plastic case of modern design. Walnut finish. Self-starting electric movement. Height 4 inches. Length 7¾ inches. Depth 4 inches.

GC7762 Mirror Clock................ $4.00
A dainty little blue mirror glass clock with bevelled edges. Etched line decorations. Popular rectangular shape. Easel back. Sessions 30 hour movement. Length 5 inches. Height 3½ inches. Excellent value.

GC7763 Electric Mirror Clock.................. $9.40
An attractive blue mirror glass clock with bevelled edges. New Haven electric movement. The upper part is securely attached to the modern step design base by chromium plated fittings. Height 4½ inches. Length of base 6½ inches. Depth 3 inches.

GC7764 Mirror Clock...................... $4.00
Distinctive half-moon shape. Blue mirror glass with bevelled edge. Easel back. Sessions 30 hour movement. Length 7 inches. Height 3½ inches. Excellent value.

GC7765 Brazilian Onyx Clock................ $31.50
A beautiful clock of genuine selected Brazilian green onyx with a lovely mottled effect. Hammond electric movement. Height 7½ inches. Length of base 8 inches. Depth 3 inches.

GC7766 Waltham Electric Clock..... $11.80
Modernly styled clock in a genuine walnut case with marquetry inlay. Rectangular base with triangular shaped upper part. Waltham self-starting electric movement. Height 6⅛ inches. Size of base 7⅞ x 4¾ inches.

GC7767 Brazilian Onyx Clock.............. $31.50
A very effective style. Case is genuine selected Brazilian green onyx with a charming matched effect. Hammond electric movement. Height 7 inches. Length of base 8 inches. Depth 3 inches.

1940 $75.00

 $100.00

No. 09666—MOGUL—A delightfully different mirror clock of exceptional beauty. In two of this season's best colors: silver mirror with black dial and silver etched numerals, or gold mirror with black dial and gold etched numerals. Height, 7¼ inches; width 12¾ inches. Silver Key wind ....Each **$14.40**
No. 09667—Same as above, Gold Key wind. ....Each **$14.40**

No. 09668—NAPOLEON—Handsome new design. Silver etched numerals on blue. Length, 15½ inches; height, 7 inches. Blue Key wind. ....Each **$21.60**

The best colors for Art Deco Clocks are-Peach, Blue, Black, Green, Smoke, and Crystal. In that order.

$75.00

$50.00

No. 09669—ARCHON—Smart, modern design, peach color base, gunmetal dial. Gold etched numerals with polished brass hands. Length, 11½ inches; height, 6½ inches. Electric........Each **$18.00**
No. 09670—Same as above, Key wind.........................Each **$18.00**

No. 09671—ROMAN—A modern black and mirror design, with white inlaid roman numerals, presenting a beautiful color contrast. Attractive finish, silver mirror with hands to match. Height, 7¼ inches; width, 6¾ inches. Silver Key wind. ....Each **$12.00**

$40.00

$25.00

$25.00

No. 09674—MERCURY—Beautiful, popular priced clock furnished in two excellent colors: crystal or green. Silver encrusted numerals with hands to match. Height, 5¾ inches; width, 5¼ inches. Crystal Electric ....Each **$9.60**
No. 09675—Same as above, Green Key wind ....Each **$9.60**

No. 09672 — BISHOP — Distinctly new shape. Modern gold encrusted black dial with hands to match. Gold mirror base. Height, 7 inches; width, 5¾ inches. Electric ....Each **$12.00**

No. 09673 — DIANA — A stunning, low priced small model clock, raised white opal dial on light blue. Black figures and hands to match. Height, 4¾ inches; width, 4¼ inches. Light Blue Key wind....Each **$9.00**

$75.00

No. 09640—Walnut case, faced with champagne glass. Two-tone champagne glass dial with covered hands and gold bezel ring. Size: 7½ inches wide by 6½ inches high. With Waltham Electric Self-Starting Movement ....Each **$20.00**

No. 09641—Same as above, with Seth Thomas 8-Day movement ....Each **$21.40**

NH 30 Hr. . . $25.00
NH Elec. . . . 15.00
Lux 80 . . . . 40.00

No. 09642—Champagne with black stripes, laminated. 4½ inches wide by 4¼ inches high, with New Haven 30-hour Spring Wound movement.
....................................Each **$8.00**

No. 09643 — Same as above, with New Haven Electric movement ....Each **$9.50**

No. 09644—Same as above, with Lux 8-Day movement.
....................................Each **$12.50**

$25.00

No. 09645—Walnut case, faced with champagne glass. Two-tone champagne glass dial with covered hands and gold bezel ring. 8 inches wide by 6 inches high. With Waltham Electric Self-Starting movement ....Each **$21.40**

No. 09646—Same as above, with Seth Thomas 8-Day movement ....Each **$22.70**

Seth Thomas,
New Haven and
Lux Movements.

1940

$40.00

No. 09649 — Agate color, two-tone dial with covered hands and gold bezel ring, 6 inches wide by 6 inches high. With Waltham Electric Self-Starting movement.
....................................Each **$21.40**

No. 09650 — Same as above, with Seth Thomas 8-Day movement..........Each **$22.40**

Radio, Desk and Boudoir Clocks.

Waltham . . $40.00
S.T. 8D. . . . 50.00

No. 09651—Agate color. Two-tone dial with covered hands and gold bezel ring. 7½ inches wide by 5½ inches high. With Waltham Electric Self-Starting movement.
....................................Each **$24.00**

No. 09652—Same as above, with Seth Thomas 8-Day movement ....Each **$25.50**

$40.00

No. 09647 — Agate color, covered hands with gold bezel. 5 inches wide by 4½ inches high. With New Haven Electric movement ....Each **$12.00**

No. 09648—Same as above, with Lux 8-Day movement ....Each **$14.70**

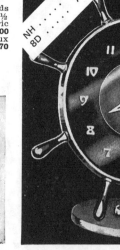

$25.00

No. 09653 — Walnut case, faced with champagne glass, 7 inches wide by 4½ inches high. With New Haven Electric movement ....Each **$14.70**

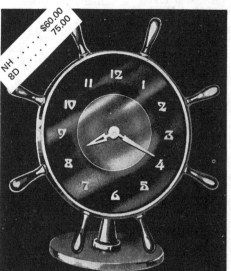

$60.00 . . . . . 75.00

NH 8D

No. 09654—Blue glass. Two-tone dial with covered hands, chromium plated finish. 6 inches wide by 6 inches high. With New Haven Electric movement ....Each **$12.00**

No. 09655—Same as above, with Lux 8-Day movement ....Each **$14.70**

$25.00

No. 09656 — Walnut case faced with champagne glass, covered hands with gold bezel ring, 4¾ inches wide by 4¾ inches high. With New Haven Electric movement ....Each **$8.00**

No. 09657—New and Distinctive Pilot Wheel Electric Clock. Pilot Wheel frame of natural wood finish. Smartly enhanced by the gilt handles. Guaranteed Electric movement, operating on A.C. current, 60 cycles, 110-120 volts. Attractive raised figured dial and sweep second hand. Overall diameter: 10½ inches....Each **$4.50**

$20.00

1940

$25.00

No. 09658 — Nautical Thermometer Electric Clock, natural wood case, gilt pilot wheel handles. Fitted with a guaranteed Electric Motor, operating on 60 cycles, 110-120 volts. Base: 12 inches. Height: 11¾ inches ....Each **$6.20**

$25.00

No. 09659—New Nautical Designed Mantel Clock. Case natural wood finish, smartly enhanced with strip of Marquetry inlay. Pilot Wheel handles in gilt. Guaranteed Electric movement operating on A.C. current, 60 cycles, 110-120 volts. Attractive raised figured dial, sweep second hand. Base: 18½ inches. Height: 11¾ inches. ....Each **$5.50**

$25.00

No. 09660—A Nautical Electric Clock, combining quality and beauty. Walnut finish wood case with contrasting brass handles on wheel. Fitted with guaranteed A.C. electrical movement. Attractive dial, red sweep second hand. Height: 10½ inches. Width: 11 inches. Cord and plug attached.........Each **$5.20**

$10.00

No. 09661—Attractive wood case Wall or Kitchen Clock finished in natural wood, red, green or ivory colors. Guaranteed A.C. motor, operating 60 cycles (110-120 volts). Base: 8¼ inches. Height: 6¾ inches ....Each **$4.20**

$20.00

No. 09662 — New Hanging Nautical Clock. Case natural wood finish, smartly enhanced by the gilt handles. Guaranteed Electric movement, operating A.C. current, 60 cycles, 110-120 volts. Raised figured dial and sweep second hand. Overall diameter: 10 inches. ....Each **$4.30**

$20.00

No. 09663—Chic in appearance this Radio or Desk Electric Clock. Case natural wood finish, highly polished, enhanced with Marquetry inlay. Motor thoroughly guaranteed. Base: 7¾ inches. Height: 6 inches. ....Each **$4.80**

$15.00

No. 09664 — Tambour Mantel Clock, richly polished natural wood finish or two-tone walnut finish. Guaranteed A.C. motor, operating 60 cycles (110-120 volts). Base: 17½ inches. Height: 6 inches..............Each **$4.50**

$25.00

No. 09665 — Electric Mantel Clock, richly polished natural wood, two-tone effect. Smart dial, sweep second hand. Guaranteed A.C. motor, operating 60 cycles, 110-120 volts. Base: 8 inches. Height: 8 inches. ....Each **$4.80**

$25.00

No. 09696—NEW HAVEN BOUDOIR No. 3 ALARM—Solid mahogany frame. Polished brass bezel. Etched, gold-color numerals. Polished brass hands. Unbreakable, convex crystal. Full-toned alarm bell. 30-hour movement—compensated for temperature changes. Size: 5 inches high; 6¾ inches wide ....Each **$4.60**

$15.00

No. 09697 — SPICA ELECTRIC ALARM CLOCK, NEW HAVEN—Ivory-colored beetleware clock of gay and refreshing appearance. Inlaid brass numerals and hour indicators. Metal dial. Fitted with a patented bell alarm not of the ordinary buzzer type. Height 5⅛ inches. Width 4½ inches ....Each **$4.50**

$35.00

No. 09698—NEW HAVEN IDEAL—Ivory color metal case with polished brass bezel. White metal dial with polished brass hands. Unbreakable, convex crystal. Full-toned alarm bell with top shut-off. 30-hour movement. Height, 4⅛ inches. Width, 5⅞ inches ....Each **$2.40**

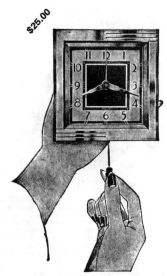

$25.00

1940

No. 09699 — NEW HAVEN "KEYLESS ARTLARM." Save your fingers, just pull to wind. No keys to turn. Easier to wind than your watch. Unusually soft tick. An entirely new idea—A Keyless Alarm Clock. A novel method of winding that eliminates the usual winding key—a few pulls on the cable and the time and alarm mechanisms are wound simultaneously. A new development in alarm clocks that will appeal to everyone. Smart simplicity. A sash of chromium-plate, with simple linear design, frames this modern, square clock. A large indicator conveniently sets the alarm from the center of the dial. 30-hour movement with full-toned alarm bell and top shut-off. A self-adjusting easel supports the clock at an angle which affords the best visibility. Size, 4½ x 4½ inches....Each **$3.90**

$25.00

No. 09700 — NEW HAVEN IDEAL JR. ALARM—A small attractive alarm clock that takes but one winding operation to wind both time and alarm mechanisms—winding the clock, automatically winds the alarm. Case of ivory-color metal with polished brass bezel. Ivory metal dial with polished brass hands and an unbreakable, convex crystal. Full-toned alarm bell sets from center of dial and has a top shut-off. 30-hour movement compensated for temperature changes. Height, 2⅞ inches. Width, 4 inches ....Each **$2.70**

$10.00

No. 09702—NEW HAVEN NEW AUTOMOBILE ELECTRIC CLOCK—Attaches to steering post. The dial is illuminated when the light switch is turned on. Will operate accurately on low voltage; dust-proof case, jeweled balance; effective illumination of dial ....Each **$10.80**

$35.00

No. 09701 — NEW HAVEN BICYCLE CLOCK—Slotted bracket attaches clock to bicycle by slipping under handlebar post bolt. Chrome, streamlined case. Visible aviation type dial. Unbreakable crystal. Stem wind, stem set 30-hour movement. Size: Width, 2 inches; height, 2½ inches; depth, 2⅛ inches ....Each **$2.60**

$15.00

No. 09703—LUX ROAMER TRAVELING CLOCK—A Utility Clock also suitable for desk or boudoir, but particularly the smallest and most suitable traveling companion—The square movement is enclosed in a nickel polished bezel and surrounded by a moulded frame which comes in colors red, green, blue or black. The collapsible bracket is a part of the frame itself and makes a very compact little unit. The metallic dial with elaborately designed gold numerals and red outlines adds to the attractiveness of the clock. Comes with unbreakable crystal. Size: Width, 2¾ inches; height, 3¼ inches..........Each **$3.30**
No. 09704—Same as above, with radium dial and numerals ....Each **$4.60**

$50.00

No. 09705—NEW HAVEN No. 90AV (GUNMETAL)—30-Hour Pull Wind movement with back-set. White and grey dial with black center panel and numerals. Selected, beveled-edge, plate glass, Convex mirror in non-glare gunmetal. Size: 2½ inches by 8 inches ....Each **$5.50**

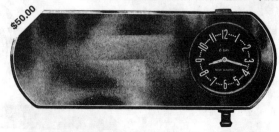

$50.00

No. 09706—NEW HAVEN No. 165AV (GUNMETAL)—8-Day Pull Wind movement with back-set. Black dial with white numerals and radium hands. Selected, non-glare Gunmetal plate glass mirror with beveled edges. Size: 2½ inches by 7 inches..............Each **$13.00**

$75.00

Archon

16HC686—8-Day - - - - - - - - $18.00
(Mfrs. Sug. Retail $15.00)

16HC687—New Haven Electric - - - - 16.80
(Mfrs. Sug. Retail $14.00)

A French design, in either mirrored gun metal face with peach colored base, or mirrored light blue face with dark blue base. Gold etched numerals with hands to match. Size 6½" x 11½". Specify color.

$40.00

Vassar

16HC695—8-Day - - - - - - - $10.80
(Mfrs. Sug. Retail $9.00)

Small modern clock with engraved design on mirror face. An occasional clock with a variety of uses. Size 5½" x 5". Colors: Silver, Aquamarine, Peach. Specify.

$50.00

16HC691—Cameo; 8-Day - - - - - - $13.20
(Mfrs. Sug. Retail $11.00)

An attractive Gothic styled mirrored mantel clock, with beautifully engraved design. Size 5¼" x 10½". Colors: Clear Crystal, Blue, or Rust. Specify.

We are Proud to Present this new and Colorful Selection of Distinctive Mirror Clocks.

Guaranteed Self-starting Electric movements for A.C. current. Eight-Day Clocks have Hershede Movements.

1941

$100.00

Statesman

16HC689—8-Day - - $19.20
(Mfrs. Sug. Retail $16.00)

16HC690—New Haven Electric - - 18.00
(Mfrs. Sug. Retail $15.00)

A distinctive gold mirrored clock with a black carara base. The Concave recesses contain legible black Roman numerals. Size 9" x 7½".

Convex Crystals enclose dials and hands of All Mirror Clocks.

Patented Friction Pins hold Glass in Place. Note absence of metal rims.

$100.00

Napoleon

16HC688—Electric - - - - - - - $18.00
(Mfrs. Sug. Retail $15.00)

A modern design in three pieces of mirrored dark blue or green glass. Silver etched numerals on blue, and gold on green, with hands to match. New Haven movement. Size 7" x 15½". Specify color.

$40.00

Eureka

16HC692—8-Day - - - - - $19.20
(Mfrs. Sug. Retail $16.00)

Perfect for desk or boudoir. A rectangular clock with black carara base. Neat dull-gold color finished brass ornaments and frame; gold bronze color dial. Size 5" x 7½". (Not a mirror clock.)

$40.00

Rhapsody

16HC693—Electric - - - - - $18.00
(Mfrs. Sug. Retail $15.00)

A delightful little boudoir or desk clock. Case is a combination of three mirrored glasses. Size 7" x 8⅝". New Haven movement. Colors: Peach or Blue. Specify.

$40.00

16HC694—Senator; 8-Day - - - - - - $14.40
(Mfrs. Sug. Retail $12.00)

A practical little clock with exquisite etched flower design on the mirror. Size 7¾" x 9". Colors: Silver or Blue. Specify.

$40.00

Monarch

16HC696—Electric - - - - - - - $12.00
(Mfrs. Sug. Retail $10.00)

Beautiful in its simplicity. This mirror clock has beveled edges, and is 6½" x 6¾" in size. Sessions self-starting movement. Colors: Burgundy, Peach or Blue. Specify.

New York   **BENNETT BROTHERS, Inc.**   Chicago

16HC1048—The Arcturus—$9.40
(Mfrs. Suggested Retail $7.95)
A well-designed self-starting electric clock of piano finish walnut. "Time at a Glance." Modern and appropriate in any setting. Pennwood movement. A.C. only. Size: 8½" wide, 4¼" high.

$10.00

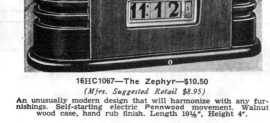

16HC1067—The Zephyr—$10.50
(Mfrs. Suggested Retail $8.95)
An unusually modern design that will harmonize with any furnishings. Self-starting electric Pennwood movement. Walnut wood case, hand rub finish. Length 10¼", Height 4".

$35.00

16HC707—Swank—$7.00
(Mfrs. Suggested Retail $5.95)
The "Up to the Minute" method of telling time. This clock comes in a modern Tenite case. Pennwood self-starting electric Numechron movement. Size 6" x 3⅝" x 3". Choice of Walnut or Ivory.

$10.00

16HC709—Petite—$4.10
(Mfrs. Suggested Retail $2.95)
A modern achievement in the art of time-telling. Self-starting electric Pennwood Numechron movement. Bakelite case, size 5½" x 3⅞" x 3⅜". Choice of Walnut or Black. Gold-color Base.

$10.00

1941

16HC1010—Cleopatra—$7.60
(Mfrs. Suggested Retail $5.50)
A Solid walnut clock richly styled with genuine Ebony, Rosewood, and Satinwood inlays. 4" gold color raised numeral dial. An ideal "Man's Clock." Sessions self-starting electric movement. Size 8" x 4½" x 6⅝". Appropriate for table, desk, mantel, shelf, or radio.

$20.00

16HC710—Moderne—$6.50
(Mfrs. Suggested Retail $4.95)
Pennwood Numechron self-starting electric clock. Irresistibly handsome case in Tenite with metal trim in polished gold-finish. Base dark red. Will give time accurate as the stars for years on end. Size 5⅝" x 3¾" x 3¼". Choice of Mottled Walnut or Ivory.

$10.00

16HC1028—Chatham—$8.20
(Mfrs. Suggested Retail $6.95)
A popular Pennwood self-starting electric clock that is beautifully and sedately designed, and will blend well with any background. Walnut wood case, hand rubbed finish. Size 7¾" x 4" x 3½".

$15.00

16HC384—Ideal Jr. Alarm—$2.66
(Mfrs. Suggested Retail $1.95)
The truly "ideal" alarm clock, with Ivory finished metal case, and dial, polished brass bezel and hands, unbreakable crystal. Alarm has front set, top shut-off, and winds simultaneously with time wind. New Haven 30-hour movement. Size 2⅞" x 4".

$25.00

Keyless 30 Hour Pull-Wind
16HC346 — — — — —**$4.18**
(Mfrs. Suggested Retail $3.25)
Chromium-plated case of simple linear design. Two-tone silvered dial. Clock is supported by self-adjusting easel. Subdued bell alarm. Size 4½" square, 2" deep. New Haven movement.

$25.00

16HC711—Topper—$5.60
(Mfrs. Suggested Retail $3.95)
Refined elegance. This infinitely practical clock comes in Tenite case, size 5¾" x 3⅝" x 3⅝", trimmed with base of polished gold-color metal. Self-starting Pennwood Numechron movement. Choice of Walnut or Ivory.

$10.00

16HC1043—The Gondolier—$5.50
(Mfrs. Suggested Retail $4.00)
An unusually beautiful and artistic clock. A superb decoration for table, desk, or fireplace. Combination of midnight blue and silver colored metal and chrome. New Haven 30-hour wind movement. Size 9" x 9".

$75.00

16HC389—Mars Jr. Alarm—$4.56
(Mfrs. Suggested Retail $3.50)
A small self-starting electric alarm clock. New Haven movement. Black plastic case. Chrome bezel. Gold-color metal dial. Convex crystal. Bell-Alarm. (Not of the ordinary buzzer-type.) Size 5½" x 4½" x 2".

$10.00

Den Alarm
16HC390 — — — — — **$4.90**
(Mfrs. Suggested Retail $3.75)
A neat new alarm clock in beautiful catalin case. 30-hour New Haven movement. Bell Alarm. One key winds alarm and time simultaneously. Etched Ivory color dial, with gold-color numerals. Size 4" x 3⅜". Choice of Ivory or Dark Green.

$10.00

16HC712—Shipswheel—$9.30
(Mfrs. Suggested Retail $7.00)
A Phinney-Walker pull-wind desk clock. 30-hour movement. Jet plastic clock frame with gold debossed numerals. Lustrous plastic oval base 2¾" x 5". Gold plated spokes and fixture.

$25.00

America's most beautiful cases plus Europe's finest movements distinguish all Herman Miller Clocks. They differ widely in their individuality. All tastes are appealed to. Genuine Honduras mahogany, rich in color and texture, is used exclusively. Rare woods, including Amboyna, Maidou and Tulipwood, English Oak and Satinwood, Ebony, and Rosewood—woods precious for their rarity and unusual color and beauty—are used to adorn each clock. This is largely responsible for the individuality and high character of Herman Miller Clocks.

No. J-258.........$174.00

Height, 16"; width, 11¾"; depth, 6¾".
Case: Solid Honduras Mahogany. Front: Maidou Burl. Movement: No. 110 Imported 8-day Westminster Rod Chime. Dial: Silver with raised numerals. Bezel: Ornamental gold-plated.

No. J-162......... $114.00

Height, 14¼"; width, 9½"; depth, 6¼".
Case: Solid Honduras Mahogany. Front: Maidou burl. Dial: Silver etched with raised numerals. Bezel: Gold-plated. Movement: No. 110 Imported 8-day Westminster Rod Chime.

No. J-138..........$138.00

Height, 15"; width, 10½"; depth, 6½".
Case: Solid Honduras Mahogany. Front: All Mahogany with carved ornamentation. Dial: Silver etched with raised numerals. Bezel: Gold-plated. Movement: No. 110 Imported 8-day Westminster Rod Chime.

No. J-328..........$105.00

Height, 13½"; width, 11"; depth, 7".
Case: Solid Honduras Mahogany. Dial: Silver etched with raised numerals. Movement: No. 110 Imported 8-day Westminster Rod Chime.

No. J-144..........$111.00

Height, 14¼" width, 13"; depth, 6¼".
Case: Solid Honduras Mahogany. Front: Mahogany Fret Overlay. Dial: Plain Silver. Movement: No. 110 Imported 8-day Westminster Rod Chime.

No. J-161..........$111.00

Height, 13½"; width, 10¼" depth, 6¾".
Case: Solid Honduras Mahogany. Front: Maidou Burl with marqueterie inlays. Dial: Silver etched with raised numerals. Bezel: Gold-plated. Movement: No. 110 Imported 8-day Westminster Rod Chime.

1928

The movements used in Herman Miller Clocks represent the finest in workmanship and quality of any of the importing factories.   These high grade movements are tested by experts to keep time to 1 minute per week.

No. J-166...........$66.00
Height, 13½"; width, 10"; depth, 6¼".
Case: Solid Honduras Mahogany. Dial: Silver with black raised numerals. Movement: No. 110 Imported 8-day Westminster Rod Chime.

No. J-167...........$66.00
Height, 13"; width, 10" depth, 6¼".
Case: Solid Honduras Mahogany. Maidou Overlay. Dial: Silver with black raised numerals. Movement: No. 110 Imported 8-day Westminster Rod Chime.

No. J-156...........$78.00
Height, 13"; width, 10¼"; depth, 6¾".
Case: Solid Honduras Mahogany. Front: Maple Burl. Dial: Silver with black raised numerals. Movement: No. 110 Imported 8-day Westminster Rod Chime.

No. J-157...........$87.00
Height, 12"; width, 9½"; depth, 6".
Period: Modern French.
Case: Solid Honduras Mahogany. Hood: Mahogany Veneer. Front: Maidou Burl. Macassar Ebony Base. Dial: Silver etched with raised numerals. Bezel: Gold-plated. Movement: No. 110 Imported 8-day Westminster Rod Chime.

No. J-155...........$84.00
Height, 11½"; width, 11"; depth, 6½".
Case: Solid Honduras Mahogany. Maidou Overlays. Dial: Silver with black raised numerals. Movement: No. 110 Imported 8-day Westminster Rod Chime.

No. J-257...........$93.00
Height, 12"; width, 9½"; depth, 6".
Period: Modern French.
Case: Solid Honduras Mahogany. Hood: Mahogany Veneer. Front: Maidou Burl. Ivory Feet. Dial: Silver etched with raised numerals. Bezel: Gold-plated. Movement: No. 110 Imported 8-day Westminster Rod Chime.

$175.00

No. J-164..............$66.00

Height, 9¾″; width, 22″; depth, 6¾″.
Case: Solid Honduras Mahogany. Maidou Overlay. Dial:
Silver with black raised numerals. Movement: No. 110 8-day
Westminster Rod Chime.

$250.00

No. J-154..............$87.00

Height, 10½″; width, 19¾″; depth, 6½″.
Case: Solid Honduras Mahogany. Maidou Overlay. Dial:
Silver with black raised numerals. Movement: No. 110 Imported 8-day Westminster Rod Chime.

$175.00

No. J-163..............$63.00

Height, 9¾″; width, 20½″; depth, 6″.
Case: Solid Honduras Mahogany. Maidou Overlay. Marqueterie Border. Dial: Silver with black raised numerals.
Movement: No. 110 Imported 8-day Westminster Rod Chime.

$175.00

No. J-165..............$66.00

Height, 10″; width, 20½″; depth, 6″.
Case: Solid Honduras Mahogany. Maidou Overlay. Dial:
Silver with black raised numerals. Movement: No. 110 Imported 8-day Westminster Rod Chime.

$275.00

No. J-126..............$120.00

Height, 10″; width, 23″; depth, 7″.
Case: Solid Honduras Mahogany. Front: Maidou Burl. Carved
Mahogany Scrolls. Dial: Silver etched with raised numerals.
Bezel: Gold-plated. Movement: No. 110 Imported 8-day
Westminster Rod Chime.

$175.00

No. J-153..............$63.00

Height, 9½″; width, 20¼″; depth, 6″.
Case: Solid Honduras Mahogany. Maidou Overlay. Dial:
Silver with black raised numerals. Movement: No. 110 Imported 8-day Westminster Rod Chime.

PRICES SHOWN ON THIS PAGE ARE KEYSTONE

The new Mauthe Mantel Chime Clocks offer a wide range of design representative of the present-day taste in home decoration—Louis XVI, Georgian, Chippendale, Sheraton, Hepplewhite and Adam. Genuine Honduras mahogany cases, made in America. Selected burl fronts and overlays, hand carvings. The cases are fitted with a new improved Mauthe 8-day pendulum movement. It has a direct strike, self-regulation of chime and strike, individual detachable barrels. Dial is silver-finished, six inch. Raised black numerals. Convex bevelled glass. Solid brass bezel.

No. 1240. ENGLISH GOTHIC DESIGN
$102.00
English burl oak front. Height, 12½″; width, 9″; depth, 6¼″.

1928

No. 1225. HEPPLEWHITE DESIGN....$104.00
Maidou burl overlays. Length, 21″; height, 10½; depth, 6″.

No. 1235. ADAM DESIGN...........$109.00
Amboyna burl front. Length, 21½″; height, 11″; depth, 6¼″.

No. 1245. SHERATON DESIGN
$109.00
Cherry burl front. Inlay borders. Height, 12½″; width, 9¾″; depth, 6″.

No. 1250. LOUIS XVI DESIGN.....$109.00
Amboyna burl overlay. Polished brass finials and feet. Height, 12¾; width, 14″; depth, 6″.

No. 1215. LOUIS XVI DESIGN.......$100.00
Amboyna burl overlay. Length, 20½″; height, 10½″; depth, 6½″.

PRICES SHOWN ON THIS PAGE ARE KEYSTONE

1928

$175.00

No. 7000.....................$99.00
Height, 9½″; width, 22″.
8 Day Four Quarter Westminster Chime. Five Rod Gongs.
Mahogany. Six-inch Sun Silver Dials. Raised Numerals.

$275.00

No. 6110..........$112.50
Height, 14½″; width, 10⅝″.
8 Day Four Quarter Westminster Chime.
Five Gongs. Mahogany. Silver Dial with
applied ornaments and raised numerals.

$175.00

No. 6423..............$83.50
Height, 8⅞″; width, 19 11/16″.
8 Day Four Quarter Westminster Chime. Five Gongs.
Mahogany. Five-inch Spun Silver Dial.
Raised figures.

$175.00

No. 7001..............$100.00
Height, 9½″; width, 22″.
8 Day Four Quarter Westminster Chime. Five Rod
Gongs. Mahogany. Six-inch Spun Silver Dial.
Raised numerals.

$165.00

No. 6419.......................$81.00
Same general description as No. 6423.

Sangamo Electrically Wound Clocks are divided into two series—Eleven Jewel and Seven Jewel. Both are fitted with an "Illinois" double roller escapement.

These clocks run on either 50 or 60 Cycle Current, and Current Interruptions Do Not Interfere with Their Constant Running. Each clock is supplied with a 30-hour maintaining spring, thus insuring uninterrupted service.

1928

$250.00

TAMBOUR
STYLE NO. 5720B.....................$45.00

Seven Jewel Movement
Height, 9″; width, 19¾″; depth, 5½″.
A distinctive tambour—contrasting applied panels. Selected genuine mahogany.
Melodious hour and half hour strike.

$300.00

$250.00

TAMBOUR
STYLE NO. 5110.....................$96.00

Eleven Jewel Movement
Height, 9½″; width, 21″; depth, 6¼″.
Graceful mahogany tambour with contrasting panels. Melodious hour and half hour strike. Illustrated with Dial No. 13—5¼″.

UPRIGHT
MAHOGANY, FRENCH GREY PANEL
STYLE NO. 5009......$114.00

Eleven Jewel Movement
Height, 11¾″; width, 11⅛″; depth, 6⅛″.
An upright with rich duo-tone wood effect and graceful spires. Dial No. 43—5¼″. Raised gold letters on silver background. Gold hands.

$300.00

TAMBOUR
STYLE NO. 5014.....................$138.00

Eleven Jewel Movement
Height, 9½″; width, 24¼″; depth, 6¾″.
Hand carved case of unusual beauty and richness—a distinctive clock for a large living room or library. Mahogany or walnut. Melodious hour and half hour strike. Illustrated with Dial No. 33—5¼″.. Raised bronze figures on silver background.

PRICES SHOWN ON THIS PAGE ARE KEYSTONE

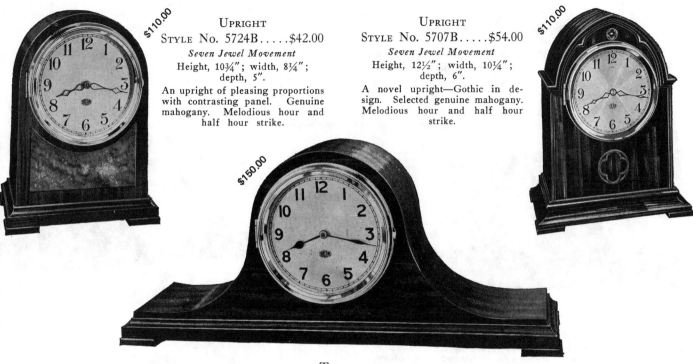

$110.00

UPRIGHT
STYLE No. 5724B.....$42.00
Seven Jewel Movement
Height, 10¾″; width, 8¼″;
depth, 5″.
An upright of pleasing proportions
with contrasting panel. Genuine
mahogany. Melodious hour and
half hour strike.

UPRIGHT
STYLE No. 5707B.....$54.00
Seven Jewel Movement
Height, 12½″; width, 10¼″;
depth, 6″.
A novel upright—Gothic in de-
sign. Selected genuine mahogany.
Melodious hour and half hour
strike.

$110.00

$150.00

TAMBOUR
STYLE No. 5726A.....................$30.00
Seven Jewel Movement
Height, 9″; width, 19⅝″; depth, 5½″.
A plain tambour—rich mahogany in graceful lines. Furnished non-strike only.
Illustrated with 5″ dial.

1928

SANGAMO WALL CLOCKS

Sangamo Office and Factory Clocks cost less than 50 cents per year to
operate. They can be connected to any *alternating* current and have
maintaining power.

SQUARE WALL CLOCK
Eleven Jewel Movement
Mahogany, walnut or oak with wood door.
Large second circle.
STYLE No. 12003-C.........$69.60
Height, 16″; width 16″; depth, 4½″.
12″ Dial.
STYLE No. 14003-C.........$81.60
Height, 19″; width, 19″; depth, 4⅝″.
14″ Dial.

$120.00

$140.00

SQUARE WOOD WALL CLOCK
No. 12703.................$48.00
Seven Jewel Movement
Height, 16″; width, 16″; depth, 4½″.
Mahogany, walnut or oak. Wood bezel.
12″ Dial.
without Second Hand.

$150.00

ROUND ALUMINUM WALL CLOCK
No. 5701.................$30.00
Seven Jewel Movement
Diameter, 7½″; depth, 3¾″.
Dial, 5″.
White, black (plain or flock), olive green,
mahogany or walnut.
No. 5001.................$54.00
Eleven Jewel Movement
Diameter, 8″; depth, 3¼″.
Dial, 5″.

$60.00

$80.00

PRICES SHOWN ON THIS PAGE ARE KEYSTONE

1928

Telechron Clocks are motor driven by a tiny synchronous motor, which receives its timing impulses right from the light current. Once connected and set, it records Observatory Time. The operation of the Telechron is marvelously simple, controlled by the wonderful little Telechron motor. There is no "clock" mechanism, no springs, no escapement—nothing to cause trouble.

The prices quoted on this page are SUGGESTED RETAIL PRICES.
Dealers' costs furnished on application.

Prices shown are for 60 cycle current only. Add $1.00 each to retail for clocks furnished with 50 cycle motors. Kindly state cycle motor wanted when ordering.

No. 656.
"The Aristocrat"

Height, 9"; depth, 5½"; base, 20½" wide.

This distinctive Telechron is made of mahogany with rosewood burl inlay—the effect being one of unusual beauty. Dial, silver finish, 6" in diameter.

Suggested Retail Price - - - - - - - - $77.00

No. 331.
"The Plymouth"

Height, 5⅛"; depth, 3⅛"; base, 13¼" wide.
A small tambour Telechron with good looks that match its un equalled accuracy. Mahogany case. A silver finish dial 3½ in diameter.

Suggested Retail Price - - - - - - - - - - $24.50

No. 655.
"The Versailles"

Height, 9"; depth, 5½"; base, 21" wide.

"The Versailles" represents the ultimate in case design and manufacture combined with Telechron accuracy and dependability. The dial is six inches in diameter. Mahogany with two-tone finish on front.

Suggested Retail Price - - - - - $66.00

Warren Clocks are historically important.

No. 601. "The Normandy"

Height, 11⅜"; width, 8½"; depth, 5½".
A stately Telechron, with a case of mahogany, inlaid. The etched silver dial is six inches in diameter.

Suggested Retail Price - - $55.00

No. 551. "The Lexington"

Height, 6⅞"; depth, 4"; base, 17".

This striking model of the world's most dependable timekeeper is meeting with unusual favor. The dial is of etched silver five inches in diameter. Case, mahogany.

Suggested Retail Price - - - - - - - - - $33.00

No. 322. "The Vanity"

Height, 5¾"; width, 5⅜"; base, 4¼".
Tastefully designed—for milady's bed chamber. In mahogany, with silver finished dial, 3½" in diameter.

Suggested Retail Price - - - - - $22.00

"Observatory Time from Your Light Socket"

1928 The prices quoted on this page are SUGGESTED RETAIL PRICES. Dealers' costs furnished on application. The prices shown are for 60 cycle current only. Add $1.00 each to retail for clocks furnished with 50 cycle motors. Kindly state cycle motor wanted when ordering.

No. 522.
"THE SALEM"

Brings dignity and charm to colonial mantel or library table. In mahogany with etched silver dial, 5" in diameter. Its height is 7", base 7¼" and depth 5".

Suggested Retail - - - - $32.00

No. 355.
"THE CATHEDRAL" MODEL

Made of the famous Bakelite in a rich walnut color. Is 5½" wide, 7¼" high and 3½" deep. The 3-inch dial is finished in silver. The Cathedral model withstands changes in temperature, moisture; retains its high lustre, will not scratch easily, and requires no polishing.

Suggested Retail - - - - $21.00

No. 455.
"THE RADIO" MODEL

This model, one of the most popular designs, is of cast metal, developed in Verde Antique. Its beautiful lines and finish are on a par with its unfailing accuracy. Stands 6⅞" high, 8" wide and 4⅛" deep.

Suggested Retail - - - - - $29.00

WOOD CASE TELECHRONS

No.		SUGGESTED RETAIL
101.	Oak	$31.00
101.	Mahogany	32.00
201.	Oak	33.00
201.	Mahogany	34.50
301.	Oak	37.50
301.	Mahogany	40.00
401.	Oak	55.00
401.	Mahogany	57.50

THE METAL CASE TELECHRON
Statuary Bronze Finish

No.	SUGGESTED RETAIL
405.	$ 29.00
406.	31.00
407.	35.50
408.	51.00
410.	110.00

For Business Use.

THE SEMI-FLUSH TELECHRON
Statuary Bronze Finish

No.	SUGGESTED RETAIL
415.	$29.00
416.	31.00
417.	35.50
418.	51.00

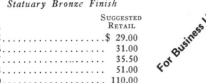

1928   Revere Telechron Chime Clocks play the Westminster Chimes at all four quarters, on 5 tuned rods, and record the correct time from your light socket, eliminating winding, oiling, regulating or cleaning. This accuracy is made possible through the installation in the power house of a Master Telechron, which enables the power company to regulate the speed of its generators.

The prices quoted on this page are SUGGESTED RETAIL PRICES.

Add $1.00 to retail for all clocks fitted with 50 cycle motors.

No. R 104

Westminster Chime
Lacquer Finish
Spanish Highlighted
Height 9″ Width 21″ Depth 6″
Suggested Retail Price.................$81.00

No. R 116

Westminster Chime
Lacquer Finish
Spanish Highlighted
Height 9″ Width 21″ Depth 6″
Suggested Retail Price.................$81.00

No. R 114

Westminster Chime
Lacquer Finish
Spanish Highlighted
Height 9″ Width 21″ Depth 6″
Suggested Retail Price.................$79.0

No. R 406

Westminster and Canterbury Chimes
Lacquer Finish
Spanish Highlighted
Height 10¾″ Width 21½″ Depth 7″
Suggested Retail Price.................$100.00

No. R 108

Westminster Chime
Lacquer Finish
Spanish Highlighted
Height 9″ Width 21″ Depth 6″
Suggested Retail Price.................$84.00

No. R 122

Westminster Chime
Lacquer Finish
Spanish Highlighted
Height 9″ Width 21″ Depth 6″
Suggested Retail Price.................$86.0

No. R 130

Westminster Chime
Lacquer Finish
Spanish Highlighted
Heighth 12½″ Width 9¾″ Depth 6¾″
Suggested Retail Price.............$97.00

No. R 132

Westminster Chime
Lacquer Finish
Spanish Highlighted
Heighth 12¾″ Width 8½″ Depth 6¾″
Suggested Retail Price.................$81.00

DEALER'S COSTS ON APPLICATION

MAY & MALONE, INC.

1932

Kenmore ELECTRIC SPRINGLESS CLOCKS
(A KODEL PRODUCT)
NO WINDING.... NO ADJUSTING.... ALWAYS ACCURATE

The electric clock is not a clock but merely a FREQUENCY or CYCLE counter. Strange as it may seem, it contains absolutely nothing which in itself keeps time. It has no springs, escapements, pendulums, etc. Instead, it is a very simple type of electric meter which counts and records the total frequency impulses of an A.C. current circuit. This is done in much the same manner as a house meter records the electric current consumed.

In every Kenmore Electric Clock there is a tiny, electric motor revolving at a speed EXACTLY proportional to the frequency of the electric current supplied. This motor counts the electric cycles pulsating through the house lighting circuit and moves the clock hands exactly ONE MINUTE every 3,600 cycles.

All modern generating units (electric power stations) are equipped with dependable, speed governing apparatus which maintains the frequency of their generating units absolutely constant. Thus the electric motor of all Kenmore Electric Clocks, connected to such a current, cannot run fast or slow but must rotate at a similar and proportionate speed thus always indicating absolutely correct time—accurate to the split second.

$10.00

MARGARET
Upright model in dainty genuine Bakelite case, exquisite raised pebbled panels. For milady's boudoir or suited for desk, table or mantel use. 3½-inch silver-finished dial, convex glass. In beautiful dark walnut finish.
Size: 5 inches high, 4 inches wide.
A502H01.....................$10.95

$15.00

PRINCESS PAT
Gracefully designed in five-inch octagon Bakelite case, beautifully grained and pebbled and is mounted with easels. 3½-inch silver finished dial. In mottled walnut only.
Size: 6¾ inches wide, 6¼ inches high, 3¼ inches deep.
A502H02.....................$17.50

$25.00

KENWOOD
Compact and graceful Tambour, unusually attractive. 5½-inch silver finished dial. The handsome wood case is embellished with beautiful raised high-lighted panels. In popular walnut only.
Size: 19½ inches long, 7 inches high.
A502H03.....................$21.90

$15.00

DOVER
A popular Gothic Cathedral model, in beautiful walnut, appealing in its simplicity. High lighted panels, 5-inch silver-finished dial. In popular walnut finish only.
Size: 8½ inches wide, 11 inches high, and 3½ inches deep.
A502H06.....................$20.65

$25.00

DELTA
The case is solid cast bronze and is held in an upright position supported by an easel back. Furnished with raised bronze Arabic numerals on frosted silver band dial with statuary bronze background. Gold finished hands. Furnished either in Statuary Bronze or Chromium finish.
Size: 6½ inches square.
A502H04.....................$37.50

$15.00

BETSY
A beautiful circular wall model, ideal for the kitchen and also suited for office, store or wherever a neat wall clock is desired. 5½-inch dial is silver-finished. The beautiful case is furnished in standard Duco enamel optional colors of pastel green, or ivory.
Size: 8 inches in diameter.
A502H05.....................$13.45

$20.00

KENALARM MODERNE
Modern Electric alarm clock and Master home clock combined. Ideal for bedroom. Instead of antiquated clanging bell—a pleasant vibrating tattoo which awakens gently—but surely. Alarm easily set. In handsome Bakelite case of semi-futuristic design. Dark Walnut only.
Size: 7¼ inches high, 5½ inches wide.
A502H09.....................$18.15

$35.00

LEVERHULME
A semi-futuristic creation with graceful wood pillars, artistic hands, and silver finished heart-shaped dial 7½ inches high. Genuine walnut case.
Size: 13 inches long, 11 inches high, and 4 inches deep.
A502H07.....................$50.05

$75.00

CARLTON
An attractive wall model of square type, designed for offices, public buildings, factories, etc. Staunchly constructed for industrial use, with large 13-inch dial, including second hand. Easily read, adding distinction to any location. Walnut finish.
Size: 15½ inches square, 3½ inches deep.
A502H08.....................$31.30

CAN BE USED ONLY ON 110 VOLTS 60 CYCLE SYNCHRONIZED CURRENT. OTHER CURRENTS, EXCEPT DIRECT, BY ORDER ONLY.

Kenmore ALL-ELECTRIC MASTER Clock
ACCURATE HOME TIME... ALWAYS

Every Kenmore Electric is guaranteed for 25 years—the world's most amazing clock guarantee. This is possible only because of the revolutionary, new lifetime Kenmore motor construction. Think what this guarantee means to you—to your customers—build for the future with the Kenmore all-electric—the clock with a 25-year guarantee!

IMPORTED CHIME CLOCKS OF EXCEPTIONAL MERIT

Full Westminster Chimes on Four Straight Gongs
Eight-Day Quarter-Hour Chime Movement

Junghans Chime Clocks have silvered dials, with raised bronze numerals. All have beveled glasses, and those with round glasses are Bombe.

DESCRIPTION OF THE CHIME MOVEMENT

The Junghans Westminster Chime Clocks strike sections of the melody at each quarter and the full Westminster Chime on the hour, followed by the hour strike, in imitation of the famous London Chimes.

The Tambour Models have four Horizontal gong rods, with the hour strike on three rods struck simultaneously by three hammers.

We draw especial attention to the strike. The gongs are straight (not spiral)—the chimes are sonorous, yet mellow and soft, distinct, but with the suggestion of distance that causes the listener to imagine they emanate from cathedral bells. The movements are of superior finish and have polished plates, detachable mainspring barrels which can easily be removed without taking the movement apart, and an Automatic Chime Adjustment which regulates the chime automatically within the hour.

$180.00

1932

$160.00

AUCKLAND
Genuine mahogany case, height 13¾ inches, width 12 inches, silver plated dial, 9x7 inches, with raised bronze numerals, bronze finish door with bevel glass. Full Westminster chimes on four straight gongs. Eight-day quarter-hour chime movement.
A501H01. List.................................$85.00

NEW YORK
Genuine mahogany case. Tambour shape, silver plated dial 6½ inches, raised bronze numerals, gilt bezel, bevel convex glass. Height 10⅜ inches, width 22 inches.
A501H02. List.................................$80.00

Two-Jewel Pendulum Movement Fine Timekeeper

$160.00

$150.00

WASHINGTON
Genuine mahogany case. Tambour shape, silver plated dial 6½ inches, with raised bronze numerals, gilt bezel, bevel convex glass. Height 10½ inches, width 22½ inches.
A501H03. List.................................$85.00

Height 9¼ inches. Length 19½ inches. Depth 6½ inches. Beveled convex glass. Solid brown mahogany case. 5-inch silvered dial with raised numerals. Diameter of minute circle, 4½ inches.
A501H04.................................$60.00

$150.00

KIENZLE CLOCKS

Height 9 inches. Length 19½ inches. Depth 6½ inches. Beveled Convex Glass. Solid brown mahogany case. 5-inch silvered dial with raised numerals. Diameter of minute circle 4½ inches.
A501H05.................................$62.00

If you now look at the Kienzle Chime Movement we are sure that you will appreciate more clearly than before the beauties of the construction. There is no wheel and no lever without a special duty to perform, and which has not been the subject of long study and experiment on the part of a staff of reliable experts in the manufacture of clocks. The rivalry between the constructors has resulted in the maximum achievement of rendering the movement simple, clear, and comprehensible. A movement has been created which is thoroughly up-to-date and the last word in clock making and we venture to say represents to-day the most perfect production in the trade.

$25.00

$40.00

$25.00

$25.00

$30.00

$35.00

J9564—3⅜ x 3¼, fancy metal case, pink, blue, and ivory crackled finish, 2 in. white dial, 30-hour American movement. 1 in box. Asstd. 12 in carton. **Each $1.05**

J9429—"Hummer," 5⅛x4 in., metal case and base, crackled ivory and green finish, concealed loud alarm, side-shut-off, 30-hour brass movement. 1 in box. **Each $1.25** 24 or more, Each 1.20

J9563—2½x2 in., square gilt dial, asstd. red, blue and green bakelite case with floral decoration, 30-hour American movement. 3 in box. **Each $1.30**

J9552—5⅝x3¼ in., asstd. blue, pink and white gilt crackled finish wood, 2 in. white dial, 30-hour American movement. 3 in pkg. **Each $1.35**

J9550—3 styles, average 3¼x3½ in., blue, pink and white pearl on amber "Ivorith," metal easel back, 30-hour American movement. 1 in box. Asstd. 3 in pkg......**Each $1.65**

J9551—2 styles, 6½x3½ in., jade and coral "Ivorith," 2 in. white dial, 30-hour American movement. 1 in box. Asstd. 2 in pkg. **Each $1.95**

$45.00

$35.00

$50.00

$60.00

$75.00

$150.00

J9553—2 styles, pink and blue on amber "Ivorith," fancy shape, 2 in. gilt dial with perforated heart showing swinging escapement, 30-hour American movement. 1 in box. Asstd. 2 in pkg......**Each $2.25**

J9554—4¼x4½ in., tinted and embossed "Art Nouveau" wood, floral wreath decoration, tilt background, 2 in. gilt dial, metal easel back, 30-hour American movement. 1 in box. **Each $2.50**

J9560—4⅜ in., octagon shape, tinted floral spray decorated mahogany effect frame, silver plated embossed rim, 2½ in. silvered dial, velvet back, metal easel, 30-hour American movement. 1 in box. **Each $3.65**

J9555—6x4¼ in., "Art Nouveau" wood, blue enameled latticed background with tinted floral festoon, 2 in. gilt dial, metal easel back, 30-hour American movement. 1 in box. **Each $2.65**

J9456—4x5 in., light blue alabastine, gold plated edge, embossed ornamentation, metal silvered dial, 30-hour American movement. 1 in box. **Each $2.50**

J9556—Juvenile clock, 7x5¼ in., tinted and enameled "Art Nouveau" wood, rustic fence with tinted garden flowers and rabbit, 30-hour American movement. 1 in box......**Each $2.95**

$45.00

$150.00

J9559—"Homestead," 9¾x6¼ in., "Art Nouveau" wood, tan and brown toned English cottage with tinted lawn and garden, 30-hour American movement. 1 in box. **Each $3.50**

$80.00

J9557—Pendant wall clock, 11x6 in., tan & gray toned "Art Nouveau" wood, tinted and enameled embossed floral sprays, silvered oval dial, suspended on 2¼ in. tangerine silk grosgrain ribbon. 30-hour American movement. 1 in box. **Each $3.95**

J9558—Juvenile wall clock, 9¼ in. octagon shape, tinted and embossed "Art Nouveau" wood, Bunny and floral spray decoration, 4 in. dial, raised blue numerals, 8-day American pendulum movement. 1 in box. **Each $3.95**

Lux $50.00—75.00

No. 853. Mechanical Watermill Clock. Set in rose gold plated frame; octagon shape with beautifully colored dial showing country home and watermill which works mechanically while clock is going. Fitted with Lux 30-hour, guaranteed movement, easel back and unbreakable crystal; size 4¾x4¾ inches. Each **$7.50**

Lux $125.00

No. 90. Miniature Hall Clock. One-day time, 2-inch gilt dial with visible pendulum. Height 12½ inches, base 3½ inches. Can be had in following finishes: **mahogany, walnut, natural, and red, blue, green, brown and black crackle finish.** Each **$7.50**

No. 812/12.
DE LUXE ARTISTIC LAMP CLOCK . $11.50

Width, 5″   Height, 20″

Made of an unbreakable wood product, in three finishes. Executed in rich colorings. Hand painted circular parchment shade with silk braid binding, supported on removable harp. Furnished with five feet silk cord and socket plug. Fitted with 30-hour, Oval Heart-beat movement.

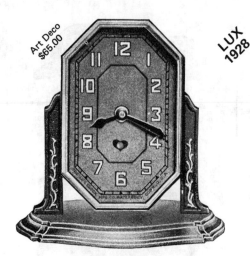

Art Deco $65.00   *LUX 1928*

No. 10/249.
BOUDOIR OR DESK CLOCK, $5.30

Length, 4⅛″; height, 4¼″.

Fancy designed metal base, mounted on ornamented columns which permit clock being put in any position. Fitted with an Octagonal shaped movement, with decorated gold and silver combination dial.
Colors: French Bronze and Royal Copper.

Art Deco $75.00

No. 202/85.
FOUNTAIN PEN AND COMBINATION CLOCK DESK SET, $8.00

Length, 8″; width, 5″; height, 5″

Octagonal shape, with depression for pens and pencil rests. Funnels accommodate any size fountain pens. Fitted with a 30-hour movement, with gold dial made in Jade.

$100.00

No. 122/25.
COLONIAL BANJO HANGING WALL CLOCK, $8.50

Width, 5¼″   Length, 18¾″

Made of an unbreakable wood product, yellow finish. Exact reproduction of popular Banjo Clocks. Carved and decorated in effective colors. Fitted with 3½″ metal etched dial, frontwind, non-overwind movement.

Art Deco $125.00

No. 40.
MARBLESQUE ELEPHANT CLOCK . . . $6.30

Length, 7¾″   Height, 6½″

Made of synthetic marble, wax finish and antiqued, supported on carved effect pedestal. Fitted with a 2″, 30-hour movement, with silver dial and bowled glass.

$165.00

No. 10/511.
SUNBURST PENDULUM WALL CLOCK, $2.30

Width, 4″   Length, 6″

Artistically designed in three colors of shaded metal, with gold etched dial. Fitted with a 2″, guaranteed, non-overwind, patented Lux movement.

$135.00

No. 10/97.
NOVELTY PEDESTAL PENDULUM CLOCK, $5.30

Length, 4″   Height, 6½″

Fancy designed base. Fitted with a 30-hour, guaranteed, non-overwind, swinging Pendulum Dome shaped Lux movement, with gold white-lettered dial and bowled glass.

PRICES SHOWN ON THIS PAGE ARE KEYSTONE

LUX – 1928

Art Deco $50.00

No. 104. GOTHIC CLOCK......$6.30

Length, 6½″; height, 6½″.

Made of an unbreakable wood product. Richly designed, carved and hand colored front, in a variety of color effects. Fitted with a Dome designed, 30-hour, guaranteed, non-overwind Lux movement.

$30.00

No. 1161. BOUDOIR OR DESK CLOCK, $2.10

Length, 5″; height, 4″.

In ornate design, in six assorted colors, crackle finish, metal front. Fitted with a 2″ 30-hour movement, on easel back.

$40.00

No. 404/12.
SPHINX ALARM CLOCK, $5.30

Length, 6½″; height, 5¼″.

Made of an unbreakable wood product, green finish. Fine alarm clock with gold dial and bowled glass.

$35.00

No. 174/23.
"TIMES SQUARE" ART CLOCK, $5.10

Length, 3″; height, 3″.

Made of an unbreakable wood product, in gold finish. In carved effects, raised dial numbers, under artistically designed unbreakable crystal front. Fitted with a 30-hour movement, with easel back.

Also available in five assorted colors.

$40.00

No. 170/9.
"TIMES SQUARE" ART CLOCK, $6.00

Length, 5″; height, 5″.

Made of an unbreakable wood product, in blue finish. In carved effects, raised dial numerals under artistically designed unbreakable crystal front. Fitted with a 30-hour, non-overwind, patented Lux movement, with easel back.

Also available in five assorted colors.

$55.00

No. 501/9.
"KENWOOD" ART CLOCK, $7.50

Length, 5¼″; height, 6″.

Made of an unbreakable wood product, blue finish. Beautifully decorated with raised letter dial under unbreakable crystal front, mounted with filigree decorated rim. Fitted with a 30-hour movement, with easel back.

Made in six finishes.

1928
Lux

No. 106/22.
"CAMBRIDGE" ART CLOCK, $5.10

Length, 4"; height, 4¾".

Made of an unbreakable wood product, in scroll design, in parchment finish. Beautifully hand decorated in two-tone colorings. Fitted with a 30-hour Lux, non-overwind, new patented Heartbeat movement, with fancy dial, bowled glass and easel back.

$75.00

$60.00

No. 500/12.
"DU BARRY" ART CLOCK, $6.80

Length, 5¼"; height, 6".

Made of an unbreakable wood product, green finish. Beautifully decorated with raised letter dial under unbreakable crystal front. Fitted with a guaranteed, 30-hour, non-overwind, Lux movement, with easel back.

Made in six finishes.

A fascinating and delightful new alarm. Made of an unbreakable wood product. Artistically decorated with gold on an apple green background. Fitted with 30-hour patented Lux alarm movement. Measures 7 inches wide by 5 inches high.

2E25030   PRICE............**$8.50**

$55.00

AMERICA'S MOST HANDSOME ALARM

$50.00

CUPID'S BEATING HEART CLOCK

Blue and white pearl hearts with gold dial clock in center. Dial shows heart beat pendulum. Size 3½ by 3¾ inches. 30-hour guaranteed non-overwind movement.

2E25021   PRICE..........................**$6.50**

$100.00

. No. 183/19.
"BOUCHER" MANTEL CLOCK, $19.50

Length, 11½"; height, 12½".

Made of an unbreakable wood product, red finish, in artistically carved effects, beautifully colored, and has a platform base. Fitted with a fine quality 8-day jeweled movement, with metal etched oval designed dial.

Also in gold, green or walnut.

$115.00

No. 1700/12
"BLOSSOM TIME"
TABLE ART CLOCK, $19.50

Width, 9¼"; height, 15¾".

Made of an unbreakable wood product, artistically decorated in beautiful green colorings in Japanese subject. Carved effect frame design, with raised numeraled dial. Fitted with 8-day fine quality jewelled movement.

Available in four colors.

$85.00

Lux
1928

No. 502/2.
"LANSDOWN" ART CLOCK, $7.50

Length, 4¾"; height, 9".

Made of an unbreakable wood product, walnut finish. Carved and hand decorated, with oval-shaped raised letter dial, under unbreakable crystal front. Fitted with 30-hour, non-overwind Lux movement, with easel back.

Available in six colors.

POPULAR PRICED AMERICAN-MADE CLOCKS

$75.00

ART TABLE CLOCK

No. 11E276 Each.....................$6.50

Octagonal shape. Made of synthetic wood, showing a beautiful design of a bird with plumage in natural tints. Fitted with Lux 30-hour, guaranteed, non-overwind, thin model movement, gold dial, unbreakable crystal and easel back. Length, 5¾ inches; height, 5¾ inches.

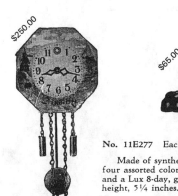

$250.00

NOVELTY PENDULETTE WALL CLOCK

No. 11E274 Each.....$2.70

Beautifully designed in colors, showing Dutch scene, on hard enameled metal front. Fitted with fine quality Lux 30-hour, pendulum movement, fully guaranteed, showing weights and chains. Width, 2¾ inches; height, 2¾ inches.

$65.00

1930 LUX

ART TABLE CLOCK

No. 11E277 Each...............................$15.00

Made of synthetic wood, in ornate design. Carved effects in hand-decorated colorings, four assorted colors. Fitted with large size fancy designed metal etched dial under glass, and a Lux 8-day, guaranteed, fine quality, non-overwind movement. Length, 10¾ inches; height, 5¼ inches.

$250.00

NOVELTY PENDULETTE WALL CLOCK

No. 11E273 Each.....$2.60

Artistically designed in delft blue, showing Dutch water scene on hard enameled metal front. Fitted with fine quality Lux 30-hour, pendulum movement, fully guaranted, showing weights and chains. Width, 2¾ inches; height, 3½ inches.

$60.00

LOUIS XIV ART CLOCK

No. 11E251 Each.....................$4.50

Made of an unbreakable wood product, handsomely designed and painted in unique color effects. Ornately trimmed with wreaths of flowers. Fitted with a 30-hour guaranteed non-overwind Lux movement. This clock can be had in three assorted color effects. Length, 4½ inches; height, 6¼ inches.

$60.00

LOUIS XV ART CLOCK

No. 11E252 Each.....................$5.00

Made of an unbreakable wood product. Artistically carved and hand colored, showing beautiful flower wreaths in relief. Fitted with a 30-hour guaranteed non-overwind oval Lux movement. This clock can be had in three assorted color effects. Width, 5¼ inches; height, 7 inches.

$250.00

NOVELTY PENDULETTE WALL CLOCK

No. 11E275 Each.....$2.80

Artistically designed in colors, showing country scene, on hard enameled metal front. Fitted with fine quality Lux 30-hour, pendulum movement, fully guaranteed, showing weights and chains. Width, 2¾ inches; height, 3½ inches.

$60.00

$85.00

No. 11E255 ART WALL CLOCK

Each..................$5.00

Made of synthetic wood, in carved designs, richly hand decorated, non-overwind, in colors. Fitted with 30-hour guaranteed thin model movement, with gold dial and unbreakable crystal. Suspended on daintily corded hanger. Length, 3 inches; height, 3 inches.

MODERNISTIC 8-DAY ART CLOCK

$85.00

No. 11E278 Each.....................$9.00

Made of synthetic wood, in carved effects, beautifully colored, raised numeral dial, with unbreakable crystal front. Fitted with fine quality 8-day Lux, non-overwind movement, easel back. Length, 8 inches; height, 4¼ inches.

MODERNISTIC 8-DAY ART CLOCK

No. 11E279 Each.........................$12.00

Made of synthetic wood, carefully executed in beautiful colorings of futuristic design, with raised numerals and unbreakable crystal front. Fitted with fine quality 8-day, non-overwind movement, easel back. Length, 9½ inches; height, 8¼ inches.

Lux Art and Novelty Clocks

Cocker Spaniel
Pendulette Clock

Made of synthetic wood showing a Cocker Spaniel overlooking a fence. Head of dog in high relief, with glass eyes. Hand decorated in natural colors. Has swinging pendulum at the bottom. **Shipped postpaid.** No. 8714. Price.... **$1.89**

1940 $250.00

$65.00

Rotary *Calendar* Clock

Most unusual clock made. Regular automatic alarm clock that tells time; gives day of the week; and date of month. Complete calendar and alarm clock. Dependable 30 hour movement. Beautiful ivory, bronze or Chinese red case. 5½ x 5½". No. 8167. Price.... **$6.25**

1950 $160.00

THE BOBBING BIRD WALL CLOCK—REPLICA OF SWISS CHALET

No. V328. Bird bobs up and down with every tick of the clock. Operates on the same principal as the expensive Swiss clocks. Equipped with pendulum, a long winding chain and a balanced weight to assure accurate time keeping. Runs 24 hours without winding. Manufacturer's guarantee enclosed with each clock. Constructed of wood and artistically carved and decorated. Individually boxed. Ship. wt. 2¼ lbs.

SUGGESTED SELLING PRICE $5.50
Sample $3.79; 10 Clocks—$36.00

1931 $65.00 Each

Miniature Clock Assortment. 6 Miniature Bugalow, 30-hour pendulum clocks; assorted colors, hand decorated ornamental weights and chains; on hardwood display stand, 18 inches high. **Six Clocks and Stand. Net........ $8.00**

1941 $55.00

Mystery
ROTARY CLOCK

The Time at a Glance

An outstanding achievement in clock creations. Instead of telling time the old fashioned way with hour and minute hands, the Rotary Clock tells time without them. The indicator points to the time—told at a glance. Tells time with dependable accuracy. Guaranteed for a full year of service. A.M. and P.M. figures distinguished—A.M. figures printed white on black background; P.M. figures black on white background. Colors—Monterey Blue, Mandarin Red or Moderne Black. 5" diameter. 3" high. No. 9138. Price.. **$2.49**

1941 $75.00

GLOBE Pendulum Clock

Combines two features into one clock to make it an accurate time teller of startling beauty! Has a 30 hour, spring movement which is controlled by the swinging pendulum. The weight on the end of the pendulum can be moved up and down, and thus you can accurately adjust the clock to keep almost perfect time. Greater accuracy and dependability! In appearance the clock is surprisingly smartly styled. Large 3" globe at top, raised numerals, hands curved to lay close to the globe. Globe is mounted on base as illustrated. Polished hands and decorations. Clock is finished in rich enameled colors such as blue, ivory, etc. 9½ inches high. No. 3817. Price **$3.95**

1940 $250.00

Kitty Kat
Pendulette Clock

Attractive clock showing cat looking over top. Hand painted in natural colors with glass eyes. Made of synthetic wood to resemble carving. Pendulum swings back and forth. 30 hour movement, accurate timekeeper. 3¾" wide, 7" deep. No. 8715. Price.... **$1.89**

1941 $55.00

Rotary Clock

The smartest novelty clock of the year—in an electric model! New style modernistic design gives the time at a glance. Rotary disc. 60 cycle, 110 volt. No. 8175. Electric Rotary Clock. Postpaid **$2.95**

1928 $25.00

RADIO FANS, ATTENTION!

Here is a clock that radio fans have been waiting for—a new invention. It tells, at a glance, the correct time all over the world. This clock stands 4 inches high and 5 inches wide, has an attractive two-tone green metal front with gold sash and dial. Tells you standard time at home and in every other important city at a glance. Very simple. Dependable DeLuxe 30-hour movement. An ideal gift for anyone who has a good radio set.

2E25018 PRICE...........................$6.00

$125.00

No. 1408. Elf Electric Light Clock. An artistic reproduction in carved effect of woodland scene, depicting **"The House in the Tree and Elfs,"** in natural colors. The windows in the house are illuminated. Contains an electric bulb with 5 feet of silk cord and combination socket plug. 30-hour Lux movement; width 11 inches, height 10½ inches. Each...**$9.00**

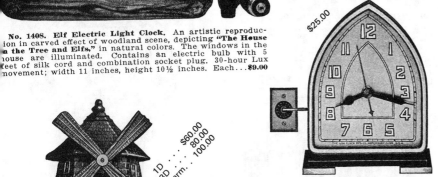

$25.00

No. 444. De Luxe Silvertone Electric Boudoir Clock. $1.90

Combination of black and nickel effects. Modernistic designed base, supporting arch shaped electric clock; fitted with Lux electric guaranteed movement; silver dial; white lettered; sweep second hand; plug and cord. Operates only on 60 cycle alternating current. Height 3¼ inches, width 3 inches.

1933

Lux 1931

4 Styles $200.00

No. 610. Pendulum Stand Clock. $4.70

On metal base, enamel finish in blue and green, with artistically carved effect fancy designed front. Fitted with 30-hour Lux guaranteed Pendulum movement and ornamented chains and weights. Width of base 4¼ inches; height 6¼ inches.

$25.00

No. 437. De Luxe Silvertone Electric Boudoir Clock. $1.90

Combinatoin of black and nickel effects. Modernistic designed base, supporting dome shaped electric clock; fitted with guaranteed Lux electric motor; silver dial; white lettered; sweep second hand; plug and cord. Operates only on 60 cycle alternating current. Height 3¾ inches, width 3 inches.

1D $60.00
8D 80.00
Alarm.. 100.00

No. 1402. Windmill Clock. Made of unbreakable wood product, in natural colors; fitted with 30-hour Lux non-overwind movement; dome shaped with gold dial. Height 10½ inches, length 8 inches. Each **$6.00**

$90.00

No. 1404. Deluxe Watermill Clock. Made of synthetic wood artistically colored in rustic colors, an exact reproduction of a Country Village Mill. Particularly well adapted for Radio Cabinets; 30-hour Lux movement, gold dial; height 9¼ inches, width 11 inches. Each **$6.75**

$55.00

No. 105. Oxford Art Clock. Made of unbreakable wood product; decorated in relief colors; fitted with 30-hour Lux Heartbeat movement; fancy dial and easel back. Length 6 inches, height 4¾ inches. Each..**$4.00**

$80.00

No. Y130. Louis XIV Fob Clock. Made out of an unbreakable wood product. Artistically carved and decorated in dainty colorings. Suspended on fine quality grained silk ribbon. Width 6 inches, length 12 inches; fitted with a 30-hour, guaranteed, non-overwind, Lux movement. Net......**$1.00**

$125.00

No. 854. Mechanical Watermill Clock.......$7.50

Set in rose gold plated frame, with beautifully colored dial showing picture of windmill which works mechanically while clock is going, with hard enameled corner ornamentations, in DOME shape. Fitted with Lux 30-hour guaranteed movement, easel back and unbreakable crystal. Width 4½ inches, height 5⅝ inches.

Novel and original designs in clocks are portrayed herein at prices which permit more than the usual saving. Interest and enthusiasm manifests itself in such unusual, exclusive and distinctive merchandise.

IDEAL AS A GIFT ARTICLE

These decorative and highly serviceable clocks greatly please any recipient. They are different and vary so much from commonplace designs that they create greater interest than an ordinary gift.

Illustrations are reduced size. **Prices Each**

1933

$45.00

NOVELTY CUCKOO PENDULETTE CLOCK

(Pictured at left)

This is a miniature reproduction of the large cuckoo clock. Same richly carved effect, also beautifully executed in natural colors. It is fitted with a 30-hour guaranteed movement with pendulum and ornamented chains, including weights. It will prove attractive in that spare corner of the living room, kitchen or breakfast nook. Even though the price is very low, it is of excellent construction.
No. K461 Each...**$2.75**

GIFTS OF UTILITY

$75.00

DE LUXE SILVERTONE (PATENTED) THERMO ALARM CLOCK

A Combination Alarm Clock and Thermometer in One. Rich black and Nickel combination case. Lovely Buff colored dial. Fitted with one-day guaranteed LUX (Inside Bell) alarm and guaranteed accurate thermometer. Supported on four metal feet. Height 4 inches. Width 3¾ inches. Purchased by us in large quantities and priced very low to you.
No. K462 Each...**$2.75**

$250.00

"Happy Days" Novelty Electric Clock. Moulded composition front, grotesque design with hand painted natural colors, sweep second hand, gilt finish dial and bezel, guaranteed synchronous manual starting motor, height 5 inches, width 3 inches.
No. 60W877.
Each **1.32**

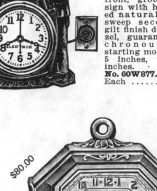

$80.00

$150.00

ART NOVELTY CLOCK
Ideal for the Radio—Retails for $8.50

If you can perceive the elegance of the colors employed in finishing this clock and visualize its massiveness, you will appreciate the exclusiveness of this attractive new design. Made of composition white metal, heavily gold plated, and all colored parts are hand painted. Tusks, white; woman's dress, blue; hair, black; hair ornament, red; fan, white; saddle cover, red; frame surrounded clock dial, white; fringe, gold and yellow; border ornament, red, green and blue. Fitted with a one-day time American make dependable movement. Masterly modeled and finished. Weight unpacked close to 5 pounds. Size, 9½x9 inches. Attractive and decorative in the home.
No. 2264 Each...**$6.00**

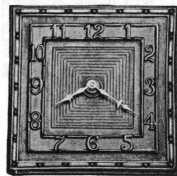

4" — $35.00
5" — $40.00

TIMES SQUARE ART CLOCK

A highly decorated and very attractive serviceable clock for the boudoir, spinet or secretary. Made of an unbreakable wood product, in carved effects, raised dial numerals, under artistically designed unbreakable convexed crystal front. Finished in rich Ivory and deftly trimmed in harmonizing blue. Fitted with an American make 30-hour non-overwind, patented Lux movement, with easel back. Unusual in character, exquisite in fine workmanship and finish. Length, 4 inches; width, 4 inches.
No. 2265 Each...**$3.25**

HANGING WALL CLOCK

Made of composition white metal and finished in a bright Chinese Red. Colorful and attractive. Fitted with American make 30-hour fully guaranteed movement, octagonal shape, with gilt etched metal dial and beveled glass. Height 11 inches. Width 5½ inches. Exacting workmanship. Priced very low.
No. 2262 Each...**$6.10**

$85.00

All Clocks on this page are Lux — Keebler 1933

No. 503. Adelphia Art Clock. Made of unbreakable wood product; carved and decorated in colors; oval shaped; raised letter dial with unbreakable crystal; filigree decorated rim; 30-hour Lux movement with easel back. Length 4¾ inches, height 9 inches. Each...**$6.00**

$45.00

LOUIS XVI ART CLOCK

Made of unbreakable wood product, Walnut finish. Richly designed and hand colored, making an effective color contrast which is captivating. Exquisite carvings on frame. Fitted with a 30-hour, guaranteed, non-overwind Octagonal Lux movement, with gold dial and bezel. Easel back. Height, 7¼ inches; length, 3¾ inches. So distinctive and unusual in design. So rich and charming in colors and finish.
No. 2253 Each...**$3.50**

$50.00

MIGNARD ART TABLE CLOCK

Made of an unbreakable wood product in carved effects, richly decorated, in Walnut finish, and enriched with gold and red, making the contrast most effective. Fitted with a guaranteed 30-hour non-overwind, new patented, "HEART-BEAT" OCTAGONAL shaped Lux movement, with gold dial and bezel. Length, 6 inches; height, 6½ inches. It's a real stylish clock nicely made and finished.
No. 2263 Each...**$4.35**

Animated and Novelty Alarm Clocks

ATTRACTIVE AND APPEALING   **GOOD TIMEKEEPERS**

$175.00

Ingersoll Waterbury Three Little Pigs Alarm Clock. The Big Bad Wolf's hungry jaws open and close in rhythm. The clock and case are bright red. The display carton has original drawings on it. A good timepiece and a big seller.

No. 60W895.
Each 1.03

$175.00

Ingersoll Waterbury New Mickey Mouse Alarm Clock. An animated Mickey Mouse on the dial, head wags and hands point the time. Green case. A self display carton makes selling easy.

No. 60W941.
Each 1.03

Lux
$125.00

Animated Alarm Clock. 30-hour lever movement. Attractively designed square case on ornamental base, brass polished edges, ebony finish with nickel polished edges. Peanut roaster is in motion while clock operates. Height 4 inches, width 4⅞ inches.
No. 60W843. Each.......................... 1.02

$75.00

Mickey Mouse Electric Clock. Metal case finished in light green, chromium plated bezel; height, 4⅜ inches. Mickey is continually turning hand-springs. Decorated with action pictures of Minnie and Mickey Mouse around three sides of clock. Mickey's own hands point the time. In attractive self-display cartons.

No. 60W896. Each 1.03

ca 1950
$85.00

CC352—Popeye Alarm—$2.00
The famous Popeye attractively reproduced in full colors on the case and on the dial. The tick of this alarm clock is unusually soft. Ivory-colored metal case with black trim; and full-toned, concealed alarm with top shut-off. Height, 4½"; Width, 4".

Lux
$125.00

Happy Day Animated Novelty Clock. 30-Hour lever movement. Square nickel polished and lacquered frame, glass front, with animated subject showing two Dutchmen drinking over a keg of beer. Design shows man lifting glass while clock is in motion. Size, 3¾ inches square. Easel back.

No. 60W875. Each............ .90

Lux
$125.00

Animated Novelty Clock. 30-hour lever movement. Square nickel polished and lacquered frame, glass front, with animated subject showing caricatured darky shining girl's shoes. Design is attractive and novel and is in motion while clock operates. Easel back. Size, 3¾ inches square.

No. 60W876. Each............ .90

Lux
$125.00

Animated Novelty Clock. Square frame, glass front with animated scene showing steeple in colors with tower bell swinging back and forth while clock is in operation. Size, 3¾ inches square. Assorted colors, rose, blue, and green. 30-hour lever movement.

No. 60W954. Each.......... 1.10

Animated Novelty Clocks - Dependable Timekeepers

Action Clocks

Watch the Motion

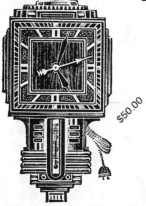

$50.00

$35.00

$165.00
Original Tail

Enchanted Forrest **$125.00**

Modernistic Clock

Appealing new design with modernistic square dial decorated in attractive colors. A room thermometer is fitted at the bottom. The clock is 12 ¾ inches in height and comes complete with cord and plug. **$4.10**
No. 8180. Postpaid....

Bluebird Clock

Beautifully designed walnut finish composition that looks like genuine wood carving. Many people prefer this to the famous Cuckoo Clock. 30 hour movement. 6 inches high, 4 inches wide. Each packed well to insure safe delivery. **$1.85**
No. 8709. Postpaid...

Black Cat Clock

The tail swings back and forth in much the same way as a pendulum and at the same time the eyes move from side to side. Fine 30 hour movement. 7 ¼ inches high, 4 ⅜ inches wide.
No. 8708. Black Cat Clock. Price Postpaid **$2.35**

Pendulette Clock

When in operation the dwarf and the pendulum swing back and forth. The enchanted forrest design surrounds the clock in dark walnut finish. Dependable 30 hour movement. Height 5 ¾ inches, width 4 inches. **$1.95**
No. 8177. Postpaid....

$35.00

$375.00
Original Tie

All Clocks on this page are Lux or Keebler 1937–1938

$375.00
Original Tie

$350.00

Cuckoo Clock

The best copy of a real Cuckoo clock we have ever seen. With each swing of the pendulum the Cuckoo bird hops in and out. Interesting and amusing to watch. Fine 30 hour movement. 7 in. high and 4 in. wide.
No. 8720. Bobbing Cuckoo Clock, Price.. **$1.95**

Dixie Boy Clock

The necktie swings back and forth in the same manner as a pendulum and the eyes roll from side to side. After you once have one in your house you'll never be without it. Dependable 30 hour movement. 8 ½" high, width 3 ¾". **$2.35**
No. 8710. Postpaid..

Circus Clown Clock

Instead of the usual pendulum this one has a swinging tie and with each swing of the tie it makes goo goo eyes that are ridiculously funny to watch. Rugged, accurate 30 hour movement. 8 ½" high, 3 ¾" wide.
No. 8721. Circus Clown Clock. Price Postpaid **$2.35**

Fan Dance Clock

When the clock is in operation the fan wiggles back and forth in a realistic manner that is extremely amusing. No matter who sees the clock, you can be sure that they will wish they had one. Height, 6 ¼ inches. **$2.75**
No. 8176. Postpaid....

Life-Like Swinging Bird Clock

$35.00

(Right) Bird swings back and forth continuously while clock is running. You will enjoy watching him on his perch, at the top of his house, colorful & happy. Makes you happy too! Attractively carved - design in moulded wood with ornamental weights & chain. 30 hour movement. Measures 7-in. high. **$3.33**
No. 8720. Price

$75.00

Pirate Clock

Cast metal case with rich finish. 30 hour movement, fancy dial. Width, 4 ½ inches.
No. 8174. Pirate Clock. Price Postpaid **$2.35**

$95.00

Scottie Dog Clock

Miniature Scottie dog clock. It has two scottie dogs seated on the base. Gold and black ribbon dial adds greatly to its appearance. 30 hour movement.
No. 8712. Scottie Clock. Price Postpaid **$2.55**

$250.00

Scotty Dog Clock

With each swing of pendulum, Scottie cocks his head in an inquisitive pose. Face is made in an imitation carved and artistically decorated compound. 30 hour, guaranteed movement. 6" high and 4 ½" wide. **$1.95**
No. 8722. Price Postpaid

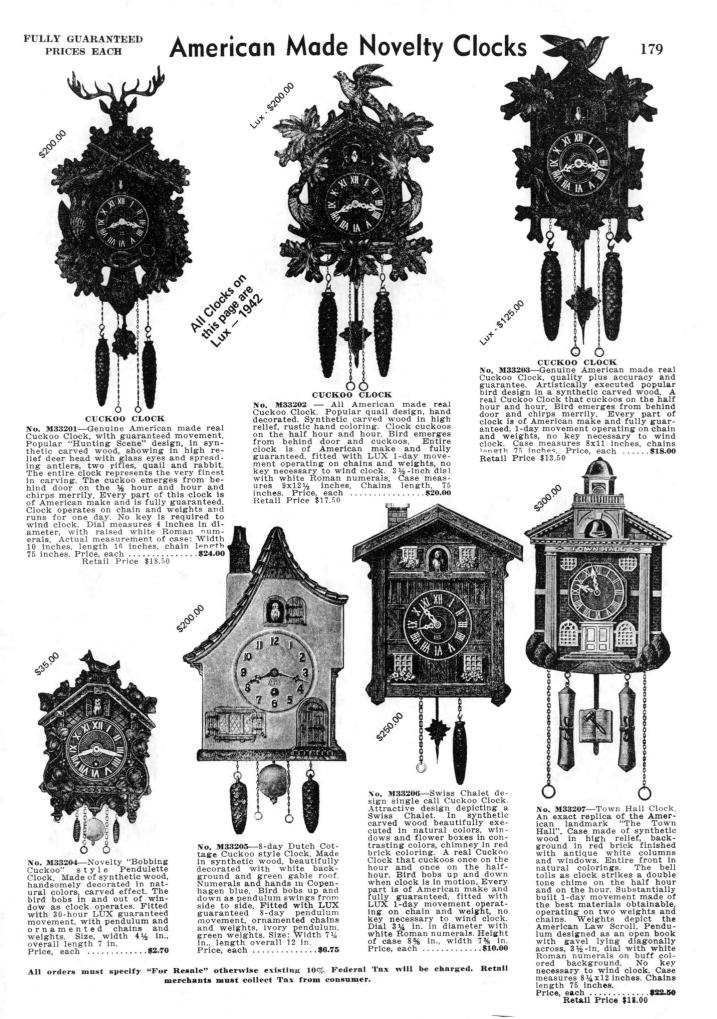

$200.00

Lux – $200.00

All Clocks on this page are Lux – 1942

Lux - $125.00

$300.00

$35.00

$200.00

$250.00

CUCKOO CLOCK

No. M33201—Genuine American made real Cuckoo Clock, with guaranteed movement. Popular "Hunting Scene" design, in synthetic carved wood, showing in high relief deer head with glass eyes and spreading antlers, two rifles, quail and rabbit. The entire clock represents the very finest in carving. The cuckoo emerges from behind door on the ½ hour and hour and chirps merrily. Every part of this clock is of American make and is fully guaranteed. Clock operates on chain and weights and runs for one day. No key is required to wind clock. Dial measures 4 inches in diameter, with raised white Roman numerals. Actual measurement of case: Width 10 inches, length 16 inches, chain length 75 inches. Price, each **$24.00**
Retail Price $18.50

CUCKOO CLOCK

No. M33202 — All American made real Cuckoo Clock. Popular quail design, hand decorated. Synthetic carved wood in high relief, rustic hand coloring. Clock cuckoos on the half hour and hour. Bird emerges from behind door and cuckoos. Entire clock is of American make and fully guaranteed, fitted with LUX 1-day movement operating on chains and weights, no key necessary to wind clock. 3½-inch dial with white Roman numerals. Case measures 9x12½ inches. Chains length, 75 inches. Price, each **$20.00**
Retail Price $17.50

CUCKOO CLOCK

No. M33203—Genuine American made real Cuckoo Clock, quality plus accuracy and guarantee. Artistically executed popular bird design in a synthetic carved wood. A real Cuckoo Clock that cuckoos on the half hour and hour. Bird emerges from behind door and chirps merrily. Every part of clock is of American make and fully guaranteed, 1-day movement operating on chain and weights, no key necessary to wind clock. Case measures 8x11 inches, chains length 75 inches. Price, each **$18.00**
Retail Price $13.50

No. M33204—Novelty "Bobbing Cuckoo" style Pendulette Clock. Made of synthetic wood, handsomely decorated in natural colors, carved effect. The bird bobs in and out of window as clock operates. Fitted with 30-hour LUX guaranteed movement, with pendulum and ornamented chains and weights. Size, width 4½ in., overall length 7 in.
Price, each **$2.70**

No. M33205—8-day Dutch Cottage Cuckoo style Clock. Made in synthetic wood, beautifully decorated with white background and green gable roof. Numerals and hands in Copenhagen blue. Bird bobs up and down as pendulum swings from side to side. Fitted with LUX guaranteed 8-day pendulum movement, ornamented chains and weights, ivory pendulum, green weights. Size: Width 7¼ in., length overall 12 in.
Price, each **$6.75**

No. M33206—Swiss Chalet design single call Cuckoo Clock. Attractive design depicting a Swiss Chalet. In synthetic carved wood beautifully executed in natural colors, windows and flower boxes in contrasting colors, chimney in red brick coloring. A real Cuckoo Clock that cuckoos once on the hour and once on the half-hour. Bird bobs up and down when clock is in motion. Every part is of American make and fully guaranteed, fitted with LUX 1-day movement operating on chain and weight, no key necessary to wind clock. Dial 3¼ in. in diameter with white Roman numerals. Height of case 8⅝ in., width 7⅜ in. Price, each **$10.00**

No. M33207—Town Hall Clock. An exact replica of the American landmark "The Town Hall". Case made of synthetic wood in high relief, background in red brick finished with antique white columns and windows. Entire front in natural colorings. The bell tolls as clock strikes a double tone chime on the half hour and on the hour. Substantially built 1-day movement made of the best materials obtainable, operating on two weights and chains. Weights depict the American Law Scroll. Pendulum designed as an open book with gavel lying diagonally across, 3½-in. dial with white Roman numerals on buff colored background. No key necessary to wind clock. Case measures 8¼ x12 inches. Chains length 75 inches.
Price, each **$22.50**
Retail Price $18.00

All orders must specify "For Resale" otherwise existing 10% Federal Tax will be charged. Retail merchants must collect Tax from consumer.

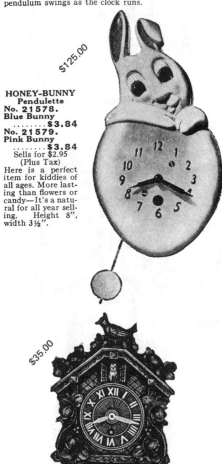

1951

$100.00

RUDOLPH
THE RED NOSED REINDEER
By Lux

No. 21574. Red Nosed Reindeer..........**$3.84**
Sells for $2.95 (Plus Tax)

Rudolph—The Red Nosed Reindeer—America's favorite animal character prances gaily on the front of this Pendulette. His Luminous Rosy Nose that makes him Santa's favorite leader **actually glows.** Handsome mahogany colored cottage front has simulated carved decorations. Backed by Lux Guaranteed 30-hour movement. Yes, the pendulum swings as the clock runs.

$6.00

LUX MINUTE-MINDER

No. 21575. Mahogany Color Case.......**$6.40**
No. 21576. Ivory Color Case............. **6.40**
Sells for $4.95 (Plus Tax)

The Minute Minder—long a kitchen "must" for good cooking. Now with its new distinctive styling and decorative colors. Take this handy timer into the living room, bedroom or for use anywhere around the house. Remind one of appointments—favorite radio and TV programs. Use for Game timing—Photo developing—Sun and Heat lamps and for timing home permanents. Let the kiddies use to time their games, chore time and clean up time or study time and practice time.
Rich Mahogany, Plastic Ivory Numerals.
White Plastic with Bright Red Numerals.

$35.00

BLUE BIRD PENDULETTE

No. 21577. Swinging Bird Pendulette....**$3.**
Sells for $2.95 (Plus Tax)

BLUEBIRD PENDULETTE CLOCK (It does all except Cuckoo). Attractively designed Novelty clock made Moulded Wood—A rustic house with Leaf trimmed tre featuring Bluebird swinging to and fro, feeding its yo as clock is in operation—LUX 30-hour Guaranteed k wind Movement with ornamented Chains and Weight A practical Time Keeper for any room in the home an natural for a child's room. Mahogany color case—Hei 7", width 4".

$125.00

HONEY-BUNNY
Pendulette
No. 21578.
Blue Bunny
.......**$3.84**
No. 21579.
Pink Bunny
.......**$3.84**
Sells for $2.95
(Plus Tax)

Here is a perfect item for kiddies of all ages. More lasting than flowers or candy—It's a natural for all year selling. Height 8", width 3½".

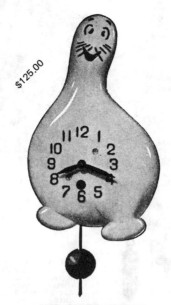

$125.00

$185.00

FIRE-CHIEF PETUNIA
PENDULETTE

No. 21580. Petunia Pendulette..........**$3.**
Sells for $2.95 (Plus Tax)

Everyone loves the Flowers and the Bees!—The Petu has both. The case is a Brilliant "Fire Chief" Red w Green stalk and leaves and Brown and Yellow "peek Bee" Pendulum. Guaranteed Lux 30-hour moveme Height 6½", width 4".

SHMOO—PENDULETTE

No. 21582. White Case..................**$3.84**
No. 21583. Shmoo Pink.................. **3.84**
No. 21584. Shmoo Blue.................. **3.84**
Sells for $2.95 (Plus Tax)

SHMOO PENDULETTE CLOCK. The most popular new cartoon character—Tells time exclusively through Lux—The case is smooth to simulate the skin of the Shmoo—Swinging Pendulum gives an eye catching animation—30-hour Guaranteed Lux Movement—An outstanding item in the Juvenile Trade. Width 3¾"—Overall Height 7¾".

$35.00

CUCKOO STYLE PENDULETTE

No. 21581. Bobbing Bird Pendulette.....**$3.84**
Sells for $2.95 (Plus Tax)

BOBBING CUCKOO STYLE PENDULETTE CLOCK (It does all except Cuckoo). A Miniature of the everpopular Cuckoo style clock made of Moulded Wood in **Walnut Finish**—with Leaves in high relief and Bird on top of house—**Red Bird bobs in and out of window** as clock is in operation—30 hour LUX Guaranteed Keywind Movement—Ornamented Chains and Weights—A practical Time Keeper for any room in the home and a natural for a child's room. Height 7½", width 4¼".

$35.00

CUCKOO TYPE PENDULETTE

No. 21585. Old Cuckoo Style Pendulette..**$3.**
Sells for $2.95 (Plus Tax)

OLD STYLE CUCKOO TYPE PENDULETTE CLOC (It does all except Cuckoo). Made of Synthetic Woo Handsomely decorated in natural colors—Carved Effec The bird bobs in and out of window as clock is in operat —Fitted with 30 hour LUX Guaranteed Keywind Mo ment—With Pendulum & Ornamented Chains & Weig —A practical Time Keeper for any room in the home a a natural for a child's room. Verde-Green color—Hei 7¼", width 4¼".

New Lux 48 Hour Alarms—Thin Movement—Slimmed for Beauty

FAIR VIEW ALARM
By Lux
. 21561. Fairview Alarm.................$3.44
Sells for $2.69 (Plus Tax)
ne Red color case 5x4¼ in. with rural scene in full
ors on dial, the Red Barn and the Bridge over the
ream in the foreground. Lux guaranteed movement.

1951

PETIT—ALARM
No. 21562. Plain Dial...................$6.60
Sells for $4.95 (Plus Tax)
No. 21563. Luminous Dial..............$7.74
Sells for $5.95 (Plus Tax)
The most beautiful Boudoir clock in the popular priced
range—Made in Connecticut, USA, it looks like a fine
Swiss product which sells for much more—Single Key
winds both Clock and Alarm—Guaranteed Lux move-
ment—Ivory Color Baked Enamel Finish—Extremely
readable porcelain dial—Heavy pedestal base—Width
2⅞", height 3⅛".

SPINNING WHEEL—ALARM
By Lux
No. 21564. Spinning Wheel Alarm........$3.80
Sells for $2.95 (Plus Tax)
The spinning wheel comes with Home Scene in full colors
with the turning wheel on the dial. Action gets action.
The Homey scene has the charm and appeal of yesteryear.
Case is finished in Wine-Red Scratch-Resistant Baked
Enamel with the famous Lux guaranteed 48-hour move-
ment.

NEW HARVESTER ALARM
By Lux
. 21565. New Harvester Alarm.........$3.24
Sells for $2.39 (Plus Tax)
. 21566. With Luminous Dial..........$4.40
Sells for $3.29 (Plus Tax)
e Harvester styled-to-the-Minute comes in the new
rly "Hammered Grey" Finish Case with a white dial.
e new slim case is fitted with the latest Lux 48-hour
n movement and quieter "Tick." They're out of this
rld when it comes to looks and performance.

SLUMBER MINDER ALARM
By Lux
No. 21567. Slumber Minder Gunmetal.....$4.80
No. 21568. Slumber Minder Ivory........ 4.80
Sells for $3.69 (Plus Tax)
The new Slumber-Minder is an old friend in a new, stream-
lined "figure" and a fresh modern design Dial. Ivory color
case has hours and hands in Gilt Color. Gunmetal Grey
color case has silvery hours and hands.

PAGE ALARM
By Lux
No. 21269. Page Grey...................$3.02
Sells for $1.99 (Plus Tax)
The finish of the Page is a Hammered Grey—Height
4¼ Inches. One-day movement.

HARVESTER ALARM
. 21571. ....$3.00
Sells for $2.39 (Plus Tax)
quare Alarm Clock on Smartly Designed Base—Top
ut-off Alarm Switch—Artistically styled Buff Dial—
wed Glass—Metal Case—Polished Brass Bezel—Ivory
lor "Baked Enamel" prevents marring and peeling off of
ish—Precision made Movement. Height 4⅝", width
¼".

SYMPHONY ALARM
No. 21572. ....$4.72
Sells for $3.59 (Plus Tax)
A new and distinctive Alarm Clock of Individual Design—
Full Molded Walnut color Plastic Case with Dial Numerals clearly embossed on a contrasting background—Sides
of case made with Ornamental Ridges—Bowed Glass covers hands and minute marks only—Fitted with Precision
made Movement. Height 4½"; width 6⅛".

CHILTON ALARM
No. 21573. ....$4.00
Sells for $3.0) (Plus Tax)
Streamlined Pedestal Alarm Clock—Back shut-off Alarm
Switch. Base in modern trend with polished metal strips—
Artistic two-tone Metallic dial—Bowed Glass—Ivory
color "Baked Enamel" prevents marring and peeling off
of finish—Precision made Movement. Height 5⅛",
width 4⅝".

THE LUX CLOCK MANUFACTURING CO., INC.
WATERBURY 20, CONNECTICUT

WHOLESALER PRICE LIST

THE LUX CLOCK COMPANY, INC.
1107 BROADWAY, NEW YORK 10, N. Y.

Effective April 16, 1956

RETAILS—$1.1

RETAILS—$1.2

RETAILS—$1.2

ALARMS

	STYLE NO.	
$5.00	203	Lebanon Ivory Case $2.98
$5.00	220	Chilton Ivory Case — $3.85
	220R	Chilton/Luminous Ivory Case — $4.95
$12.00	236	Fairview Wine Red Case $3.50
$6.00	237	Conqueror Ivory Case — $3.35
	237R	Conqueror/Luminous Ivory Case — $3.95
$85.00	270	Spinning Wheel Wine Red Case $3.60
$85.00	272	Grist Mill Hammered Gray $3.60

PENDULETTES

	STYLE NO.	
$35.00	301	Swinging Bird Mahogany $3.75
$45.00	315	Hunter Walnut $3.98
$35.00	312	Bobbing Bird Walnut $3.75
$45.00	314	Dove Mahogany $3.98

MINUTE MINDERS

	STYLE NO.	
$6.00	2428	Single Ding White, Red Yellow $3.95
$6.00	1928	Long Ring White, Ivory Mahogany $4.95

DATE MINDER CALENDAR CLOCK

	STYLE NO.	
$35.00	5120	Grey and White dial with raised polished Brass Numerals. $10.95
$35.00	5121	Gold, White and Black dial with Black Numerals. $10.95
		Available in Metallic Bronze, Antique Yellow, Flame Red, Ebony and Ice White.

RETAILS—$1.6

RETAILS—$1.7

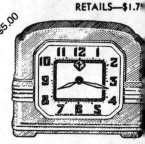

RETAILS—$2.00

1928

Beauty of design, excellence of materials and craftsmanship, and perfection of imported movements, enter into the making of every Colonial Clock. The Colonial line fully meets the requirements of all types of home furnishings. "There is a Colonial Clock for every good home." Solid Honduras mahogany is used in all Colonial Clocks. Colonial movements are the finest products of renowned clock makers of Europe.

$2500.00-3000.00

$700.00-900.00

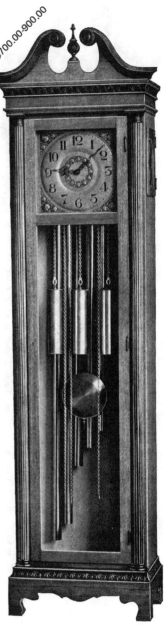

$700.00-900.00

$350.00-450.00

No. 1500/68 . . . . . $688.00
Height, 81"; width, 22"; depth, 16".
...nders the Westminster Chimes every quarter on four tubular -inch bells, and strikes the hour on the fifth bell.

No. 1500/88 . . . . . $738.00
...ys the Canterbury on six, and Westminster on four, tubular ...ls and strikes the hour on the seventh bell.

No. 1500/82 . . . . . $846.00
...imes on each quarter either the ...hittington on eight, Canterbury ...six, or Westminster on four, ...inch tubular bells, and strikes the hour on the ninth bell.

No. 1525/38 . . . . . $539.00
Smaller case with 5 tubes, Westminster Chime.

No. 1505/36 . . . . . $340.00
Height 79"; width, 21"; depth, 12".
Plays the Westminster Chimes on every quarter on four rods, and strikes the hour on four rods. Key wind. 8-Day weight movement.

No. 1505/54 . . . . . $280.00
Description same as No. 1505/36 but is chain wound.

No. 1506/53 . . . . . $338.00
Height, 81"; width, 21"; depth, 12".
Renders the Westminster Chimes on four tubular bells and strikes the hour on the fifth. Chain wind. 8-Day weight movement.

No. 1506/11 . . . . . $206.00
8-Day. Hour and half hour strike on large Cathedral Gong. Chain wind.

No. 1513/22 . . . . . $136.00
Height, 66"; width, 12"; depth, 7".
Chimes the Westminster on four rods and strikes the hour on four rods. Spring wind. 8-Day self-adjusting movement.

No. 1513/14 . . . . . $110.00
8-Day. Hour and half hour strike on three rods. Called Echo Chimes.

PRICES SHOWN ON THIS PAGE ARE KEYSTONE

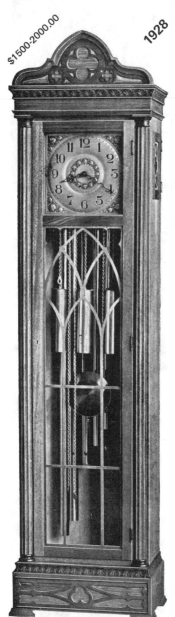

$1500-2000.00

1928

All Colonial Hall Chime Movements are encased in solid brass plates of various sizes. They have dead beat escapements. Maintaining power, cut steel pinions and self-adjusting chime and strike. Shut-off levers on all models.

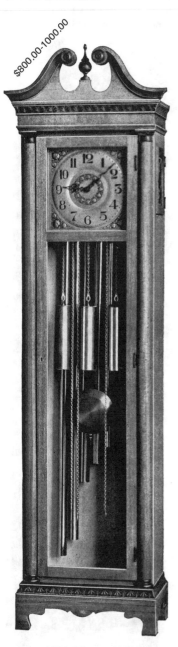

$800.00-1000.00

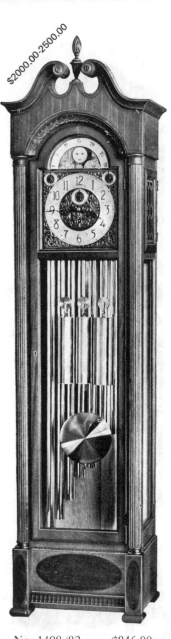

$2000.00-2500.00

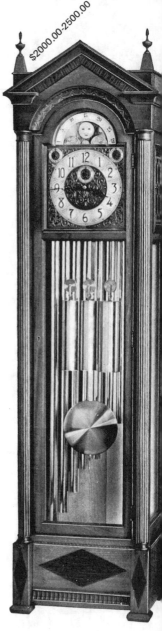

$2000.00-2500.00

No. 1496/36.....$354.00

Height, 82"; width, 21"; depth, 12".

Renders Westminster Chimes on four rods and strikes the hour on four rods. Three brass weights. Key wind. 8-Day.

No. 1496/53.....$354.00

Plays Westminster Chimes on four 1⅜-inch tubular bells, and strikes hour on fifth. Three weights. Chain wind. 8-Day.

No. 1496/54.....$293.00

Chimes Westminster on four rods, and strikes hour on four rods. Three weights. Chain wind. 8-Day.

No. 1494/39.....$386.00

Height, 81"; width, 21"; depth, 12".

Renders Westminster Chimes on four 1⅜-inch tubular bells, and strikes the hour on the fifth. Three brass weights. Chain wind.

No. 1498/82.....$846.00

Height, 85"; width, 22"; depth, 16".

Plays on each quarter either the Whittington on eight, or the Canterbury on six, or Westminster on four, 1¼-inch tubular bells, and strikes the hour on the ninth. Three weights. Key wind. Self-adjusting 8-day movement.

No. 1499/88.....$738.00

Height, 81"; width, 22"; depth, 16".

Chimes the Canterbury on six, Westminster on four, tubular bells and strikes the hour on the seventh. Three weights. Key wind. Self-adjusting 8-day movement.

No. 1499/68.....$688.00

Renders Westminster Chimes on four tubular bells, and strikes hour on fifth. Three weights. Key wind. Self-adjusting 8-day movement.

"GRANDMOTHER MODELS"

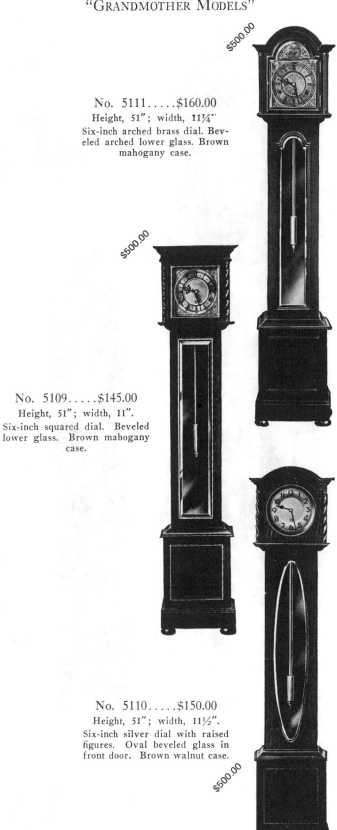

$450.00-550.00

1928

$450.00-550.00

$500.00

$500.00

$500.00

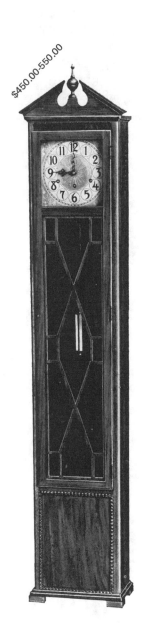

No. 5111.....$160.00
Height, 51"; width, 11¼"
Six-inch arched brass dial. Beveled arched lower glass. Brown mahogany case.

No. 5109.....$145.00
Height, 51"; width, 11".
Six-inch squared dial. Beveled lower glass. Brown mahogany case.

No. 1514/22..$136.00
Height, 68"; width, 12"; depth, 7".
Renders Westminster Chimes on four rods, and strikes the hour on four rods. Spring wind. -Day. Self-adjusting movement.

No. 1514/14..$110.00
Half hour strike on three rods. Called Echo Chimes. 8-Day.

No. 1515/22..$136.00
Height, 67"; width, 12"; depth, 7".
Description same as No. 1514/22.

No. 1515/14..$110.00
Description same as No. 1514/14.

No. 5110.....$150.00
Height, 51"; width, 11½".
Six-inch silver dial with raised figures. Oval beveled glass in front door. Brown walnut case.

1928

Revere Telechron Clocks offer observatory time by electricity with Symphony Chimes, all from the light circuit. When once set correctly, the clock can be depended upon as accurate—the light socket holding the secret. There is a Revere Telechron Chiming Clock for every home, whether large or small. They are available in chiming Westminster on four rods with hour-strike on deep tone symphony rod, making five in all; or a combination chiming Westminster and Canterbury on six rod with the hour-strike on a triple-chord using three of the chiming rods.

The prices quoted on this page are the SUGGESTED RETAIL PRICES.

$450.00

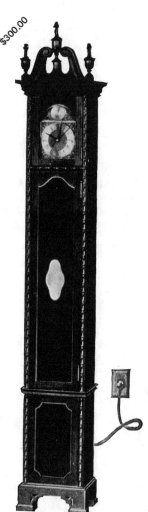

$300.00

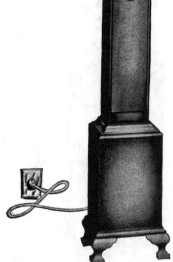

$300.00

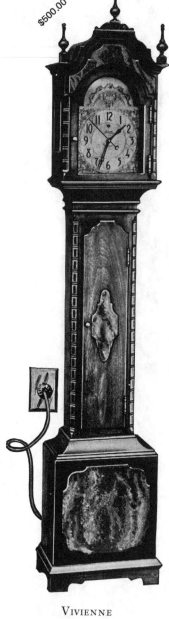

$500.00

ROSEMARY
Westminster and
Canterbury Chimes
Lacquer Finish
Spanish Highlighted
Heighth 72"   Width 11½"
Depth 7½"
Suggested Retail Price . . . $209.00

JENNY LIND
Westminster Chime
Lacquer Finish
Spanish Highlighted
Heighth 68"   Width 11¼"
Depth 8¼"
Suggested Retail Price . . . $176.00

PRISCILLA
Westminster Chime
Lacquer Finish
Spanish Highlighted
Heighth 73"   Width 10"
Depth 7¼"
Suggested Retail Price . . . $198.00

VIVIENNE
Westminster and
Canterbury Chimes
Lacquer Finish
Spanish Highlighted
Heighth 73"   Width 13"
Depth 8"
Suggested Retail Price . . . $220.00

HALL CLOCKS OF ARTISTIC BEAUTY AND CRAFTSMANSHIP

$5,000.00—6,500.00

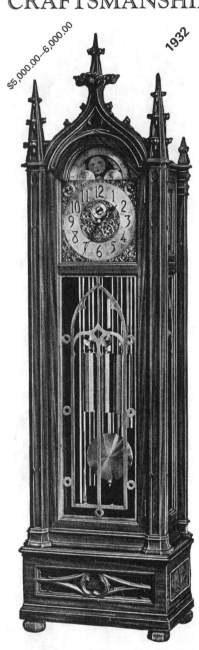

$5,000.00—6,000.00

1932

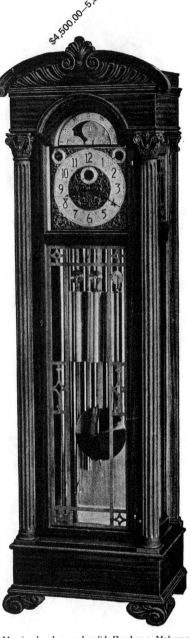

$4,500.00—5,500.00

Solid Honduras Mahogany Case.

Height 84 inches, width 25 inches, depth 17 inches. Carved from solid wood. Base overlaid with figured veneer offset with finely carved ornaments. Hand carved fret in door. Filigree weights and pendulum. Beveled plate glass door and sides. Fitted with imported eight day, three chime, nine tube bell movement. Solid brass plates measuring 6¼x8 inches. Renders on each quarter either the Whittington Chime on eight, Canterbury on six or Westminster on four 1½ inch tubular bells and strikes the hour on the ninth. It has steel cut pinions, Graham dead beat escapement, maintaining power, brass cables, key wind, three large filigree weights, 6¾ inch pendulum ball and steel pendulum rod. Chimes and hour strike can be silenced, or chimes changed from Westminster to Whittington or Canterbury by shifting levers on dial.

A heavy brass filigree dial, 13x19 inches, mounted with raised silvered hour ring, arch ring, second and setting circles. Hour, second and setting circles and hemispheres nicely engraved. Finely finished beveled gilt raised hour figures. Saw pierced, chased and engraved gilt corner and center ornaments. Hand painted moving moon wheel showing marine view and landscape.

A483H01. .... $1470.00

F. O. B. Central Michigan

Gothic design with hand carved solid Honduras Mahogany case.

Height 97 inches, width 27 inches, depth 18 inches. Beveled plate glass door and sides fitted with imported eight day, three chime, nine tube bell movement with solid brass plates measuring 6¼x8 inches. Renders on each quarter the Whittington chime on eight, Canterbury on six or Westminster on four 1¼ inch tubular bells and strikes the hour on the ninth. It has steel cut pinions, Graham dead beat escapement, maintaining power, brass cables, key wind, three large weights, gridiron pendulum which has four brass and three steel rods placed alternately and is fitted with a nine inch spun brass pendulum ball with brass lyre on top. Chimes and hour strike can be silenced or chimes changed from Westminster to Whittington or Canterbury by shifting levers on dial.

A heavy brass dial 13x19 inches, mounted with raised silvered hour ring, arch ring, second and setting circles. Hour, second and setting circles nicely engraved. Finely finished, pierced, chased and engraved gilt corner and center ornaments. Hand painted moving moon wheel showing marine view and landscape.

A483H02.................................$1148.00

F. O. B. Central Michigan

Massive hand carved solid Honduras Mahogany case.

Height 80 inches, width 25 inches, depth 16 inches. Beveled plate glass.

Fitted with imported eight day, three chime, nine tube bell movement with solid brass plates measuring 6¼x8 inches. Renders on each quarter either the Whittington chime on eight, Canterbury on six or Westminster on four 1¼ inch tubular bells and strikes the hour on the ninth. It has steel cut pinions, Graham dead beat escapement, maintaining power, brass cables, key wind, three large weights, 6¾ inch pendulum ball and steel pendulum rod. Chimes and hour strike can be silenced, or chimes changed from Westminster to Whittington or Canterbury by shifting levers on dial.

A heavy brass dial, 13x19 inches, mounted with raised silvered ring, arch ring, second and setting circles. Hour, second and setting circles and hemispheres, nicely engraved. Finely finished beveled gilt raised hour figures. Saw pierced, chased and engraved gilt corner and center ornaments. Hand painted moving moon wheel showing marine view and landscape.

A483H03.................................$890.00

F. O. B. Central Michigan

MAY & MALONE, INC.

FINE CHIME CLOCKS OF SUBSTANTIAL QUALITY

1932

$4,500.00—5,000.00

$4,000.00—5,000.00

$4,500.00—5,500.00

Oak Antique Finished Case. Height 79 inches, width 19 inches, depth 14 inches.

Fitted with imported large size heavy construction, eight day, two chime, seven tube bell movement. Renders on each quarter either the St. Johns chime on six, or Westminster on four 1⅛-inch tubular bells and strikes the hour on the seventh. It has steel cut pinions, Graham dead beat escapement, maintaining power, brass cables, key wind, three large weights, eight-inch pendulum ball and steel pendulum rod. Self adjusting chime arrangement. To set the clock hands can be turned backward without shutting off the chime or strike and it will chime correctly when it reaches the hour. Chimes and hour strike can be silenced or chime changed from St. John to Westminster by shifting levers on dial.

Heavy brass dial, mounted with raised silver hour ring, saw pierced and beautifully engraved ornaments and raised numerals. Hand painted, moving moonwheel showing Marine view and landscape.

A484H01.   Price.........................$750.00

F. O. B. Northern Illinois
Shipping weight 310 lbs.

Solid Brown Mahogany Hand Rubbed Case. Height 85 inches, Width 23 inches, Depth 16 inches.

Fitted with imported large size heavy construction, eight day, two chime, seven tubular bell movement. Renders on each quarter either the St. Johns chime on six, or Westminster on four 1⅛-inch tubular bells and strikes the hour on the seventh. It has steel cut pinions, Graham dead beat escapement, maintaining power, brass cables, key wind, three large weights, eight-inch pendulum ball and steel pendulum rod. Self-adjusting chime arrangement. Chimes and hour strike can be silenced or chime changed from St. Johns to Westminster by shifting levers on dial.

Heavy brass dial, mounted with raised silver hour ring, saw pierced and beautifully engraved ornaments and raised numerals. Hand painted moving moonwheel showing Marine view and landscape.

A484H02.   Price.........................$669.00

F. O. B. Northern Illinois
Shipping weight 372 lbs.

Solid Honduras Mahogany Case. Height 87 inches, Width 22 inches, Depth 16 inches.

Fitted with imported eight day, two chime, seven tubular bell movement with solid brass plates measuring 8x8½ inches. Renders on each quarter, the Canterbury on six, or Westminster on four 1¼-inch tubular bells and strikes the hour on the seventh. Movement is self adjusting, that is, you can turn the hands backward or forward without shutting off the chime or strike and it will chime and strike correctly when it gets to the hour. It has steel cut pinions, Graham dead beat escapement, maintaining power, brass cables, key wind, three large weights, 8-inch pendulum ball and steel pendulum rod. Chimes and hour strike can be silenced, or chimes changed from Westminster to Canterbury by shifting levers on dial.

A heavy brass dial, 11x16 inches, mounted with raised silvered hour ring, arch ring, second and setting circles. Hour, second and setting circles and hemispheres, nicely engraved. Finely finished beveled gilt raised hour figures. Saw pierced, chased and engraved gilt corner and center ornaments. Hand painted moving moon-wheel showing Marine view and landscape.

A484H03.   Price.........................$739.00

F. O. B. Central Michigan
Shipping weight 300 lbs.

MAY & MALONE, INC.

THESE CLOCKS ARE BUILT TO KEEP ACCURATE TIME FOR GENERATIONS

1932

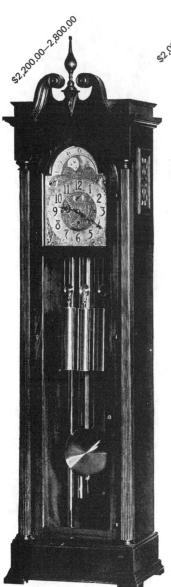

$2,200.00—2,800.00

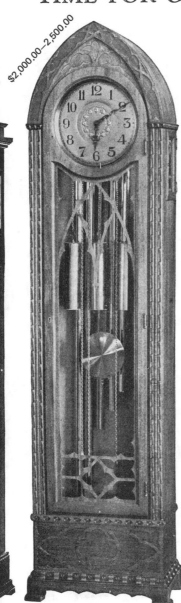

$2,000.00—2,500.00

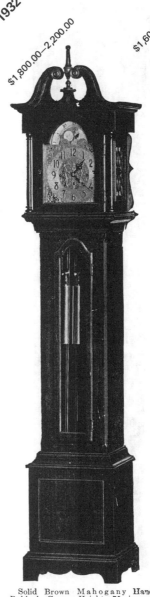

$1,800.00—2,200.00

$1,600.00—2,000.00

Solid Brown Mahogany Hand Rubbed Case. Height 82 inches. Width 20 inches. Depth 14 inches.

Fitted with imported large size heavy construction eight day three chime, nine tubular bell movement. Renders on each quarter either the Whittington Chime on eight, St. Johns Chime on six, or Westminster on four 1⅛-inch tubular bells and strikes the hour on the ninth. It has steel cut pinions, Graham dead beat escapement, maintaining power, brass cables, key wind, three large weights, eight inch pendulum ball and steel pendulum rod. Self adjusting chime arrangement. Chimes and hour strike can be silenced or chime changed from Whittington to St. Johns or Westminster by shifting levers on dial.

Heavy brass dial 11x16 inches, mounted with raised silver hour ring, saw pierced and beautifully engraved ornaments and raised numerals. Hand painted moving moon-wheel showing marine view and landscape.

A485H01. Price............$580.50

F.O.B. Northern Illinois
Shipping Weight 330 Pounds

ELECTRIC

Solid Honduras Mahogany Case. Height 78 inches. Width 21 inches. Depth 12 inches.

Fitted with movement which is wound by a Universal motor that is plugged in any light socket, and is suitable for all cycles and either alternating or direct current. It automatically winds every twenty-four hours, but will operate without current until weights reach bottom of clock. Approximately three to four days. Renders Westminster chime on every quarter on four 1⅜-inch tubular bells and strikes the hour on the fifth. Movement is encased in heavy solid damask brass plates 9x6 inches. Has Graham dead beat escapement, maintaining power, steel cut pinions, three large brass weights, wooden pendulum rod, chain wind, and has a 6¼-inch brass pendulum ball. The movement is self adjusting, that is you can turn the hands backward or forward without shutting off the chime or strike, and it will chime and strike correctly when it gets to the hour. Chimes and hour strike can be silenced by shifting levers on dial.

A485H02. Price............$479.00

F.O.B. Central Michigan
Shipping Weight 200 Pounds

Solid Brown Mahogany Hand Rubbed Case. Height 75 inches. Width 14 inches. Depth 11 inches.

Fitted with imported small size eight day one chime, five tubular bell movement. Renders on each quarter the Westminster chime on four 1⅛-inch tubular bells and strikes the hour on the fifth. Encased in heavy brass plates, steel cut pinions, Graham dead beat escapement, solid damask brass plates, maintaining power, brass cables, key wind, three medium weights and 6½-inch pendulum ball. Self adjusting chime arrangement. To set the clock hands can be turned backward without shutting off the chime or strike and it will chime correctly when it reaches the hour. Chime and hour strike can be silenced by shifting levers on dial.

Brass dial, 9x12 inches, mounted with raised silver hour ring, saw pierced and beautifully engraved ornaments and raised numerals. Hand painted moving moon-wheel showing marine view and landscape.

A485H03. Price............$433.00

F.O.B. Northern Illinois
Shipping Weight 150 Pounds

ELECTRIC

Solid Honduras Mahogany.

Height 77 inches. Width 21 inches, Depth 12 inches.

Fitted with imported electrically wound Westminster rod chime movement. It is wound by a Universal motor by plugging in any light socket and is suitable for all cycles and either alternating or direct current. Automatically winds every twenty-four hours, but will operate without current until weights reach bottom of clock, approximately three to four days. It has a Westminster chime which operates on every quarter on four rods and strikes the hour on one accord on four rods. A chime of high quality and pleasing tones. The movement is encased in heavy brass plates 5¾x8¾ inches, Graham dead beat escapement, maintaining power, steel cut pinions, three large brass weights, wooden pendulum rod, chain wind and has a 6½-inch brass pendulum ball. Chimes are self adjusting. Hour strike and chimes can be silenced by shifting levers on side of movement.

A485H04. Price............$333.00

F.O.B. Central Michigan
Shipping Weight 200 Pounds

MAY & MALONE, INC.

THE MOVEMENTS ARE BUILT TO A DEGREE OF FINENESS AND ACCURACY, UNSURPASSED BY ANY CLOCK MAKER IN THE WORLD

$300.00—500.00

$200.00—300.00

1932

$175.00—250.00

$150.00—225.00

ELECTRIC

Solid Honduras Mahogany Case. Height, 73 inches. Width, 14 inches. Depth, 8 inches. Top arch overlaid with Madiou Burl and mouldings. Base and door nicely offset with mouldings and ornaments.

Fitted with imported Westminster chime movement which is wound by a Universal electric motor, by merely plugging in any light socket, and is suitable for all cycles and either alternating or direct current. Automatically winds at stated intervals, but will operate without current until spring is completely unwound, or approximately seven days. This movement renders on each quarter the Westminster chime on four rods and also strikes the hour on two rods. It is encased in heavy brass plates 5½ x 5¼ inches. Chimes are self-adjusting, dead beat escapement, wooden pendulum rod and a cylindrical brass pendulum ball.

A486H01. Price..........**$182.00**

F.O.B. Central Michigan
Shipping Weight 80 Pounds

ELECTRIC

Solid Honduras Mahogany Case nicely offset with fine mouldings. Height, 72 inches. Width, 15 inches. Depth, 9 inches.

Imported Synchronous Westminster chime movement which operates only on 60-cycle alternating current. The rotor of the American motor revolves at the comparatively slow speed of 225 R.P.M. Every shaft or gear which rotates at a speed greater than 30 R.P.M. runs in oil completely enclosed in the mechanism. Will keep absolutely accurate time when properly started and set, through controlled generating stations, by plugging into the light socket. The movement renders, at each quarter, the Westminster chime on four rods, strikes the hour in one accord on four rods, with a chime of high quality and pleasing tones. It is encased in heavy solid brass plates 5x5¼ inches, and is self adjusting, that is, you can turn the hands backward and forward without shutting off the chime or strike, and it will chime and strike correctly when it gets to the hour.

A486H02. Price..............**$162.50**

F.O.B. Central Michigan
Shipping Weight 60 Pounds

Solid Brown Mahogany Hand Rubbed Case. Height, 61 inches. Width, 11 in. Depth, 9 in.

Fitted with imported eight-day Westminster, six-rod chime movement. Renders on each quarter the Westminster chime on four rods and strikes the full hour in one accord on four rods; a chime of high quality and pleasing tones. Spring wind, encased in heavy brass plates, steel cut pinions and Graham dead beat escapement. It has three l a r g e highest quality springs enclosed in barrels, and all three springs are detachable in a new and extremely simple manner. Self-adjusting, in that, you can turn the hands backwards and forwards without shutting off the chime or strike, and it will chime or strike correctly when it gets to the hour.

Dial, brass and silver beautifully etched with sunken black numerals.

A486H03. Price......**$154.50**

F.O.B. Northern Illinois
Shipping Weight 79 Pounds

ELECTRIC CORNER CLOCK

Honduras Mahogany Case neatly offset with fine mouldings, having a door with suitably designed grill.

Height, 73 inches. Width, 15 inches. Depth, 9 inches.

A synchronous time electric movement operating on 60-cycle alternating current only. The rotor of the American motor revolves at the comparatively slow speed of 225 R.P.M. Every shaft or gear which rotates at a speed greater than 30 R.P.M. runs in oil completely enclosed in the mechanism. Movement will keep absolutely accurate time when properly started and set, through controlled generating stations, by plugging into the light socket.

The case is in the shape of a triangle and will fit back into the corner of a room. Books or curios may be attractively placed on the four shelves behind the glass door.

This is an entirely new idea in a combined master clock and shelf case.

A486H04. Price................**$56.00**

F.O.B. Central Michigan
Shipping Weight 60 Pounds

THE LOVELY CHIMES *of* FAMOUS CATHEDRALS

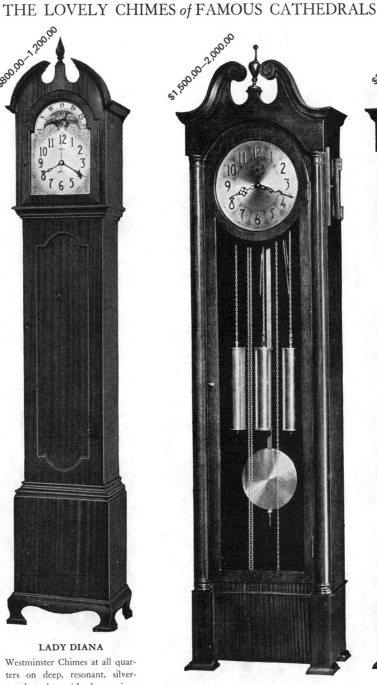

$1,200.00—1,800.00

1939

$800.00—1,200.00

$1,500.00—2,000.00

$2,000.00—2,500.00

MIDLAND

Westminster Chimes at all quarters on four tubular bells. Chimes can be silenced. Silver Dial. Mahogany case. 73½ inches high. 16 inches wide. 9½ inches deep.
$150.00

LADY DIANA

Westminster Chimes at all quarters on deep, resonant, silvertoned rods, with harmonious chord hour strike. Chimes can be silenced. The dial has gold plated scroll corners, raised numerals, and ornamental non-operating moon. Mahogany case. 71½ inches high. 12½ inches wide. 8¼ inches deep......**$100.00**

No. 509

Eight-day chain wind, weight-action Floor Clock. Self-adjusting movement, Westminster chimes each quarter hour on four deep-toned harmonious chime tone rods. Chord hour strikes on four separate deep-toned harmonious chime tone rods. Cases of genuine Honduras mahogany. Height, 80 inches. Width, 21 inches. Depth, 12 inches......**$200.00**

No. 511

Eight-day chain wind, weight-action Floor Clock. Self-adjusting movement. Westminster chimes each quarter hour on four deep-toned harmonious chime tone rods. Chord hour strikes on four separate deep-toned harmonious chime tone rods. Cases of genuine Honduras mahogany. Height, 80 inches. Width, 21 inches. Depth, 12 inches......**$270.00**

THE ABOVE CLOCKS FITTED WITH
SYNCHRONOUS ELECTRIC MOVEMENT

HERSCHEDE TUBULAR CHIMING FLOOR CLOCKS

THE LOVELY CHIMES *of* FAMOUS CATHEDRALS

1939

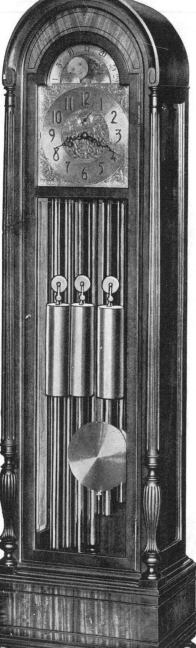

$2,750.00—4,500.00

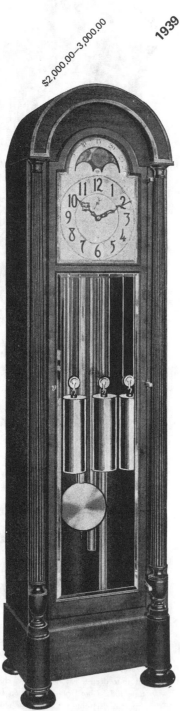

$2,000.00—3,000.00

$2,000.00—2,750.00

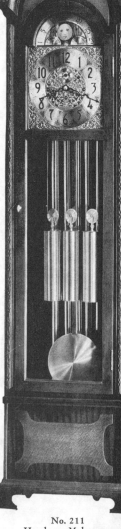

$2,000.00—3,000

No. 276—Honduras Mahogany
Satinwood top and base. Height, 78 inches. Width, 21 inches. Depth, 14¾ inches. Gold Dial with Moving Moon. Westminster Chimes on 5 tubular bells **$540.00**
Westminster and Canterbury Chimes on 7 tubular bells **$625.00**
Westminster, Canterbury and Whittington Chimes on 9 tubular bells **$670.00**

No. 214—Honduras Mahogany
Height, 78 inches. Width, 24 inches. Depth, 15 inches. Gold Dial with Moving Moon. Westminster Chimes on 5 tubular bells
$395.00

No. 217
Honduras Mahogany
Height, 80 inches. Width, 21 inches. Depth, 15 inches. Gold Dial with Moving Moon. Westminster Chimes on 5 tubular bells **$350.00**

No. 211
Honduras Mahogany
Height, 75¼ inches. Width, 19 inches. Depth, 12¼ inches. Go Dial with Moving Moon. Westminster Chimes on 5 tubular bel
$310.00

THE ABOVE CLOCKS FITTED WITH HAND-WOUND EIGHT-DAY WEIGHT ACTION MOVEMENTS

H═══H

Clocks for Every Purpose

Novel ideas in Clocks built for precision-skill and accuracy.

The Clocks on this page are fitted with guaranteed electrical movements.

$60.00

$75.00

$75.00

401CP-770—Aeroplane Clock
A handsome Clock keyed to the times by adapting the graceful lines of an aeroplane propeller with its hub as the setting for a modern Clock dial. The walnut finished case and wings are mounted on crome-plated metal landing gear, with balloon tires. Sessions self-starting electric clock movement. Width 23″, height 7″.　　Mfr's. Sugg. Retail $12.85

402CP-945—Airliner Clock
An Airliner Clock with a wingspread of 21 inches, gleaming chrome metal wings and chrome tri-blade propellers. Sessions self-starting electric clock movement set in front of Brown plastic cabin. Chrome landing gear and balloon tires. It makes a handsome and decorative, as well as an accurate timepiece. Height 10″, width 21″.

Mfr's. Sugg. Retail $15.75

1085CP-1005—"Golden Girl" Electric Clock
This clock gracefully combines fine Art with accurate time-telling. Hand-rubbed walnut finished base and clock case. Metal figure and clock bezel finished in 22K gold plate. Sessions electric self-starting clock movement. Height 13¼″, width 11¼″.

Mfr's. Sugg. Retail $16.75

$75.00

$25.00　*1947*　*$25.00*

$75.00

1091CP-770 "Ballerina" Electric Clock
An interesting statuette of a lovely Ballerina is posed above this handsome clock. The gold plated figure stands out in strong relief against the background of walnut finish on the wood case. Sessions self-starting electric movement set in a frame with ornamental gold plated rim. Height 11½″, width 8¾″.　Mfr's. Sugg. Retail $12.85

1084CP-770 "Eagle" Electric Clock
The graceful spread-winged, gold finished metal American Eagle on the handsome hand-rubbed walnut finished base holds aloft a clock of the same walnut finish. Equipped with genuine Sessions self-starting electric clock movement. The clock for the place of honor today in any American home or office. Height 10½″, width 6¼″.　Mfr's. Sugg. Retail $12.85

1094CP-770 "Marine" Electric Clock
For the den or office of the marine minded. This nautical clock is mounted on a walnut finished wood base with round wood frame of the same hand-rubbed walnut finish. Anchor, standard and bezel are in brightly contrasting chrome finished metal. Equipped with Sessions self-starting electric clock movement. Height 10¾″, width 7½″.

1089CP-945 "Pals" Statuette Electric Clock
Dog and boy figures of cast metal with gold plated finish against rich, hand-rubbed walnut finish of the wood base and panel. Genuine Sessions self-starting electric clock. Height 11″, width 9¼″.

Mfr's. Sugg. Retail $15.75

$50.00

1088CP-1095 "Two-Lip" Statuette Electric Clock
A design of whimsical but universal appeal wrought in gold plated on metal statuette effect on an attractive walnut finished wood clock case and base. Dutch motif is carried out in the tulip design front panels as well as the boy and girl figures. The clock has Sessions self-starting electric clock movement. Height 10″, width 14½″.

Mfr's. Sugg. Retail $18.25

Clock with TWO FACES Can Be Read from FRONT AND BACK

TWIN FACE Electric CLOCK

With its twin dials this new and definitely unusual clock can face two ways and is attractive from any angle. There is no unsightly back which must be hidden against a wall. Twin Face Clock is designed for convenience and dependability in the modern manner.

$25.00

1107CP-521—Desk Clock
Dependable Sessions self-starting electric time movement set in wood case beautifully finished in rich mahogany color with gold colored decorations, sash and hands. Height 7½″, width 6¾″.　Mfr's. Sugg. Retail $7.90

$120.00

1105CP-431—Commercial Wall Clock
Exceptionally fine Wall Clock with the famous Sessions self-starting electric time movement. Metal case is handsomely finished in bronze color. Silver lithographed metal dial and bottom hand set. 14½″ square case.　　Mfr's. Sugg. Retail $6.55

$25.00

1103CP-900—Twin Face Clock
Novel and convenient Twin Face Clock in beautiful square design walnut case. Has gold colored numerals and hands. Case is 6″ square.

Mfr's. Sugg. Retail $15.00

Prices Do Not Include Federal Excise Tax

$150.00

1106CP-624—Commercial Wall Clock
Ideally suited for schools, offices, auditoriums, etc. The black moulded plastic case is 17″ in diameter and has black and gilt lacquered numerals. Equipped with Sessions self-starting time movement. Convenient bottom hand set.

Mfr's. Sugg. Retail $9.45

Fine Clocks
1951

Precision—Dependability—skill of the master craftsman. Clocks built to present-day exacting standards of time accuracy. Traditional—modern—designed for beauty and years of unfailing service.

1218CU2100—Onyx Clock
An unusually fine direct reading clock for desk or mantel. Movement case is made of heavy-duty bank bronze and is mounted on a solid Pedrara White Onyx base. Base is 7" long and 4½" wide. Height overall, 4½".
Mfr's. Sugg. Retail $31.50

1219CU2025—Onyx Clock
Uniquely styled in heavy-duty bank bronze and Pedrara White Onyx with direct reading time movement. Bronze movement case is mounted on Onyx base, 10½" x 4½" and is decorated with Onyx on both sides. Height overall, 4½".
Mfr's. Sugg. Retail $39.40

$75.00

400 Day Anniversary Clock
1257CU3200—Here is a clock that will run over one year on one winding. Beautifully styled—the base posts and trimmings all of polished brass; movement of solid brass with porcelain enameled dial with flower wreath design. Entire clock covered with glass dome. Height overall with glass dome 12", without dome 10½"; base 7½", dial 3¾".
$15.00   Sugg. Retail $47.95

1256CU5370—"Madison" Chiming Clock
$100.00

Distingushed and charmingly styled in the traditional colonial Eli Terry type cabinet, dark, hand-rubbed Mahogany. The "Madison" is a gracious addition to your home. It has an etched solid brass dial. Entirely electrical in operation, completely modern in mechanism with the self-starting Telechron Movement, and Westminster Chimes that sound four notes on the half hour and eight on the hour. Has volume control and automatic "Midnight to 6:30 A.M." Chime cut-off. Size 10½" wide, 6" deep, 16½" high.
Mfr's. Sugg. Retail **$89.50**

$30.00

The "Duplex" Timekeepers

Yes! Here is an electric clock that never stops—thunder storms, current failures or loose plugs do not affect it, because of the Timekeeper Duplex movement that lets spring power take over until current is resumed. The spring movement does not need rewinding but once a year. The Timekeeper is always on time—take it on vacations or move it from room to room, plug it in and you still have the time—on time.

1258CU1625—Plexiglas "Duplex" Timekeeper
The Timekeeper comes in the new streamlined Plexiglas case. Its transparent appearance is as smooth as the movement that lies within. Adds a modern touch to any room.
Mfr's. Sugg. Retail **$25.00**

$15.00

1259CU975—Mahogany "Duplex" Timekeeper
The Timekeeper in rich hand-finished Mahogany is perfection in design and construction. A beautiful addition to any room and as a gift—there is no equal.
Mfr's. Sugg. Retail **$15.00**

$15.00

1260CU975—Blond Oak "Duplex" Timekeeper
The popular Blond Oak Duplex Timekeeper is fashioned for ultra smartness and is perfect for the bed table with its soothing color, and you can depend on it—it couldn't be wrong.   Mfr's. Sugg. Retail **$15.00**

$20.00

The "Clipper"
1145CU1332—Sparkling solid brass wheel, movement cover and base are highly polished; hand rubbed solid mahogany case. Brass dial, black numerals, brass sweep second hand. Self-starting electric movement, 110 volts, AC only. Size 5¾" x 9½" x 2¼".   Mfr's. Est. Retail **$19.98**

$25.00

The "Penthouse"
1149CU1332—Exciting, modern clock in clear Lucite with faceted edges. Movement cover is solid copper highly polished; gold colored dial, black numerals, white hands, gold colored sweep second hand. Self-starting electric movement, 110 volts, AC only. Size 4⅞" x 4⅞" x 2½".   Mfr's. Est. Retail **$19.98**

$25.00

The "Nautilus"
1148CU2633—Highly polished brass wheel, movement cover, base and dial. Brass sweep second hand. Hand engraved tinted nautical designs in clear Plexiglas, illuminated by tiny bulb, switch controlled. Self-starting movement, 110 volts, AC only. Size 5¾"x9½"x2¼".   Mfr's. Est. Retail **$39.95**
1147CU1997—The "Sea Witch"—Same without engraving and lighting.   Mfr's. Est. Retail **$29.95**

UNITED
CLOCKS do more than *tell* TIME
...they *sell* it!

KNOWN AS *the Leadership line*

$30.00

975

ENCHANTÉ ANNIVERSARY

An old world treasure interpreted in an up-to-the-minute pendulum action. Preserves the beauty of the original. Today's proud possession.

$25.00

385

GRANDFATHER CLOCK

Pendulum movement adds quaint charm to this *early American* teller of today's time. Simulated walnut or mahogany. Height 15 ins.

22K "gold plated"

$30.00

1955

72

BALLERINA MUSICAL

Daintily attired artiste rhythmically twirls to sweet music. "Gold metal," mirrors, lights and smart framing add to its attraction.

$85.00

811 "SHIP-OF-THE-LINE." WITH PORT LIGHTS

From its sturdy, simulated walnut hull, port and deck lights gleam — reflect softly against the brilliance of fully unfurled chrome sails, bunting and rigging. Oh!...to be the proud skipper of this three-master! Appropos, clock case is rendered in ship's wheel styling.

$40.00

Eternal Light of American Liberty

44

STATUE OF LIBERTY

Lighted symbol of our priceless possession. Enshrined, with Time, in statuary bronze. Ever-popular. Especially appropriate.

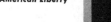

$35.00

BANJO CLOCK

375

PENDULUM

Interest-sustaining design. Shadow-box story of the sea framed in hardwood and brilliant metal. On-view "gold" pendulum movement.

$15.00

22K "gold plated"

309

WESTERN THOROBRED

Few sculptures can match the scaled proportions and fine detailing of United's gleaming thorobred. Those "who take to the saddle," treasure it.

$50.00

870

BALLERINA CLOCK

As a twosome, Time and its gay little dancing partner are certain to please their possessor. Music, too, at the turn of a switch.

$10.00

75

MANTEL CLOCK

Contrasting structural components of selected hardwood. These pillars and panels frame Time in a manner that reflects smart styling.

$30.00

730

WOODLAND WATERFALL

Romance pauses to refresh, note the time and enjoy the illuminated scene of "cascading water" A colorfully encased action assembly.

$30.00

420

MODERN FIREPLACE

Memories of baby shoes, stacked books and fireplace logs—the more pleasantly mellowed by Time! Appropriately staged in hardwood.

FIFTIETH
1905
UNITED
1955
ANNIVERSARY

1955

—The RIGHT TIME is _United_ TIME!

$40.00

345
FLORENTIME

An ornate swirl of 24K "gold plated" curves interrupted only by the timing sweep of its columnar pendulum. Based on shaped hardwood.

$35.00

555
WISE MANTEL OWL

Our feathered friend rolls his eyes as he keeps watch over your Time. Smartly mounted to hardwood for mantel or table placement.

Modernized with dependable electric movements, United's beautifully inspired designs accurately interpret clockcraft's most treasured classics. Each United...

Underwriters Laboratories Approved

Charmingly Told—
"TIME"
—Accurately Kept!

$50.00

870 BALLERINA CLOCK WITH MUSIC

Time escorts and chaperones this miniature ballerina... a figurine which at the flick of a selective backstage switch, pirouettes to music. Theatrically, the routine takes place on a spotlighted dais in front of mirrors, and behind glass. You see, you hear, and you applaud for repeat performances.

$20.00

111 SUN FLOWER

A burst of color set off by raised numerals — and an interestingly framed dial. Mischievous butterfly animates pendulum action.

$10.00

46E
Enamel

46C
Chrome

KITCHEN WALLTIME

Large, round, pleasant-to-look-at, easily readable dial. Sweep second-hand. Time-set adjuster knob. Gay kitchen colors.

$40.00

940
VENETIAN PENDULUM

Twin nymphs modeled after an early Italian masterpiece. Mercury-simulated pendulum action. Crystal clear, shatter-proof dome.

$30.00

$30.00

$30.00

419
TRADITIONAL FIREPLACE

"Warmth" from an ornamented wood hearth, directs the beam of its light at the Time it accurately and ever-interestingly tells.

326
CHROME SAILBOAT

Cabin lights blink brightly against the brilliance of lofty chrome sails. Hull and model-type mantel-mounting are of hardwood.

605
SENTIMENTAL COACH

The plush carriage of the royal past, decoratively dramatized and exquisitely detailed in bronze. Modern in that it is up-to-the-minute!

UNITED CLOCK

$550.00

$525.00

$600.00

VANNER & PREST'S MOLLISCORIUM
BAIRD CLOCK CO.
Plattsburgh, N.Y. — 12 inch dial
18x30. Open Front Model.
Red case, gold letters.

MAYO'S TOBACCO
BAIRD CLOCK CO.
Plattsburgh, N.Y. — 12 inch dial
18x30. Closed front model.
Red case, rust letters.

DUFFY'S PURE MALT WHISKEY
New Haven. 12 inch dial.
18x32, Pine color.

The following 7 pages of Advertising
Clocks are presented with the kind per-
mission of Mr. Bernard J. Edwards from
his book, "Clock and Watch Advertising",
first published in 1976.

$75.00

$250.00

$225.00

ANSONIA NOVELTY, No. 44
Model for Hamilton Logo
1886 — 8x4½

CHICAGO—MILWAUKEE—ST. PAUL
1898 — 6½x10½

AMERICAN FLYER 'MODEL TRAIN'
1927 — 4x5½

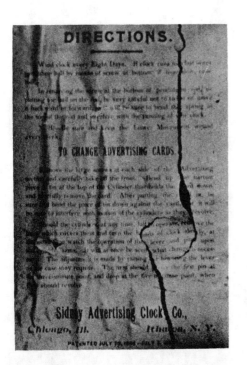

All Original . . .$6,000.00
Reproduction . .$3.500.00

SIDNEY ADVERTISING CLOCK – 1888
A gold leaf; silver leaf; Mother of pearl throat. 12 ads rotate
every 5 minutes after bell rings. Length 68'' – Width 28''.
Seth Thomas 8 day.

Sessions Clocks

Get Your Name and Business Before the Public and Keep it there!

Make the people talk about you and what you are doing!

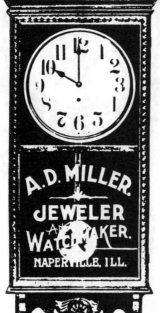

$375.00

REGULATOR "E"
Oak Case   Eight Day
Time $11.71 Time Cal. $15.71

$375.00

Reliable
Eight-Day
Advertising
Clocks
For
Stores
and
Offices

REGULATOR No. 2
Oak or Mahogany
Height 28½ in.   12 in. dial
8DT $14.71   8DS $16.81
REGULATOR No. 1
Height, 25½ in.   10 in. dial
8DT $11.05

DIRECTIONS.

TO CHANGE ADVERTISING CARDS.

Sidney Advertising Clock Co.,
Chicago, Ill.   Ithaca, N. Y.

$375.00
Collection of
Steve Longo
Illinois

CHEW STRONGHOLD PLUG

3 Sizes
$175.00

MR. BOSTON
5 Gallon Container

Generally, subtract $50 to $75 from these clocks with reproduction glass.

ORANGE CRUSH

$475.00

Collection of
Bernie Edwards
Northbrook, Illinois

Collection of
Steve Longo
Illinois
$500.00

CALUMET BAKING POWDER

$395.00

CIGAR CUTTER CLOCK

$275.00

$275.00

Modern Reproduction Glasses
LA REFORMA CIGARS

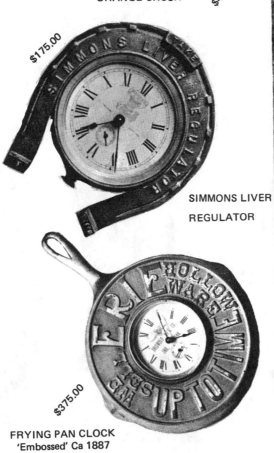

$175.00

SIMMONS LIVER
REGULATOR

$375.00

FRYING PAN CLOCK
'Embossed' Ca 1887
9 inch diameter

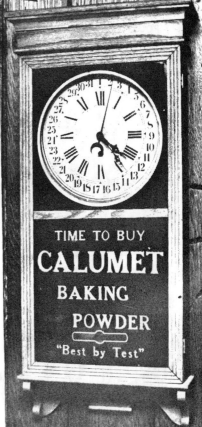

Modern Reproduction Glasses
CALUMET BAKING POWDER

$550.00

NINE O'CLOCK
WASHING-TEA

$40.00

CENTRAL LIFE
Pin Clock — 5 inch diameter

$325.00

VICTROLA
ca 1912-16 — 15 inch

$450.00

POUCH CLOCK
Canvas over wood
Ansonia — 8x12

G.E. REFRIGERATOR

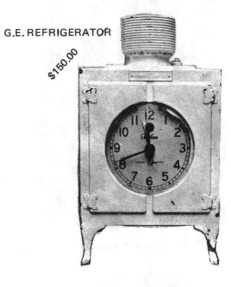

$150.00

GEO. M. REED BITTER CO.
Reed's Tonic — 10x24
L. Hubbel Mvt., 1865

$550.00

LUCKY STRIKE CLOCK.
R.A. Patterson Tobacco Co.
16x25, 11½ inch dial
Dial center, orange with lettering
in black.

$40.00

WESTINGHOUSE ELECTRIC RANGE
WESTERN CLOCK CO.

$600.00

$25.00

BIG BEN' JEWELER'S AD

GOLD LION TONIC

Collection of
Bob Couch
Chicago

$425.00

$750.00

KRAMER BACKWARDS BARBER SHOP
Waterbury. Reverse viewing from barber's
chair. 14x22, 9 inch dial. 8 Day.
Unique reflective advertising.

$425.00

CHANCELLOR CIGAR

Collection of
Richard Roelle
Chicago

$1,000.00

**CHAMBERLAIN
CIGARS & CIGARETTES**
BAIRD CLOCK CO. Pine case, dove
tailed 20x30. Blue & white tin dial, 12
inch. Seth Thomas movement.

**COCA COLA
BAIRD CLOCK CO.**
Pine case dove tailed. 20x30.
Blue & white tin dial, 12 inch.
Seth Thomas movement.

$3,500.00

$475.00

U.S.G. HARNESS OIL
6½ inch dial on 13 inch face.
17x25 Embossed Oak. - 8 Day

THREE BEE POLISH
Ansonia 1890

$275.00
Collection of
Claude Kennedy
Rockford

$35.00

MONTGOMERY WARD
8-Day Alarm

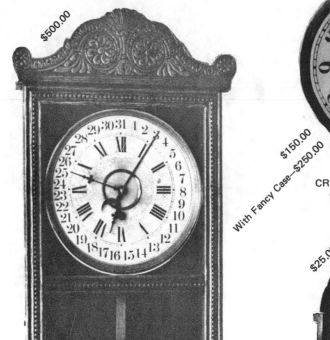

$500.00

LET GEORGE DO IT
G.W. BARBOUR
JEWELER
353 CONGRESS ST.
PORTLAND, ME.

LET GEORGE DO IT
G.W. Barbour Jeweler

Collection of
Don Davidson
Skokie, Illinois

Collection of
Claude Kennedy
Rockford

$150.00

With Fancy Case—$250.00

CRESCENT WATCH CASE CO.
(Gas Light Clock)

$25.00

STAR BRAND SHOES
New Haven

$200.00

WALTHAM AUTO CLOCK
In shape of early Lincoln grill.

$45.00

ANSONIA SHOE AD

$225.00

ST. CHARLES EVAPORATED CREAM
8x14

ARM & HAMMER BRAND
CHURCH & CO'S
SODA
NEW YORK.

$500.00

ARM & HAMMER
4¼ x 3¼
Beige, red & blue

EARLY TIMES CLOCK
13x14

$250.00

$1,350.00

EVER-READY 'SAFETY RAZOR'

$200.00

ANSONIA 'JUG CLOCK'
American Jewelry, Cincinnati
8½x13

$275.00

WESTERN UNION DELIVERY BOY

$150.00

TYPICAL SWISS CLOCK
ca 1890's — 18" diameter

$100.00

COLUMBUS CLOCK
1892 — 7x12½

$1,500.00

GEM DAMASKEENE RAZOR
'UGLY BABY CLOCK'

$250.00

SIMMONS REGULATOR
13x16

ABOUT THE ADVERTISING IN THIS BOOK

TO OUR ADVERTISERS: We here at Heart of America Press want to thank you for your help in making possible the publishing of this book.

TO OUR READERS: We encourage you to consider using the services of our advertisers when needed.

FUTURE ADVERTISING: Our staff, Roy, Red, Shirley and Sherry, are working on Clock Book 4 now and we are planning to release it about May or June of 1984. If you would like to advertise in Book 4, or any of our other future publications, let us know "NOW" and we will get in touch with you when it is time to send in your advertising copy. We do not necessarily need "camera ready" copy, as we have an excellent facility nearby (Smith Secretarial Service) who has prepared several of the pages you see here.

We think this is an excellent idea for advertising because it is before the customers for years rather than just days. We hope you will think so too.

* *

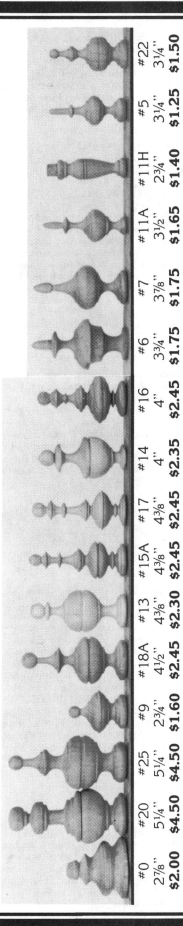

CLOCK IDENTIFICATION & PRICE GUIDE, BOOK 3
ROY EHRHARDT AND RED RABENECK, 1983
208, 8½x11 pages. $15.00. Order No. 10500

This latest publication is certainly another milestone in the evolution of clock collecting. It takes you on a historical journey, beginning in the 1870's with Wm. L. Gilbert, Ansonia, E.N. Welch, Waterbury, New Haven, Florence Kroeber, Nicholas Muller's Sons, and fine imported banjos, Viennas, and German cuckoo clocks; then on to the 1900's with an extended section on alarms, fantastic grandfathers, 39 English clocks (ca 1915), banjos, novelties and antimateds. You'll find Chelseas, Walthams, Lux, and on through the 1900's to the 1940's with Art Deco, advertising clocks, and the electrics that are now in use and being collected everywhere. And, last but not least, **16 pages illustrating 117 different French clocks of the early 1900's.** You will love this one even more than **Book 1 and 2.** Retail mail orders autographed and mailed first. Planned delivery date is July 4, 1983.

CLOCK IDENTIFICATION & PRICE GUIDE, BOOK 1
Roy Ehrhardt & Red Rabeneck, 1977. Price Guide Revised 1979
198, 8½x11 pages. $15.00. Order No. 10233

THE OLD STANDBY — NO CLOCK LIBRARY IS COMPLETE WITHOUT ONE.

American and imported clocks from 1840 to the 1940's were selected as the best representation for the clocks of this era. The following information is given for each clock: One of the years it was offered for sale; The factory description; The price it sold for originally; The present retail collector value. Over 4,000 clocks are pictured or described. Of interest to both beginning and advanced collectors is the sections on "Conditions or Considerations as They Affect Value", "Periods in Clock Production", and "Replicas, Reproductions & Fakes". In addition, "Identification and Dating of 150 of the Most Important U.S. Clock Makers" is shown in chart form. **The first book of this kind ever published.** This book and the later publication, **"Clock Identification & Price Guide, Book 2"**, are more useful on a day-to-day basis than all other clock books put together.

CLOCK IDENTIFICATION & PRICE GUIDE, BOOK 2
ROY EHRHARDT & RED RABENECK, 1979.
192, 8½x11 pages. $15.00. Order No. 10276

In the tradition of **Clock Identification & Price Guide, Book 1,** ask any of the thousands of collectors who own one for his personal recommendation. A continuation of **Book 1,** with all new and different illustrated clocks. Many additional clock companies are covered. Some examples are: Jennings Bros.—Western Clock Co.—1873 Terry Clock Co.—More complete Ansonia, New Haven, Gilbert, Seth Thomas, Ingraham, Sessions, Welsh—More Jeweler's Regulators and Battery Regulators—Hall—Grandfathers—Calendars—Connecticut Shelf—Novelty—Statue—etc. An important section of the book is a complete, non-illustrated **Price Guide to all Known Calendar Clocks,** with references to all books (by page number) illustrating calendar clocks. An article entitled "Understanding the Victorian Period of Clock Production" features a "time line" of important world and clock events from 1870 Daniel Burnap to the failure of Sessions in 1970. Also included is information on repairing and restoring old finishes, woods used in clock cases, and how to detect replicas and fakes.

THE OFFICIAL 1983 PRICE GUIDE TO ANTIQUE CLOCKS
ROY EHRHARDT AND RED RABENECK, 1983
572 page color-cover paperback. $10.00. Order No. 10643

A HANDY SIZE FOR TRAVELING AND AUCTIONS.
THE LATEST PRICES FOR OVER 4,700 CLOCKS

The most DEPENDABLE SOURCE for COMPLETE, ACCURATE listings of all the pricing information you've been looking for — now, for the first time — an up-to-date volume guiding you through the fascinating world of COLLECTIBLE CLOCKS. Over 10,000 current market values for the most comprehensive listing of antique collectible clocks in print. INSIDE INFORMATION — learn how to obtain top value in the antique clock market — Where to go; Who to contact; When to bid; How to bid; How to spot fakes and replicas; tips on repairs and restorations — from alarm clocks to grandfather clocks. OVER 1,000 ILLUSTRATIONS from actual manufacturers catalogs dating back to the 1840's, to insure the most detailed identification of your antique clock available; plus an eight page color section, displaying a breathtaking array of Novelty, Gilt, Statue, Steeple and Cabinet clock designs. DESCRIPTIONS OF MANUFACTURERS AND VARIATIONS — how to recognize and understand clock labels, distinguishing characteristics, period of time, style, and makers: discriminate between rare and common specimens. PERSONALIZED COLLECTOR INFO — on displaying, cleaning, storing your collection. Learn how to keep your antique clocks in MINT condition, spiraling your professional status upward in the antique marketplace. With this book the tiniest detail of your clock's condition will become a valuable tool in buying and selling. DETAILED GLOSSARY — defining clock cases, works and terminology. Eliminates confusion with dealers, buyers and catalogues. LOCATE new and old clock suppliers, museums, libraries, periodicals and book sources, clubs, swap meets, conventions and NAWCC regional meetings, all over the United States. BUY IT — USE IT — BECOME AN EXPERT.

F. KROEBER CLOCK CO. IDENTIFICATION & PRICE GUIDE
ROY EHRHARDT AND RED RABENECK, 1983
36, 8½x11 pages. $10.00. Order No. 10497

A very important book for F. Kroeber collectors and dealers. Information has heretofore been rare and vague on Florence Kroeber and his clocks. Contains 292 actual clock illustrations from two rare, original F. Kroeber factory sales catalogs, one dated 1888 and one dated 1893, and pictures from factory advertisements and sale flyers from the 1888-1895 era. The same format and style as **Clock Identification & Price Guide, Books 1, 2 and 3.** The following information is given for each clock: One of the years it was offered for sale; The factory description; The present retail value. After reading the special article by Red, titled "Florence T. Kroeber, The Mysterious Clockmaker", you will have a much better understanding of the man and his clocks, as well as a market advantage.

Order from: Heart of America Press, P.O. Box 9808, Kansas City, MO 64134
Send amount of book plus $1.00 postage & handling.

OTHER BOOKS AVAILABLE FROM HEART OF AMERICA PRESS

POCKET WATCH BOOKS

**ERICAN POCKET WATCH IDENTIFICATION & PRICE
DE, BOOK 2.** Ehrhardt, 1974. (Prices Revised in 1980).
. 8½x11 pages. 1 lb. 10 oz.................$15.00

**REIGN & AMERICAN POCKET WATCH IDENTIFICATION
RICE GUIDE, BOOK 3.** Ehrhardt, 1976. 172, 8½x11 pages.
8 oz.................$10.00

6 POCKET WATCH PRICE INDICATOR.
hardt, 1975. 64, 8½x11 pages. 14 oz...........$5.00

7 POCKET WATCH PRICE INDICATOR.
hardt, 1976. 110, 8½x11 pages. 1 lb.........$7.00

8 POCKET WATCH PRICE INDICATOR.
hardt, 1978. 110, 8½x11 pages. 1 lb. 2 oz.....$10.00

9 POCKET WATCH PRICE INDICATOR.
hardt, 1979. 110, 8½x11 pages. 1 lb. 2 oz.......$10.00

0 POCKET WATCH PRICE INDICATOR.
hardt, 1980. 110, 8½x11 pages. 1 lb. 2 oz.......$12.00

KET WATCH INVENTORY & PRODUCTION DATES
cket Book with 50 inventory pages). Ehrhardt, 1979.
3½x5½ pages. 2 oz.................$3.00

STER INDEX TO 13 WATCH BOOKS. (Books published
re 1980.) Ehrhardt, 1979. 16, 8½x11 pages. 6 oz....$4.00

IN POCKET WATCH ID. & PRICE GUIDE.
hardt, 1976. 120, 8½x11 pages. 1 lb. 2 oz.....$10.00

NOIS SPRINGFIELD WATCHES ID. & PRICE GUIDE.
hardt, 1976. 136, 8½x11 pages. 1 lb. 4 oz.......$10.00

THAM POCKET WATCH ID. & PRICE GUIDE.
hardt, 1976. 172, 8½x11 pages. 1 lb. 4 oz.......$10.00

MILTON POCKET WATCH ID. & PRICE GUIDE
hardt, 1976. (Revised 1981). 53, 8½x11 pages.
4 oz.................$10.00

**KFORD GRADE & SERIAL NUMBERS WITH
DUCTION FIGURES.** Ehrhardt, 1976. 44, 8½x11 pages.
z.................$10.00

DEMARKS.
hardt, 1976. 128, 8½x11 pages. 1 lb. 2 oz.......$10.00

PRICELESS POSSESSIONS OF A FEW. A brief history
e Gruen Watch Company, their 50th Anniversary Watch,
contemporary prestige watches: Edward Howard—Premier
imus—C. H. Hurlburd—Lord Elgin—Hamilton Masterpiece.
ne T. Fuller, 1974. 64 perfect bound pages. 10 oz. .$10.00

**ERICAN POCKET WATCH ENCYCLOPEDIA & PRICE
DE.** Ehrhardt, 1982. 216, 8½x11 pages. 1 lb. 10 oz.
me 1, June 1982.................$25.00
me 2, Tentative—................$25.00
me 3, Tentative— (Price of Volume 1,2,3 & 4 subject . $25.00
me 4, Tentative— to change after April 1, 1983).......$25.00

orders to:

ART OF AMERICA PRESS
   P. O. Box 9808
sas City, Missouri 64134-0808

POCKET WATCH BOOKS

**EVERYTHING YOU WANTED TO KNOW ABOUT
AMERICAN WATCHES & DIDN'T KNOW WHO TO ASK.**
Col. George E. Townsend, 1971. (With 1983 Price Guide by
Roy Ehrhardt). 88, 6x9 pages. 8 oz...............$8.00

AMERICAN RAILROAD WATCHES.
Col. George E. Townsend, 1977. (With 1983 Price Guide by
Roy Ehrhardt). 44, 6x9 pages. 8 oz...............$8.00

THE WATCH THAT MADE THE DOLLAR FAMOUS.
Col. George E. Townsend, 1974. (With 1983 Price Guide by
Ralph Whitmer). 45, 6x9 pages. 8 oz...............$8.00

SET OF 3 PRICE GUIDES TO TOWNSEND BOOKS....$9.00

E. HOWARD & CO. WATCHES 1858–1903.
The last word on Howard watches: Identification — Production—
Price Guide. Col. George E. Townsend, Author. (With Price Guide
by Roy Ehrhardt). 1983. This manuscript was ready for publica-
tion when Col. Townsend died. The Price Guide was written by
Roy Ehrhardt after his death. 48, 8½x11 paperback. 6 oz. .$8.00

CLOCK BOOKS

CLOCK IDENTIFICATION & PRICE GUIDE, BOOK 1.
Malvern "Red" Rabeneck & R. Ehrhardt, 1977. (Prices Revised
in 1979). 198, 8½x11 pages. 1 lb. 12 oz...........$15.00

CLOCK IDENTIFICATION & PRICE GUIDE, BOOK 2.
M. "Red" Rabeneck & R. Ehrhardt, 1979. 192, 8½x11 pages.
1 lb. 10 oz.................$15.00

VIOLIN BOOKS

VIOLIN IDENTIFICATION & PRICE GUIDE, BOOK 1.
E. Atchley & R. Ehrhardt, 1977. 192, 8½x11 pages.
1 lb. 10 oz.................$25.00

VIOLIN IDENTIFICATION & PRICE GUIDE, BOOK 2.
E. Atchley & R. Ehrhardt, 1978. 206, 8½x11 pages.
1 lb. 10 oz.................$25.00

VIOLIN IDENTIFICATION & PRICE GUIDE, BOOK 3.
E. Atchley & R. Ehrhardt, 1978. 152, 8½x11 pages.
1 lb. 5 oz.................$15.00

MISCELLANEOUS BOOKS

AMERICAN COLLECTOR DOLLS PRICE GUIDE, BOOK 1.
S. Ehrhardt & D. Westbrook, 1975. 128, 8½x11 pages.
1 lb. 2 oz.................$9.00

AMERICAN CUT GLASS PRICE GUIDE, (Revised 1977).
Alpha Ehrhardt. 120, 8½x11 pages. 1 lb. 2 oz.......$7.00

POCKET KNIFE BOOK 1 & 2 PRICE GUIDE (Revised 1977).
J. Ferrell & R. Ehrhardt. 128, 8½x11 pages. 1 lb. 2 oz...$7.00

The books listed above are sold on a satisfaction guarantee. If
you are not sure about the books you want, send a self-
addressed, stamped envelope and we will send you detailed brochures on all of the publications. For orders in the U.S. and
Canada, send the price of the book plus $1.00 postage and
handling for the first book and 30 cents for each additional.
Foreign countries—Check with your Post Office for rate, your
choice, Air or Sea Mail, Book Rate. Book and carton weights
listed.

THE BANJO TIMEPIECE

BY CHIPMAN P. ELA

An in-depth study of the weight driven banjo clock by Chipman Ela. 210 pages, 10" x 7", soft cover with over 300 illustrations, drawings and photographs. Beginning with Simon Willard, the first maker of the banjo, it traces the famous and not-so-well known makers of the styles and points out their construction habits for easier identification of unmarked clocks. In addition there is a section of definitions as well as comparison listings of cases, dials and movements. It's a necessary book for the serious banjo collector and the lover of early American clocks.
055106 . . . . $29.95

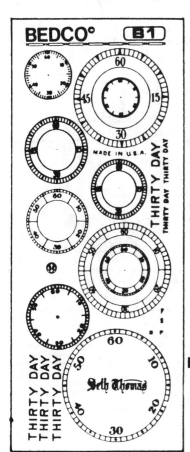

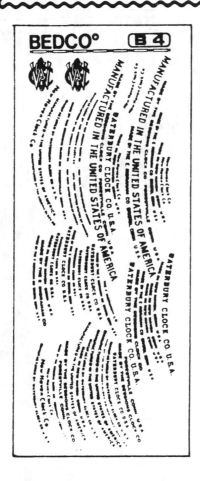

Timesavers

P.O. Box 171   Wheeling, IL 60090

312-394-4818

URGOS SUSPENSION SPRINGS
Genuine replacement suspension springs. Mix sizes for quantity discounts. FREE DELIVERY! A complete selection of clock suspension springs are now in stock.
No. 12083.................Small Spring
No. 12084 ....Large Spring
$2.00 each $21.00/12 ($1.75)

PEN OILERS
Now a lower price on our popular pen oilers. Filled with a quality clock oil. Refillable. Has a pocket clip. FREE DELIVERY!
No. 13717
$1.00 each $2.85/3 ($ .95) $10.20/12 ($ .85)

K&D/KWM BUSHING TOOL
NEW...Made by K&D to use the KWM bushing system. Complete with six anvils, five reamers, five pushers, chamfering cutter, centering point and a wood accessory holder. Top quality all the way through at a price you can afford. Instructions are included. Guaranteed. FREE DELIVERY!
No. 13569

$198.00 each

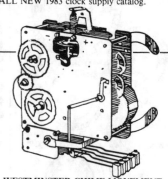

WESTMINSTER CHIME MOVEMENT
Quality 8-day German Westminster chime floating balance movement. Measures 5" wide x 5½" high and 3¼" deep. The hammers are mounted on the bottom. A five rod gong, hands and key are included. And don't forget FREE DELIVERY!
No. 14508
$65.00 each $180.00/3 ($60.00)

KITCHEN CLOCK MOVEMENT
Our eight day kitchen clock movement is a quality reproduction of the original. The movement measures 5½"x6"x2⅜" deep. The pendulum is 9¼" from the center of the handshaft to the pendulum tip. Each movement is complete with pendulum, gong, gong base, hands and key. And don't forget FREE DELIVERY! Guaranteed.
No. 14442
$38.00 each $105.00/3 ($35.00)

KWM BUSHINGS
All bushings are in stock for immediate delivery. Sizes L-01 through L-137. Twenty bushings in a bag. FREE DELIVERY!
L-01 through L-127:
$1.95 each bag $19.20/12 ($1.60)
$75.00/50 ($1.50) $140.00/100 ($1.40)
L-128 through L-137: (10 bushings in a bag)
$3.50 each bag $39.00/12 ($3.25)
SPECIAL....bags of 100 bushings are available in sizes L-01 through L-127-only **$7.00 per 100** delivered.

WATCH PENS
Stainless steel WATCH PENS tell the time and date on an LCD display. Replaceable battery and ink cartridge (both are included). Guaranteed for one full year. FREE DELIVERY!
No. 11205
$5.00 each $14.25/3 ($4.75) $27.00/6 ($4.50)
$48.00/12 ($4.00) $93.75/25 ($3.75) $175.00/50 ($3.50)
WRITE FOR PRICES ON LARGER QUANTITIES

ORANGE SHELLAC FLAKES
Used for setting jewels. Just heat, set jewel and allow to cool. Available in a 6 ounce package. FREE DELIVERY!
No. 13750   **$4.35 each $12.45/3 ($4.15)**

CUCKOO PENDULUM CLOSEOUT
Save on this closeout oakleaf pendulum. Medium size brown color. Supplies are limited so order NOW. FREE DELIVERY!
No. 10271
$2.00 each
$5.70/3 ($1.90)
$21.00/12 ($1.75)

SUSPENSION RODS
Quality suspension rods for American clocks. Twelve to a bundle. Order in quantity and save. FREE DELIVERY!
No. 12288
$2.40 each bundle $6.90/3 ($2.30) $27.00/12 ($2.25)

MAINSPRING WINDER
A quality tool for removing and installing mainsprings in barrels and open springs. Complete with instructions and extra arbors. GUARANTEED. FREE DELIVERY!
No. 13407   **$89.00**

CUCKOO HAND BUSHINGS
Hard to find cuckoo clock hand bushings. Twelve bushings in a package. FREE DELIVERY!
No. 11208
$1.50 each pack
$4.20/3 packs ($1.40)
$15.00/12 ($1.25)

ANSONIA HANDS
Steel replacement hands for Ansonia 11" dials. Bushing on the hour hand and square hole in the minute hand. FREE DELIVERY!
No. 13116   **$1.00 each set**
$2.85/3 sets ($ .95) $10.20/12 sets ($ .85)

QUARTZ "MINI" MOVEMENT
CHECK OUT OUR NEW LOWER PRICES
Made by Tokigi Tokie Co. Ltd. This movement is used in many Seiko © and Pulsar © clocks. It measures 2⅜" x 2⅜" and ⁹⁄₁₆" thick. Each movement is complete with an hour, minute and stepping sweep second hand and a set of mounting hardware. Factory fresh. First quality. Mix handshaft lengths for discount prices. Guaranteed for two full years. FREE DELIVERY! Please call to receive our battery movement flyer and for pricing on larger quantities.
No. 14400 ....⅝" Handshaft
No. 14401 ....1" Handshaft
$6.00 each $15.00/3 ($5.00) $48.00/12 ($4.00) $187.50/50 ($3.75)
$350.00/100 ($3.50) $650.00/200 ($3.25) $1500.00/500 ($3.00)

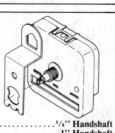

FREE DELIVERY FAST SERVICE

IN A HURRY?

CALL 312-394-4818

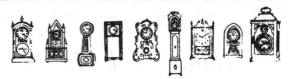

SHIPS CLOCKS, DECKWATCHES AND CHRONOMETERS

Collector wants nautical timepieces from any country. Please send complete description and price. Some duplicates in my collection are for sale. **Lelland M. Fletcher, DDS, 3737 Moraga Ave., San Diego, California 92117. (619) 273-3181 or 275-0161.**

CLOCKS FOR SALE: We have a constant and rapidly changing inventory of about 200 antique clocks at all times. Condition and originality are absolutely guaranteed on everything we sell. Our shipping is safe and very reasonable. To assist you in your shopping we publish a brochure which illustrates, describes, and prices each clock. It is reprinted every 3 or 4 months with an entirely new listing of clocks and is free for the asking with a self-addressed stamped envelope. We also keep an active "wants" file, so if your needs are specific, just let us know. Larson's Clock Shop. Lindy and Karen Larson, RR 2, Barre, VT 05641. 802-476-7524.

MUSEUM PIECES — HEIRLOOMS — QUALITY REPRODUCTIONS

Dials restored or completely duplicated, exactly as original, in every detail. Due to frequent consulting trips and varying amounts of work, please contact us before shipping. **RICHARD & MARTHA SMALLWOOD, Rt. 7, Box 532, Dallas, Georgia 30132. 404-445-2877.**

THE CLOCK EXCHANGE DESPERATELY NEEDS ALL TYPES OF CLOCKS IN ANY CONDITION WE WILL PAY CASH ANYWHERE, IN USA. . . ENTIRE COLLECTIONS WELCOMED. . . CALL OR WRITE; "THE CLOCK EXCHANGE" 278 PLANDOME RD. MANHASSET, NY 11030 JERRY BOXENHORN 212 978-9089 OR STEVE SADOWSKI 212 429-6251 OR 516 627-5506

WANTED: Watches such as Ingersoll & other dollar watches. Admiral Dewey, South Africa Boer War, Universelle Paris Expo., Kaiser Wilhelm, 1904 St. Louis Worlds Fair, 1939 New York Worlds Fair, 1901 Pan American Expo., 1904 Roosevelt & Fairbanks and 1904 Parker & Davis political watches. Original Betty Boop, Donald Duck, Mickey Mouse lapel, Tom Mix, Moon Mullins, Popeye and other original character watches. Ingersoll Puritan, Quaker, Royal, Champion, Climax, Pilgrim and others. Ingersoll advertising items, signs, and display racks. **RALPH WHITMER, 7731 Lisle Avenue, Falls Church, VA 22043. 708-893-7467.**

ROLEX SPECIALIST, Patek, Vacheron, Constantin, American Railroad. Complete restoration & Buy, Sell, Trade. *D.C. ALMQUIST, P.O. Box 60, Crimora, VA 24431. 703-943-5559.*

BUYING FOR INVESTMENT: Pocket or wrist watches or collections wanted. Any amount. Also, parts, movements, cases, catalogues, signs, brochures, watchmaking tools, benches & old jewelry store or watchmaker's stock of old watches, bands or parts. References. Will travel. Call or write: *ROY EHRHARDT, P.O. Box 9808, Kansas City MO 64134. 816-761-0080.*

American Pocket Watch Repair. COA & MSPG $24.00, yr. guarantee. Also pkt watch list. Repaired & guaranteed. SASE: *MIKE NELSON, Mountain Time, 217 Grove, Prescott, AZ 86301. 602-778-3426.*

Wheels, pinions, barrels or whatever, repaired or made new. Repivot arbors. No watch parts. KEN-WAY INC., KEN LEESEBERG, P.O. Box 430, County F Montello, Wisconsin 53949.

BOOKS

NEW BOOKS ON ANTIQUES & COLLECTIBLES. Write for list of over 1,100 titles covering antiques from A to Z. Visa or Mastercard accepted. *THE COLLECTORS' SHELF OF BOOKS. P.O. Box 6, Dept. R, Westfield, NY 14787. 716-326-3676.*

NEW JEWELRY GUIDE. *All About Jewelry*, a guide for buyers, wearers, lovers and investors, is now available in paperback ($6.95) and cloth ($15.95). The author is Rose Leiman Goldemberg. Order from *Arbor House Publishing Co., 235 East 45th St., New York, NY 10017.*

HOROLOGY

Adams Brown has issued their 1983 Catalog No. 106 listing books on watches, clocks, sundials, and related subjects. *Adams Brown* now has a new address: *P.O. Box 357, Cranbury, NJ 08512.*

IDENTIFICATION & PRICE GUIDES TO CLOCKS, POCKET WATCHES & OTHER ANTIQUES. Heart of America Press, Publisher of "Reliable Identification & Price Guides", usually produces 3 to 5 new books each year. Send for our latest catalog. *HEART OF AMERICA PRESS, P.O. Box 9808, Kansas City, MO 64134.*

Self Winding Clock Co. Literature factory instructions. Info includes adjustments of magnet motor, armature, contacts, levers, maintenance, & more. Send $4. for copies. *ROYCE HULSEY, 6563 Maplegrove, Agoura, CA 91301.*

VIOLIN IDENTIFICATION & PRICE GUIDES. Send SASE for brochures and full ordering information. *HEART OF AMERICA PRESS, P.O. Box 9808, Kansas City, MO 64134.*

POCKET WATCH PRICE GUIDE. American Pocket Watch Encyclopedia & Price Guide, Volume 1, by Roy Ehrhardt. The information in this book is not available anywhere else in any form. No book ever printed by anyone has this latest research and prices on pocket watches. If you are buying or selling pocket watches without this information you are probably paying too much or selling too cheap. No pocket watch can be valued correctly until it is properly identified as to rarity, desirability, etc. $26.00 postpaid to: *HEART OF AMERICA PRESS, P.O. Box 9808, Kansas City, MO 64134. Charge cards call 816-761-0080. Satisfaction guaranteed.*

IMPORTANT WATCH COLLECTORS READ

Roy Ehrhardt has purchased the complete inventory and copyrights of the late Col. George Townsend's famous books and is now offering them for sale to collectors through Heart of America Press.

Price Guides have been written by Roy Ehrhardt (23096) with contributions by well known collectors Bill Meggers, Ralph Whitmer and Bob Wingate, who are specialists in their field. Many of you already have three of Col. Townsend's books and may only want the set of three price guides, which is available separately for $9.00.

Col. Townsend's books were first published in 1971, 1974 and 1977. He, and other collectors, has done much research since then and Roy has added hundreds of listings to the price guides that were not in the original books, especially the Railroad Book, which now has 1,037 listings of different railroad grade watches, along with values. Many additional names have also been added to the Dollar Watch Book by Ralph Whitmer, making it as complete as research now allows.

Col. Townsend had worked and researched for 25 years on the E. Howard & Co., 1858 to 1903, and the manuscript was complete and ready to go to the typesetter when he died 15 August 1982. A Price Guide to this E. Howard manuscript has been written by experts on Howard watches and is included in this newly published work. This book represents at least five years continuous work by Col. Townsend.

1983 Price Guides to Col. George E. Townsend's Books

AMERICAN RAILROAD WATCHES, 1983 Price Guide, Illustrated. Listing of 1,037 different railroad watches with their current value. A combined effort by George E. Townsend, 1977, and Roy Ehrhardt, 1983. Very valuable information never before published. 66, 6x9 pages. $8.00

EVERYTHING YOU WANTED TO KNOW ABOUT AMERICAN WATCHES & Didn't Know Who to Ask. Col. George E. Townsend, 1971. (With 1983 Price Guide by Roy Ehrhardt). 88, 6x9 pages. $8.00

THE WATCH THAT MADE THE DOLLAR FAMOUS. Col. George E. Townsend, 1974. (With 1983 Price Guide by Ralph Whitmer). 45, 6x9 pages. $8.00

SET OF 3 PRICE GUIDES TO TOWNSEND BOOKS. $9.00

E. HOWARD & CO. WATCHES 1858—1903. The last word on Howard watches: Identification — Production — Price Guide. Col. George E. Townsend, Author. (With Price Guide by Roy Ehrhardt), 1983. This manuscript was ready for publication when Col. Townsend died. The Price Guide was written by Roy Ehrhardt after his death. 48, 8½x11 paperback. $8.00

Mix or match 6 or more of the above books and price guides and take a 20% discount for NAWCC members. Order from Heart of America Press, P.O. Box 9808-M, Kansas City, MO 64134 or call 816-761-0080

FOR SALE — CLOCKS & WATCHES

Buy and Sell Dutch, Black Forest, and early Japanese Antique Clocks. *A. MEURS, 2112 Bay Pt. La., Hartland WI 53029. 414-367-8122.*

POCKET WATCHES FOR SALE. Railroads, hunting, gold, low-end foreign, cases, dials & chains. Large SASE for list or come by my office by appointment. Pocket watches is my only business. Maybe I can help you upgrade your collection. Want lists are welcome. Thank you for your response to my last lists and I appreciate your business. *LARRY EHRHARDT, RAILROAD WATCH CO., P.O. Box 9808, Kansas City, MO 64134. 816-966-8358.*

POCKET WATCH NEWSLETTER by ROY EHRHARDT. A tool you must have if you buy, sell, or collect pocket or wrist watches. Ask your collector friends about it. Send $25.00 for 6 issues or SASE for descriptive brochure. *Pocket Watch Newsletter, P.O. Box 9808, Kansas City, MO 64134. 816-761-0080.*

SERVICES

Old clock cases rebuilt—repaired. New cases made for old movements. Movement and case repair. *H. E. HARRIS, KEEZLETOWN, VA 22832. 703-269-4541.*

POCKET WATCH REPAIRING. Staff clean and buff case — $20.00 — most American pocket watches. All work guaranteed. Please contact: *D. DAVENPORT, 118 Fir Street, Henderson, NV 89015. 702-565-8442.*

Reverse glass painting, restoration. Brochure: $1.00. *LINDA ABRAMS, 26 Chestnut Ave., Burlington, MA 01803. 617-272-8391.*

Correspondence courses in Quartz-Accutron-Watchmaking-Jewelry. Free folders. *Watchmaking Institute of Canada, 1012 Mt.-Royal East, Montreal, H2J 1X6. 514-523-7623.*

CLOCK WHEEL AND PINION CUTTING. Fast service - Write for free brochure and price list. *Fendleys, 2535 Himes St., Irving, TX 75060.*

Information of the following Clock Companies wanted:

Albert & J.M. Anderson Mfg. Co.
Boston, Mass. ca 1906
Ajax Time Stamp, ca 1920, Boston
American Coo-Coo Clock Co.
American Calendar Clock Co.
American Clock Co.
American Chime Clock Co. ca 1920
Annual Wind Clock Co.
Middletown, Conn. ca 1904
Atkins
Atkins & Downs
Atkins & Porter
Atkins Clock Co.
Atkins Clock Mfg. Co.
R & E Atkins
Atkins, Merritt & Co.
Atkins, Porter & Co.
Atkins, Whiting & Co.
Automatic Time Stamp Co.
Boston - ca 1900
Ball, Seymour & Co., Unionville
Barnes & Johnson
Thos. Barnes, Jr. & Co.
Barnes, Barth & Co.
Barnes, Philip & Co.
Barnes Wallace Co.
A. Platt & Co.
Bliss & Co.
Boston Clock Co.
Mfd. Buerk's Watch Clocks ca 1885
Made A.D. Crane's Pat. 2/10/1841
375 Day Clock
Borg Battery Clocks ca 1932
Bostwick & Burgess Co.
Bostwick—Burgess Co.
Bostwick—Burgess Mfg. Co.
Bostwick—Goodell Co.
Derry Clock Co.
Elbridge
Ellis Clock Co.
Follett Time Recording Co.
New York, NY ca 1913
Frick Clock Co.
Waynesboro, Penn. ca 1913
Gravity Clock Co.
Herchede Clock Co.
Hahl Automatic Clock Co.
Chicago & N.Y. ca 1913
E.O. Hausburg Clock Co., NY ca 1895
Irenus (?)
Ideal Clock Co.
A.D. Joslin Manufacturing Co.
Manistee, Mich. ca 1920
LeGrange Watchman's Clock Co.
Louisville, KY ca 1880
Marti (French?)
Mitchell Vance & Co.
Nicholas Muller & Sons ca 1870-80
National Clock Mfg. Co.
One Hand Clock Co.
George Owen
Peckerwood Mvt.
Pomroy Mvt.
Patti Mvt.
Plymouth Clock Co. (Seth Thomas)
A.E. Pollhans, St. Louis, Mo.
Poole Electric Clocks
Ithaca, NY
Revere Clock Co. (Herchede)
Sangamo Electric Co.
Springfield, IL 1924?
Tucker
United States Clock Case Co.
Cincinnati, OH ca 1888
Warren Clock Co.
Warren Telechron Co.
Warren Clock Mfg. Co.
Windsor Clock Co.

Bits and pieces of information usually found in advertisements, city directories, original factory sales catalogs, etc. I need anything that will help prepare a history of these companies. Let me know what you have. We will then work out the details. I attend some of the NAWCC regionals. Bring your materials with you and let's get acquainted. **Red Rabeneck, P.O. Box 11097, Kansas City, MO 64119. 816-452-4581.**

WANTS — CLOCKS AND WATCHES

WANTED: Early or unusual Howard watches. Especially "K" and "I" Models. *BOB WEBB, 594 Blanche Drive, St. Charles, MO 63301.*

LUX & KEEBLER PENDULETTES. Will pay $450 for "Mary had a Little Lamb", $300 for Country Scene, $250 for Xmas wreath, $600 for Bull Dog Face, $200 for Sambo. Will pay top prices for any Lux or Keebler clocks. *SAL PROVENZANO, 1059 Stell Place, Bronx, NY 10469. 212-655-7021.*

CLOCK AND WATCH COMPANY FACTORY PRODUC CATALOGS WANTED: Either U.S. or foreign. Also, jewelry or general merchandise catalogs with sections on clocks & watches. I need new material for future issues of my books. I will buy outright, rent, or borrow, with full credit for the parts I use in my books. Let me know what you have. We will work out the details. *ROY EHRHARDT, P. O. Box 9808, Kansas City, MO 64134. 816-761-0080.*

WRIST WATCH POINT OF SALE BOOKLETS AND FACTORY CATALOGS WANTED and other advertising that would be of use in putting together a book on wrist watches. Age not important, 1900 to 1970. I especially need information on Patek Philippe, Rolex, Audemars Piguet, Vacheron Constantin, Universal Geneve & other complicated wrist watches. *ROY EHRHARDT, P.O. Box 9808, Kansas City, MO 64134.*

CLOCK AND WATCH ADVERTISING TRADE CARDS & POST CARDS, Point of sale items & wall or window display signs, and all types of give-away advertising. Let me know what you have. *ROY EHRHARDT, P.O. Box 9808, Kansas City, MO 64134.*

FACTORY PRODUCT CATALOGS (TRADE CATALOGS) WANTED on the following subjects: Cut glass, pressed glass, pocket knives, old dolls, bicycles, clocks & watches, oriental rugs, golf clubs, violins, guitars and other stringed instruments, oil & electric living room lamps, early jewelry catalogs. Especially interested in catalogs on anything before 1875. Either English or foreign language trade catalogs needed. Write & tell me what you have and your price. *ROY EHRHARDT, P.O. Box 9808, Kansas City, MO 64134.*

POCKET WATCHES WANTED. I will be at the NAWCC Regionals in the coming months. If you are coming, bring your watches and let's talk about what you have for sale. Also, if you get a chance to trade for or buy watches and don't know what to pay, call me. I can help you. *RAILROAD WATCH CO., LARRY EHRHARDT, 10101½ Blue Ridge, Kansas City, MO. 64134. 816-966-8358.*

COLLECTOR—WATCHMAKER — HISTORIAN: Pocket or wrist watches or collections wanted. Any amount. Also, parts, movements, cases, catalogs, signs, brochures, watchmaking tools, benches, and old jewelry store or watchmaker's stock of old watches, bands or parts. References. Will travel. Call or write me about what you want to sell. *ROY EHRHARDT, P.O. Box 9808, Kansas City, MO 64134. 816-761-0080.*

LUX & KEEBLER PENDULETTES, NOVELTY & ANIMATED CLOCKS. CARRIAGE CLOCKS, CHRONOMETER CASES, CLOCKS IN ORIGINAL BOXES. Parts needed for all of the above, in any condition. *PATRICK CULLEN, 29 Pinehurst Ave., Natick, MA 01760. 617-655-3990.*

ANTIQUE WATCH & CLOCK CLUB OF KANSAS CITY, MISSOURI invites you to attend our meeting and mart at the Granada Royale Hometel, 220 W. 43rd St., Kansas City, MO. Our meeting begins with registration and setup at 9:30 a.m. Saturday, with the public invited at 10 a.m. and continues until 3:30 p.m. Live educational programs from 4 to 5 p.m. We meet at a very special Hometel, which offers very special & unusual accomodations within easy walking distance to the world famous Country Club, Spanish Style, Plaza Shopping Center (with world famous, exclusive shops), and the newly reconstructed "Old Westport". We offer an opportunity to collect, trade, or sell watches & clocks, and have a wonderful weekend. Make your reservations early as you can, as they are always sold out. *Schedule for the next few months.*

1 day . . . . July 30, 1983
1 day . . . . Sept. 10, 1983
1 day . . . . Oct. 8, 1983
2 day . . . . . Nov. 26 & 27, 1983
1 day . . . . Jan. 7, 1984

Our 2-day shows start at 6 p.m. on Friday. If you would like to come and enjoy yourself at our meeting, write for current meeting calendar and full motel information. Registrations are free, and 6 foot tables are $12.50; ½ table, $7.50 each day. Call or write: *P.O. Box 9808, Kansas City, MO 64134. 816-761-0080.*

SERVICES

* *
*
* **RESTORATION — REPAIR**
*
*   CLOCKS * MUSIC BOXES
*
*   Cases, gear work, castings,
*   plating, custom work.
*
*   JERRY FAIER, C.M.C.
*
*   *The Clock Makers*
*   *7509 W. 97th*
*   *Shawnee Mission, KS 66212*
*   *913-648-2014*
*
* *

COMPLETE POCKET WATCH RES-TORATION. Call me "when it absolutely has to done right". Expert at restoring important early American watches, especially Waltham, Pitkin, Goddard, Mozart, etc. Recasing, reguilding, making & locating parts my specialty. *BILL TAPP, 1013 Albion Road, Boulder, CO 80303. Phone: 3 a.m. to 10 p.m.: 303-499-4763.*

GIVLER CLOCK WHEEL CUTTING: Barrels, wheels, pinions, pivoting repaired or new; Two-week service most gears. Music box gears, governors rebuilt. WHEEL PINION CUTTERS, finest tool steel sharpenable, send wheel you want to cut. STAINLESS STEEL CABLE, 2 sizes, tall clock and Banjo. SASE for data & price list. FREE ESTIMATES. *RICHARD GIVLER, 146 Third Street, Wadsworth, OH 44281. 216-336-2243.*

CUSTOM BRASS CLOCK WEIGHTS. Elegant handmade brass weights custom-sized to fit your clock. Viennas my specialty, including BIEDEMEIER tops; also, Seth Thomas No. 2 and No. 3 styles. SASE for details. *DALE STAHLHUT, 7107 Montana Norte, Austin, TX 78731.*

BANJO CLOCK REPLACEMENT PICTURES. OVAL, Pirates, Ships, Mt. Vernon. 51 different pics. $3.00—$15.00. Brochure & 5x7 color photo $1.20. *FRED CATTERALL, 54 Short St., New Bedford, MA 02740.*

Restoration supplies for music boxes; New musical movements, Catalog $4.00. Disc & Cylinder antique music boxes for sale. Disc Catalog $3.00; Repro Tune Card Catalog, $1.50. Buy—Sell—Restore. *N. FRATTI, PANCHRONIA ANTIQUITIES, Box 73, Warners, NY 13164. 315-672-3697.*

WANTS — CLOCKS & WATCHES

LUX & KEEBLER CLOCKS: Will Pay: $500 Lux Bulldog Head—$400 for any Nursery Rhyme—$300 Golfer, Niagra, Country Scene—$250 for Kiddy Kat, Boy Scout, Xmas Wreath, Clown, Cocker Spaniel, Beer Drinker, Dog House, Liberty Bell, Dutch Mill Boat Scene, Fort Dearborn, U.S. Capitol (Roosevelt), ABC, Sally Rand, Sambo—$75 to $150 for Honey Bunny, Sailor, Sunflowers (wood or metal) Potted Daisy, 8-Day Cottage, Hungry Dog. Also asking price for unusual types. *JEROME LEVIN, 53 Notre Dame, Creve Coeur, MO 63141. 314-567-4848.*

CLOCK & WATCH AUCTION CATALOGS WANTED: I need catalogs from anywhere in the United States and around the world from the major auction houses. I prefer catalogs (with the prices realized, if available) from the following auction houses: Sotheby's Park Bernet, Inc.; Phillips; Crott & Schmeltzer; UTO Auktionen, Mannheimer; Antiquorum, Patrizzi & Tortella; Antiker Uhren Niedheidt; Christie, Manson & Woods, Int.; Marouf-Auktionen Antiker Uhre; etc. from cities around the world. Examples are: New York, Los Angeles, London, Geneva, Zurich, Hong Kong, Monaco, Dusseldorf, Aachen, Montreal. The above are common examples that are easier to find. I am also interested in all auction catalogs from any year and any location. In your first letter list the (1) name of the auction house; (2) the date it was held; (3) the location and a brief description as to number of pages, size, etc. If you do have a large number, just send the name and date and your price. *ROY EHRHARDT, P.O. Box 9808, Kansas City, MO 64134. 816-761-0080.*

Old Wristwatches, especially high grade, unusual, moon phase, doctors, or anything complicated. Any Rolex, Patek Phillipe, Tiffany, or Cartier - Dead or Alive. Please state price and phone No. *MICHAEL LEPIE, 85 Mt. Auburn St., Cambridge, MA 02138. (days) 617-492-7575. (nights) 617-323-0310.*

SELF-WINDING CLOCKS, New York, Good running order. International Self-winding, good running order; or other American Battery Clocks. Send pictures or description and price. *HARRY SIDON, 109 Fourth Ave., Bellaire, OH 43906. 614-676-1920.*

Art Deco clocks, all types; Grandfather clocks, Men's & women's wristwatches, half (demi) hunting cased watches, Tiffany, paperweight type, glass, spherical shaped, ball clocks. Full info & price to: *JAMES BLINDER, 2750 W. Grand, Chicago, IL 60612.*

WANTED—WANTED—WANTED: Old Books and Periodicals on Horology. Send description and price to: *LOU GENTRY, 5105 Olean St., Fair Oaks, CA 95628.*

CLOCKS BY: Brackett, Oliver; Bracket, Reuben; Corbett, T.; Jewett, Amos; Merrill, Granville; Wells, Calvin; Winkley, John; Youngs, Benjamin; Youngs, Isaac; Youngs, Seth. *BOB SOBERMAN, 3547 Webster Ave., Bronx, NY 10467.*

LUX, "Mr. Hyde" clock wanted. I have a "Dr. Jeckyll" and need a "Mr Hyde" to complete the pair. Write *ROSS WERT, P.O. Box 250, Park Ridge, IL 60068.*

WANTED: Old Cuckoo Clocks & Black Forest Clocks. Must be pre-1930. (Any type & condition wanted.) Mantels, Trumpeter, picture frame, & ornately carved pieces. (Parts & basket cases needed.) *Complete Black Forest Clock Repair & Restoration.* Please contact: *ERIC FUCHSLOCHER, 8050 Ventura Canyon Ave., Panorama City, CA 91402. 213-994-1492.*

Jeweler's Regulators or Howards. Large, ornate, complete, wall-hanging or floor-standing. Also, gold leaf signs. Send picture & price. *DAN POWERS, Box 87, Boone, IA 50036. 515-432-2600.*

I COLLECT SHIPS BOX CHRONOMETERS, POCKET CHRONOMETERS, AND HOROLOGICAL SCHOOL WATCHES, especially one of a kind hand-made Chronometers. Making friends with collectors, exchanging information, and adding to my collection, makes life interesting. *GREG REDDICK, 1860 Loras Blvd. Dubuque, IA 52001. 319-556-4399.*

OLD STOCK AND BOND CERTIFICATES WANTED, especially on railroads, watch, clock or radio companies, oil companies, mining, anything western. Any amount—one or a hundred . Sometimes found in the original books. Issued or not, the older the better. Get in touch with me if you have any. I collect some and trade some. I hope to do a book on collecting them some day. Bring them with you to the NAWCC Marts or flea markets and let's talk. *ROY EHRHARDT, P.O. Box 9808, Kansas City, MO 64134.*

Railroad Watch Company

Larry A. Ehrhardt

P.O. Box 9808
10101½ Blue Ridge
Kansas City, MO 64134

Business: (816) 966-8358
Residence: (816) 761-3662

Pocket Watches are my only business.

I sell watches from the most expensive perpetual calendar watches to the rarest in $ Dollar Watches. My specialty is watches with Railroad associated names, and historically important rare U.S. time pieces. Send a large self-addressed, stamped envelope for my latest list or phone my office for an appointment to see my current selection.

Does your collection contain duplicates or unwanted pieces? Trade them to me for the pieces you need. Let's make this work to both our advantages.

When you're ready to sell an individual piece or your complete collection, you'll get the best price when you deal with someone who knows the value of what you have for sale. Get in touch with *me* when the time comes.

Thank you for your response to my previous lists. I appreciate your business and look forward to hearing from you in the future. Give me a call or drop me a line no matter how small a problem or how large a collection. I attend most of the NAWCC Regionals, come by my table and let's get acquainted.

Larry A. Ehrhardt
Proprietor